Away for the WEEKEND®

SOUTHEAST

Away for the WEEKEND®

SOUTHEAST

REVISED AND UPDATED

Great Getaways for
Every Season in
Alabama
Georgia
North Carolina
South Carolina
Tennessee

ELEANOR BERMAN

THREE RIVERS PRESS • NEW YORK

Published by Three Rivers Press, New York, New York.
Member of the Crown Publishing Group.

Random House, Inc. New York, Toronto, London, Sydney, Auckland
www.randomhouse.com

THREE RIVERS PRESS is a registered trademark and the Three Rivers Press
colophon is a trademark of Random House, Inc.

Originally published in paperback by Crown Publishers in 1994.

Printed in the United States of America.

Library of Congress Cataloging-in-Publication Data
Berman, Eleanor
   Away for the weekend, Southeast: great getaways for every season in Alabama,
Georgia, North Carolina, South Carolina, Tennessee / Eleanor Berman.—3rd ed., rev.
and updated.
   Includes index.
   ISBN 0-609-80776-5 (pbk.)
1. Southern States—Guidebooks.
F207.3.B47   2001
917.504'44—dc21   00-054508

ISBN 0-609-80776-5

10 9 8 7 6 5 4 3 2 1

Revised and Updated Edition

Contents

Acknowledgments

My thanks to the many people throughout the Southeast who aided me with the research for this update.

Introduction

From the misty ridges of the Great Smoky Mountains to the white sands of the Atlantic, from the skyscrapers of Atlanta to the Colonial charm of Charleston, the Southeastern states are filled with travel treasure. Antebellum mansions and cozy log cabins, spectacular gardens, fast horses and lazy rivers, mountain crafts and modern art, the Appalachian frontier and the frontiers of outer space—all of these await in this beautiful and bountiful region.

With so much to choose from, the problem is where to begin. Should it be the mountains of North Carolina, Tennessee, Alabama, or Georgia? The beaches of the Outer Banks, the Grand Strand, or the Gulf Shore? The eighteenth century in Winston-Salem, the Old South in Macon, or the future in Huntsville?

Away for the Weekend®: Southeast invites you to try them all, one at a time, as memorable weekend getaways.

Unlike most guides, this book is not divided into individual states, but samples the best of five states: Alabama, Georgia, North Carolina, South Carolina, and eastern Tennessee. It offers change of pace and a recharge of spirits for every mood and interest around the calendar.

The organization of each trip suggests a weekend itinerary that brings together all the attractions within easy reach of each destination, so that you won't go home and find you've missed something special just a few miles out of your way.

Most of the trips are within an easy drive of Atlanta, the largest city in the region, and are conveniently accessible from other major cities such as Charlotte, Birmingham, and Nashville. Driving directions include instructions from Atlanta, but pinpoint destinations to make it easy to plot a course from any direction, and mileages are given for the closest cities.

Because the region is large, some of the very best places—the coasts of both Carolinas and the tip of eastern Tennessee, for example—are long drives from many metropolitan areas, but they are well worth the trip. Consider these for long weekends, or check the public transportation information in each chapter to take advantage of convenient flights that make it possible to go farther for a weekend adventure.

The book is divided into four seasonal sections to allow you to make the most of each time of year. That means, for example, the best gardens and house tours for spring, beach and mountain escapes in summer, autumn foliage routes, and special Christmas festivities. Reading ahead allows you to take advantage of special events, planning a relaxing and leisurely weekend and reserving the best of local lodging.

Don't be bound by the calendar, however. Many of these destinations are equally appealing and less crowded when nothing special is happening. Mild Southern weather invites off-season jaunts that are easy on the budget and a special delight because you can have busy destinations almost to yourself. The information listings at the end of each chapter are appropriate no matter in what season you make the trip.

It should be noted from the start that this is a personal and selective guide. Instead of listing every possibility in each state, I've selected what I feel are the cream of the weekend destinations. Nor is every single sight-seeing attraction, lodging, and restaurant in each location included. I've limited the listings to places I've visited myself or that were recommended by knowledgeable local sources and frequent visitors to these areas—people whose opinions I respect.

Since Southern inns and resorts are very special places, many are prominently mentioned and some become destinations in themselves. However, this is primarily a guide to destinations and events, not to lodgings. Where motels are the only accommodations available, the lists reflect this. The final chapter of the book, "The Last Roundup," covers resorts that did not fit into the destinations in other chapters.

Registry listings and free state guides listed in the information pages at the end of this Introduction will widen your options for inn and bed-and-breakfast accommodations.

HOW TO USE THIS BOOK

Like its predecessors for the New York area, New England, the mid-Atlantic, the Midwest, and northern California, *Away for the Weekend®: Southeast* assumes you have a normal two-day weekend to spend, arriving on Friday night and leaving on Sunday. Each trip suggests activities for a two-day stay, with added attractions to accommodate varying tastes and time schedules. I've included what I hope is just enough history and background to make each area more interesting without bogging you down in lengthy detail. If you become intrigued and want more information, you can get it on the spot.

When there is enough to do to warrant a long stay, a symbol at the start of each trip will tell you so. When you do have more than a weekend to spend, use these symbols as a cue, or use the maps at the end of the book to combine nearby weekends to fill out an extended stay. Mountain destinations in northeast and northwest Georgia, and the South Carolina coast from Charleston to Myrtle Beach, are examples of places that can easily be combined for a longer tour.

The following symbols indicate trips that seem appropriate for children or long weekends, though you are the best judge of what your family might enjoy:

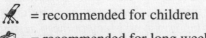

        = recommended for children

        = recommended for long weekends

Lodging prices are for a double room; dining prices indicate main entrees only, rather than an entire meal, since many people do not choose to order two or three courses with every meal.

> I (inexpensive) = under $80
> M (medium) = $80 to $135
> E (expensive) = $136 to $200
> EE (extra expensive) = over $200

When meals are included in the rates, these letters are used:

> CP = continental plan (breakfast only)
> MAP = modified American plan (breakfast and dinner)
> AP = American plan (all three meals)

Dining prices are coded as follows:

> I = most entrees under $12 per person
> M = most entrees between $12 and $20
> E = most entrees between $20 and $25
> EE = most entrees over $25 (or, when indicated, a prix-fixe menu)

When prices bridge two categories, a combination of letters is used.

Since AAA, Mobil, and other, similar guides do so well by motel ratings, I've omitted motels unless they are the only available lodgings, represent the only budget choices, or have a special appeal. You can always get a full listing of motels and hotels by writing to the local tourist office noted at the end of each chapter. Their websites have been added to this edition, as well.

Camping information is not included here, but the state listings include state park information numbers.

Admission prices to sight-seeing attractions use dollar signs to indicate price categories, as follows:

> $ = under $2.50
> $$ = $2.50–$5.00
> $$$ = $5.01–$7.50
> $$$$ = $7.51–$10
> $$$$$ = Over $10

Rates increase steadily, often before a book makes it from author to publisher to bookstore. Rates given here are as accurate as could be determined at the time of publication, and are included as a general indication of what to expect. Please use them just that way—as a general guide *only*. Always use the telephone numbers included to check for current prices when you plan your trip. It is a good idea to verify current hours and holiday closings, as well.

When it comes to restaurants and lodgings, remember that a new owner or chef can make a big difference, and changes and closings cannot always be predicted. If you find that any information here has become seriously outdated, that a place has closed or gone downhill, I hope that you will let me know by writing to me in care of Clarkson Potter, 299 Park Avenue, MD 6-3, New York, NY 10171, so that the entry can be corrected. If you discover new places or know some appealing ones that I have missed, I hope you will let me know about these as well.

The maps in this book are simplified to highlight locations of suggested destinations. They are not necessarily reliable as road maps. You can get an excellent overall map free from the tourism offices listed on the next page.

One last tip: Reserve well ahead of time if you want to stay in country inns or to visit beach resorts or Great Smoky Mountain National Park and other foliage meccas in autumn. Most lodgings offer refunds on deposits if you can cancel with reasonable notice, so plan ahead and take your pick, instead of settling for leftovers.

For this native Southerner who has lived in the Northeast for many years, the year and a half spent researching this book was truly a joy, as were my return trips for this update. Though I have gone back home frequently to visit family, my trips seldom allowed time for exploring. I have been reminded anew of the pleasures found everywhere in the Southeast: the haunting beauty of the mountains, the glorious gardens, the beaches beyond compare. Everywhere the special history and flavor of the past continue to make this one of America's most uniquely interesting and colorful regions. My waistline has felt the effects of the wonderful cuisine, from low-country shrimp and grits to flaky fried chicken and fresh-caught mountain trout.

I was delighted to see the remarkable progress that has transformed so many Southern cities, particularly my hometown of Birmingham.

I hope that my very real enthusiasm for these places and pleasures comes through, inspiring both Southerners and more of my Northern neighbors to share these discoveries—and to make some of their own.

STATE TOURIST INFORMATION

Contact any of these state tourist offices for free maps and literature on attractions throughout their states.

Alabama Bureau of Tourism and Travel
401 Adams Avenue,
P.O. Box 4927
Montgomery, AL 36103
(334) 242-4169
(800) ALA-BAMA
www.touralabama.org

Georgia Tourism Division
P.O. Box 1776
Atlanta, GA 30311
(404) 656-3590
(800) VISIT-GA
www.georgia.org

North Carolina Division of Travel and Tourism
301 North Wilmington Street
Raleigh, NC 27699
(919) 733-8372
(800) VISIT-NC
www.visitnc.com

South Carolina Division of Tourism
1205 Pendleton Street,
P.O. Box 71
Columbia, SC 29202
(803) 734-1700
www.travelsc.com

Tennessee Department of Tourist Development
Rachel Jackson Building,
5th floor
320 Sixth Avenue North
Nashville, TN 37243
(615) 741-8299
(800) GO2-TENN
www.tnvacation.com

STATE PARKS

For camping, lodging, and recreation information, contact the following:

Alabama State Parks
Department of Conservation and
Natural Resources
64 North Union Street
Montgomery, AL 36130
(334) 242-3333
(800) ALA-PARK
www.dcnr.state.al.us

Georgia State Parks and Historic Sites
Department of Natural Resources
205 Butler Street, Suite 1354
Atlanta, GA 30334
(770) 389-7275
(800) 864-PARK
www.gastateparks.org

North Carolina Division of Parks and Recreation
512 North Salisbury Street
Raleigh, NC 27611
(919) 733-4181
www.ils.unc.edu

South Carolina Office of State Parks
1205 Pendleton Street
Columbia, SC 29201
(803) 734-0156
(888) 887-2757
www.southcarolinaparks.com

Tennessee State Parks
Department of Environment and Conservation
L and C Tower,
401 Church Street
Nashville, TN 37243
(888) TN-PARKS
www.state.tn.us

BED-AND-BREAKFAST LISTINGS

Contact the following for directories of bed-and-breakfast accommodations in their areas. (Some associations do not provide telephone numbers, so must be contacted by mail or e-mail.)

Bed and Breakfast Association of Alabama
P.O. Box 707
Montgomery, AL 36101
www.bbonline.com/al/bbaa

Bed and Breakfast Atlanta
1608 Briarcliff Road, Suite 5
Atlanta, GA 30306
(404) 875-0525
(800) 967-3224
www.bedandbreakfastatlanta.com

Great Inns of Georgia
541 Londonberry Road N.W.
Atlanta, GA 30327
(404) 843-0471
(800) 501-7328
www.bbonline.com/ga/greatinns/

North Carolina Bed and Breakfasts and Inns
P.O. Box 1077
Asheville, NC 28802
(800) 849-5392
www.bbonline.com/nc/ncbbi

South Carolina Bed and Breakfast Association
P.O. Box 1275
Sumter, SC 29150
(888) 599-1234
www.bbonline.com/sc/scbba

Historic Charleston Bed and Breakfast
57 Broad Street
Charleston, SC 29401
(843) 722-6606
(800) 743-3583
www.charleston.net/com/bed&breakfast

Tennessee Bed & Breakfast Innkeepers Association
5431 Mountain View Road, Suite 150
Antioch, TN 37013
(800) 820-8144
www.bbonline.com/tbbia

Spring

Overleaf: Harbour Town, Hilton Head, Photo courtesy of Sea Pines Plantation, South Carolina

Making the Pilgrimage to Eufaula

It was noon on a sunny April day in 1865 when a messenger came racing over the hill. Though the Civil War had officially ended two weeks earlier at Appomattox, General Benjamin H. Grierson was demanding further "truce," and a regiment of Union cavalry was on the way to Eufaula, Alabama.

Knowing the fate of other towns that had been burned down by the enemy, the mayor and other local dignitaries rode out personally to escort the general and his staff into town and entertain them at dinner. Southern charm prevailed, and Eufaula was spared.

Today it is a showcase of "high cotton days," the good years before the war, when the "white gold" of the Old South enriched this small town on the Chattahoochee River with a treasury of lovely homes. The Seth Lore and Irwinton Historic District includes more than 700 architecturally significant structures dating back as early as 1836. Set among tall trees draped with Spanish moss, they make for a pretty picture.

The annual spring Eufaula Pilgrimage draws hundreds for the chance to tour some of these homes, many still furnished with family heirlooms. This is Alabama's oldest house tour and one of its finest, a tradition since 1966. Favorite features are the evening candlelight tours, each led off by a wine-and-cheese party at the town's showplace Shorter Mansion. The weekend also includes a prestigious annual antiques show and an outdoor art exhibit.

Add the color of azaleas and dogwoods in the early spring, and the beauty of the Southern belles in period hoop skirts serving as hostesses at the homes and gardens on the tour, and there's every good reason to plan a Eufaula visit.

For a change of pace, spend some time at a neighboring state resort park on Lake Eufaula, the body of water formed by the construction of the Walter F. George Lock and Dam on the Chattahoochee River. Or do some bird-watching at the Eufaula National Wildlife Refuge, a haven for waterfowl.

The name Eufaula comes from one of the Indian tribes found living beside the river when early settlers arrived in 1823. The streets of the oldest part of town were laid out by Captain Seth Lore, and the initial letters of their names spell out his surname—Livingston, Orange, Randolph, and Eufaula. The town changed its name briefly to Irwinton in the 1830s to honor General William Irwin, the largest slaveholder and landowner in the state, who used his influence in the legislature to create a steamboat landing in town. His name remains in the title of the historic district, along with Lore's.

Eufaula prospered, both from its cotton plantations and from the commerce brought by the boats that steamed into the dock to take on bales of cotton. The walking-driving tour of the historic district, available from the Chamber of Commerce or at the Shorter Mansion, leads down streets such as North Eufaula, lined with stately, pillared Greek Revival homes such as the 1863 Conner-Taylor house, the 1854 Couric-Smith House, and the 1848 Drewry-Moorer house with its fancier Italianate columns.

Fendall Hall, built in 1856–60 and renovated in the 1880s, is one of the most beautiful of the Italianate structures, with fine marble floors and stenciled walls. It offers the chance to see a restoration in progress, a look at what it takes to return a historic home to its original state.

Another town showplace is the Tavern, Eufaula's oldest frame structure, built in 1836 on the bluffs as a riverside inn amid ancient, moss-draped trees. Now a private home and photographer's studio, it is often included on Pilgrimage tours.

Some of the old homes have new uses. The Historic Chattahoochee Commission has quarters in the Greek Revival–style Hart House, built in the early 1800s. Visitors are welcome on weekdays, free of charge.

The Shorter Mansion, headquarters of the Eufaula Heritage Association, is also open for tours. Built in 1894 by a wealthy cotton planter and remodeled in 1906, when 17 Corinthian columns were added, the home is lavishly furnished with period pieces, thanks to an appropriation from the Alabama legislature. It includes a "Governor's Parlor," honoring six Alabama governors who came from Barbour County.

Eufaula has several fine early churches as well as homes, and a stroll down Broad Street, the commercial center of town, reveals more history, since many current businesses are housed in nineteenth-century buildings. Broad Street rates its own printed walking tour guide. On this street also is Kendall Manor, an Italianate home with a cupola; the house is now a spectacular bed-and-breakfast inn.

Eufaula's Pilgrimage events can easily fill a weekend, but you might choose to save Sunday for the out-of-doors and Lakepoint Resort State Park. The 85-mile lake, on the Alabama-Georgia border, is famous for its large catches of bass, but the park offers more than fishing. The grounds include a lakeside beach, a marina, an 18-hole golf course, tennis courts, picnic grounds, and, in season, a pool for guests who stay in the park's modern motel rooms or cabins. The attractive lodge dining room offers lake views.

Even if you're not a fisherman, you'll likely enjoy a visit to Tom Mann's Fish World Aquarium, a 38,000-gallon tank filled with bass and other native fish. Phone to find out hours when the fish are fed; the mad rush for food is a sight to behold. There's a monument here to the late Leroy Brown, the fish that Mann swore by as a tester for his lures. If Leroy bit, Tom knew he had a winner. The aquarium is located on Route 431 north of Eufaula, on the way to the state park.

If you have still more time, you can cross the Georgia border to Lumpkin and see the restored village of Westville and the amazing formations of Providence Canyon State Park (see page 152).

There's plenty to do and see in the area, but none of it compares to the simple pleasure of a stroll through Eufaula, a return to the best of the Old South.

Area Code: 334

DRIVING DIRECTIONS Eufaula is located on US Routes 431 and 82 in southeast Alabama, near the Georgia border. From Atlanta, follow I-85 to I-185 south to US 431, about 167 miles. From Birmingham, take I-65 south to Montgomery, then US 82 east to US 431 south, about 169 miles.

ACCOMMODATIONS *Kendall Manor,* 534 West Broad Street, 36072, 687-8847, M–E, CP • *Lakepoint Resort State Park,* P.O. Box 267, 36072, 687-8011 or (800) 544-LAKE, central reservation service (800) ALA-PARK; 101 motel rooms, I; 29 cabins, I–E • *Jameson Inn,* 136 Towne Center Boulevard, 36072, 687-7747 or (800) 541-3268, pleasant choice among local motels, pool, some whirlpools, I, CP • *Best Western Eufaula Inn,* 1337 South Eufaula Avenue, 36072, 687-9300, pool, I, CP • *Ramada Inn,* East Barbour Street, 36072, 687-2021, pool, I.

DINING *Lakepoint Resort State Park* (see Accommodations above), I–M • *Adijan Diner,* 325 Copeland Street, 687-5848, country cooking, I.

SIGHT-SEEING *Eufaula Pilgrimage,* Eufaula Heritage Association, P.O. Box 486, 36072, 687-3793 or (800) EUF-AULA. Three days of tours by day and by candlelight, held in April. Phone for current rates • *Shorter Mansion,* 340 North Eufaula Avenue, 687-3793. Hours: Monday to Saturday 9 A.M. to 4 P.M., Sunday from 1 P.M. $$ • *Fendall Hall,* 917 West Barbour Street, 687-8469. Hours: Monday to Saturday 10 A.M. to 4 P.M. $$ • *Tom Mann's Fish World,* US 431 north, 687-7044. Hours: Daily 8 A.M. to 5 P.M. $$ • *Lakepoint Resort State Park,* off US 431, 7 miles north of Eufaula, P.O. Box 267, 36072, 687-6676. Daylight hours, park is free, fees for golf and other activities • *Eufaula National Wildlife Refuge,* off State Road 165, Box 97-B, 36072, 687-4065. Hours: Daily during daylight hours.

INFORMATION Eufaula/Barbour County Chamber of Commerce, 102 North Orange Avenue, Eufaula, AL 36072, 687-6664 or (800) 524-7529, www.ebcchamber.org.

Welcoming Spring in Wilmington

Azaleas light up the spring landscape all over the South, but nowhere are they more bountiful or beautiful than in Wilmington, the home of the annual North Carolina Azalea Festival. Not only do billions of blossoms turn the whole city into a garden, the many plantations nearby are also in their glory.

It's the state's premier celebration of spring, and a perfect time to discover a delightful Colonial port city enjoying a lively renaissance. To make things even nicer, April is warm along the Cape Fear coast, and the white sands of Wrightsville and other local beaches are just 15 miles away.

Saturday is the big day for the festival, which celebrated its fiftieth anniversary in 1997. The Azalea Queen's parade is in the morning, followed by the opening of a lavish two-day street fair along River Front Park.

Saturday evening brings a free street dance downtown, or you can attend the Queen's gala Coronation Pageant. The Azalea Queen each year is a popular entertainer, her court a retinue of local beauties. Big-name entertainment is also a traditional feature of the weekend.

In between the hoopla, take time for a walk through Wilmington's historic district, armed with the free guide map available from the Visitors Bureau. The main sights on the map are near the center of town. If you can join the Wilmington Adventure walking tour, you'll not only learn a lot of history from Bob Jenkins, the colorful guide with the hat and cane, but have a very good time sharing his knowledge. Among the tidbits, you'll find out why North Carolinians are known as Tarheels.

The town's wide streets remain as they were laid out in 1734. The city was incorporated in 1739, named for the royal governor, the Duke of Wilmington. Prosperity came quickly from two sources, the Cape Fear River and the pine tree.

The river was the deepest in the colony, and the only one leading directly into the Atlantic Ocean. It helped Wilmington thrive as an export center for cotton and for the rice that was grown on dozens of area plantations.

The name Fear (from *fere,* Middle English for "danger") was inspired by the tricky shoals offshore, easy for the natives to maneuver but perilous for any ship whose pilot was unfamiliar with local tides and currents. Local pilots helped blockade-runners evade the Union navy during the Civil War. Fort Fisher, which guarded the entrance to the river, held out against Union assault until a major sea battle in 1865.

The pine forests found in abundance in the area were a valuable source of the desirable products known as naval stores. Tough heart of pine could be used for shipbuilding, and pine resin could be reduced to the pine tar necessary to coat ships' bottoms and ropes. With a rich supply of pine and an easy route for shipping, this region was America's largest supplier of naval stores until the twentieth century. It was pine tar that inspired the nickname "Tarheels."

Like many early ports, Wilmington languished over time, until a strong preservation movement began in the 1960s. A town survey identified more than 200 historic blocks. Many of these sites are now occupied by businesses and offices; some still have the original brick and heart-of-pine walls erected in the 1840s.

The spirit of revival has transformed the waterfront and turned old waterfront warehouses such as Chandler's Wharf and the Cotton Exchange into atmospheric shopping and dining enclaves. These changes have attracted many new young residents to Wilmington, a number of them living in apartments over shops in the downtown area, just as merchants did in Colonial times.

Another new facet of the town is its emergence as a film production center. EUE/Screen Gems Studio is the largest movie production facility east of Hollywood, and it can be toured on weekends. The city also holds several film festivals each year; check the Visitors Bureau for the current schedules.

Many of the city's earliest buildings were lost to a fire in 1840, so most of those still standing were built after that year, and many of the loveliest Victorians are now bed-and-breakfast inns. An exception is the Burgwin-Wright House, circa 1770, a Colonial gentleman's town house with lovely parterre gardens and a three-story outside kitchen. General Cornwallis used it as his headquarters during the American Revolution. The triple-tier porches are typical of the early coastal Carolina building style, showing the Caribbean influence of early settlers from Barbados. The finest room in the house is the upstairs drawing room, rich with elaborate paneling.

Look carefully at the foundation stones of buildings as you stroll and you will notice another legacy from the Caribbean. The angular stones came as ballast from Barbados, the regular shapes came from England.

Watch also for plaques marking buildings that were lost before the preservation movement took hold. Among them is the home of Whistler's mother, the subject of the famous painting by James Whistler.

The columned Zebulon Latimer House, Wilmington's second showplace, was built in stately Italianate in 1852 by a wealthy merchant and remained in the Latimer family until 1963, when it was restored as the headquarters for the local historical society.

Wilmington is known as the city of churches, and many are well worth noting. The standout is St. James Episcopal Church at 1 South Third Street, a Gothic Revival building erected in 1840 for a congregation dating to 1781. Among the many fine details are the carved wooden ceiling and the rose window.

St. Paul's Evangelical Lutheran Church, at 603 Market Street, has stained-glass windows thought to have been created by Tiffany. The Moorish-style Temple of Israel, at 1 South Fourth, is the oldest Jewish house of worship in the state, completed in 1876.

Downtown museums also merit a visit. The Cape Fear Museum tells of the area's history and heritage with life-size dioramas and interactive displays. When you try to stir a paddle through sticky pine tar, you'll understand why it was so valuable as protection for ships.

St. John's Museum of Art, a complex of three restored buildings, has a major collection of the work of Mary Cassatt and a big selection of Jugtown pottery, one of North Carolina's time-honored crafts. The museum also shows work by many state artists.

Railroad buffs will want to look in on the Wilmington Railroad Museum, with articles dating from the original Wilmington and Weldon Railroad, circa 1840, to today. Outside the building are a steam locomotive and caboose that can be boarded.

The final historic attraction not to be missed is Thalian Hall, part of the 1855–58 City Hall Building. This theater, built when Wilmington was the largest city in the state, was grand and a major stop on the traveling theatrical circuit. In the years following the Civil War, it played host to the likes of Lillian Russell, "Buffalo Bill" Cody, and John Philip Sousa. Recently restored and expanded, the elegant hall now hosts more than 600 performances every year in three theater spaces. Check for the current offerings.

One of Wilmington's most popular attractions is the battleship *North Carolina*. Board the river taxi shuttle for a chance to tour the ship that took part in every major Pacific naval battle during World War II. Sightseeing cruises on the water are also available via riverboat.

Antiquers should pick up the current shopping guide. There are more than two dozen antiques shops in town, many located on Front Street, with more clustered north of town on Market Street. A second guide highlights the proliferating crafts galleries found downtown, more than a dozen at last count.

No spring stay in Wilmington is complete without a tour of nearby plantations and gardens. Orton Plantation is an example of the eighteenth-century rice plantations that were once common in the area. The rice fields and marshes are now a wildfowl refuge. The 1725 main house is private, but 20 acres of beautiful gardens are open to the public from spring through fall.

History buffs may want to make a detour from Orton to the nearby Brunswick Town/Fort Anderson State Historic Site, the excavated remains of the oldest Colonial settlement on the Cape Fear coast.

Poplar Grove, once a peanut plantation, is the place to tour an antebellum mansion. The plantation house now features demonstrations of old-time crafts such as weaving and blacksmithing and includes a restaurant for a lunchtime break.

Airlie Gardens, famous for its 50 acres of scenic gardens, is open to the public on weekends. The estate's serene lakes, rare plantings, majestic moss-draped live oaks, and views of Wrightsville Sound are an unforgettable backdrop for the brilliant color of the azaleas in spring.

Greenfield Gardens is another spring spectacle, with a five-mile scenic drive surrounding a lake. It was to raise funds for this city park that the Azalea Festival was born.

When you've had your fill of festivals and flowers, the beaches beckon. Though hard hit by hurricanes in 1996 and 1999, they have quickly rebuilt. The closest is Wrightsville Beach, only about 15 minutes east via US 74. This small island community is a longtime family resort with miles of sand for sunning and quiet walks. There are lodgings such as the Blockade Runner and the Holiday Inn Sunspree right on the beach, making for a nice counterpoint to the attractions of Wilmington. If the weather is right, Wrightsville may well tempt you to extend your stay.

Area Code: 910

DRIVING DIRECTIONS US Routes 74, 421, 17, and 117 all lead into Wilmington. From Raleigh, take I-40 to US 17 west, 123 miles. From Charlotte, follow US 74 east to Route 17, 203 miles. From Atlanta, take I-20 east to I-95 north, then US 74 east, approximately 413 miles.

ACCOMMODATIONS *Graystone Inn,* 100 South Third Street, 28401, 763-2000, or (888) 763-4773, grand 1905 mansion, E–EE, CP • *Rose Hill Inn,* 114 South Third Street, 28401, 815-0250 or (800) 815-0250, 1848 home once owned by the Lincoln Memorial architect, M–E, CP • *The Verandas,* 202 Nun Street, 28401, 251-2212, award-winning restoration of 1853 Victorian, M–E, CP • *Catherine's Inn,* 410 South Front Street, 28401, 251-0863 or (800) 476-0723, handsome home with river view, M, CP • *Front Street Inn,* 215 South Front Street, 28401, 762-6442, art-filled, eclectic, appealing, M–E, CP • *Curran House,* 312 South Third Street, 28401, 763-6603 or (800) 763-6603, 1837 Victorian, M, CP • *Taylor House,* 14 North Seventh Street, 28401, 763-7581 or (800) 382-9982, M, CP • *Worth House,* 412 South Third Street, 28401, 762-8562 or (800) 340-8559, cozy 1883 Queen Anne Victorian, M, CP • *The Inn at St. Thomas Court,* 101 South Second Street, 28401, 343-1800 or (800) 525-0909, luxury suites with balconies, modern amenities, E, CP • *Hilton Wilmington Riverside,* 301 North Water Street, 28401, 763-5900, E • **Wrightsville Beach** (rates go down off-season): *Blockade Runner,* 275 Waynick Boulevard,

28480, 256-2251 or (800) 541-1161, oceanfront hotel and adjoining cottage-style inn, E–EE • *Holiday Inn SunSpree Resort,* 1706 North Lumina Avenue, 28480, 256-2231 or (800) 532-5362, M–EE.

DINING *Caffe Phoenix,* 9 South Front Street, 343-1396, casual, sophisticated, much-praised Italian, M–E • *Pilot House,* 2 Ann Street, Chandler's Wharf, 343-0200, restored 1870 quarters on the river, M–E • *Elijah's,* 2 Ann Street, Chandler's Wharf, 343-1448, nautical decor, river view, informal, seafood specialties, M • *Deluxe,* 114 Market Street, 251-0333, arty, eclectic menu, M • **Wrightsville Beach:** *Oceanic,* 703 South Lumina Avenue, Wrightsville Beach, 256-5551, seafood, outside pier, M • *Ocean Terrace,* Blockade Runner (see Accommodations on page 9), romantic setting, live jazz, M–E • *Bridge Tender,* Airlie Road at Wrightsville Beach Bridge, 256-4519, seafood, view of Intracoastal Waterway, M–E.

SIGHT-SEEING *North Carolina Azalea Festival,* P.O. Box 51, Wilmington 28402, 763-0905. Three-day weekend held in early April; check for current dates and events • *Wilmington Adventure Tour Company,* 763-1785. Hours: Walking tours meet at the foot of Market Street daily April through October at 10 A.M. and 2 P.M. $$$ • *Battleship* **North Carolina,** junction of US 74/76, 17, and also reachable by ferry from Wilmington, 251-5797. Hours: Daily 8 A.M. to 5 P.M.; to 8 P.M. mid-May to mid-September. $$$$ • *Cape Fear Museum,* 814 Market Street, 341-4350. Hours: Memorial Day to Labor Day, Tuesday to Saturday 9 A.M. to 5 P.M., Sunday 2 P.M. to 5 P.M.; rest of year closed Monday. $$ • *St. John's Museum of Art,* 114 Orange Street, 763-0281. Hours: Tuesday to Saturday 10 A.M. to 5 P.M., Sunday 12 noon to 4 P.M. $ • *Wilmington Railroad Museum,* Red Cross and Water Streets, 763-2634. Hours: Memorial Day to Labor Day, Monday to Saturday 10 A.M. to 5 P.M., Sunday 1 to 5 P.M.; rest of year to 4 P.M. and closed Wednesday. $$ • *Burgwin-Wright House,* 224 Market Street, 762-0570. Hours: Tuesday to Saturday 10 A.M. to 4 P.M. $$ • *Zebulon Latimer House,* 126 South Third Street, 762-0492. Hours: Monday to Friday 10 A.M. to 3:30 P.M., Saturday and Sunday noon to 5 P.M. $$ • *Screen Gems Studios,* 1223 North 23rd Street, 343-3433. Hours: Tours Saturday and Sunday noon to 2 P.M. $$$$.

Boat rides: Phone all for current schedules and rates. *Cape Fear Riverboats,* P.O. Box 1881, Wilmington, 28402, 343-1661 or (800) 676-0162: riverboat cruises on the *Henrietta III,* river taxi to Battleship Memorial, sight-seeing tours • **Guided Kayak Nature Tours:** *Cape Fear Outfitters,* 256-1258; *Carolina Kayaks,* 458-9111.

Plantations and gardens: *Orton Plantation Gardens,* 9149 Orton Road, Southeast, Winnabow, reached via N.C. Route 133, 18 miles south of Wilmington, 371-6851. Hours: March through August; 8 A.M. to 6 P.M.; September through November, 10 A.M. to 5 P.M. $$$$ • *Poplar Grove Historic Plantation,* US 17, 14 miles north of Wilmington, 686-4868. Open February through December, Monday to Saturday 9 A.M. to 5 P.M., Sunday 12 noon to 5 P.M. $$$ • *Airlie Gardens,* Airlie Road, 7 miles east on US 74/76, 793-7531. Hours: Tuesday to Saturday, 9 A.M. to 5 P.M., Sunday, 1 P.M. to 5 P.M. $$$ • *Greenfield Park and Gardens,* US 421, 2.5 miles south, 341-7855. 5 mile scenic drive. Hours: Daily, daylight hours. Free

INFORMATION *Cape Fear Coast Convention and Visitors Bureau,* 24 North Third Street, Wilmington, NC 28401, 341-4030 or (800) 222-4757; www.cape-fear.nc.us.

Tapping the Waters Near Cave Spring

Northwest Georgia is full of discoveries, refreshing places that are off the usual tourist track.

Take Cave Spring, for example. With a population of around 1,000, it is only a hamlet, yet it boasts 90 buildings and sites on the National Register of Historic Places—not to mention an abundance of choice antiques and talented craftspeople. And don't forget the wonder that inspired the town's name, a spring that's hidden in a cave and that flows at an amazing three to four million gallons a day.

In nearby Rome is Oak Hill, the antebellum mansion and magnificent gardens that were home to Martha Berry. She founded a remarkable school in a log cabin nearby, and it grew into Berry College, with one of the largest college campuses in the world. It's right across the street from Oak Hill, a testament to Berry's achievements.

And what about Barnsley Gardens, not far away, near Adairsville? They were begun by an Englishman in the 1840s and completed by a German prince in the 1990s to show off, among other beautiful blooms, many roses whose vintage predates the Civil War. In 1999, the property was turned into a super-luxurious resort on 1300 acres, complete with 18-hole golf course, spa and fitness center, tennis courts, and a Grecian-style swimming pool, hardly what you would expect out here in the country. Seventy suites decorated in English country style are in 33 newly constructed cottages on the grounds. Late spring, when the roses are at their peak, is just the right time to pay a call.

More modest lodgings can be found in Rome, the biggest town in the area, with a choice of motel accommodations as well as a gingerbread Victorian Gothic bed-and-breakfast inn, the Claremont House.

There are other choices in nearby towns as well, depending on your tastes and the temperature. Red Top Mountain State Park, on Lake Alla-toona, is an ideal gateway to the area, allowing you to add the great out-doors to your agenda. The 33-room park lodge and 18 two-bedroom cabins are modern, with many rooms offering lake views. Opportuni-ties abound for hiking, biking, swimming, and picnicking; there are many ranger-led walks; and boats can be rented to take advantage of the 11,860-acre lake. At mealtime, the big picture window in the lodge's dining room gives a close-up view of deer and other animals at feeding troughs just a stone's throw away. The feeding area is lit at night.

Bed-and-breakfast fans may prefer the historic Hearn Academy Inn, a modest but nicely restored nineteenth-century building in Cave Spring that is filled with antiques and warmth. It serves as headquarters for the Cave Spring Historical Society. Adairsville offers Old Home Place, an 1855 country house on six acres, and those who admire the Craftsman style of the early 1900s will find it at Stoneleigh in Calhoun.

Wherever you stay, allow plenty of time for shopping and meeting the creative folks in Cave Spring. Driving into town is taking a step back in time. The tiny green, surrounded by old-fashioned shops, might well have been lifted from a painting. Inside those shops are some very interesting wares.

Antiques and curios of all kinds are found around the square, on Broad Street, and on US 411/State Route 53, which bends at a right angle near the center of town and takes two different names, Alabama Street and Rome Road. The biggest selection of wares is found at the Antique Mall on Rome Road, where there are many dealers.

Pick up a shopping guide in any of the stores for the full listing—and don't forget a stop at Martha Jane's, as famous for its fudge as for its unique gifts. For still more variety, come for the annual arts festivals, held the second weekend in June and the fourth weekend in September.

Turn off the square to Rolater Park and you'll spy people lined up with bottles and jugs, scooping up the cool, crystal-clear water pro-duced by the abundant spring. Guided tours are offered through the big limestone cave that is the spring's source. Some of the water is bottled and distributed commercially, but there is easily enough left over to supply the two-and-a-half-acre town swimming pool, constructed in the shape of the state of Georgia.

The park grounds were once the campus of the Manual Labor School, founded in 1839. Two of the original buildings and the church are being restored, and the original student lodging has been turned into the Hearn Academy Inn.

Cave Spring has been home to the Georgia School for the Deaf since 1846; that is the reason many local residents are fluent in American

Sign Language. The original administration building served as a field hospital during the Civil War. The school is now located on a more modern campus on the edge of town.

From Cave Spring, the next stop is Rome, about 18 miles north on State Route 53, on the Coosa River. You'll find a nicely revitalized downtown and riverfront and a couple of interesting galleries.

The 28,000 acres of Rome's Berry College are impressive, but its history and purpose rather than its size are what make this school unique.

It was a fateful Sunday in the late 1890s when Martha Berry looked out the window of her log playhouse on the grounds of Oak Hill to see a group of mountain children watching her read. She invited them in to listen to Bible stories. Soon she was teaching Sunday school to these neglected but eager students. Next she started a day school, and finally the "Berry Schools," which grew into a college on 83 acres of land that Miss Berry inherited from her father. The college provided a chance for youngsters who would otherwise have had no hope of getting an education.

The first stop for visitors is the the Martha Berry Museum, constructed in Greek Revival style to complement the columns of nearby Oak Hill's mansion. The film shown here, telling her story, is quite moving. Adjacent to the museum, in its original setting, is the modest cabin that was the school's birthplace.

The next stop is Oak Hill, the 1847 antebellum mansion where Miss Berry lived. The furniture was handmade by Berry students in the style of Miss Berry's day. The house is surrounded by the giant oaks and formal gardens that were the family's pride.

Finally, using the map guide available at the museum, drive across the road to see what Miss Berry accomplished. The older campus is Georgian in design. A large and rather opulent English Gothic complex, added in the 1920s, was a gift from Henry Ford, who was not noted for philanthropy but who was mightily impressed with Miss Berry's goals and accomplishments.

Drive into the Log Cabin Area to the first location of the Martha Berry School for Girls, a pioneer in education for women.

Rome's other attractions include the Rome Area History Museum downtown and the Eubanks Museum and Gallery on the campus of Shorter College. The latter is filled with personal artifacts collected by the Eubanks family from safaris to Africa and India, from an antique telephone to a stuffed Indian Honey Bear.

Those who are interested in Native American history will be drawn to the Chieftain's Museum, which was once the residence of the Cherokee leader Major Ridge. Far different from most visions of Indian dwellings, this is a fine house, part of a plantation that included a ferry landing and a trading post, reflecting the prosperity of the nation that was broken apart by the removal of the Cherokees from their land.

This museum is a stop on the Chieftain's Trail, which explores the history of the Native Americans of northwest Georgia. Another nearby site is the Etowah Indian Mounds, southwest of Cartersville.

The most important site is in Calhoun. Here you'll see a reconstruction of the New Echota Cherokee Capital as it looked in 1825, when it was the seat of government for the nation that once covered northern Georgia and parts of four other southeastern states. It includes the supreme court building, the print shop where the Cherokee newspaper was produced, a tavern, and the home of a Christian missionary. The more one learns about the Cherokees, the sadder becomes the story of their removal.

From Rome, those interested in folk art will surely want to drive 26 miles north to Summerville and the studio of Howard Finster, a former minister who has become one of America's best-known unschooled artists. Just ask anyone in town where he lives. It is worth the trip just to see the "Paradise Garden" that Finster spent more than 20 years creating outside of his studio, an indescribable mélange of three-dimensional constructions, paintings, and writings inspired by his visions of other worlds. Finster's wooden cutouts and some of his paintings are on sale here for prices far below those asked by city galleries. Come to visit on Sunday afternoon and you'll often find the artist himself, now well past his eightieth birthday but usually still ready to chat nonstop about his views of the world, earthly and heavenly. He'll sign his work for you.

Area Codes: 706 and 770

DRIVING DIRECTIONS   Cave Spring is at the intersection of US 411 and State Route 100. From Atlanta, take US 278 west to State Route 100 north, about 75 miles. From Birmingham, take I-59 east to US 411 east, about 100 miles. For Red Top Mountain State Park, take I-75 north from Atlanta to exit 123, Cartersville, and drive 2 miles east.

ACCOMMODATIONS   *Barnsley Inn and Golf Resort at Barnsley Gardens,* 597 Barnsley Gardens Road, Adairsville, 30103, (770) 773-7480, EE • *Hearn Academy Inn,* 13 Cedartown Street Southwest, Cave Spring, 30124, (706) 777-8865, I, CP • *Red Top Mountain Lodge,* 653 Red Top Mountain Road Southeast, Cartersville, 30120, (770) 975-0055 or (800) 573-9658, lodge rooms and cottages, I–M • *Old Home Place,* 764 Union Grove Church Road Southeast, Adairsville, 30103, (770) 625-3649, I, CP • *Stoneleigh,* 316 Fain Street, Calhoun, 30701, (706) 629-2093, I, CP • *Claremont House Bed & Breakfast,* 906 East 2nd Avenue, Rome, 30161, (706) 291-0900 or (800) 254-4797, M, CP • *Holiday Inn–Sky Top Center,* US 411, Rome, 30161, (706) 295-1100, I.

DINING *Gray Horse,* on the square, Cave Spring, (706) 777-3766, bountiful Southern buffet lunches, dinners on weekends, I • *Adairsville Inn,* 100 South Main Street, on the square, Adairsville, (770) 773-2774, steaks, seafood, great homemade yeast rolls, I • *Country Gentleman,* 26 Chateau Drive, Rome, (706) 235-2108, country decor, varied menu, some Italian specialties, I–M • *Partridge Café,* 330 Broad Street, Rome, (706) 291-4048, hearty Southern cooking in a restored movie theater, I • *Schroeder's,* 406 Broad Street, Rome, (706) 234-4613, informal, jazz on weekends, I • *Magretta Hall,* 201 Broad Street, Rome, (706) 234-6636, lavish lunch buffets in a restored bank building, I • *Rice House,* Barnsley Inn (see Accommodations on page 14), formal Southern-style dining in an 1854 homestead, E–EE • *Woodlands Grill,* Barnsley Inn (see Accommodations on page 14), English hunt decor, charbroiled meats and fish, M–EE.

SIGHT-SEEING *Chieftain's Museum,* 501 Riverside Parkway between State Route 53 spur and US 27, Rome, (706) 291-9494. Hours: Tuesday to Saturday 10 A.M. to 4 P.M. $$ • *Etowah Indian Mounds,* 813 Indian Mounds Road Southwest, Cartersville, (770) 387-3747. Hours: Tuesday to Saturday 9 A.M. to 5 P.M., Sunday 2 to 5:30 P.M. $$ • *New Echota State Historic Site,* State Route 225, Calhoun, (706) 629-8151. Hours: Tuesday to Saturday 9 A.M. to 5 P.M., Sunday 2 to 5:30 P.M. $ • *Oak Hill and Martha Berry Museum,* Berry College, Martha Berry Boulevard (US 27), Rome, (706) 291-1883. Hours: Monday to Saturday 10 A.M. to 5 P.M., Sunday from 1 P.M. $$ • *Rome Area History Museum,* 303-305 Broad Street, (706) 235-8051. Hours: Tuesday to Saturday 10 A.M. to 4 P.M. $$ • *Eubanks Museum & Gallery,* Shorter College, Rome, (706) 291-2121. Hours: Monday to Friday 9 A.M. to 5 P.M. Free. • *Red Top Mountain State Park,* Red Top Mountain Road, Cartersville, (770) 975-0055. Hours: Daily 7 A.M. to 10 P.M. Office open daily 8 A.M. to 5 P.M. Car fee. $.

INFORMATION *Rome Convention & Visitors Bureau,* 402 Civic Center Drive, Rome, GA 30161, (706) 295-5576 or (800) 444-1834; www.romegeorgia.com • *Cartersville-Bartow County Convention & Visitors Bureau,* 16 West Main Street, P.O. Box 200397, Cartersville, GA 30120, (770) 387-1357 or (800) 733-2280; www.notatlanta.org.

Having a Ball at Hilton Head

Name your favorite sports target—golf ball or tennis ball. Or maybe it's a beach ball you'd rather bounce around. Whatever your game, you can indulge it to your heart's content on Hilton Head Island, where more than 20 golf courses and over 300 tennis courts beckon.

This is also the place to watch the pros put the ball into play in some very prestigious tournaments each spring and to sign on for top-notch instruction to improve your own strokes.

It's hard to believe, but South Carolina's prime resort island used to be a remote, sparsely settled place. Twelve miles long and up to four miles wide, it is rimmed with beaches for almost its entire length, with lush palms and palmettos growing right up to the sand.

Hilton Head was named for Sir William Hilton, the English explorer who sailed into Port Royal Harbor in 1663. Early settlers prospered by establishing plantations growing indigo, a plant that produces blue dye valued for its intense color. When plantation life ended with the Civil War, Hilton Head slumbered.

Then, in the 1950s, a bridge was completed connecting Hilton Head to the mainland and the word *plantation* took on a new meaning, as the Sea Pines Plantation began development on the southern tip of the island. It was a fresh concept at the time, a limited-access residential community with golf courses, bike paths, marinas, and beaches, all carefully planned and placed so as to retain as much of the surrounding natural environment as possible. Over 600 acres were left as a forest and nature preserve.

Sea Pines flourished, and pretty soon there were other posh "plantations" all over the place—Shipyard, Port Royal, and Hilton Head, for example—each with a private gate guarding its villas, beach, golf courses, and other recreational facilities. Most have resort hotels within their property. These plantations now occupy two thirds of the island.

As a result of all this development, there are over 28,000 permanent residents and over 2 million visitors each year—far too many to suit a lot of people who knew the island in its early days. Visitors now arrive via a divided highway whizzing with cars and lined with shops, restaurants, and outlet stores. The stretch of beach along Forest Beach Drive has become motel-condo row.

So don't look for solitude on Hilton Head—but you'll have to look far to find a better place for sports or beaching. It's a great family vacation haven, with accommodations in a wide enough range to suit any budget. You'll see families all over, happily pedaling along the island's

miles of bike paths. Life is tranquil behind the gates of those plantations. And there are still a few carefully guarded nature preserves to
show you why people loved Hilton Head in the first place. Since the climate is semitropical, the weather is conducive to sports most of the
year, allowing you to take advantage of lower off-season rates.

The Chamber of Commerce Welcome Center and Museum, half a
mile past the bridge, is a wonderful welcome to the island. The cedar
building blends gracefully into its surroundings, and the deck offers
peerless views of lowland marshes. The museum tells you about the
island's rich bird life and even has buttons to push to hear bird calls. It
also offers summer morning and afternoon nature activities for
youngsters.

Sea Pines, at the far end of the island, remains the largest of the plantations, with 5,000 acres. It is also the most popular, with a big Welcome Center building at the gate. For those who want to tour or dine in
the plantation, day passes are available here for a small fee.

Tucked among the moss-draped trees beyond the gates are winding
lanes of villas, many of them adjoining one of the three golf courses,
including the famous Harbour Town links, home of the MCI Heritage
Classic in April. The Harbour Town clubhouse is worth visiting just to
see the original oil paintings showing the Classic's winners over the last
20-plus years, a "who's who" of the golfing world. A wide range of
instruction is available at the Sea Pines Academy of Golf.

The highly regarded Sea Pines Racquet Club offers tennis lessons
for all levels, from tots to almost-pros.

The Wildlife and Forest Preserve offers seven miles of groomed
trails. You can take guided tours on foot or on horseback from Lawton
Stables, or take it easy on a hayride or horse-drawn carriage tour
through the forest.

Favorite activities also include cycling on 15 miles of paved bicycle
paths, with rentals available at the Sea Pines Sports and Conference
Center. Many bikers enjoy taking a spin on the hard-packed beach.

Almost everyone who comes to Hilton Head visits Sea Pines at least
for a meal and a stroll in Harbour Town, where the lighthouse and a
marina full of sleek yachts make for the island's most picturesque
scene, especially at sunset. The recently opened Inn at Harbour Town
makes it easy to stay here if you don't want to rent a villa.

South Beach, at the very tip of South Sea Pines Drive, has its own
marina and village, and an inn with a look that is more Cape Cod than
South Carolina.

The scene is quite different just north of the Sea Pines gate. Adjoining the public Coligny Beach Park area are South and North Forest
Beach roads, wall-to-wall with more modest villas, condos, and motels.
This stretch has the largest concentration of people—and some of the
most reasonable rates. If you choose to stay here, you can still play

golf for a fee at many of the private courses, including Harbour Town, as well as at many fine public links such as the Hilton Head National. The island's largest public tennis facility is the 24-court Van der Meer Tennis Center, where excellent instructional tennis weeks and clinics are held.

Continuing north, back toward the bridge, brings you to Shipyard Plantation, 800 acres including 27 holes of golf, another racquet club, and the Holiday Inn Crowne Plaza Resort.

Palmetto Dunes ranks after Sea Pines in size, and its 2,000 acres include both the fancy Hyatt Regency and the Hilton Resort. Facilities are lavish, including three golf courses, the Tennis Racquet Club, and Shelter Cove Harbour, a yacht basin with restaurants and shops. Near the harbor is the new Disney's Hilton Head Island Resort; it is planned as a time-share property but presently allows guests to stay in its town houses and enjoy its myriad activities.

Folly Field, the second public beach area, is a little less manicured than the rest of the island and has its own moderately priced motels and villas.

Hilton Head Plantation incorporates a growing shopping/dining/office development called Main Street, with its own inn and nature walks. The final major plantation, the Port Royal Resort, at the northeastern corner of Hilton Head, is the location of the upscale Westin Resort.

Tennis buffs can get inspiration at the free exhibitions usually held in the late afternoon at the racquet clubs at Sea Pines, Palmetto Dunes, and Shipyard, and at the Van der Meer Tennis Center. Check for current schedules. With so many options for instruction, there's no better place to brush up on your game.

When you're not swinging at a ball or watching one whiz by, you can explore some of the natural beauty that remains on the island. The Coastal Discovery Museum holds interpretive beach walks and marine study trawler trips on the water. Pinckney Island National Wildlife Preserve, on an island between the two bridges connecting Hilton Head to the mainland, offers 4,000 unspoiled acres with paths for hiking and biking and great opportunities for bird-watching. A variety of boat trips is available, some taking you into some of the backwater creeks and salt marshes that are the unique beauty of the low country.

If the unthinkable happens and it rains, you can always check out the art galleries and dozens of shops on the island, or take a drive to Bluffton, just across the bridge, where many interesting boutiques have opened. And there are dozens of dining options, from casual crab houses to haute cuisine. After dinner, the Self Family Arts Center provides handsome quarters for theater and concerts.

With all the activity available on Hilton Head, you have only yourself to blame if you don't have a ball.

<u>Area Code: 843</u>

DRIVING DIRECTIONS Hilton Head Island is located along the southernmost point on the South Carolina coast, 95 miles south of Charleston and 45 miles north of Savannah, Georgia. From the north, take I-95 to exit 28 (Coosawhatchie) and head east on State Route 462 until it merges with US 278. Follow 278 into Hilton Head. From the south, take I-95 to exit 5 and follow the signs to Hilton Head. It is 292 miles from Atlanta, 262 miles from Charlotte, 164 miles from Columbia.

PUBLIC TRANSPORTATION Hilton Head has its own airport, or you can fly to Savannah, less than one hour away. Limos bring passengers from Savannah to Hilton Head; taxis and rental cars are available at both airports.

ACCOMMODATIONS All are zip code 29938. Rates vary with seasons and proximity to the beach; villa rates given are for one bedroom. Ask about golf and tennis packages at all resorts. *Sea Pines Plantation,* P.O. Box 7000, (800) 732-7463, villas, M–EE; *Inn at Harbour Town,* (888) 807-6873, E–EE • *Palmetto Dunes Resort,* P.O. Box 5606, (800) 845-6130 (in South Carolina, 785-1161), villas or hotel-type rooms with daily maid service, M–EE • *South Beach Marina Inn,* South Beach, Sea Pines Plantation, (800) 367-3909, M–EE • *Hyatt Regency,* P.O. Box 6167, Palmetto Dunes, (800) 233-1234, EE • *Hilton Oceanfront Resort,* 23 Ocean Lane, Palmetto Dunes, (800) 221-2424, E–EE • *Crowne Plaza Resort,* 130 Shipyard Drive, Shipyard Plantation, 842-2400 or (800) 334-1881, EE • *Westin Resort and Villas,* 2 Grasslawn Avenue, Hilton Head Plantation, (800) 228-3000 or 681-4000, E–EE • *Disney's Hilton Head Island Resort,* Shelter Cove Harbour, (800) 453-4911, M–EE • *South Beach Marina Inn,* 232 South Sea Pines Drive, 671-6498 or (800) 367-3909, small all-suite hotel, M • *Sea Side Villas,* 23 Forest Beach Drive, 842-9005 or (800) 995-4075 (in South Carolina, 842-9005), on the beach, M–E; daily rates spring and summer, weekly only fall and winter • *Comfort Inn,* 2 Tanglewood Drive (off South Forest Beach Drive), 842-6662, across the road from the beach, good value, I–E • *Hilton Head Island Beach & Tennis Resort,* 40 Folly Field Road, (800) 777-1700 or 842-4402, M–E • *Best Western at Hilton Head,* 40 Waterside Drive, 842-8888 or (800) 528-1234, 5 minutes from the beach, a budget best bet, M.

CENTRAL RESERVATION SERVICES With so many options, over a dozen services provide advice and reservations anywhere on the island. This is a sampling; write or call for a complete list. *Hilton Head Central Reservations,* (800) 845-7018 or 785-9050 • *Hilton Head Accommodations,* (800) 444-4772 or 686-6662 • *Vacations on Hilton*

Head, (800) 232-2453 or 686-3500 • *Island Rentals,* (800) 845-6134 • *Central Tee-Time Center,* golf packages, (800) 767-5423 or 681-6681.

DINING *Charlie's L'Etoile Verte,* 1000 Plantation Center, 785-9277, French, one of the island's best, E • *Starfire Contemporary Bistro,* 37 New Orleans Road, 785-3434, fine dining, E–EE • *Brian's,* 1301 Main Street Village, 681-6001, Continental menu, M–E • *Lagniappe,* 1000 William Hilton Parkway, Village at Wexford, 341-3377, creative chef and colorful ambience, M • *Stripes,* 32 Office Park Road, Courtyard Building 114, 686-4747, American grill, M–E • *Juleps,* 14 Greenwood Drive, Gallery of Shops, 842-5827, cooking with a Southern accent, M–E • *The Captain's Table,* 10 North Forest Boulevard, 686-4300, oceanfront dining, M–E • *Gaslight,* 303 Market Place, 785-5814, French cuisine, candlelight, M–E • *CQ's,* Harbour Town, Sea Pines Plantation, 671-2779, varied menu, casual, long-time favorite, M • *Café Europa,* Harbour Town, 671-3399, varied menu, super view, M • *Crazy Crab* (two locations), Harbour Town, 363-2722 or US 278, Jarvis Creek, 681-5021, steamed, boiled, or fried seafood, I–M • *Harbourmaster's,* off US 278 on Shelter Cove, 785-3030, overlooking the harbor and marshes, M–E • *Damon's,* Village at Wexford, US 278, 785-6677, popular chain known for ribs and onion ring loaf, I–M • *Remy's Restaurant,* Arrow Road and Dunnagan's Alley (near Sea Pines Circle), 842-3800, locals' favorite for generous portions at reasonable prices, M • *Santa Fe Cafe,* 700 Plantation Drive, 785-3838, excellent Southwestern food, M • *San Miguel's Mexican Cafe,* Shelter Cove Lane, Shelter Cove Marina, 842-4555, top spot for inexpensive dining, M • *Truffles Cafe and Market,* Sea Pines Center, 671-6136, top choice lunch or light dinner menu, I–M • *Salty Dog Café,* South Beach Marina, 671-2233, great for lunch on the docks, try the crab salad, I.

ACTIVITIES Check for current schedules and prices. **Nature walks and programs:** *Coastal Discovery Museum,* 100 William Hilton Parkway, 689-6767 • **Bicycle rentals:** *Fishcreek Landing,* 785-2021; *Peddling Pelican,* 785-5470; *South Beach Cycles,* 671-2453; *Hilton Head Bicycle,* 686-6888 • **Boat cruises:** *Adventure Cruises,* 785-4558; *Vagabond Cruises,* 842-7179 • **Canoe rentals:** *Fishcreek Landing,* 785-2021 • **Kayak rentals:** *Outside Hilton Head,* 686-6996 • **Horseback riding:** *Lawton Stables,* 671-2586 • **Nature preserves:** *Pinckney Island National Wildlife Refuge,* 642-4415; *Sea Pines Forest Preserve,* 842-1449; *Audubon-Newhall Preserve,* 785-5775 • **Sailing:** *Cheers,* 671-1800; *Island Water Sports,* 671-7007. Contact Chamber of Commerce for full list of current activities and operators.

INFORMATION *Hilton Head Island Chamber of Commerce,* P.O. Box 5647, Hilton Head, SC 29938, 785-3673; www.hilton headisland.org.

Arts and Flowers in Winston-Salem

Start with an eighteenth-century community famed for its Old World crafts skills. Combine with a twentieth-century manufacturing center whose benevolent business tycoons strongly support the arts.

The result: Winston-Salem, North Carolina, a surprising city. Known best for history and its textile and tobacco industries, Winston-Salem is gaining an equal reputation as a Southern center for the arts.

The community known as Old Salem, founded in 1766, remains the most popular of the city's visitor attractions, but it now has strong competition. Two art showplaces are in former mansions of industrial magnates. The R. J. Reynolds home, Reynolda, has become a noted house museum of American art. The Hanes mansion is now part of the Southeastern Center for Contemporary Art (SECCA), the region's foremost showcase for cutting-edge modern art.

The Museum of Early Southern Decorative Arts, a division of Old Salem, is an underpublicized treasure of period rooms and galleries featuring the decorative arts of seven Southern states from 1690 to 1820. Decorative arts of the future are being influenced by students at the Sawtooth Center for Visual Design, located in a converted 1910 textile mill. The school houses three art galleries with rotating presentations by local artists.

Winston-Salem is also the home of the North Carolina School of the Arts, the first state-supported school of arts in the United States, nurturing young talent in music, drama, dance, and art. The school offers a wealth of concerts and performances at the handsome Roger L. Stevens Center, a renovated movie palace.

The best place to start a visit is Old Salem. Tucked away in the shadow of downtown, this is one of the most authentic restorations in America, with some 90 buildings from the eighteenth and nineteenth centuries. Visit in spring for garden tours and a treasured tradition, the Moravian Easter sunrise service, which attracts thousands of worshippers.

Salem was founded by Moravians, a German-speaking Protestant sect based in what is now Czechoslovakia. Fleeing religious persecution in Europe in the mid-1700s, members established missions in various parts of the world. The communities and their missionary work were supported by making and selling high-quality handicrafts.Their first American settlement was in Pennsylvania; the second was in North Carolina at Historic Bethabara, outside Winston-Salem. That original settlement, at the 110-acre Bethabara Park, features restored and reconstructed community buildings—a church, a cabin, a French and Indian War fort—and community and medical gardens.

Established 13 years after Bethabara, Salem, like all Moravian communities, was under the control of the church. Residents lived in "choirs" according to age, sex, and marital status. Skilled work and worship were stressed, and religious music was an important part of life.

Salem ceased to be a church-owned town in the mid-nineteenth century but remained an active community until it was merged with the larger and more prosperous industrial city of Winston in 1913. In 1950, when the old buildings were threatened with demolition, Old Salem was formed to preserve the unique heritage.

When you enter Old Salem today, there's a sense of life and continuity that is missing in many such restorations. This is partly because it shares a green with the architecturally compatible buildings of Salem College, a liberal arts school for women, and Salem Academy, a girls preparatory school, first established in 1772. The first boarding school building, dating to 1805, still serves as a college dorm.

Each Moravian family not only had a garden for its needs but was assigned a lot outside town where field crops like corn, wheat, pumpkins, and sweet potatoes were grown and the family cow was pastured. Over 30 gardens have been reconstructed using plants documented as the same varieties cultivated 200 years ago. Most of the historic brick and clapboard houses in the historic area are now private residences.

The dozen Old Salem buildings that are open to the public run mostly along Main Street. Taking the self-guided tour is almost like dropping in on a town two centuries ago. Cooking, baking, sewing, tinsmithing, pewter making, blacksmithing, weaving, and dyeing are some of the crafts you might see demonstrated by costumed residents re-creating the life of an earlier day. On Monday, you might encounter a woman carrying a 25-pound bucket of water in each hand to wash the linens. Return on Tuesday, you might find her pressing those same linens using a six-pound iron heated in front of the fire.

Most of the artisans are found in the largest restored building, the Single Brothers House, a 1769 half-timbered structure with a brick addition. Boys were required to live there from the age of 14 while they learned a trade from one of Salem's renowned craftsmen.

Other stops include individual shops where a shoemaker may be cutting out leather, a potter may be turning his wheel with a foot treadle, and a joiner may be showing off his fine carpentry skills.

So highly regarded were these artisans that the town tavern thrived simply by accommodating customers who came to purchase local products. The original tavern remains furnished as it was in the past.

The Salem Tavern Restaurant is the place to stop for a wonderful lunch, especially the flaky pot pies and homemade rolls. For dessert, you won't do better than the Winkler Bakery, where goodies such as

Moravian sugar cake are baked in a wood-fired oven and sold to the public. It is the most crowded of all the exhibit buildings.

At the end of Main Street is the Museum of Early Southern Decorative Arts (MESDA), a one-of-a-kind showcase that merits your full attention, so try to get there before your energy is spent or come back the next day. Tickets can be purchased separately or in combination with an Old Salem visit.

Twenty-four fully furnished rooms and seven galleries show different aspects of the South before 1820, an unrivaled display of the talent of the region's early craftsmen. Representing everything from a Palladian manor on Virginia's James River to a log house from the Carolina back country, each room is filled with furnishings of its time and place.

The core of the materials is from the private collections of Frank L. Horton and his mother, Theo L. Taliaferro, who also endowed the institution. The museum serves an important role as a center for the study of early Southern arts.

Also in the museum building are the Gallery at Old Salem, with changing exhibits, and the Children's Museum at Old Salem, designed for youngsters ages four to nine.

The other "must" attraction in Winston-Salem is Reynolda House, a treasury of American art in an exquisite setting. This was the country home built between 1912 and 1917 by Richard J. Reynolds, the founder of the enterprise that became the largest tobacco company in the world. The white-columned, bungalow-style 100-room mansion with a low-hanging green roof is surprisingly livable, grand yet comfortable at the same time.

Unfortunately, both Reynolds and his wife, Katharine, died not many years after the house was completed. Their daughter, Mary, acquired the property in 1934 and lived there with her husband, Charles Babcock. They were responsible for opening the house to the public in 1967 as a museum of American art and culture.

The distinguished collection spanning the years from 1755 to the present is a significant survey of American art from Copley and Peale to O'Keeffe and Calder. An outstanding example of the Hudson River School is Frederic E. Church's masterpiece *The Andes of Ecuador.*

A very human side of the family can be seen on the third floor, where clothing dating from 1905 and worn by members of the Reynolds family is displayed. Included is the outfit hand-sewn by Mrs. Reynolds for her wedding; she was a girl of modest means who married the boss.

Downstairs, indoor amusements for the family, such as a glass-enclosed indoor swimming pool, squash courts, a bowling alley, and a shooting gallery, give an idea of their lavish lifestyle.

The grounds were also planned for recreation, including polo, golf, and tennis. The fine gardens were located so that they could be enjoyed by the public without impinging on the family's privacy. They make for a glorious spring stroll.

Reynolda was planned as a model farm and village as well as a private estate. It had its own telephone and power systems, post office, school, church, and staff residences. The stables, barn, workshops, and homes of workmen living on the property, all done with the same white walls and green roofs as the main house, are now Reynolda Village, one of Winston-Salem's most attractive shopping and dining complexes.

Beyond is the 340-acre Reynolda campus of Wake Forest University. Founded in the town of Wake Forest in 1834, the school was relocated in 1956 to this site, thanks to the generosity of the A. Smith Reynolds Foundation and the Reynolds family, which donated 300 acres of land for the campus and an annual grant of $500,000. With their aid, the campus has grown in less than 40 years from an original 14 structures to more than 40 major buildings.

Stop at the Welcome Center at the Reynolda Road entrance for a map. Besides admiring the expansive modern campus, you can visit the Museum of Anthropology, displaying objects from around the world, including materials collected by Moravian missionaries.

Across the road from the Reynolda mansion is a stop that is a must for anyone who wants to know what is happening now in the world of modern art. The modernistic galleries of the Southeastern Center for Contemporary Art (SECCA) are a startling contrast to their entrance, the 1929 stone mansion of the late textile magnate James G. Hanes, the original building on the 32-acre site.

A prime mission of SECCA is to bring artists and the public together in a dialogue about modern art. The changing shows each year are an unpredictable variety of styles and media. Guided art walks by the staff help visitors understand the concept of the exhibitions and allow them to ask questions. Some pieces you may like, some you may hate, but all will likely arouse your interest. As the brochure promises, you'll be seeing the future of art.

Contemporary crafts also can be seen in the making in small studios along Trade Street, a downtown area becoming known as the Arts District. The Studios, 560 North Trade, is the largest workshop, home to potters, painters, jewelers, calligraphers, and the Artworks Gallery, a co-op of visual artists.

Add to Winston-Salem's arts list Piedmont Craftsmen, an organization representing over 300 top Southeast artisans who must meet juried standards to join. Their works in a variety of media are on display in a gallery on Reynolda Road.

If children are along, plan a stop at SciWorks, an indoor-outdoor museum of nature and science that includes live animals and a planetarium.

While you are in this part of the state, you may want to take time out to take advantage of another North Carolina specialty, furniture bargains. It is just 19 miles to the dealers in High Point, where the Furniture Discovery Center is the nation's only museum showing how furniture is manufactured, or 70 miles to Hickory's vast Furniture Mart, the largest manufacturers' outlet in the country selling directly to the public, with dozens of showrooms exhibiting pieces from quality manufacturers such as Drexel-Heritage and Henredon.

Another possibility is an hour's drive southeast: the North Carolina Zoo, near Asheboro. One of the country's largest animal parks, comprising some 1,400 acres, the zoo has many outstanding naturalistic displays, including African plains, chimpanzee and lion habitats, and the R. J. Reynolds Forest Aviary, a miniature jungle that is home to more than 150 exotic birds.

If the day is fine, you can also enjoy the outdoors closer to town at Tanglewood Park, located in Clemmons, about 15 minutes west of Winston-Salem. This was the estate of William Neal Reynolds, another heir to the tobacco fortune, who willed it to the county. Now it is a forested playground that includes picnic grounds, nature trails, a wildlife park where deer and peacocks stroll, lakes, a pool, tennis courts, stables, and 54 holes of golf, including the challenging Robert Trent Jones course that is the site of the Vantage Championship, one of the richest Senior PGA golf tournaments. The park is the setting for many other special events, from concerts to steeplechase races, an annual Chili Cook-Off to a dazzling display of Christmas lights.

Area Code: 336

DRIVING DIRECTIONS   Winston-Salem is reached via I-40 from east or west, or via US 52 from north and south. From Atlanta, take I-85 east to I-77 north, then I-40 east, 340 miles. From Charlotte, take I-77 north to I-40, 81 miles.

PUBLIC TRANSPORTATION   The closest major airport is in Greensboro, about half an hour away. A car is necessary to see the sights.

ACCOMMODATIONS   *Brookstown Inn,* 200 Brookstown Avenue, Winston-Salem, 27101, 725-1120 or (800) 845-4262, M, nicely restored old mill with brick walls, exposed beams, M–E, CP • *Augustus T. Zevely House,* 803 South Main Street, Old Salem, 27108, 748-9299 or (800) 928-9299, historic Old Salem home turned bed-and-breakfast, M, CP • *Colonel Ludlow Inn,* Summit and West Fifth Streets, Winston-Salem, 27101, 777-1887 or (800) 301-1887, Queen Anne–style home, upscale bed-and-breakfast, E–EE, CP • *Henry F. Shaffner House,* 150 South Marshall Street, Winston-Salem, 27101, 777-0052, another nicely restored Victorian bed-and-breakfast, M–EE, CP • *Lady Anne's Bed & Breakfast,* 612 Summit Street, Winston-Salem, 27101, 724-1074, homey Victorian, M–E, CP • *Tanglewood Manor House,* Tanglewood Park, Highway 158 (off I-40), Clemmons, 27012,

778-6370, manor house and guest houses, M, CP • *Adam's Mark Winston Plaza,* 425 North Cherry Street, Winston-Salem, 27101, 725-3500, downtown hotel with indoor pool, sauna, sun deck; ask about weekend package rates, M–E.

DINING *Noble's Grille,* 380 Knollwood Street, 777-8477, contemporary decor, open grill, one of the city's best, E • *Fabian's,* 1100 Reynolda Road, 723-7700, sophisticated cuisine, good value five-course prix fixe menu, EE • *Michael's,* 848 West Fifth Street, 777-0000, restored mansion, French/American menu, E • *Southbound Bistro & Grille,* 300 South Liberty Street, 723-0322, innovative dishes in a restored warehouse, M–E • *Zevely House,* 901 West Fourth Street, 725-6666, dining in an 1815 landmark with fireplace and patio, M–E • *Leon's Café,* 924 South Marshall Street, 725-9593, eclectic interesting menu, popular, M • *The Vineyards,* 120 Reynolda Village, 748-0269, Continental, M • *Paul's Fine Italian Dining,* 3443-B Robinhood Road, 768-2645, the name says it, M • *South by Southwest,* 241 Marshall Street, 727-0800, popular Southwest fare, M–E • *Salem Tavern Restaurant,* 736 Main Street, Old Salem, 748-8585, great food and ambience, don't miss the pot pie, lunch, I; dinner, M • *Village Tavern,* 221 Reynolda Road, 748-0221, casual, good value, lunch, I; dinner, I–M • For barbecue lovers, the place is *Pig Pickins of America,* 615 Deacon Boulevard, 777-0105, I, or drive half an hour south to Lexington, a town wall-to-wall with barbecue restaurants.

SIGHT-SEEING *Old Salem,* 600 South Main Street, 721-7300 or (888) OLD-SALEM; www.oldsalem.org. Write for calendar of special events. Hours: Monday to Saturday 9:30 A.M. to 5 P.M., Sunday from 12:30 P.M. $$$$$ • *Museum of Early Southern Decorative Arts,* 924 South Main Street, Old Salem, 721-7360. Hours: Monday to Saturday 9 A.M. to 5 P.M., Sunday from 1 P.M. $$$; combination tickets available with Old Salem; building includes the *Children's Museum of Old Salem* • *Reynolda House Museum of American Art,* Reynolda Road, 725-5325. Hours: Tuesday to Saturday 9:30 A.M. to 4:30 P.M., Sunday from 1:30 P.M. $$$ • *Historic Bethabara Park,* Bethabara Road, 924-8191. Hours: Monday to Friday 9:30 A.M. to 4:30 P.M., Saturday and Sunday from 1:30 P.M. $ • *Wake Forest Museum of Anthropology,* Reynolda Station, Wake Forest University, 759-5282. Hours: Tuesday to Saturday 10 A.M. to 4:30 P.M., modified hours in summer. Donation • *Sciworks,* 400 Hanes Mill Road, 767-6730. Hours: Monday to Saturday 10 A.M. to 4:30 P.M., Sunday 1 P.M. to 4 P.M. $$$.

Contemporary art galleries: *Southeastern Center for Contemporary Art,* 750 Marguerite Drive (off Reynolda Road), 725-1904. Hours: Tuesday to Saturday 10 A.M. to 5 P.M., Sunday from 2 P.M. $$ • *Sawtooth Center for Visual Design,* Winston Square, 226 North Marshall

Street, 723-7395. Hours: Monday to Friday 9 A.M. to 9 P.M., Saturday to 5 P.M. Free • *Piedmont Craftsmen,* 1294 Reynolda Road, 725-1516. Hours: Tuesday to Saturday 10 A.M. to 6 P.M., Sunday 1 to 5 P.M. Free • *Diggs Gallery,* 601 Martin Luther King Drive, Winston-Salem State University, 750-2458, showcase for changing exhibits of African-American art. Hours: Tuesday to Saturday 11 A.M. to 5 P.M. Free.

Other diversions: *North Carolina Zoological Park,* 4401 Zoo Parkway, 6 miles southeast of US 64, Asheboro, 879-7000 or (800) 625-0170. Hours: Daily, April to October 9 A.M. to 5 P.M., rest of year to 4 P.M. $$$$ • *Tanglewood Park,* US 158 (off I-40), Clemmons, 778-6300 Hours: Daily, dawn to dusk. Admission to grounds, $.

Furniture shopping: *Hickory Furniture Mart,* 2220 US 70, exit 125 from I-70, Hickory, (800) 462-MART, largest showroom in the Southeast. Hours: Monday to Saturday 9 A.M. to 6 P.M. For High Point shopping information, contact *High Point Convention & Visitors Bureau,* 1101 North South Main Street, P.O. Box 5025, High Point, NC 27262, 889-8151.

INFORMATION *Winston-Salem Convention & Visitors Bureau,* 601 West Fourth Street, P.O. Box 1409, Winston-Salem, NC 27102, 728-4200 or (800) 331-7018; www.wscvb.com • *Visitor Center* is at 601 North Cherry Street, 777-3796 or (800) 331-7018.

Mr. Callaway and Mr. Roosevelt of Pine Mountain

Cason J. Callaway, a textile mogul and founder of Callaway Mills, was known as a man who believed that the most interesting ideas were "conceived in superlatives." But even his wife, Virginia, was surprised back in the 1930s when she asked for a magnolia tree for her birthday and a truckload of 5,000 trees arrived.

Those trees were a harbinger of what was to come. They can still be seen in full bloom each spring at what is now Callaway Gardens, the family's superlative legacy to the South. The gardens they grace today comprise 14,000 acres of horticultural displays, as well as one of the largest conservatories in North America for colorful butterflies that are aptly described as "flowers on the wing."

Mr. Callaway was not the only prominent man who influenced this region, whose scenery surprises many who do not expect mountains in central Georgia. The ridgetop Pine Mountain Trail traverses land that once belonged to Franklin Delano Roosevelt, whose Little White House may be visited in Warm Springs, 11 miles from Callaway Gardens. When you see the natural beauty of the area, you'll understand why these two powerful men came to love it.

One of the nation's major floral attractions came into being almost by accident when the Callaway family took a drive in the country and discovered a spot near Hamilton called Blue Springs. On a walk in the woods, Cason picked a sprig of a bright red wild azalea for his wife, who loved wildflowers. She identified it as a prunifolia or plumleaf, a species so rare it was on the verge of extinction. Callaway reacted by buying up 2,500 acres to save the shrubs. The family built a compound that became their treasured weekend getaway, Blue Springs Farm.

A heart attack in 1948 caused Cason Callaway to change his priorities. He and Virginia divided their land among their four children and deeded a fifth portion to the Ida Cason Callaway Foundation, named for his mother. That last portion became their focus. According to a biographer, the Callaways determined to create "one corner of Georgia in which every sight was beauty."

Callaway Gardens, which opened to the public in 1952, was the fulfillment of that mission. It is a showcase for the world's largest display of hollies, more than 700 kinds of azaleas, and endless varieties of wildflowers. Mr. Cason's Vegetable Garden, a 7.5-acre showplace where more than 400 varieties of vegetables, fruits, and herbs are grown, uses many of the growing techniques developed at Blue Springs Farm. The grounds also include a 3,000-acre protected wilderness area.

The gardens can be seen via walking trails, as well as a 13-mile paved drive and a ten-mile biking trail. Stops along the way allow for visiting each of the special gardens. The Azalea Trails are in their glory from March to May, accented with dogwoods, rhododendrons, and a rainbow of wildflowers. Spring also brings an annual celebration from late March to mid-April that includes entertainment, art shows, and other special events.

Callaway's attractions continue to grow. The Ida Cason Callaway Memorial Chapel was dedicated in 1962. The English Gothic church is a favorite setting for weddings and is noted for its organ, whose music may be heard outside the church through the louvered tower. In 1984 the John A. Sibley Horticultural Center added a dramatic five-acre greenhouse complex featuring a two-story waterfall and year-round floral displays.

A rare treat is the Cecil B. Day Butterfly Center, a 15,000-square-foot garden enclosed by soaring glass walls, where more than 1,000 exotic butterflies are allowed to fly free. These graceful, airy creatures are given their bold colors by nature as protection; the bright hues and bold patterns signal predators that these butterflies are not good to eat. However, these same brilliant shades are an endless delight for humans, who rarely get such a close-up vantage point for admiring nature's palette. Some of the fluttering beauties are so tame they will light on your hand. The center was opened in 1988, with the major contribution a gift from Deen Day Smith in honor of her late husband Cecil Day, the founder of Days Inns of America.

The latest major development is a new orientation area for visitors called the Virginia Hand Callaway Discovery Center. A recently-built entrance at the intersection of Georgia Highways 18 and 354 leads to the center, which provides ample parking spaces and entree to bicycles, trams, and a lake ferry as well as entrances to walking trails and road-ways. An information desk, an orientation theater, and interpretive exhibits help guests make the most of their visits. The building also contains an auditorium for lectures, an exhibit area, a shop, and the Mountain Creek Café, serving breakfast and lunch. The café deck surrounds a lovely water garden.

Callaway Gardens attracts nearly one million visitors yearly, a popularity that has helped develop the little town of Pine Mountain a few miles away on US 27. Pine Mountain has dining places and several antiques shops and galleries. The Anne Tutt Gallery is of interest for its paintings of Callaway landscapes by Alexander Kalinin. The Pine Mountain Antique Mall on Main Street has 100 dealers and holds auctions on the first and third Saturday nights each month.

An unusual stop is the Pine Mountain Wild Animal Park, where 300 kinds of exotic animals, from alligators to zebras, can be seen via "safari bus." There's also a petting zoo for the very young.

The Callaway Gardens Country Store is the place to pick up traditional Southern foods, including the store's own muscadine products, and to have substantial Southern breakfasts and lunches at the Country Kitchen, overlooking the valley.

Right across the road from the store begins the Pine Mountain Trail, an outstanding hiking trail. Since 1975, volunteers young and old have worked to build and maintain the spectacular 23-mile footpath along the mountain ridge. An inexpensive map is available at the FDR State Park Welcome Center.

As noted, much of the land this trail traverses was owned by Franklin Roosevelt. Roosevelt was a young attorney in New York in 1924, in despair over the polio that had seemingly ended a promising career, when he heard about a Georgian with the same disease who had regained sensation in his legs after bathing in the bubbling hot waters at Warm Springs.

Those close to Roosevelt claimed that his spirits revived along with the sensation in his numbed limbs as he swam in the Warm Springs pool. While there he also regained his drive and ambition, and he went on to become the president who led the nation to recovery from the Depression and to victory in World War II.

Roosevelt loved Warm Springs, where he spent many of his happiest days fishing, riding, and enjoying country life in spite of his disability. In 1932 he built a six-room white clapboard house with Southern-style pillars, the home that would become known as the Little White House, on a site above a deep wooded ravine. He became a familiar figure in the area, cruising the country roads in a runabout convertible specially fitted with hand controls, stopping to chat with anyone he spotted in a front yard. Two of his 1938 roadsters are on display at his home.

Many historic decisions were made at Warm Springs, and it was there that Roosevelt died on April 12, 1945, while posing for a portrait, seated in his favorite brown leather chair.

The house remains just as he left it, with the unfinished portrait still on the easel. The modest pine-paneled rooms, fieldstone fireplace, shelves of books, and comfortable furnishings are a contrast to Roosevelt's formal public life. The house is filled with the ship models and maritime paintings he admired.

FDR's wife was rarely among the guests at Warm Springs, according to local gossip. It was his longtime friend Lucy Mercer who was with him when he suffered his fatal stroke in 1945, a side of his life only recently made public. This is not discussed at the home, which is now a State Historic Site.

On the grounds is a museum telling the story of his life and of FDR's battle with polio. A film showing a laughing Roosevelt romping with children in the pool and picnicking in the nearby woods reveals a playful side of the great man that is seldom seen. He even allowed photographers to show his shrunken legs, usually so carefully hidden from the public.

With polio conquered, Roosevelt's original foundation encountered funding difficulties, and in 1974 the house was sold to the state for one dollar. It has since become a state rehabilitation facility serving people with a wide variety of physical disabilities. The original springs and outdoor pools have been maintained as a historic attraction.

The land the president loved to roam has become Georgia's largest state park, with a special marking at Dowdell's Knob, the point overlooking Pine Mountain Valley that was FDR's favorite picnic retreat. The park's stone swimming pool and stone-and-log buildings were built as part of Roosevelt's Civilian Conservation Corps program.

The village of Warm Springs, which had declined over the years, has been rediscovered and restored by private developers. With its quaint turn-of-the-century structures transformed into shops and cafés, it is now ideal for strolling. The old hotel is once again receiving visitors.

This is just one of several lodging options in the area. Bed-and-breakfast lovers have their pick of Magnolia Hall in Hamilton or Raintree Farms in Waverly Hill, each an easy drive to Callaway Gardens. Aunt Stella's House is unique; guests have the whole four-room house to themselves, complete with porch swing, fireplace, TV/VCR, and a refrigerator stocked with breakfast. Two rustic resort retreats that take advantage of the mountain scenery are Pine Mountain Club Chalets, on a private lake, and Mountain Top Inn and Resort, with log cabins and a lodge on a secluded ridge adjoining the wilderness of the state park. Both offer pools and tennis. Rustic cabins are also available in Roosevelt State Park, where amenities include two lakes, the pool, 30 miles of hiking trails, and horseback riding.

Those who elect to stay at Callaway Gardens can take advantage of even more extensive resort facilities, such as 63 holes of golf, 10 lighted tennis courts, indoor racquetball courts, bicycle and jogging paths, and 14 man-made lakes for swimming, waterskiing, fishing, boating, or just reflecting on the lovely reflections. Lodgings range from 349 hotel-style rooms in a wing adjoining the main lobby and dining rooms to cottages and luxurious villas.

If you can't afford the tab at on-site lodgings, not to worry. Most of Callaway's sports facilities, including golf and tennis, are available to all for a fee.

Area Code: 706

DRIVING DIRECTIONS Callaway Gardens is about 70 miles south of Atlanta. From Atlanta, take I-85 to I-185, continue 7 miles farther to US 27 south, and proceed 11 miles to the gardens. From Birmingham, take US 280 east to I-85 north to Georgia Route 18 east. From Nashville, take I-75 south to I-85 and follow directions above. For Warm Springs, take I-85 south to US 27A south. Georgia Route 190 is a scenic connector between Callaway Gardens, on US 27, and US 27A leading to Warm Springs.

ACCOMMODATIONS *Callaway Gardens Resort,* Pine Mountain, 31822, 663-2281 or (800) 225-5292; Gardens Inn, M; cottages, E–EE; villas, EE • *Mountain Top Inn & Resort,* Georgia Route 190 and Hines Gap Road, P.O. Box 174, Pine Mountain, 31822, 663-4719 or (800) 533-6376; lodge rooms, I–M, CP; log cabins, E • *Pine Mountain Club Chalets,* Georgia Route 18, P.O. Box 477, Pine Mountain, 31822, 663-2211 or (800) 535-7622, E • *Davis Inn,* US 27 south and State Park Road, Pine Mountain, 31822, 663-2522 or (888) 346-2668, motel near Callaway Gardens, M–E • *Hotel Warm Springs,* P.O. Box 351, Warm Springs, 31850, 655-2114, I–M, CP • *Franklin D. Roosevelt State Park,* 2970 Georgia Route 190, Pine Mountain, 31822, 663-4858, rustic cabins, I.

Bed-and-breakfast inns: *Magnolia Hall B & B,* P.O. Box 326, Hamilton, 31811, 628-4566, handsome Victorian ambience, M, CP • *Raintree Farms of Waverly Hall,* 8060 Highway 208, Waverly Hall, 31831,

582-3227 or (800) 433-0627, 1833 home, friendly hostess, M, CP •
Aunt Stella's House, Hamilton Square Street, Hamilton, 31811, 628-
4733, individual home accommodating two to six, M.

DINING *Cricket's Restaurant,* Georgia Route 18, Pine Mountain,
663-8136, excellent menu, Creole and Cajun specialties, I–M • *Oak
Tree Victorian Restaurant,* US 27, Hamilton (5 miles south of Callaway), 628-4218, Old World ambience, Continental, M–E • *Bulloch
House,* US 21, Warm Springs, 655-9068, Southern cooking in an 1892
home, outdoor dining, I • *Marco's Italian Restaurant,* 9635 Highway
208, Waverly Hall, 582-3295, rustic ambience, very popular, M • **Callaway Gardens restaurants 663-2281:** *Plantation Room,* Southern-
style buffets, all three meals; dinner, M; light dining, I; *Georgia Room,*
candlelight and "nouveau Southern" cuisine, M–E; *The Veranda,* Italian cuisine, views of the golf course, I–M; *Gardens Restaurant,*
casual, I–M; *Country Kitchen,* bountiful breakfast or lunch with
panoramic view, I; *Mountain Creek Cafe,* light cafeteria-style dining, I.

SIGHT-SEEING *Callaway Gardens,* US 27, Pine Mountain, 663-
2281 or (800) 225-5292; www.callawaygardens.com. Hours: Daily
9 A.M. to 5 P.M., 7 A.M. to 7 P.M. in warmer months. $$$$ • *Little White
House Historic Site,* Georgia Route 1, P.O. Box 10, Warm Springs,
655-5870. Hours: Daily 9 A.M. to 5 P.M., last admission 4 P.M. $$ •
Franklin D. Roosevelt State Park, 2970 Georgia Route 190E, Pine
Mountain, entrances on US 27 and Georgia Route 190, 663-4858.
Hours: Daily 7 A.M. to 10 P.M., office hours daily 8 A.M. to 5 P.M. $ •
Pine Mountain Wild Animal Park, 1300 Oak Grove Road, Pine Moun-
tain, 663-8744 or (800) 367-2751. Hours: Monday to Friday 10 A.M. to
7:30 P.M., Saturday and Sunday to 7:30 P.M. $$$$.

INFORMATION *Pine Mountain Tourism Association, Inc.,* P.O.
Box 177, Pine Mountain, GA 31822, 663-4000 or (800) 441-3502;
www.pinemountain.org.

Making the Most
of Montgomery

Montgomery is going to surprise you. With a population under 200,000, this is not a huge city, yet it is chock-full of Southern history and alive with arts. Civil War and civil rights, Hank Williams and Zelda Fitzgerald, Shakespeare, Greek sculpture, and American art—all of these are part of the unexpected mix that makes up Alabama's varied and vital capital.

If you come in early spring, you can add to your agenda the oldest and largest rodeo east of the Mississippi.

Begin with a visit to the Visitor Center to pick up maps and information and watch a video on Montgomery's highlights, and you're ready to explore the sights. One good plan is to cover nearby downtown, then move on to the many outlying attractions.

As with many cities these days, Montgomery's center is no longer the shopping heart of the city, and it can't be called scenic, but it does hold many sight-seeing treasures.

One of the most instructive is Old Alabama Town, a three-block complex just behind the Thompson mansion that shows how people lived in central Alabama from 1800 to 1900. More than 30 restored buildings interpret changing lifestyles in the state. Lucas Tavern, the reception center, is where the first pioneers socialized when they came into the territory in 1817. An audiotape by Alabama's favorite story-teller, Kathryn Tucker Windham, serves as a colorful guide while you stroll through the rest of the town. Among the stops are a log cabin, a one-room school, a grocery, and a doctor's office. Grandest of all is the Ordeman-Shaw home, a circa-1850 town house filled with antiques of the period. Interpreters are on hand to tell you what life was like for the Ordeman family and the rising middle class before the Civil War.

The Drugstore Museum and Rose House Craft Center, located around the corner on Columbus Street, also are worth a stop. At the Craft Center you will find artisans in action, spinning, weaving, wood-carving, and building musical instruments.

Montgomery was founded in 1818, when two smaller settlements merged and named their town for a Revolutionary War hero, Brigadier General Richard Montgomery. It prospered as a cotton market and transportation center and, with the promise of a privately financed capitol building atop Goat Hill, replaced Tuscaloosa as the state capital in 1846. When the first capitol was lost to fire, a second went up in 1851.

In 1861 this building served as the first capitol of the Confederacy. Thousands celebrated in front of the capitol portico on February 16, 1861, as Mississippian Jefferson Davis was inaugurated as president of the Confederate States. Alabama governors are still sworn in with the Bible that Davis used. After extensive restoration, the capitol building is now a combination working capitol and museum. It is beautiful to see, and full of Southern history.

Another interesting place to see downtown is the White House of the Confederacy, the 1835 home where Jefferson Davis and his family lived while in Montgomery.

Montgomery recovered quickly from the Civil War. By the 1880s it was prospering once again as a railroad center, and downtown boasted the nation's first electric trolley system, called "the Lightning Route" for its amazing speed of six miles an hour.

Not far away is a monument to a different period in Montgomery's history. The city's Civil Rights Memorial was designed by Maya Lin, who also designed the Vietnam Veterans Memorial in Washington, D.C. Like her earlier creation, this one is moving in its simplicity. It is a curved circular black granite table with the names of 40 martyrs of the Civil Rights Movement radiating from the center like the hands of a clock. Water flows from the center across the surface. On the wall behind are the words of Dr. Martin Luther King Jr.: "We will not be satisfied until justice rolls down like waters and righteousness like a mighty stream."

Dr. King became the minister of the nearby Dexter Avenue Baptist Church in 1954. That church was the focal point for meetings of blacks who organized an 18-month bus boycott that eventually resulted in the Supreme Court decision outlawing segregation on public transportation. It set in motion the Civil Rights Movement of the later 1950s and 1960s. Dr. King went on to win the Nobel Peace Prize for his work. A folk mural in his former church depicts King's work.

Not far from the church is Centennial Hill, a prominent black residential area developed in the 1870s, with fine homes along Jackson and Union Streets. At 1524 St. John Street is the more modest Cole-Sanford House, the birthplace of singer Nat "King" Cole.

A much-visited shrine to another famous Montgomery entertainer is the grave of country music great Hank Williams. Williams is buried on a hilltop in the Oakwood Cemetery Annex, just north of the state capitol, with a granite ten-gallon hat as a memorial. A life-size statue of the singer stands across from City Hall, and a museum devoted to memorabilia of his life, including the 1952 blue Cadillac in which he died, opened recently.

Having traced the past of Montgomery, it's time to see its vibrant present, the Wynton Blount Cultural Park, where the Alabama Shakespeare Festival Theater and the Montgomery Museum of Fine Arts face each other across a serene pond populated by majestic swans.

The elaborate red-brick theater does not try to emulate Stratford, but the Bard would no doubt be pleased if he could see the handsome quarters where his works are staged by a 200-member repertory company.

The theater holds two stages, and contemporary works are also on the program. This is one of the largest and most productive regional theaters in the country, and it attracts more than a quarter of a million visitors each year.

The $21 million gift by former U.S. Postmaster General Wynton Blount and his former wife, Carolyn, to rescue a struggling Anniston, Alabama, Shakespeare troupe and build its new home in Montgomery was the largest single contribution ever made to a U.S. theater.

The imposing Museum of Art, built in a style to complement the theater, holds another Blount contribution, his significant collection of American art, ranging from Colonial times to the present, from John Singer Sargent to Georgia O'Keeffe. One of the most impressive parts of the museum is called Artworks, a hands-on gallery and studio introducing art to children.

This arts-conscious town also has a number of art galleries, including the Alabama Artists Gallery, operated by the Arts Council of Alabama. Some galleries specialize in "outsider" art, works by talented but unschooled artists who are gaining national renown. Alabama has its full share of these artists.

Off US 231, north of Montgomery, is Jasmine Hill, which should delight both art and flower fanciers. The gardens were conceived by Benjamin and Mary Fitzpatrick, an Alabama couple who spent their lives establishing a successful chain of stores in the South, sold out just before the Depression, then retired to their hilltop estate to create a living memorial to ancient Greece. They made more than 20 trips to Greece to study the sculpture and to purchase exact copies of the greatest art of ancient Greece, pieces such as the Venus of Melos, the Lions of Delos, and the remains of the Temple of Hera at Olympia.

New owners have carefully preserved the gardens, which are particularly lovely in April when the azaleas are at their peak.

Fans of F. Scott Fitzgerald should not miss the home in the fashionable Cloverdale suburb where he and his wife, Zelda, lived in 1931. Zelda Sayre, daughter of an Alabama Supreme Court judge, was born in Montgomery in 1900. Fitzgerald met her at a dance while he was stationed at nearby Camp Sheridan, and they returned to the city for a time after Zelda suffered her first mental breakdown in 1930. The house is filled with memorabilia, photos, and Zelda's paintings and poignant letters, both hopeful early love letters and later ones written during her bouts with mental illness.

This is one of several older neighborhoods on the National Register of Historic Places that make for a pleasant driving tour. Others include the Garden District and Cottage Hill. Check a local map or ask for directions at the Information Center.

If you've brought kids along, perhaps you'd rather head for the zoo, whose residents include many rare and endangered species. Animals are clustered by their native lands and allowed to roam with a minimum of barriers. A fun way to see it all is aboard the Montgomery Express, a miniature train that traverses the grounds.

Another attraction recommended for families is the Alabama Science Center, a museum filled with hands-on exhibits to engage kids in learning. If you come on a weekday, the Alabama Cattleman's Association Mooseum has an electronic host who makes learning about cattle lots of fun.

Finally, about that rodeo. For more than 35 years the Southeastern Livestock Exposition has been held in early spring to promote Alabama's cattle-and-livestock industry and the Alabama Agricultural Center. The proceeds, more than $1 million to date, help fund youth activities. The event includes a livestock and horse show and the rodeo, with more than 400 cowboys and cowgirls showing off at bareback riding, barrel racing, and bronco busting. It's a taste of the Old West in the Old South—just one more unexpected pleasure in Alabama's surprising capital city.

Area Code: 334

DRIVING DIRECTIONS   Montgomery is at the intersection of I-65 and I-85. From Atlanta, direct access is via I-85 west, 175 miles. From Birmingham, via I-65 south, 95 miles.

PUBLIC TRANSPORTATION   Montgomery is served by several major airlines.

ACCOMMODATIONS   *Red Bluff Cottage,* 551 Clay Street, 36101, 264-0056, charming bed-and-breakfast convenient to downtown, best bet and best buy, I, CP • *Holiday Inn Hotel & Suites,* 120 Madison Avenue, 36104, 264-2231, convenient downtown location, I–M • *Best Western State House Inn,* 924 Madison Avenue, 36104, 265-0471, I • *Holiday Inn East,* 1185 Eastern Boulevard at I-85, 36117, 272-0370, best of the city's many motels, convenient for Shakespeare Festival, I–M • *Bed & Breakfast Montgomery,* P.O. Box 1026, 36101, 264-0056, reservation service with many listings.

DINING   *Vintage Year,* 405 Cloverdale Road, 264-8463, attractive arty decor, M • *Sahara,* 511 East Edgemont Avenue, 262-1215, handsome decor, longtime local favorite, excellent seafood, M–E • *Panache at Rose Hill,* 11250 Highway 80 East, 277-7620, historic plantation house, upscale Southern menu, EE prix fixe • *Jubilee Seafood,* 1057 Woodley Road, 262-6224, M • *Canyon Grill,* 127 East Boulevard, Tex-Mex change of pace, I • *Gator's Plaza Cafe,* 5040 Vaughn Road, 274-0330, Cajun/Caribbean fare, I • *Farmers Market Cafe,* 315 North McDonough, 262-1970, generous and delicious Southern fare for breakfast and lunch, I • *Bates House of Turkey,* 1060 East Boulevard,

279-9775, turkey every way imaginable, good lunch spot, I • *Sassafras Tea Room,* 532 Clay Street, 265-7277, Queen Anne home on the Alabama River, delightful place for lunch, I • *Country Barbecue* (two locations), 5335 Atlanta Highway, 270-0126, and 2610 Zelda Road, 262-6211; the locals' choice, I.

SIGHT-SEEING *Alabama State Capitol,* Capitol Hill, east end of Dexter Avenue, 242-3184. Hours: Monday to Saturday 9 A.M. to 4 P.M. Free • *Governor's Mansion,* 1142 South Perry Street, 834-3022. Hours: Monday to Friday 8 A.M. to 4:30 P.M., weekends and holidays from 9 A.M.; tours by appointment. Free • *First White House of the Confederacy,* 664 Washington Avenue, 242-1861. Hours: Monday to Friday 8 A.M. to 4:30 P.M. Donation • *Montgomery Museum of Fine Arts,* 1 Museum Drive, Wynton M. Blount Cultural Park, off Woodmere Boulevard, 244-5774. Hours: Tuesday to Saturday 10 A.M. to 5 P.M.; Thursday to 9 P.M., Sunday noon to 5 P.M. Free • *Alabama Shakespeare Festival,* 1 Festival Drive, Wynton M. Blount Cultural Park, off Woodmere Boulevard, 271-5353 or (800) 841-4ASF. Phone for current programs and prices • *F. Scott and Zelda Fitzgerald Museum,* 919 Felder Avenue, 264-4222. Hours: Wednesday to Friday 10 A.M. to 2 P.M., Saturday and Sunday 1 to 3 P.M. Donation • *Jasmine Hill Gardens & Outdoor Museum,* off US 231 north on Jasmine Road, 567-6463. Hours: March through November, Tuesday to Sunday and Monday holidays, 9 A.M. to 5 P.M. $$ • *Old Alabama Town,* 310 North Hall Street, off Madison Avenue, 263-4355. Hours: Monday to Saturday 9 A.M. to 3 P.M. $$ • *Montgomery Zoo,* 2301 Coliseum Parkway, 240-4900. Hours: Daily 9 A.M. to 5 P.M. $$ • *Hank Williams Museum,* 118 Commerce Street, 262-3600. Hours: Monday to Saturday 9 A.M. to 6 P.M., Sunday 1 P.M. to 4 P.M. $$ • *Alabama State Archives and History Museum,* 624 Washington Avenue, 242-4363. Hours: Monday to Friday 8 A.M. to 5 P.M., Saturday 9 A.M. to 5 P.M. Free • *Dexter Avenue King Memorial Baptist Church,* 454 Dexter Avenue, 263-3970. Hours: Guided tours Monday to Thursday 10 A.M. and 2 P.M., Friday 10 A.M., Saturday 10 A.M. and 2 P.M. Donation • *Alabama Cattleman's Association Mooseum,* 201 South Bainbridge, 265-1867. Hours: Monday to Friday 9 A.M. to noon, 1 P.M. to 4 P.M. Free • *Alabama Science Center,* 244 Dexter Avenue, 832-3902. Hours: Tuesday to Friday 9 A.M. to 4 P.M. Free.

Art Galleries: *Alabama Artists Gallery,* 201 Monroe Street, 242-4076. Hours: Monday to Friday 8 A.M. to 5 P.M. • *Sac's Gallery,* 2019 Clubview Street, 265-9931. Hours: Monday to Saturday 10 A.M. to 5 P.M. • *Armory Gallery,* 1018 Madison Avenue, 241-ARTS. Hours: Daily 8 A.M. to 5 P.M. **Outsider art galleries:** By appointment only. Marcia Weber, 262-5349; Anton Haardt, 263-5494.

Rodeo: *Southeastern Livestock Exposition/World Championship Rodeo,* Garrett Coliseum, 265-1867, usually held in late March, during school spring-break week. Check current schedules.

INFORMATION *Montgomery Area Chamber of Commerce,* P.O. Box 79, Montgomery, AL 36101, 261-1100 or (800) 240-9452; www.montgomerychamber.com • *Visitor Center,* 300 Water Street, Union Station, 262-0013.

Back to the Past in Rugby

An unsuspecting traveler happening upon Rugby, Tennessee, could hardly be faulted for thinking he had encountered an apparition. After all, who would expect to find an English Victorian village alive and well on a sparsely settled back road in northeastern Tennessee?

In its heyday, Rugby was the biggest town in three counties, populated with the cream of British society. Today it gives the visitor a chance to step back in time, strolling along unpaved lanes, past quaint wooden cottages rich with gingerbread trim, while learning about one of the most unusual settlements in America.

Adding to the pleasure of the trip is the timeless beauty of the Cumberland Plateau region, including the rugged Big South Fork National River and Recreation Area nearby.

The idea for "New Rugby" originated with Thomas Hughes, an English social reformer and the author of *Tom Brown's School Days.* He founded the colony in 1880 out of concern for England's "second sons," young men from wealthy families who were denied inheritance of the family fortune by the law of primogeniture, according to which the entire estate passed to the eldest son.

Hughes bought 75,000 acres of wilderness on the Cumberland Plateau, offering it as a haven for such young men, most of them cultured and well educated. His goal was "to plant on these highlands a community of ladies and gentlemen." In his utopian dream, all would work cooperatively for the good of the town.

Things went well at the start. By 1884 there were 450 residents and more than 70 buildings. A resort hotel went up to accommodate visitors, and Rugby was the scene of sporting events and fancy balls; formal teas were served at 4 P.M. each day.

But Rugby was not meant to be. Misfortunes beset the town, from a typhoid epidemic to drought to fire, and many of the original settlers moved on. By the 1920s, Rugby had dwindled to a small farming community of about 125 people. But many of the original buildings remained, and in 1964 a 16-year-old resident, Brian Stagg, began a one-man campaign to bring his historic hometown back to life. Mustering support in the community, Stagg became director of the Rugby Restoration Association, attending college only every other semester in order to carry out his work.

Rugby received historic landmark designation in 1976, but restoration money remained scarce and the obstacles were many. After Brian Stagg's untimely death at age 28, his sister Barbara took over the fight.

Some 20 buildings have been restored, and the town is being rediscovered. As many as 70,000 visitors now come each year for tours and to attend special weekends such as the annual spring Music and Crafts Festival, the Rugby Pilgrimage in early August (the only time that private homes are open for touring), and Christmas at Rugby, held the first two Saturdays in December. The Harrow Road Café was built in 1985 to provide dining facilities.

Whenever you come, a visit begins at the restored 1907 schoolhouse, now converted into a visitors' center, where you'll learn a little about Rugby's unusual history. Daily guided tours take in three important sites.

The first is the town church. With its peaked roof and tiny belfry, it is a charming example of Carpenter Gothic design. The original bell still calls worshippers to church.

Hughes's own cottage, Kingstone Lisle, is the second stop. Many original Rugby pieces are among the furnishings, showing what early life was like in the colony.

The final stop will please devotees of Victoriana. The Thomas Hughes Free Public Library, little changed from its 1882 appearance, is stocked with 7,000 volumes donated by publishers, showing the reading tastes of the late Victorian era.

All of these buildings are on Central Avenue, once a dirt road with wooden boardwalks but now the main highway running through town. To really get the feel of the past, head down the still-unpaved lanes to the rear of town, where small wooden cottages with names like Wren's Nest and Martin Roost are tucked into the trees. Most of these are privately owned, but you can learn about their histories with the self-guiding tour available at the visitors' center.

Save time for browsing in Rugby's intriguing Commissary, a reconstruction of the original village cooperative. It is filled with traditional mountain crafts, from handmade dulcimers to cornhusk dolls to a nice stock of books on the Victorian period.

If the weather is fine, buy a sandwich and dessert for a picnic and spend the afternoon by the river. Follow the loop to the left of the town cemetery and you'll see the parking area and trailhead sign for the Gentlemen's Swimming Hole. A quarter-mile walk through the forest brings you down the gorge to the Clear Fork River, with huge boulders along the bank. It is a good spot to appreciate the natural beauty that drew Hughes to this area. To the left you'll come to the swimming hole, no longer only for gentlemen. It is a scenic plate to relax, even if the weather doesn't make you want to take a plunge. Go a mile farther to the right and you'll come to the "Meeting of the Waters," where the Clear Fork and White Oak Creek converge, another nice picnicking spot. More trails are being restored.

The 1880 Newbury House and the Pioneer Cottage in Rugby's historic district have been restored as inns for modern visitors. Guests are treated to breakfast at the Harrow Road Café.

Or you can stay a mile down the road at Grey Gables, a new inn built in the style of a Victorian farmhouse, with an 80-foot wraparound porch for taking in the views. Antiques and family mementos throughout the inn give a warm feeling. Hostess Linda Brooks Jones serves her delicious meals family-style so that guests can socialize at dinner. She hosts many special events open to the public, from holiday and theme lunches and dinners to afternoon teas.

Linda and her husband also run the R. M. Brooks General Store, built by her grandfather, just down the road on Route 52. The center of commerce after the Rugby colony's decline, it still looks much like a country store of yore, with a potbellied stove and the old post office tucked in a corner. Although filled with memorabilia, it continues as an operating business and is a local lunch favorite for bologna sandwiches and stick candy. In the back of the store the Joneses have installed Granny's Attic Crafts and Gifts, selling work by mountain artisans.

You'll pass the store if you take a drive along the Cumberlands of Tennessee Heritage Trail, a route from Rugby that offers views of the great natural beauty of this region and some sight-seeing stops as well. A printed guide detailing the full tour spanning five counties is available at Historic Rugby. Driving west on State Route 52 the stops include a one-mile detour for Colditz Cove, a heavily wooded area where 60-foot Northrup Falls tumbles off the high cliffs. An easy walking loop leads through the area.

Other stops include Frozen Head State Park and Natural Area, and Yahoo Falls, where a loop trail leads to a 113-foot falls rushing over a huge rock formation. At US 127, you may want to turn south briefly for Highland Manor, Tennessee's only winery. Turning north on 127 will bring you to the Sergeant Alvin C. York Mill and Grave, a small and moving memorial to one of America's most decorated heroes of World War I. The York Grist Mill and Dam is across the road.

Come back on Route 52 to the junction of Route 154 and turn east for the most scenic stop of all, the Big South Fork National River and Recreation Area, located 35 miles from Rugby. The free-flowing Big South Fork and its tributaries pass through 90 miles of scenic gorges and valleys and a wide range of natural and historical sites. Maintained by the National Park Service, the area straddles the Kentucky-

Tennessee border and encompasses more than 125,000 acres. It is great territory for all sorts of outdoor activities, including camping, whitewater rafting, kayaking, canoeing, hiking, horseback riding, mountain biking, hunting, and fishing.

It takes a little effort to fully appreciate the beauty of the area; except for one overlook at the East Rim, near park headquarters, most of the spectacular gorge views and rock formations are not accessible by car. Guided horseback rides are available from the stables at Bandy Creek, and there are 150 miles of marked hiking trails in the dense and beautiful woodlands. The Slave Falls Trail is a moderate 1.2-mile walk leading to waterfalls, bluffs, rock shelters, and the Needle Arch, one of the natural rock bridges in the park. Despite its remoteness, the beauty of the area attracts over 800,000 visitors each year.

Nature lovers can stay amid the tall trees at Charit Creek Lodge, a collection of log cabins accessible only by horse or on foot. There is no electricity; cabins are lit by kerosene lanterns. But there's no lack of comfort, and guests are treated to simple, hearty dinners and country breakfasts in the main lodge, a weathered building dating from 1817. The shortest way in is under 1 mile. The most scenic route is the Twin Arches Trail, 1.8 miles, leading past towering Twin Arches, the most famous of the area's rock formations. Mere humans look like pinpoints beside it.

A wonderful detour awaits heading south from Rugby, off I-75 north of Knoxville. The Museum of Appalachia is a loving and authentic presentation of pioneer life. It includes a village of some 30 authentic log structures moved to this site and one of the largest collections of frontier and pioneer memorabilia to be found anywhere. What sets the exhibit buildings apart is their personal approach, using photos tracing actual families and the things they created and used.

Unlike Rugby's pioneers, these simple, hardy people tamed the frontier and survived, leaving a rich legacy for all of us who came behind.

Area Code: 423

DRIVING DIRECTIONS   Rugby is located on Tennessee Route 52, 16 miles southeast of Jamestown, 35 miles from I-40 or I-75. It is about 300 miles from Atlanta, 125 miles northeast of Nashville, and 70 miles northwest of Knoxville.

ACCOMMODATIONS   *Newbury House* **and** *Pioneer Cottage,* c/o Historic Rugby, Inc., P.O. Box 8, Rugby, 37733, 628-2441, M, CP • *Grey Gables,* P.O. Box 52, Highway 52, Rugby, 37733, 628-5252, M, MAP; write for calendar of special events • *Charit Creek Lodge,* c/o 250 Apple Valley Road, Sevierville, TN 37862, (865) 429-5704, M, MAP.

DINING *Harrow Road Café,* Rugby, 628-2350, informal dining, the only choice in town, I.

SIGHT-SEEING *Historic Rugby,* P.O. Box 8, Rugby, 37733, 628-2441; www.historicrugby.org. Tours available February 1 to December 31, Monday to Saturday 10 A.M. to 4:30 P.M., Sunday from 12 noon. $$ • *Big South Fork National River and Recreation Area,* open year-round. Bandy Creek Visitor Center, 2 miles off Highway 297, open June–October, 8 A.M. to 6 P.M., rest of year to 4:30 P.M. Free. Fees for swimming pool and backcountry permits. Information available from Superintendent, Big South Fork NRRA, Bandy Creek Visitor Center, 4654 Leatherwood Ford Road, Oneida, TN 37841, (931) 879-3625 • *Museum of Appalachia,* off I-75, P.O. Box 359, Norris, 37828, 494-7680. Hours: Daily 8 A.M. to dusk. $$$.

INFORMATION *Middle East Tennessee Tourism Council,* P.O. Box 19806, Knoxville, TN 37939, (865) 584-3553.

Thinking Pink in Macon

Move over, Washington, D.C. The title of Cherry Blossom Capital must be shared with Macon, Georgia, where the spectacular blooms of 30,000 Yoshino cherry trees crown the town each spring in clouds of pink. Macon has many more trees than the nation's capital—more, in fact, than any single town in Japan.

When all those pink blossoms become a backdrop for Macon's famous antebellum white columns, it's a glorious time to pay a call on the South's nineteenth-century "inland queen." Diverse attractions nearby add to the springtime scenery, and you can drive home via the Peach Blossom Trail.

Macon owes its extraordinary spring show to the generosity of the late William A. Fickling, who planted the first trees. The festival was launched in his honor in 1982. His family has continued the tradition of planting as many as 10,000 new trees in a single year, so that the blooming season grows ever more beautiful.

A festival takes place during the peak bloom in late March, with parades, fashion shows, riding exhibitions, art and antiques shows, and big-name entertainment. There are hundreds of events, including tours through the town's loveliest residential sections. Homeowners celebrate the season by festooning doors, mailboxes, streetlights, and even automobiles with pink bows, flags, and cherry-blossom sprays.

Between festival events, you can get acquainted with Georgia's third-largest city, one that has prospered from its founding in 1823. Cotton, the Ocmulgee River, and the railroad accounted for the trade that made fortunes in Macon's nineteenth-century heyday. Antebellum mansions and Victorian cottages built by wealthy planters and businessmen remain to delight visitors today. The city has 11 districts on the National Register of Historic Places, and hundreds of buildings dating from the 1820s. The film at the downtown Welcome Center provides a good background before you set out to see the sights.

A stop at the Welcome Center, in the handsomely restored Terminal Station at the foot of Cherry Street, will arm you with a printed walking-tour guide, or you may sign up for one of Sidney's Historic Tours, which leave from the center. You'll pick up a lot of entertaining local lore as you admire the splendid homes of the Old South.

The most lavish of the homes is Hay House, a domed, red-brick, 24-room Italian Renaissance Revival palace completed in 1860 for Macon entrepreneur William Butler Johnston. The home is not only an architectural masterpiece but was noted for such innovations as indoor plumbing, walk-in closets, and a sophisticated ventilation system, amenities that were far ahead of their time.

Other showplaces include the Confederate Museum at the Cannonball House. The home, built in 1853, is best known for the cannonball that struck it during a Union attack in 1864. The cannonball still sits at the landing.

A stroll through the historic district on the hill reveals more stately homes. The Carmichael House, a national landmark built in 1840 on Georgia Avenue, has a majestic free-standing, three-story spiral staircase. On College Street, one of the classic homes is now the 1842 Inn, the city's finest lodging. The Woodruff House on Bond Street, an 1836 Greek Revival mansion on the hill overlooking Macon, was built for one of the South's wealthiest cotton planters and has been beautifully restored by Mercer University.

Washington Park, on Magnolia Street, where natural springs once supplied water for the town, is a fine starting place for a tour of Victorian Macon. The street has several vintage cottages as well as the site of Macon's first waterworks building (circa 1850), now a gift and antiques shop. Paralleling Washington is High Street, with the 1840 cottage that was the birthplace of the poet Sidney Lanier. It is now headquarters for the Middle Georgia Historical Society, displaying period furnishings and Lanier memorabilia.

A downtown tour includes several points of interest. Macon's showplace, the Grand Opera House, was built to house the Academy of Music in 1883–84 and was restored in 1969 as the entertainment center of the city. It boasts one of America's largest stages, where legendary performers such as Sarah Bernhardt and Will Rogers once appeared.

The 1836 City Hall was the temporary capitol of Georgia from 1864 to 1865, and the Municipal Auditorium, constructed in 1925, boasts one of the world's largest copper-covered domes and has a mural inside depicting Macon's history from de Soto's visit in 1540 to World War I.

Also downtown are some outstanding houses of worship, such as the 1858 First Presbyterian Church; Temple Beth Israel, built in 1902, with a singular dome lined with stained glass; and Macon's oldest church, the 1825 Christ Episcopal, where Sidney Lanier was married in 1867. The upstairs office where Lanier practiced law with his father and uncle before turning to poetry is at 336–48 Second Street.

Next to the restored Terminal Station is the Georgia Music Hall of Fame. It's an appropriate location, since so many of the state's best-known performers have Macon roots, including Little Richard, Otis Redding, James Brown, and Lena Horne. Macon-based Capricorn Records, where the Allman Brothers Band recorded, put the city at the center of the music industry for nearly a decade.

The imaginatively designed museum offers a chance to hear a host of Georgia-born greats in settings appropriate to their music, such as a jazz club, a country café, or a chapel for gospel music. The Record Store features the music of the Allman Brothers, R.E.M., and the B-52s; the Soda Fountain offers Little Richard and other rock and roll greats on the jukebox; and the Jazz Club presents Lena Horne, Harry James, and Johnny Mercer. The Skillet Lickers Café resounds with the sounds of Ronnie Milsap, Brenda Lee, Travis Tritt, and Trisha Yearwood; the Rhythm & Blues Revue stars James Brown, Otis Redding, Gladys Knight and the Pips, and Ray Charles. In the Gospel Chapel, an 18-minute film chronicles the history of gospel singing; the Georgia Theater salutes Georgia's classical artists, including Robert Shaw and Jessye Norman.

When you are ready for more history, go see Macon's Pleasant Hill Historic District, one of the first black neighborhoods to be listed on the National Register of Historic Places. The Tubman African American Museum features history, culture, and art, and has a striking wall mural, *From Africa to America,* by a local artist, Wilfred Stroud.

One of the most fascinating historic tales is told at the Ocmulgee National Monument—the most extensively excavated of the South's major Indian sites—where 12,000 years of Southeastern Indian cultures are documented. Six temple mounds, a burial mound, and a ceremonial earth lodge remain from a ceremonial center on the Macon Plateau dating to about A.D. 900. An excellent film, *People of the Macon Plateau,* is shown every half hour.

For a change of pace, the Museum of Arts and Sciences offers natural-science exhibits, two art galleries, nature trails, and the Mark Smith Planetarium. Two of its unique attractions are the three-story Discovery House, packed with eccentric collections and participatory exhibits, and the Back Yard, mini-habitats featuring a variety of engaging animals.

The Georgia Sports Hall of Fame, the largest of its kind in America, is filled with memorabilia from Georgia's most legendary teams and athletes.

There's plenty to keep you busy in Macon, especially during festival time, but you might want to allow time for a day south of the city, where more attractions await.

Warner Robins Air Force Base is home to one of the top three most-visited museums in Georgia, boasting the biggest and best displays of aircraft south of the Smithsonian's National Air and Space Museum. The museum offers more than 85 aircraft in its collection, tracing the history of flight from the first gliders to the fighters used in the Operation Desert Storm attack on Iraq in 1991.

Massee Lane Gardens in Fort Valley, the home of the American Camellia Society, has nine acres of display gardens, at their peak in winter and very early spring. The museum here also contains the world's largest collection of Edward Marshall Boehm porcelain—exquisite, lifelike re-creations of flowers and birds that are worth a trip even when the gardens are not in bloom.

The pretty little town of Perry, located about midway between Fort Valley and Warner Robins, is the center of this region. The shops on Main Street will appeal to antiquers.

The Georgia State National Fairgrounds and Agricenter in Perry hosts the Georgia National Stock Show and Rodeo in early spring as well as the Georgia National Fair in October.

Twice a year, one of Georgia's most outstanding folk and crafts events, the Mossy Creek Barnyard Arts and Crafts Festival, is held in a wooded country setting three miles from town. There's no better place to see nationally acclaimed artists and artisans demonstrate crafts from decoy carving to dulcimer making, to hear folk songs and stories, to watch cloggers in action, and to take your own turn to a country music band.

You'll have to come back to catch Mossy Creek in action, and for the big fall fair, but March is just the right time to head north on US 341 and 41 from Perry back toward Atlanta along the Peach Blossom Trail. Cherry blossom time coincides with the period when the orchards are showing off their delicate spring blossoms, a sight guaranteed to send you home with your spirits abloom.

Area Code: 912

DRIVING DIRECTIONS Macon is at the intersection of I-75 and I-16. From Atlanta, follow I-75 south about 84 miles.

ACCOMMODATIONS *1842 Inn,* 353 College Street, Macon, 31201, 741-1842 or (800) 336-1842, elegant columned mansion, best in town, E, CP • *Crowne Plaza Hotel,* 108 First Street, Macon, 31202, 746-1461, high-rise luxury in town center, pool, M • *Best Western Riverside,* 2400 Riverside Drive, 31204, 743-6311, motel, I • *Evans-Cantrell House,* 300 College Street, Perry, 31030, 825-9611, 1916 home of former "peach king," I–M, CP • *Swift Street Inn,* 1204 Swift Street, Perry, 31069, 988-9148, I–M, CP.

DINING *Green Jacket,* 325 Fifth Street, 746-4680, steaks and seafood, salad bar, M–E • *Natalia's,* 2720 Riverside Drive, Riverside Plaza, 741-1380, northern Italian, M–E • *Len Berg's,* Post Office Alley, 742-9255, Southern specialties, I • *Fresh Air Barbecue,* 3076 Riverside Drive, Northgate Shopping Center, 477-7229, oldest barbecue restaurant in Georgia, I • *H&H,* 807 Forsyth Street, 742-9810, big Southern breakfasts, meat-and-two (vegetable) plates, Allman Brothers photos on the walls, I • *New Perry Restaurant,* 800 Main Street, New Perry, 987-1000, Southern cooking, I–M.

SIGHT-SEEING *Hay House,* 934 Georgia Avenue, 742-8155. Hours: Monday to Saturday 10 A.M. to 4:30 P.M., Sunday from 1 P.M. $$$ • *Confederate Museum at The Cannonball House,* 856 Mulberry Street, 745-5982. Hours: Monday to Saturday 10 A.M. to 4 P.M. $$ • *Georgia Music Hall of Fame,* 200 Martin Luther King Jr. Boulevard, 750-8555 or (800) GA-ROCKS. Hours: Monday to Saturday 9 A.M. to 5 P.M., Sunday 1 to 5 P.M. $$$$ • *Tubman African American Museum,* 340 Walnut Street, 743-8544. Hours: Monday to Friday 9 A.M. to 5 P.M., Saturday from 10 A.M., Sunday from 2 P.M. $$ • *Museum of Arts and Sciences,* 4182 Forsyth Road, 477-3232. Hours: Monday to Saturday 9 A.M. to 5 P.M., Friday to 9 P.M., Sunday from 1 P.M. $$ or free 9 A.M. to 5 P.M. on Monday and 5 P.M. to 9 P.M. on Friday • *Georgia Sports Hall of Fame,* 301 Cherry Street, 752-1585. Hours: Monday to Saturday 9 A.M. to 5 P.M., Sunday 1 P.M. to 5 P.M. $$$ • *Ocmulgee National Monument,* 1207 Emery Highway (US 80, 2 miles east of Macon), 752-8257. Hours: Daily 9 A.M. to 5 P.M. Free • *Sidney's Tours,* Macon-Bibb County Convention & Visitors Bureau, Inc., 200 Cherry Street, 743-3401. Hours: Monday to Saturday 10 A.M. and 2 P.M. $$$$$ • *Museum of Aviation and Georgia Aviation Hall of Fame,* Warner Robins Air Force Base, Warner Robins, 926-6870. Hours: Daily 9 A.M. to 5 P.M. Free • *Massee Lane Gardens,* One Massee Lane, Fort Valley, 967-2358. Hours: December to March, Monday to Saturday 9 A.M. to 5 P.M., Sunday from 1 P.M.; rest of year, Monday to Friday 9 A.M. to 4 P.M. $$ • *Georgia National Fairgrounds and Agricenter,* 401 Golden Isles Parkway, Perry, 987-2774. Write for current schedule of horse shows, Georgia National Fair, Georgia National Stock Show and Rodeo • *Mossy Creek Barnyard Arts & Crafts Festival,* Georgia Route 96, 3 miles from Perry, held late April and mid-October annually. Information from (912) 922-8265.

INFORMATION *Macon-Bibb County Convention & Visitors Bureau, Inc.,* Terminal Station, 200 Cherry Street, Macon, GA 31204, 743-3401 or (800) 768-3401; www.maconga.org.

On the Green in Pinehurst

Entrepreneurs, who tend to be optimists by nature, often see possibilities that the rest of the world cannot.

Take James Walker Tufts, for example. A Massachusetts man who made a fortune as one of the first American designers and manufacturers of soda fountains, Tufts was considered something of a fool when he paid one dollar an acre in 1885 for 5,890 acres of land in central North Carolina. The land had been stripped of its timber and abandoned. The useless sandy terrain had caused the region to be called the Sandhills.

But Tufts had a vision: a health retreat where Northerners would flock to enjoy the mild winter climate. Ignoring the skeptics, he hired Frederick Law Olmsted, the landscape architect famed for his design of New York's Central Park, to lay out a new village with "open park spaces and winding streets that attain their usefulness by following lines of beauty."

Olmsted did not disappoint. One year and some 222,000 trees later, Tufts had a charming retreat with a circular village green and streets sweeping from it in concentric circles. By 1896 the village he dubbed Pinehurst had a general store, a dairy, a boardinghouse, 20 cottages, a horse-drawn trolley car, and a hotel, the 45-room Holly Inn.

No one scoffed anymore. Guests arrived in growing numbers to play at Pinehurst, and they have been coming ever since, enjoying their games against a backdrop of lush pines, hollies, and magnolias that grow lovelier by the year. Most beautiful of all are the tall and stately longleaf pines, with slim needles over a foot long growing in clusters like delicate flowers on the boughs. The pines, whose fresh scent fills the air, account for the town's name and have become its trademark.

Even Tufts, who was a visionary, could not have predicted that Pinehurst would achieve its greatest fame from golf. The sandy terrain turned out to be perfect for golf courses, drying quickly even after heavy rains. Today there are an amazing 43 courses in the area, attracting ever-growing numbers of golfing retirees as well as tourists. If you are good at the game, the challenge is legendary. If you are thinking of taking up golf, Pinehurst instruction is superb, and you can attend golf schools for a weekend as well as a week.

But this is an equally fine destination if your game is tennis, croquet, or canoeing—or if all you want to do is get away to a gracious slice of yesterday. The delightful village beckons with tempting shops along its brick sidewalks. The flat terrain is ideal for biking beneath the pines; ask at the visitors' center for the bike tour brochure, called "Tour de

Moore." The Tour de Moore race each spring brings cyclists from around the world for the featured 100-mile race and the coveted Pinehurst Cup.

Old-fashioned carriage rides are a less energetic way to see the area; the carriages seem perfectly at home in this quaint setting.

The neighboring town of Southern Pines adds nature preserves, gardens, steeplechase racing, and carriage parades to the list of area activities, and Pinehurst supplies its own horsey flavor with polo games on Sunday afternoons in spring and fall. April is the month when the biggest and most colorful equestrian events are scheduled.

Excellent nearby excursions from Pinehurst will surely tempt you to make this a long weekend, allowing time for antiquing, visiting the historic pottery-making village of Seagrove, or talking to the animals at the North Carolina Zoo.

According to local legend, the first Pinehurst golf course came about in 1898 when a workman complained to James Tufts that guests were disturbing the dairy cows with the little white balls they were hitting around the fields. Tufts had a rudimentary course laid out for this pastime, then newly imported from England.

In 1901, when the grand Carolina Hotel (now the Pinehurst Hotel) was built, a young Scottish professional named Donald Ross was hired to direct golf operations. Ross remained for the next 47 years and became the foremost architect of American golf, designing more than 400 courses throughout North America.

At Pinehurst, he expanded the original No. 1 Course to 18 holes and eventually added three more courses. His crowning achievement was the No. 2 Course, which became and remains one of the best known in the country. Pinehurst has hosted scores of tournaments, including the U.S. Open Championship in 1999, an event that will return in 2005.

You can learn more about Pinehurst at the Tufts Archives at the Given Memorial Library, a collection of letters, photos, news stories, and memorabilia dating back to 1895.

The Pinehurst Hotel is still *the* place to stay in town. The white, pillared building, topped with a cupola and wrapped with canopied porches, has been fondly dubbed "the White House of Golf." It retains an Old World aura and tradition that newer resorts simply cannot match. Along with the main inn, still called the Carolina, Pinehurst resort has smaller properties, such as the original rambling, wooden Holly Inn in the village, now with 77 rooms and nicely updated while retaining its turn-of-the-century feel. The 45-room Manor Inn, circa 1923, is another option, and the resort includes a number of condominiums with access to all of the resort facilities.

Besides the golf courses, which now number eight, those facilities include 24 tennis courts, croquet, lawn bowling, five swimming pools, and a 200-acre man-made lake where boats and windsurfers can be rented.

If you can't afford the tab at the Pinehurst, at least have a drink, inspect the memorabilia in the Ryder Cup bar, and stay for the multi-course dinner served beneath sparkling chandeliers in the Carolina dining room.

Two other golf resorts, in nearby Southern Pines, are also well worth considering, each offering tennis, a pool, and a Donald Ross course to tempt golfers.

Pine Needles, a rustic resort with a chaletlike feeling, is owned by the family of noted golfer Peggy Kirk Bell, a charter member of the LPGA. The Women's U.S. Open was played here in 1996 and 2001. Bell herself teaches at the resort's Golfari schools. Programs are available for ladies only, for couples, for adults, and for children ages 10 to 18.

Mid-Pines, a stately, Southern-style hotel built in 1921, has warm wood paneling, a charming garden dining room, and a gracious setting on 250 acres. It was recently purchased by Pine Needles.

Those who prefer smaller inns have several choices beside the Pinehurst properties. The Magnolia Inn, dating from 1895, has been completely renovated while maintaining period touches like the old claw-foot bathtubs. The Pine Crest Inn, a homey hotel dating from 1913, has a dining room and piano bar that are local favorites.

Knollwood House, a 1927 mansion in Southern Pines, has the air of an English manor and rooms and suites that are elegant indeed. The lawn rolls down to the Mid-Pines golf course. All inns offer packages for golfers.

If shopping is your game, the Sandhill Women's Exchange in Pinehurst is the place to find handicrafts and a little lunchroom, all under the low ceilings of an 1810 log cabin. Within the nearby village circle, all manner of clothing and gift shops await, along with a café housed in a former movie theater.

Midland Road, once the route of the trolley that brought guests to Pinehurst from the train depot in Southern Pines, stretches for six scenic miles between the towns, with august rows of tall pines on either side and in the median. Along this road is the area's outstanding shop, Midland Crafters, a fine-arts gallery with a magnificent collection of contemporary American crafts.

Southern Pines presents more shopping possibilities along an old-fashioned main street that runs on either side of the railroad tracks. The town remains an Amtrak stop on the run from the Northeast to Florida.

Drive out Connecticut Avenue to see some of the cultural and equestrian heritage of Southern Pines. Weymouth Center, listed on the National Register of Historic Places, was the home of author and publisher James Boyd, and is now a gracious setting for lectures and concerts. Across the way, the Campbell House, a handsome Georgian home occupied by the Moore County Arts Council, has a gallery showing local art.

There are more than 80 farms in this area where racehorses are bred and trained. Make a right turn onto sandy, unpaved Old Mail Road to see some of the loveliest of these farms—and signs reading "Slow, Horse and Dog Crossing." The Southern Pines Horse Farm Tour in April is a favorite event.

The Five Points Horse Park, a facility of competitions and horse trails, is scheduled to open in 2001. One of its first events will be the legendary Stoneybrook Steeplechase, celebrating its 50th running on April 7, 2001.

Two other major April horse happenings include an international carriage-driving competition, held in the open fields along Old Mail Road, and an annual Spring Carriage Drive, a parade from Southern Pines through Pinehurst of beautifully groomed, high-stepping horses pulling shiny carriages, with drivers dressed in fancy period attire. It's a fantastic show.

The horsey side of Pinehurst centers around the Harness Track, a major training center for harness racers. Come over any morning, fall through spring, to watch the trotters and pacers working out, and return on Sunday afternoon for polo matches held on the track grounds.

Flower fanciers will want to visit the Sandhills Horticultural Gardens, featuring the largest holly collection on the East Coast, a specialized conifer garden, and the Sir Walter Raleigh Garden, a formal 1.5-acre English garden. The gardens are maintained by horticultural students at the Sandhills Community College.

Those who want to get out and breathe the pine-scented air will find peaceful nature trails at Weymouth Woods, a 571-acre preserve in Southern Pines. Nature programs are offered on Sundays in spring and summer. Other nature trails can be found at the Southern Pines Reservoir on Highway 22, where there are also picnic tables beside a lake.

The only problem you may encounter is fitting in all of this and still finding time for the nearby attractions. Ten miles away, just off US 1 in the tiny town of Cameron, are a host of antiques stores in quaint nineteenth-century quarters and two delightful stops for lunch, the Dewberry Deli, in the old hardware store, and Miss Belle's Antiques and Tea Room.

The 45-minute drive to the Seagrove area, via Highway 211 west to Highway 705 north, allows you to visit the shop-studios of more than 60 potters who live and work in a community where the pottery-making tradition dates back to the 1700s. Some of the young potters are the ninth generation of their families to ply this craft. Watch for the shops of the Coles, Owens, Cravens, Lucks, and Teagues, the earliest families in the area, and for the North Carolina Pottery Center.

Just a few miles north of Seagrove, in Asheboro, is the superb and still growing North Carolina Zoo. This 1,448-acre sanctuary is one of the first American zoos built around the natural-habitat philosophy, a revolutionary vision that would most certainly have appealed to that other nature lover and visionary, Mr. James Walker Tufts of Pinehurst.

Area Code: 910

DRIVING DIRECTIONS Pinehurst is located on US 15/501, US 1, and North Carolina Routes 2, 211, and 5. From Raleigh-Durham, follow US 1 south to US 15/501, 70 miles. From Charlotte, follow US 74 east to US 1 north, 104 miles. From Atlanta, take I-85 to Charlotte, exit at Brookhaven Expressway southbound, watch for the connection to US 74, and follow Charlotte directions above, about 352 miles. From Columbia, South Carolina, take I-20 east to US 1 north, about 130 miles.

PUBLIC TRANSPORTATION US Air has commuter service directly to Pinehurst from Charlotte, and Amtrak serves Southern Pines, 6 miles away. Raleigh-Durham International Airport is 70 miles from Pinehurst, a drive of about 75 minutes, and Greensboro is 85 miles away; transportation is available from the airports.

ACCOMMODATIONS Area rates are highest in spring and fall, but considerably lower in winter, when the weather is often mild enough for sports. Many MAP lodgings are also available without meals; all lodgings offer special golf packages. *Pinehurst Resort,* Carolina Vista, P.O. Box 4000, Pinehurst, 28374, 295-6811 or (800) ITS-GOLF, main hotel (Carolina), Manor Inn, Holly Inn, or condominiums, EE, MAP • *Mid-Pines Inn and Golf Club,* 1010 Midland Road, Southern Pines, 28387, 692-2114 or (800) 323-2114, EE, MAP • *Pine Needles Lodge and Golf Club,* 1005 Midland Road, Southern Pines, 28387, 692-7111, EE, MAP • *Magnolia Inn,* Magnolia Road, P.O. Box 818, Pinehurst, 28374, 295-6900 or (800) 526-5562, M–E, MAP • *Pine Crest Inn,* Dogwood Road, P.O. Box 879, Pinehurst, 28374, 295-6121, M–E, MAP • *Knollwood House,* 1495 W. Connecticut Avenue, Southern Pines, 28387, 692-9390, M, CP; suites, E, CP.

Area motels: *Comfort Inn,* 9801 US 15/501, Pinehurst, 28374, 215-5500 or (800) 228-5150, M, CP • *Holiday Inn,* US 1 at Morganton Road, Southern Pines, 28387, 692-8585, M • *Hampton Inn,* 1675 US 1, Southern Pines, 28387, 692-9266, I–M • *Microtel Inn,* 205 Windstar Place, Southern Pines 28388, 693-3719 or (877) 693-3738, good value, I, CP.

DINING Reservations are required for resort dining rooms. *Carolina Dining Room,* Pinehurst Resort, 295-6811, EE prix fixe • *Holly Inn,* 215-8257, 1895 Room, EE; The Tavern, I–M • *Manor Inn,* 295-8405:

Mulligan's Sports Bar and Grill, I–M • *Mid-Pines Inn* (see Accommodations on page 51), M–E • *Pine Crest Inn* (see Accommodations on page 51), very popular, M–E • *Magnolia Inn* (see Accommodations on page 51) M–E • *Dugan's Pub,* Market Square, Pinehurst, 295-3400, informal, I–M • *Chef Warren's,* 215 N.E. Broad Street, Southern Pines, 692-5240, popular bistro, eclectic menu, M–E • *Jefferson Inn,* 150 W. New Hampshire Avenue, Southern Pines, 692-5300, old fashioned setting, modern menu, M–E • *La Terrace,* 270 S.W. Broad Street, Southern Pines, 692-5622, French, M–E • *The Lob Steer Inn,* US 1, Southern Pines, 695-1161, informal, steak, seafood, and bountiful salad bar, M • *The Squire's Pub,* 1720 US 1 south, Southern Pines, 695-1161, casual, pub fare, lots of British beers, I–M.

SIGHT-SEEING *Sandhills Horticultural Gardens,* Sandhills Community College, 2200 Airport Road, Pinehurst, 695-3882. Hours: Daily, daylight hours. Free • *Tufts Archives,* Given Memorial Library, 150 Cherokee, Pinehurst, 295-3642. Hours: Monday to Friday 9:30 A.M. to 12:30 P.M. and 2 to 5 P.M., Saturday 9:30 A.M. to 12:30 P.M. Free • *Weymouth Center,* 555 E. Connecticut Avenue, Southern Pines, 692-6261. Hours: Monday to Friday 10 A.M. to noon and 2 to 4 P.M. Free • *Weymouth Woods Sandhills Nature Preserve,* 1024 Fort Bragg Road, Southern Pines, 692-2167. Hours: Monday to Saturday 9 A.M. to 6 P.M., Sunday noon to 5 P.M. Free • *Campbell House Galleries,* 482 E. Connecticut Avenue, Southern Pines, 692-4356. Hours: Monday to Friday 9 A.M. to 5 P.M., also third Saturday and Sunday each month. Free • *North Carolina Zoological Park,* North Carolina Route 159, 6 miles south of US 64 and 220 intersection, Asheboro, 879-7000 or (800) 488-0444. Hours: April to October, daily 9 A.M. to 5 P.M.; rest of year to 4 P.M. $$$$ • **Carriage rides:** *Pinehurst Livery Stable,* 295-8456 • **Polo games:** *Pinehurst Race Track,* 949-2106. Hours: April and May, Sundays at 2 P.M.; check for fall schedule. Free • For current dates of steeplechase, carriage competitions, and carriage drive, contact the Convention and Visitors' Bureau.

SPORTS **Bicycle rentals:** *Rainbow Cycles,* 239 N.E. Broad Street, Southern Pines, 692-4494 • **Tennis:** *Lawn and Tennis Club of North Carolina,* One Merrywood, Pinehurst, 692-7270. For locations of public courts, phone Moore County Parks and Recreation Department, 947-2504.

INFORMATION *Convention and Visitors' Bureau for the Pinehurst, Southern Pines, Aberdeen Area,* 10677 US 15/501, Southern Pines, NC 28388, 692-3300 or (800) 346-5362. Events line, 692-1600; www.homeofgolf.com.

Humming Along in Nashville

Andrew Jackson must have been a man of amazing foresight. At the Hermitage, the gracious home of our seventh president, just outside of Nashville, is a driveway in what seems unmistakably to be the shape of a guitar.

How could Jackson have known that a century and a half later his hometown would be best known as Music City, the home of the guitar-picking, toe-tapping Grand Ole Opry?

Guitars are now in evidence all over Nashville, which has become the ultimate destination for lovers of country music. But don't be fooled into thinking that this is a one-note city.

The flip side of Nashville is a landscape of green hills, Southern mansions, and gracious gardens, some of them dating back to Jackson's day. Before music stole the spotlight, Nashville was known as "the Athens of the South" for the many colleges established there. Hidden on one of the smaller campuses is a prize private art collection, only one of several displays in the city that will surely please art lovers.

As the state capital, Nashville also boasts more than its share of history, centered in the Capitol Building and state museums in the heart of the city. The present city is claiming its place as one of the liveliest and fastest growing in the South, evidenced by a host of new buildings. The Tennessee Titans football team and the Nashville Predators professional hockey team have arrived recently to mark the city's rise into the big leagues. Along the downtown waterfront, turn-of-the-century warehouses have blossomed into a center for dining and nightlife known as "The District." Planet Hollywood, the Hard Rock Cafe, and a massive dance club called the Wildhorse Saloon are among the establishments that have taken Nashville far beyond its early country roots.

Not to be missed on the riverfront is the delightful Tennessee Fox Trot Carousel created by the internationally known artist Red Grooms, a Nashville native. The carousel has 36 riding figures, from Andrew Jackson and Davy Crockett to country star Kitty Wells.

In fact, Nashville is a city with so many facets you can have a wonderful time even if you don't care a hoot for Hank or Dolly or Garth. So unless country is the reason for your visit, plan a weekend with the dial first tuned elsewhere, thereby discovering sides of a cultured and rapidly changing city where corporate is catching up with country.

This was rugged frontier when the first settlers arrived at the Cumberland River on a frosty Christmas Eve in 1799. A reconstruction of their log fort stands on the riverbank downtown to remind the visitor of what things were like. Those brave first arrivals fought off the Indians, raised racehorses, traded with the rest of the world via riverboat, and explored what was then considered the West.

To see how quickly the early settlers prospered and created an oasis of culture in the wilderness, drive a few miles south of town to a restoration of the historic Travellers' Rest, built in 1799 by John Overton, Andrew Jackson's law partner. The house was enlarged in 1808 and again in 1828, and is a chronicle of changing decorative arts.

It will set the stage for Jackson's Hermitage, the 1821 Greek Revival home that the president built for his bride, the one place he most wanted to return to after his illustrious military and political careers. This is one of the most personal of all the presidential homes, furnished almost entirely with the family's own belongings. The self-guided cassette tour, with dramatized narratives by various "family members," gives insight into "Old Hickory," the tough hero of the War of 1812 and the tender husband who never stopped grieving for his wife, Rachel, after her sudden death in 1828. He and his wife are buried together in a corner of her beloved garden, kept just as it was designed for her in 1819.

A vintage mansion telling a different kind of Nashville tale is Belle Meade Plantation, considered "the queen of Tennessee plantations" and once one of the finest thoroughbred breeding farms in the country. The mansion is fine, the racing history is fascinating, and the big carriage house and stables hold one of the largest antique carriage collections in the South. Recent additions include a new visitor center and restaurant.

While you are in the Belle Meade neighborhood, drive around to admire Nashville's best addresses in one of the most magnificent residential sections to be found in any Southern city.

Not too far away is a third mansion not to be missed. The 55-acre Cheekwood estate lives up to its formal name: Nashville's Home of Art and Gardens. The Georgian-style main house is now the Fine Arts Center, a lovely home setting for American art and collections of decorative arts that include Worcester porcelain and Old Sheffield silver. The grounds are a showplace of gardens that include boxwood, wildflowers, a Japanese garden, and changing displays of seasonal blooms. Walking trails lead through native trees and shrubs, past cascading streams and quiet pools. There's also the Botanic Hall, with a tropical atrium, sculptured fountains, and changing exhibits.

A virtual garden is the campus of Vanderbilt University, a 75-acre site not far from the city center that is also an arboretum boasting more than 60 species of trees. Outdoor sculptures are artistically placed among them.

The school was built with a gift of $1 million, a vast sum when it was given in 1873 to a city never seen by the donor, Cornelius Vanderbilt. Vanderbilt's Southern wife had some knowledge of Nashville through her connection with a local minister. She convinced her husband that it was crucial for the South to have centers of learning if it was to come back after the Civil War. Though a statue honors him, Vanderbilt never came to see the college he helped to create.

Stop at Kirkland Hall at the main campus entrance for a self-guiding map to the lovely Victorian campus, and stop in the Fine Arts Gallery in the historic Old Gym to see changing exhibits from the Vanderbilt Art Collection. The gallery in the Sarratt Student Center has changing art exhibits of contemporary art.

Not far from Vanderbilt is Nashville's most unusual art venue, the Parthenon, a full-scale replica of the Greek original down to the smallest detail, with a re-creation of the 42-foot-tall statue of Athena as a focus. Built for the 1897 Tennessee Centennial Exposition, it was kept as a museum, showing the Cowan Collection of American art as well as changing exhibits.

The true art treasure of the city is in far more modest surroundings. Fisk University, founded in 1866, is one of the oldest African-American colleges in the United States. Along with Meharry Medical College, which opened in 1876, it made Nashville a leader in education for African-Americans after the Civil War. Here again, the city benefited from a donor who had never visited. Because of her association with Carl Van Vechten, a New York writer and critic with a strong interest in Fisk, artist Georgia O'Keeffe in 1949 presented to this modest campus a major portion of the important art collection of her late husband, Alfred Stieglitz, who was not only a brilliant photographer but a noted patron of the arts.

O'Keeffe did come to Nashville personally to oversee the collection's installation in a small red-brick building that was once the school gymnasium, now called the Carl Van Vechten Gallery of Fine Arts. Included are more than 100 paintings by such artists as Cézanne, Picasso, Renoir, Toulouse-Lautrec, John Marin, George Grosz, Diego Rivera, and O'Keeffe herself, along with some 18 fine Stieglitz photographs and a selection of African sculptures. The Aaron Douglas Gallery, on the third floor of the Fisk Library, is another worthwhile stop, highlighting works by African-American artists.

Nashville will gain another fine art venue in 2001 with the opening of the Frist Center for the Visual Arts, designed to house major traveling exhibits.

Having seen some of the fine homes and fine arts of the city, head downtown for the historic 1859 state capitol building. Still the active seat of state government, the building's handsome chambers, fine details, and ceiling frescoes have been restored to their original nineteenth-century appearance. Outside are a statue of Andrew Jackson and the grave of another Tennessee resident who became a U.S. president, James K. Polk.

The Tennessee State Museum is also interesting, tracing the state from prehistoric times to the early 1900s, with a separate building set aside for military history.

The museums are high on a hill among a stately complex of

government buildings. Behind the State Museum is the Bicentennial Mall State Park, a 19-acre outdoor museum covering Tennessee's history, and the city's Farmer's Market. To the front is the nicely landscaped Church Street, and beyond is the Nashville Convention Center, and, at the corner of Broadway and Fifth Avenue, is the Gaylord Entertainment Center. This is the location of the city's Visitor Information Center and the Tennessee Sports Hall of Fame, as well as a 20,000-seat arena that is home to the city's hockey and arena football, as well as many concerts and special events.

Now it's time to liven your stay in Nashville with a chorus of country. The Country Music Hall of Fame and Museum is the place to start, ensconced in a lavish new $37 million home not far from the Gaylord at Fifth Avenue and Demonbreun Street. Now three times the size of the original building, it has saluted the greats since 1961, when Hank Williams and Jimmie Rodgers were among the first honorees. Later inductees have included Johnny Cash, Dolly Parton, Charley Pride, and, of course, Elvis. The museum is filled with memorabilia, exhibits, and over a million recordings and films telling the tale of how "hillbilly" music captured the heart of city folk and tracing the changes in styles over the years. It features live entertainment.

A few blocks away on Fifth is the Ryman Auditorium, where the Grand Ole Opry performed from 1943 until 1974. It is still a popular spot for nostalgic daytime tours; the auditorium has been renovated and lights up at night with live entertainment once again.

Come back to Broadway and walk toward the river to get a feel for the old days in Nashville. The singing starts by 11 A.M. at Tootsie's Orchid Lounge on the corner of Broadway and Fifth Avenue. Tootsie's is a bit down-at-the-heels, but it remains a nostalgic favorite because so many country greats hung out there between sets at the nearby Ryman Auditorium. In the same neighborhood you'll see an unbelievable array of glitzy guitars at Gruhn's Guitar, find just about every country music record imaginable at the Ernest Tubb Record Shop, and see a lot of glitter at Robert's Western World, where you can also hear music at night. Legends Corner is another place to hear music, and Printer's Alley, the area of Church Street between Third and Fourth avenues, is another entertainment center.

There's another Ernest Tubb shop on Nashville's famous "Music Row." The formation of the Acuff-Rose publishing company on 17th Avenue touched off the development of many music-related businesses. The quaint offices in houses have mostly given way to steel-and-glass buildings housing the big record companies, but this is still the street of dreams for those hoping to hit it big in the country world. One of the most famous sites is RCA's historic Studio B, where some of the greatest country hits were recorded. It has been updated to meet modern standards, and you may well see a recording session in progress. If you have dreams of recording your own country hit, commercial studios, such as You're the Star Recording Studio on Second Avenue, offer the chance to star on a record or video, singing against a prerecorded background.

In 1974, the Grand Ole Opry moved on to much bigger quarters about 15 minutes outside of town to the area now known as Music Valley. Still going strong, it celebrated its 75th anniversary in 2000 as the longest-running radio show in the world. The fancy Opry auditorium seats 4,400 and boasts some of the floorboards from the old Ryman, just for luck. The cast of 70 currently includes Dolly Parton, Trisha Yearwood, Vince Gill, Patty Loveless, and new stars like Garth Brooks.

The museum adjacent to the theater pays tribute to past and present stars with special audio and video electronic effects and lots of interactive devices. The building also includes a gallery featuring the private guitar collection of the late country star Roy Acuff and another gallery paying homage to an old favorite, Minnie Pearl.

There's plenty of commerce for the crowds attracted to the Opry: country entertainment theaters such as the Stardust, Texas Troubadour, and The Nashville Palace; a wide range of museums including a wax museum, an antique-cars museum, and the Willie Nelson Museum; and, of course, many places to shop—a shop selling cowboy boots and an Ernest Tubb record store built around one of Tubb's old buses are two not to miss.

The new Opry Mills complex promises "Shoppertainment," with a host of stores complemented by attractions like Gibson Guitar's Bluegrass Showcase, the chance to race in a computer simulator at NASCAR Silicon Motor Speedway, a 24-screen Cineplex and IMAX theater, and many restaurants, including Wolfgang Puck's Grand Cafe.

Opryland has its own enormous, lavish hotel, with nearly 3,000 rooms, and complete with indoor rivers and waterfalls, convenient for those who want to be as close as possible to the performances.

But unless you are devoted to country music, you'd do better to stay in the city, where there is far more variety in dining and nightlife. Join the recording stars and record producers who stay at Loew's Vanderbilt Plaza Hotel, or take a nostalgia trip at the handsomely restored Union Station or the turn-of-the-century Hermitage Suites Hotel. Center-city hotels such as the Hermitage, the Crowne Plaza, the Doubletree Hotel, Hilton Suites, and the Renaissance Nashville are within walking distance of the capitol, the Nashville Convention Center, the Gaylord Center, and the District.

In a town where almost everyone is or wants to be a music star, it's not surprising that you can hear some great music in local clubs. The queen of nightlife is the Bluebird Café, about six miles west of town, but all you have to do is wander the District and you'll find live music at many of the local restaurants, from jazz to country, rock, and blues, all of it a harmonious sampling of the Nashville sound.

Area Code: 615

DRIVING DIRECTIONS Nashville is at the intersection of I-40 and I-24 east-west and I-65 north-south. From Atlanta, follow I-75 north to I-24 west, about 250 miles. I-65 north leads directly from Birmingham, about 192 miles.

PUBLIC TRANSPORTATION Nashville is served by almost all major airlines. Downtown trolleys connect the District, Music Row, the Parthenon, and other downtown attractions, and river taxis connect Opryland with downtown.

ACCOMMODATIONS *Loews Vanderbilt Plaza Hotel,* 2100 West End Avenue, Nashville, 37203, 320-1700, E–EE • *Union Station Hotel,* 1001 Broadway, Nashville, 37203, 726-1001 or (800) 331-2123, E–EE • *Hermitage Hotel,* 231 Sixth Avenue North, Nashville, 37219, 244-3121 or (800) 251-1908, all suites, E • *Crowne Plaza,* 623 Union Street, Nashville, 37219, 259-2000 or (800) 447-9825, E • *Doubletree Guest Suites Hotel,* 315 Fourth Avenue North, Nashville, 37219, 889-8889, E • *Renaissance Nashville,* 611 Commerce Street, Nashville, 37203, 255-8400 or (800) HOTELS, M–EE • *Hilton Suites Nashville Downtown,* 121 Fourth Avenue South, 37203, 620-1000, E • *Holiday Inn Vanderbilt,* 2613 West End Avenue, Nashville, 37203, 327-4707 or (800) 777-5871, high-rise hotel, convenient location, M–E • *Days Inn Vanderbilt,* 1800 West End Avenue, Nashville, 37203, 327-0922, good budget choice, I • *Opryland Hotel,* 2800 Opryland Drive, Nashville, 37214, 871-6853, 3000 rooms!, EE.

DINING Fine dining: *The Wild Boar,* 2014 Broadway, 239-1313, widely praised, paintings, antiques, wild game specials, E–EE • *Arthur's,* Union Station Hotel (see Accommodations above), 255-1494, Continental menu, EE prix fixe • *Bound'ry,* 911 20th Avenue South, 321-3043, eclectic with a Southern/Southwestern accent, E • *Mario's,* 2005 Broadway, 327-3232, northern Italian, M–EE.

Handsome restored quarters in the District: *The Merchants,* 401 Broadway, 254-1892, M–E • *Mere Bulles,* 152 Second Avenue North, 256-1946, M–EE.

More choices: *Amerigo,* 1920 West End Avenue, 320-1740, informal Italian, I–M • *Belle Meade Brasserie,* 101 Page Road, 356-5450, contemporary decor and menu, M–E • *Capitol Grille,* Hermitage Hotel (see Accommodations above), contemporary cuisine, M–E • *F. Scott's,* 2210 Crestmoor Drive, 269-5861, eclectic and excellent menu, M–E • *Jimmy Kelly's,* 217 Louise Avenue, 329-4349, Victorian mansion, longtime favorite for steaks, chops, M–E • *Stock-Yard,* 901 Second Avenue North,

255-6464, steaks are the specialty, M–EE • *Sunset Grill,* 2001-A Belcourt Avenue, 386-3663, creative menu, arty decor, M–E • *Valentino's Ristorante,* 1907 West End Avenue, 320-7778, upscale Italian, M–E • *Zola,* 3001 West End Avenue, 320-2778, Mediterranean, M–E.

Southern cooking: *Loveless Café,* 2823 Nolensville Road, 254-9888, worth a drive, good Southern food and lots of it, legendary biscuits, country stars often on hand, great for all three meals, I–M • *Rotier's,* 2413 Elliston Place, 327-9892, traditional "meat and threes (vegetables)," I–M • *Swett's Restaurant,* 2725 Clifton, 329-4418, more country cooking, specialties, cafeteria-style, I.

NIGHTLIFE Where to hear music: Country: *Barbara's,* 207 Printer's Alley, 259-2272 • *Wildhorse Saloon,* 120 Second Avenue, 251-1000, dancing • *Robert's Western World,* 416 Broadway, 256-7937 • *Tootsie's Orchid Lounge,* 422 Broadway, 726-3739 • *Legends Corner,* 428 Broadway, 248-6334. **A short drive from town:** *Bluebird Café,* 4104 Hillsboro Road, 383-1461 • *The Broken Spoke,* 1412 Brick Church Pike, 262-7524. **Blues:** *Bourbon Street Blues and Boogie Bar,* 220 Printer's Alley, 242-5837. **Jazz:** *Mere Bulles* and *The Merchants* (see Dining listings). This is just a sampling; check current listings for more clubs and theaters presenting country shows.

SIGHT-SEEING *Belle Meade Plantation,* 5025 Harding Road, 356-0501. Hours: Daily 9 A.M. to 5 P.M. $$$$ • *Cheekwood, Nashville's Home of Art and Gardens,* 1200 Forrest Park Drive, 356-8000. Hours: Monday to Saturday 9 A.M. to 5 P.M., Sunday from 11 A.M. $$$$ • *Fisk University: Van Vechten Gallery,* 18th Avenue North, 329-8720. Hours: Tuesday to Friday 9 A.M. to 5 P.M., Saturday and Sunday from 1 P.M. Donation. *Aaron Douglas Gallery,* Jackson Street (Fisk Library, third floor), 329-8543. Hours: Tuesday to Friday 10 A.M. to 5 P.M., Saturday and Sunday from 1 P.M. $$ • *The Hermitage,* 4580 Rachel's Lane, 889-2941. Hours: Daily 9 A.M. to 5 P.M., except holidays and the third week in January. $$$$ • *Historic Traveller's Rest,* 636 Farrell Parkway, 832-8197. Hours: Tuesday to Saturday 10 A.M. to 5 P.M., Sunday from 1 P.M. $$$ • *The Parthenon,* West End and 25th Avenues, Centennial Park, 862-8431. Hours: Tuesday to Saturday 9 A.M. to 4:30 P.M.; also Sunday 12:30 P.M. to 4:30 P.M. in April to September. $ • *Tennessee Fox Trot Carousel,* Riverside Park, 254-7020. Hours: Monday to Saturday 11 A.M. to 6 P.M., Sunday noon to 6 P.M.; extended hours in summer. $ • *Tennessee State Museum,* Fifth Avenue between Union and Deaderick Streets, 741-2692. Hours: Tuesday to Saturday 10 A.M. to 5 P.M., Sunday from 1 P.M. Free • *Tennessee State Museum, Military History Branch,* War Memorial Building, 741-2692. Hours: Tuesday to Saturday 9 A.M. to 5 P.M. Free • *Vanderbilt Galleries: Sarratt Student Center,* Vanderbilt Place near 24th Avenue, 322-2471. Hours: Monday to Friday 9 A.M. to 9 P.M., Saturday and Sunday 11 A.M. to 10 P.M. When school is not in session, the gallery closes at 4:30 P.M. and is closed weekends. Free. *Vanderbilt Fine Arts Gallery,* 23rd and West End Avenues, 322-0605. Hours: Monday to Friday noon to 4 P.M., Saturday and Sunday 1 to 5 P.M. Closed Sunday and Monday in summer. Free.

Country music attractions: *Grand Ole Opry,* 2804 Opryland Drive, 889-3060 or (800) 456-6779; www.opry.com. Hours (can vary, so it's best to check): Friday 7:30 P.M., Saturday 6:30 P.M. and 9:30 P.M.; matinees Tuesday 3 P.M. in summer. Best to order tickets in advance by phone, mail, or on the Internet. • *Grand Ole Opry Museum,* including Roy Acuff and Minnie Pearl museums, 2802 Opryland Drive, 889-6611. Hours: Open during performances. Free • *Country Music Hall of Fame and Museum,* Fifth Avenue and Demonbreun Street, (800) 852-6437; www.country.com. Hours: Daily 9 A.M. to 5 P.M. $$$$$ • *Ryman Auditorium,* 116 Fifth Avenue North, 889-3060. Hours: Tours daily 8:30 A.M. to 4 P.M.; check current performance schedule. $$$ • *The General Jackson Showboat,* Opryland, 889-6611. Phone for current schedules.

INFORMATION *Nashville Convention and Visitors' Bureau,* 211 Commerce Street, Nashville, TN 37219, 259-4700 or (800) 657-6910; www.musiccityusa.com.

Plantation Pleasures Near Charleston

Once upon a time, 20 lovely plantations stood along the Ashley River northwest of Charleston, South Carolina. Growing conditions were ideal there, not only for the rice and indigo that made planters rich but also for some of the first and most magnificent gardens in early America.

The Civil War banished this way of life. In fact, when the war was over, all but three of the 20 original plantation homes had been destroyed, a vivid testimony to the terrible toll that struggle exacted from the South.

Luckily for today's visitors, however, the gardens have proven more durable. The remaining plantations and their fabulous grounds are among the loveliest springtime sights in the Southeast. Many people make the trip out South Carolina Route 61 and hurry through the plantations as part of a visit to Charleston, but these sites really deserve a weekend to themselves, with time to absorb their history, their haunting beauty, and the tales they tell of another era.

Each of these properties has something unique to offer. Drayton Hall, begun in 1738 and one of the earliest examples of Georgian-Palladian architecture in America, still looks remarkably as it did in the 1700s. It is the only plantation on the Ashley that survived the war intact. Some say the troops passed it by because they heard that small-pox victims were being treated there. The house remained in the Drayton family until 1974; it was used as a summer home only and was kept in its original state, without plumbing or electricity.

Now maintained by the National Trust for Historic Preservation, Drayton Hall is shown without furnishings and is somehow all the more memorable with nothing to distract from the details of the workmanship, including the extraordinary sculpted plaster ceilings and hand-carved paneling and moldings.

Not far away is Magnolia Plantation and Gardens, a residence for other members of the Drayton family for ten successive generations. The original house, dating to the 1680s, was lost to fire; the replacement was burned by Union soldiers. The present modest home—occupied by the family until quite recently—is of interest mainly as an example of how plantation life changed after the Civil War.

The pride here is the large and lush garden, first planted in 1685 by Thomas Drayton. By the time Drayton died in 1717, his small English garden had grown to ten acres. The earliest portion, still known as Flowerdale, remains virtually unchanged, but it is now part of 50 sumptuous acres of gardens overhung with Spanish moss romantically reflected in dark lakes that once nurtured rice fields.

This is one of the nation's floral showplaces, resplendent in winter with 900 varieties of camellias and in spring with some 250 types of azaleas. Brick paths laid out centuries ago lead to a biblical garden, a topiary garden, a maze, and an herb garden.

Also on the property is the Audubon Swamp Garden, where boardwalks allow you to see alligators and the many varieties of birds that inhabit South Carolina's low country.

The two Drayton properties will fill a day nicely; Middleton Place deserves a day on its own. This site contains America's oldest formal landscaped gardens, laid out personally by Henry Middleton, who became president of the First Continental Congress, over 250 years ago.

Creating the formal parterre lawn terraces leading up from the river, the butterfly lakes, and the many paths and geometric patterns required ten years of work by 100 Middleton slaves.

Middleton died in 1784, too soon to appreciate the additions made two years later by the French botanist André Michaux, who, according to family legend, planted exotic trees such as mimosa and ginkgo and brought as a gift the first four camellia bushes to be grown in America, three of which still bloom near the terraces.

In the nineteenth century, winding walks in wooded settings and naturalistic plantings were added, a contrast to the formal early sections.

The main house was burned by Sherman's army in the 1860s; one wing was restored after the war to serve as a residence and is now a museum where you can share the colorful history of the Middleton family and see family collections of art, Charleston-made furniture, English silver, and a sampling of the library, which is said to have contained some 10,000 volumes in 1865.

The gardens languished until a Middleton descendant, J. J. Pringle Smith, and his wife came on the scene in the 1930s and began the daunting task of restoration. Today the gardens are as beautiful as ever, magnificent in every season.

The plantation stableyards have also been restored to show animals and early crafts, and workshops that re-create the era when plantations were self-sufficient. Also remaining is Eliza's House, built in 1870 as a two-family dwelling for the freed blacks who remained on the plantation.

One other attraction on this side of the river is Charles Towne Landing, the site of the original English settlement in South Carolina, founded in 1670. This is a state-owned preserve that brings to life the experience of the first settlers. A full-scale replica of the seventeenth-century trading vessel *Adventure* can be boarded, and there are replicas of buildings and crop gardens of the original town. Also on the property is the Animal Forest, a 20-acre natural-habitat zoo.

Though you can easily stay in Charleston and enjoy plantation touring by day, there is one unusual inn on the Ashley, right in the midst of the attractions. Even though it is on an old plantation's grounds, Middleton Inn is starkly modern in style and seems almost unattractive at first sight. Yet inside it is quite special, with handsome handmade furnishings and big windows with river views. The inn serves breakfast, and a short path along the river leads to the restaurant at Middleton Place, which specializes in Southern cooking for lunch or dinner. Horseback riding from Middleton Stables and miles of trails for nature walks are available, along with swimming and tennis.

If you have more time and want to complete a tour of area plantations and gardens, travel northeast across the Cooper, the river on the other side of Charleston, and follow US 17 north to Boone Hall Plantation. This puts you close to Mount Pleasant, across the river from Charleston, where you'll find a particularly charming bed-and-breakfast, the Long Point Inn, and good dining. This is also the site of the Patriots Point Naval and Maritime Museum, home to the USS *Yorktown,* a World War II aircraft carrier, and several other historic ships.

The classic columned mansion at Boone Hall is called America's most photographed plantation. The three-quarter-mile arching Avenue of Oaks approaching the mansion can be seen in countless illustrations. The oaks were planted in 1743 by Captain Thomas Boone, a descendant of the original settler, Major John Boone, who arrived to claim his land grant in 1681.

Boone Hall became a thriving cotton plantation, covering 17,000 acres in its heyday. The house itself was rebuilt in 1935, respecting the original 1750 Georgian architecture and using the original brick and woodwork.

The original "Slave Street," with nine brick slave cabins circa 1743, is one of the few such original quarters remaining in the Southeast.

The gardens at Boone Hall are loveliest in spring, when masses of bulbs add to the color of the azaleas and camellias.

A final special garden awaits farther north in Moncks Corner. Cypress Gardens was originally part of Dean Hall, one of the Cooper River's major rice plantations. The 163-acre swamp garden was the center of the antebellum estate and was used as a reservoir to flood the surrounding rice fields. This blackwater swamp is now the centerpiece of the gardens that were created by owner Benjamin Kittredge in the late 1920s. Three miles of walking paths lead you through the plantings, a profusion of azaleas, camellias, and daffodils in spring, or you can relax and see the garden by traversing its scenic waters by boat.

Area Code: 843

DRIVING DIRECTIONS   See Charleston directions, page 238. From Charleston to the plantations, take US 17 south, cross the Ashley River Bridge, and follow South Carolina Route 61 north.

ACCOMMODATIONS   *Middleton Inn,* Ashley River Road (South Carolina Route 61), Charleston, 29414, 556-0500, M–E, CP • *Long Point Inn,* 1199 Long Point Road, Mount Pleasant, 29464, 849-1884, ME, CP. Also see Charleston listings, pages 239–40.

DINING   *Middleton Place Restaurant,* Ashley River Road, Charleston, 556-6020, lunch, I; dinner, M • *Gilligan's Steamer & Raw Bar,* 160 Main Road (US 17 south), 766-2244, informal seafood, I–M • *Plantation Kitchen Restaurant,* Boone Hall, 884-1730, lunch served Monday to Saturday, I • *Coco's Cafe,* 863 Houston Northcutt Boulevard, Patriots Plaza, Mount Pleasant, 881-5550, chef-owned, creative seafood, M • *Slightly Up the Creek,* 130 Mill Street, Mount Pleasant, 884-5005, seafood with picturesque water views, M. Also see Charleston listings, page 240.

SIGHT-SEEING   *Drayton Hall,* Ashley River Road (South Carolina Route 61), Charleston, 769-2600. Hours: March to October, daily 10 A.M. to 4 P.M.; rest of year, to 3 P.M. $$$$ • *Magnolia Plantation and Gardens,* Ashley River Road (South Carolina Route 61), Charleston, 367-3517. Hours: Mid-February to early November, daily 8 A.M. to dusk, last tickets sold 5 P.M. or 5:30 P.M.; rest of year phone for hours. Gardens, $$$$; house tour, every half hour beginning at 9 A.M., $$ in addition to garden admission • *Audubon Swamp Garden,* at Magnolia Plantation, 571-1266. Hours: Daily 8 A.M. to 5:30 P.M. $$ • *Middleton Place,* Ashley River Road (South Carolina Route 61), Charleston, 556-6020. Hours: Daily 9 A.M. to 5 P.M. $$$$$ • *Charles Towne Landing,* South Carolina Route 171, Charleston, 852-4200. Hours: Daily 9 A.M. to 5 P.M.; until 6 P.M. June through August. $$ • *Boone Hall Plantation,* US 17, Mount Pleasant, 884-4371. Hours: April through Labor Day, Monday to Saturday 9 A.M. to 5 P.M., Sunday 1 to 4 P.M.; rest of year, Monday to Saturday 1 to 5 P.M., Sunday 1 to 4 P.M. $$$$$ • *Cypress Gardens,* 3030 Cypress Gardens Road (off US 52), Moncks Corner, 553-0515. Hours: February to December, daily 9 A.M. to 5 P.M. $$$.

INFORMATION *Charleston Area Convention and Visitors Bureau,* 81 Mary Street, P.O. Box 975, Charleston, SC 29402, 853-8000 or (800) 774-0006; www.charlestoncvb.com

Ambling Around in Atlanta

Old and New South meet head-on in Atlanta, Georgia.

Scarlett O'Hara, Atlanta's best-known fictional resident, would be dumbfounded if she could see the present-day skyline of the city that was burned to the ground during the Civil War. High-rise architecture, from John Portman's shiny hotel towers to the cupola of Philip Johnson's much-lauded Atlanta Center, is an unmistakable monument to a metropolis on the rise. Indisputably the major business center of the South, Atlanta claimed its place on the international scene as host to the 1996 Summer Olympic Games.

Growth has spawned four distinct business areas—Downtown, Midtown, Buckhead, and the city's Perimeter—and has brought lavish shopping and dining and ever-spreading residential suburbs in four counties, all connected by a whizzing spaghetti maze of freeways.

Look beyond the flash and the freeways, however, and the grace of the older South remains. What Atlantans like best about their town is a lifestyle that mixes the modern with some of America's loveliest, leafiest residential neighborhoods. Come to visit in spring, when the dogwoods or magnolias are in bloom, and it's all but impossible not to fall under the city's spell.

Sight-seeing begins in Downtown, where Ted Turner's CNN Center, headquarters of the Cable News Network and Headline News, offers guided studio tours—plus a chance to shop for souvenirs at the Clubhouse Shop of Turner's Atlanta Braves. The stately halls of the state capitol are nearby.

An early Downtown neighborhood of streets near the railroad terminal became a forgotten warehouse district after the roads were paved over by viaducts. But they have bloomed anew as Underground Atlanta, a lively shopping and entertainment complex that now extends to street level and offers 12 acres of shops, eateries, and clubs.

Peachtree Fountain Plaza, the gateway to Underground Atlanta, is easy to spot with its showy ten-story light tower and cascading fountains. A dazzle of neon marks the area's most popular attraction, the World of Coca-Cola. A million patrons a year enjoy this slick, highly entertaining look at how Coke grew to become one of the world's best-known products. Free soda samples are served at the end of the tour by a high-tech fountain of the future that swirls the liquid ten feet into the air before spouting it in a ten-foot arc—neatly into the visitor's cup.

Atlanta's Olympics reign has left a convenient legacy for sports-minded visitors. Easily reached from Downtown are the 70,500-seat Georgia Dome, headquarters for Atlanta Falcons football, and the 85,000-seat former Olympic Stadium, converted into Turner Field, the home of Atlanta's beloved Braves baseball team. The Atlanta Hawks basketball team and the Atlanta Thrashers hockey team also play in Downtown at the new Philips Arena.

All of Downtown looks better since streets were repaved and trees were planted to show the city at its best for the Olympics, and the Centennial Olympic Park was developed where vacant lots and derelict buildings had been.

Take the MARTA subway system or drive north on Peachtree Street to Midtown to visit Richard Meier's striking High Museum of Art. It is part of the Woodruff Arts Center, the city's fine-arts hub, where the Alliance Theatre Company and the Atlanta Symphony perform.

Other Midtown attractions include Scitrek, Atlanta's much-lauded interactive science and technology museum, and the elegantly restored Fox Theater, now used for plays and concerts. The Margaret Mitchell House, where the famous author lived, now houses a *Gone with the Wind* Museum filled with movie memorabilia.

Piedmont Park, a 185-acre urban oasis, is adjacent to the city's Botanical Garden, with acres of woods and walking trails; perennial, herb, and rose gardens; and a striking indoor conservatory.

Wherever you are in Atlanta, rolling hills and lush greenery are only a block or two from even the busiest arteries. More sight-seeing awaits in these sylvan neighborhoods.

Begin with a drive farther north to Buckhead and the long lineup of multimillion-dollar mansions on and around Paces Ferry Road, the city's most prestigious area. The governor's mansion is one of those along the way.

In the middle of the mansions is the Atlanta History Center, where you can tour one of the grandest of the homes, the Swan House, built and lavishly furnished in 1928 by Edward Hamilton Inman, heir to a cotton fortune.

This is one of the city's top attractions. After a guided tour of the house, admire the formal gardens and stroll among the stately trees of the 32 wooded acres. The grounds also include an 1840 farmhouse and outbuildings, showing what rural life was like before the Civil War.

The History Center's museum building is Georgia's largest urban history museum. The major gallery traces the city from 1835 to the present, and there are notable changing exhibits, as well. The museum houses several noted private collections, such as the DuBose Civil War Collection and the John A. Burrson Folklife Collection, as well as its own renowned assembly of costumes and textiles and *Gone with the Wind* memorabilia.

Buckhead is the place to sample the sophisticated shopping and dining that are Atlanta trademarks. The Lenox Square Mall is one of the largest in the South, and Phipps Plaza, across the street, offers elegant stores in a setting that looks more like a plush hotel lobby than a mall.

One of the city's posh antiques centers is at 2300 Peachtree Road in Buckhead. For artier shopping, seek out Bennett Street, a side street off Peachtree Road at the southern end of Buckhead, where you'll find some 75 galleries, antiques shops, and intriguing boutiques within a short stroll.

There's a funkier scene in Virginia-Highland, an older neighborhood being rediscovered by young Atlantans. Drive past the gracious homes beneath tall trees, then walk along Highland Avenue to see the blues bars, cafés, and offbeat galleries, such as the Modern Primitive Gallery, a folk art haven at 1393 North Highland Avenue.

Another area ripe for exploring is Druid Hills, whose gardenlike streets were the setting for the movie *Driving Miss Daisy*. They were laid out in 1893 by landscape architect Frederick Law Olmsted, who was also responsible for Piedmont Park.

One of the best ways to appreciate the beauty of Druid Hills is to go on the walking tours sponsored by the Atlanta Preservation Center. The center offers other walks as well, which take in sights ranging from modern architecture to the Victorian beauties of Inman Park, the city's first garden suburb, which includes the homes of early Coca-Cola magnates Asa Candler and Ernest Woodruff.

Inman Park is where you will find the Carter Presidential Center and Museum of the Jimmy Carter Library. It is located on Copenhill, the site from which General Sherman directed the battle of Atlanta. Set on 30 lush acres including lakes, a Japanese garden, and a waterfall, the library features a film showing how the president's role has changed under succeeding incumbents. Displays include a life-size replica of the Oval Office and exhibits reminding the visitor of Carter's accomplishments, including fostering peace between Israel and Egypt.

Another famous Georgian, Martin Luther King Jr., was born on Auburn Avenue, the heart of an early progressive upper-class black community known as "Sweet Auburn" for the good life it represented. America's Civil Rights Movement was born here, even before King became its leader. The National Park Service operates a visitor center, conducts tours through King's birthplace, and is slowly restoring the remaining buildings on the block. Also open to visitors is the Ebenezer Baptist Church, where Dr. King, following in the footsteps of his father and grandfather, was co-pastor from 1960 until 1968. His grave is nearby, at the Martin Luther King Jr. Center for Nonviolent Social Change, an organization headed by Coretta Scott King and dedicated to her late husband's goals.

Civil War buffs will want to pay a visit to the Atlanta Cyclorama, an enormous painting-in-the-round depicting the Battle of Atlanta. It is in Grant Park, which is also home to the Atlanta Zoo and its famous pair of giant pandas, Lun Lun and Yang Yang.

The famous mammoth carving of Confederate leaders Davis, Lee, and Jackson can be seen on the mountain at Stone Mountain Park, 17 miles to the north. This wooded, 3,200-acre recreational area, the site of Olympic canoeing, cycling, rowing, and tennis events, can fill a day or more on its own with golf, tennis, lakes, hiking trails, and other recreational facilities. Gondola and steam train rides and a paddle-wheel steamboat are among the other diversions. And while it isn't Tara, it is where you can tour the buildings of a Georgia plantation.

Those who want to stay there will find two attractive lodgings, the Stone Mountain Inn and the Evergreen Conference Center and Resort.

The Fernbank Science Center, on the city outskirts near Decatur, is the place to take a walk along a two-mile trail through one of the largest virgin forests in any U.S. metropolitan area. The center also boasts the Southeast's largest planetarium. The Fernbank Museum of Natural History is the largest natural-history museum south of the Smithsonian. The spectacular Dinosaur Hall has seven life-size inhabitants; the Okefenokee Swamp Gallery surrounds visitors with realistic sights and sounds of the swamp.

The best way to experience Atlanta's gracious lifestyle firsthand is to stay in a bed-and-breakfast home or an inn in one of the wooded residential areas.

When it comes to hotels, the Ritz Carlton properties, both in Downtown and at a five-star location in Buckhead, are acknowledged as tops for luxury lodging as well as dining in the city. Since Buckhead is convenient to shopping and many of the city's best restaurants, another good bet is the dramatic Swissotel, adjacent to the Lenox Square Mall. There are less pricey Buckhead choices, but even the Ritz and Swissotel are comparative bargains on the weekend.

For those who want to be near the downtown attractions and the Convention Center, the downtown Ritz Carlton is comfortable, as is the less expensive Westin Peachtree Plaza, the round tower that is one of John Portman's best-known designs. Wherever you stay, don't miss the Westin's revolving rooftop Sun Dial Restaurant, Bar and View. It is the best overview of the growing city, with a self-guided walking tour to identify the major buildings below. You can enjoy the sights over dinner or a drink, or pay a small fee to visit the Sun Dial View, rightfully advertised as "Atlanta's best view of Atlanta."

Atlanta is a terrific restaurant town, with new entries all the time. Trendy restaurants come and go at a rapid pace, and there will undoubtedly be new stars by the time you read this. The Dining Room at the Ritz Carlton Buckhead seems to hold its top place in spite of all the competition. The Virginia-Highland district has many of the current favorites of young Atlantans and is less expensive than the trendy power scene in Buckhead.

If Southern fried chicken is what you had in mind, join the long line at Mary Mac's Tearoom, which has been serving cafeteria-style at the same stand for 50 years—proving that despite all that modern glitter, there's still a lot of the Old South left in new Atlanta.

Area Code: 404

DRIVING DIRECTIONS   Atlanta is reached by I-20 east and west, and by I-75 or I-85 north and south. It is 149 miles from Birmingham, 249 miles from Charlotte, 252 miles from Nashville, 112 miles from Chattanooga, and 144 miles from Greenville, South Carolina.

PUBLIC TRANSPORTATION   Atlanta is the hub city for Delta Air Lines, and is served by virtually every other airline, as well as by Amtrak.

ACCOMMODATIONS   All are considerably less expensive on weekend packages.

Downtown: *Ritz Carlton Downtown,* 181 Peachtree Street, 30303, 659-0400 or (800) 241-3333, E–EE • *Hyatt Regency Atlanta,* 266 Peachtree Street Northeast, Peachtree Center, 30303, 577-1234, E • *Westin Peachtree Plaza,* Peachtree Street at International Boulevard, 30343, 659-1400, M–E • *Omni Hotel at CNN Center,* 100 CNN Center, 30335, 659-0000, M–EE • *Courtyard by Marriott–Downtown,* 175 Piedmont Avenue Northeast, 30303, 659-2727, M • *Best Western Inn at the Peachtrees,* 330 West Peachtree Street Northwest, 30308, 577-6970, M.

Midtown: *Four Seasons,* 75 14th Street, 30309, 881-9898, E–EE • *Courtyard by Marriot–Midtown,* 1132 Techwood Drive, 30318, 607-1112, M; weekends, I.

Buckhead: *Ritz Carlton Buckhead,* 3434 Peachtree Road Northeast, 30326, 237-2700 or (800) 241-3333, EE • *Swissotel,* 3391 Peachtree Road Northeast, 30326, 365-0065 or (800) 253-1397, E–EE • *Grand Hyatt,* 3300 Peachtree Road Northeast, 30305, 364-3888 or (800) 223-1234, EE • *Embassy Suites Buckhead,* 3285 Peachtree Road, 30305, 261-7733, M–E • *Holiday Inn Buckhead,* 3377 Peachtree Road, 30326, 264-1111, M–E • *Hampton Inn Atlanta Buckhead,* 3398 Piedmont Road Northeast, 30305, 233-5656, M • **Courtyard by Marriott–Buckhead,** 3332 Peachtree Road Northeast, 30326, 869-0818, M.

Stone Mountain: *Stone Mountain Inn,* Robert E. Lee Boulevard, Box 778, Stone Mountain, 30086, (770) 469-3311 or (800) 277-0007, M • *Evergreen Conference Center and Resort,* Stone Mountain, 30086, (800) 722-1000, M–E.

Inns: *Ansley Inn,* 253 15th Street Northeast (north of Downtown), 30309, 872-9000, M–E, CP • *Shellmont,* 821 Piedmont Avenue Northeast (Midtown), 30308, 872-9290, M, CP • *Buckhead Bed & Breakfast,* 70 Lenox Point Northeast, 30324, 237-9224, M, CP.

Bed-and-breakfast reservation services: *Bed-and-Breakfast Atlanta,* 1801 Piedmont Avenue Northeast, 30324, 875-0525 • *R.S.V.P. Grits, Inc.,* 541 Londonberry Road Northwest, 30327, 843-3933 or (800) 823-RSVP.

DINING   Downtown: *Atlanta Grill,* Ritz Carlton Hotel, Downtown (see Accommodations on page 68), elegant, E–EE • *City Grill,* 50 Hurt Plaza, 524-2489, handsome setting, chandeliers and marble, E • *Lombardi's,* 94 Upper Pryor Street, 522-6568, decent northern Italian, best choice in Underground Atlanta, M • *Pittypat's Porch,* 25 International Boulevard, 525-8228, corny setting (natives say for tourists only) but good traditional Southern food and great crabcakes, M–E.

Midtown: *Bacchanalia,* 1198 Howell Mill Road, 365-0410, one of the city's best, E • *South City Kitchen,* 1133 Crescent Avenue, 873-7358, superb contemporary Southern cooking, M–E • *Mary Mac's Tearoom,* 224 Ponce de Leon Avenue, 876-0727, fried chicken and fixings, I • *Pleasant Peasant,* 555 Peachtree Street Northeast, 874-3223, informal, I–M.

Virginia-Highlands: *Babette's Cafe,* 471 North Highland Avenue, 523-9121, bistro, popular, I–M • *Camille's,* 1186 North Highland Avenue, 872-7203, Italian café, M • *Dish,* 870 North Highland Avenue, 897-3463, funky New American in a converted gas station, M • *Indigo Coastal Grill,* 1397 Highland Avenue, 876-0676, Key West ambience, Caribbean food, M.

Buckhead: *Anis Bistro,* 2974 Grandview Avenue, 233-9889, charming French bistro, M–E • *Atlanta Fish Market,* 265 Pharr Road, 262-3165, good fresh fish in a great-looking, crowded, noisy setting, M–E • *Canoe,* 4199 Paces Ferry Road, 432-2663, take a drive for the riverside setting and eclectic, highly praised Continental fare, M • *Blue Ridge Grill,* 1261 West Paces Ferry Road, 233-5030, Southern/soul food, M–E • *Bones,* 3130 Piedmont Road Northeast, 237-2663, wood paneling, fireplace, prime beef, E–EE • *Brasserie Le Coze,* 3393 Peachtree Road, Lenox Center, 266-1440, outstanding, especially for seafood, M–E • *Buckhead Diner,* 3073 Piedmont Road, 262-3336, trendy choice, I–M • *Bluepointe,* 3455 Peachtree Road, 237-9070, current hot spot for fusion cuisine, M–E • *Chops,* 70 West Paces Ferry Road, Buckhead, 262-2675, art deco scene, steaks, M–EE • *The Dining Room,* Ritz Carlton Buckhead (see Accommodations on page 69), best in town for traditional Continental dining, EE • *Fusebox,* 3085 Piedmont Road, 233-3383, where the in crowd goes for Asian fusion fare, M–E • *Nava,* 3060 Peachtree Road, 240-1984, Southwestern change-of-pace menu, knockout decor, M–E • *O.K. Cafe,* 1284 West Paces Ferry Road, 233-2888, all-American diner fare, I–M • *103 West,* 103 West Paces Ferry Road, 233-5993, antiques, Victoriana, excellent food, M–EE • *Pano & Paul's,* 1232 West Paces Ferry Road, 261-3662, classic Victorian decor, longtime top choice, M–EE • *Seeger's,* 111 West Paces Ferry Road, 846-9779, Continental, rated one of Atlanta's best, EE • *Soto,* 3330 Piedmont Road, 233-2005, the place for sushi and other Japanese dishes, E.

SIGHT-SEEING Museums: *Atlanta History Center,* 130 West Paces Ferry Road, Buckhead, 814-4000. Hours: Monday to Saturday 10 A.M. to 5:30 P.M., Sunday noon to 5:30 P.M. $$$$ • *High Museum of Art,* 1280 Peachtree Street Northeast, 733-4400. Hours: Tuesday to Saturday 10 A.M. to 5 P.M., Friday to 9 P.M., Sunday noon to 5 P.M. $$$ • *High Museum of Art Folk Art and Photography Galleries,* Georgia Pacific Center, 30 John Wesley Dobbs Avenue, 577-6940. Hours: Monday to Saturday 10 A.M. to 5 P.M. Free • *Jimmy Carter Library and Museum,* 442 Freedom Parkway, 331-3942. Hours: Monday to Saturday 9 A.M. to 4:45 P.M., Sunday noon to 4:45 P.M. $$ • *Atlanta Cyclorama,* 800 Cherokee Avenue Southeast, Grant Park, 658-7625. Hours: Daily 9:30 A.M. to 4:30 P.M.; June to Labor Day, to 5:30 P.M. $$ • *Margaret Mitchell House and Museum,* 990 Peachtree Street Northeast, 249-7015. Hours: Daily 9 A.M. to 4 P.M. $$$.

Nature and science: *Fernbank Museum of Natural History,* 767 Clifton Road Northeast, 929-6300. Monday to Saturday 9 A.M. to 5 P.M., Sunday noon to 5 P.M. Includes Museum of Natural History, Science Center and Planetarium, woodlands, trails, $$$$. IMAX Theater, $$$$. • *Scitrek—The Science and Technology Museum of Atlanta,*

395 Piedmont Avenue, 522-5500. Hours: Monday to Saturday 10 A.M. to 5 P.M., Sunday noon to 5 P.M. $$$ • *Atlanta Botanical Garden,* Piedmont Avenue at the Prado, Piedmont Park, 876-5859. Hours: Tuesday to Sunday 9 A.M. to 6 P.M. $$$.

Other attractions: *CNN Studio Tour,* One CNN Center, Marietta Street at Techwood Drive, 827-2300. Hours: Daily 9 A.M. to 6 P.M.; tours leave every 15 minutes. $$$ • *Martin Luther King Jr. National Historic Site,* 501 Auburn Avenue, 331-3919. King's birthplace, church, and other sites; guided tours by National Park Service. Hours: Daily 9 A.M. to 5 P.M.; to 6 P.M. Memorial Day to Labor Day. Free • *Georgia State Capitol,* Capitol Hill at Washington Street, 656-2844. Hours: Monday to Friday 8 A.M. to 5 P.M., guided tours, 10 A.M., 11 A.M., 1 P.M., and 2 P.M. Free • *World of Coca-Cola,* 55 Martin Luther King Jr. Drive, 676-5151. Hours: Monday to Saturday 9 A.M. to 5 P.M., to 6 P.M. June to August, Sunday noon to 6 P.M. $$$ • *Zoo Atlanta,* 800 Cherokee Avenue, Grant Park, 624-5600. Hours: Monday to Friday 9:30 A.M. to 4:30 P.M., Saturday and Sunday to 5:30 P.M. $$$ • *Stone Mountain Park,* Highway 78, Stone Mountain, 498-5690. Hours: Memorial Day to Labor Day, park open daily. $$$ (per car). Individual or combination tickets available for Antebellum Plantation, antique car museum, skylift, riverboat cruises, scenic railroad, wildlife preserve.

Walking tours: *Atlanta Preservation Center,* 537 Peachtree Street, 876-2041. Phone for current schedule of guided tours of Atlanta neighborhoods, $$.

INFORMATION *Atlanta Convention and Visitors Bureau,* 233 Peachtree Street Northeast, Suite 100, Atlanta, GA 30303, 521-6600 or (800) ATLANTA; www.atlanta.com.

Summer

Peak Season at Roan Mountain

Rhododendrons like cool weather. Give them a mountain slope at a high elevation, and they thrive in remarkable fashion.

If you want spectacular proof, come for the show at Roan Mountain State Park in Tennessee. Located astride the state border with North Carolina at an elevation of 6,285 feet, the rugged mountain is one of the highest in the eastern United States, and it provides the perfect growing climate for one of the largest natural displays of rhododendrons in the world, some 600 acres of purple and pink blossoms. Knockout views of the dusky ridges of the mountains are a bonus backdrop.

This glorious natural garden usually reaches its peak just in time to welcome the arrival of summer. For over 50 years the weekend closest to June 20 has been the occasion for a local celebration on both sides of the state line, featuring old-time music, dancing, Appalachian crafts, food, and all the hoopla of a gala festival.

But then this Tennessee state park is worth discovering any time, whether you are looking for activity or beautiful serenity. Those who reserve far enough ahead to snag one of the 20 attractive cabins will enjoy a mountain setting and resort facilities that include a pool, tennis, and an amphitheater with a schedule of country entertainment every weekend, ranging from cloggers to storytellers to mountain music.

Ranger-guided programs of nature walks, bicycle tours, and evening adventures such as "owl prowls" are all free. And then there are special events such as the July Fourth fireworks jamboree, with music, fireworks, and clogging exhibitions, and several nature weekends with guest naturalists leading hikes and tours.

Away from the activity, Roan Mountain offers breathtaking views and quiet solitude above the clouds. Hiking is superb. Seven miles of trails from a quarter mile to four miles in length meander through the park. Some ascend to highland peaks, others follow the mountain streams and the Doe River. One of the most popular stretches of the Appalachian Trail crosses Roan High Knob, the highest point in the park.

The view at the top hasn't changed much since Dr. Elisha Mitchell described it back in 1836: "the most beautiful of all the high mountains . . . the top of the Roan may be described as a vast meadow without a tree to obstruct . . . with Carolina at the feet on one side and Tennessee on the other, and a green ocean of mountains rising in tremendous billows immediately around."

Dr. Mitchell, incidentally, is the scientist who measured the mountains and established that the highest peak east of the Rockies was located not in New Hampshire, as had been thought, but in North Carolina, where that mountain, Mount Mitchell, and a county are named for him.

The Roan summit area offers picnic areas, hiking and interpretive trails, and scenic overlooks, all accessible by car.

A world of wildflowers also awaits walkers. Roan Mountain has long drawn botanists for its rich varieties of plants. In the last century, Dr. Asa Gray, considered the father of American botany, called Roan "without doubt the most beautiful mountain east of the Rockies."

One of the most interesting sights in the park is the Dave Miller Homestead, a home built in the early to mid-1900s and restored to represent the lifestyles of residents of the southern Appalachians durng the early twentieth century. The barn, chicken house, smokehouse, and root cellar of the original farm remain, telling of a time when isolated mountain families were self-sufficient, using lye soap made from ashes and medicines made with herbs and plants. On Saturdays in summer, the Homestead hosts programs showcasing traditional arts such as spinning and music from old-time fiddling to bagpipes.

Since the park cabins go fast and preference is given to weeklong stays in summer, you may have to stay elsewhere in the area and enjoy the activites of the park as a day visitor. In Tennessee, the best bet is Jonesborough, about 45 minutes northwest. This is the oldest town in the state, and it is a charmer. Read more about it on pages 153–158.

Or you can go through the park and over the mountain, descending into North Carolina's Mitchell County, a drive of about 20 minutes. The North Toe River has carved out a scenic valley here between high mountains. Mount Mitchell, at 6,684 feet, is one of a dozen peaks in the area over 6,000 feet. There's a North Carolina state park with a road to the summit of Mount Mitchell and an observation tower if you want another peak view.

This is a relatively quiet and often overlooked area of North Carolina, but you'll find ample rewards for a visit.

Even if you've never set foot in Mitchell County, you may have had some part of it in your home. Roan Mountain Fraser fir, with its rich green needles and pungent aroma, is the king of Christmas trees, and it is grown here in abundance at more than 50 nurseries.

Mitchell County mines produce lovely gemstones, as well as significant amounts of the feldspar and quartz used to manufacture everything from mayonnaise jars to bathroom fixtures. A large percent of the United States supply of ultrapure quartz used in semiconductors comes from the region. You can actually go underground in some of the historic mines.

The biggest is the North Carolina Mining Museum at Emerald Village near Little Switzerland, a town named for its scenic mountain setting. Some 45 different rocks, minerals, and gems have been found in the Emerald area, including aquamarines, emeralds, garnets, and smoky quartz. The museum is located in a mine where feldspar was the principal find, valued as an ingredient for the popular cleansing powder known as Bon Ami. The cavernous space and tunnels dug by the miners remain, along with the crushers, cable cars, and machines used to extract the feldspar.

It's quite a fascinating little tour, and afterwards you can have a go at finding your own gems. You pay for a bucket of stones, then wash and sift through them at a heated indoor flume. You may not find a priceless prize, but every bucket is guaranteed to contain at least one small gem. Several other area mines offer the same opportunity to hunt for treasures.

The Emerald Village gift shop displays gem jewelry and loose gems priced from $3 to $100. Half a dozen more gem shops in Spruce Pine sell not only jewelry but beautiful geodes, stones that have been split to reveal a colorful mineral-lined cavity. Geodes, when split evenly, make uniquely attractive bookends.

As capital of the state's mining and mineral-processing industry, Spruce Pine is the logical place for an annual Mineral and Gem Festival, an event that has been held on the first weekend in August for over 40 years. Some 60 retail dealers, offering everything from inexpensive clear quartz crystals to flawless gems worth thousands of dollars, set up shop in the Pinebridge Center.

Spruce Pine itself is the commercial center for the area. It's not a tourist town, but it is being spruced up and has recently been discovered by retirees.

You can see gorgeous gems displayed at the Museum of North Carolina Mines, just off the Blue Ridge Parkway in Spruce Pine.

The Penland School of Crafts in Penland, a few miles north of Spruce Pine, is renowned. It was founded in 1923 by Miss Lucy Morgan, who came to the area to help her brother Rufus run the Appalachian School, a school for mountain children supported by the Episcopal Church. Miss Morgan saw crafts as a way to help mountain women earn money, and began to revive the dying art of hand-weaving. More than 60 women took part in the weaving project, initially in their homes. Eventually a "weaving Cabin" was built at the school, using logs and labor donated by the weavers' families. The school has grown to offer a wide variety of classes in fiber, wood, clay, glass, metalwork, and other arts taught by master craftsmen from around the world. The gallery is well worth a detour; excellent work is for sale there.

Many former students have established permanent studios in the area, and towns like Burnsville have many galleries. In Spruce Pine, the Twisted Laurel Gallery at 333 Locust Avenue shows the work of 120 area craftspeople in a wide variety of mediums. If you want to visit artists' studios tucked away in the hills and hollows, stop at the Mitchell County Chamber of Commerce for a listing.

Among several lodgings in the area, the choicest is the Switzerland Inn in Little Switzerland, built in chalet-style architecture with panoramic vistas that would do credit to the Alps. Guests have use of a spring-fed pool, tennis courts, and lovely hiking trails.

If you spend a day atop Roan Mountain State Park and a day admiring gems and exploring underground mines, there's plenty to fill a weekend, but if time allows, Little Switzerland is less than half an hour from Grandfather Mountain and Blowing Rock to the east, with some of the best scenery and highest waterfalls along the Blue Ridge Parkway on the way.

Area Codes: Roan Mountain, TN, 423; Mitchell County, NC, 828

DRIVING DIRECTIONS Roan Mountain is on Route 143, reached in Tennessee via Route 19E. From I-40 east, continue south on I-40 at the I-81 intersection. Exit at Highway 321 east and follow it to Route 19E at Elizabethton. Turn south on 19E, then make a right on Route 143 to the park. Roan Mountain is 130 miles from Knoxville. From Atlanta and other southern points, the best route is through North Carolina. Take I-85 north to I-26 north to Asheville, follow I-240 north into Highway 70/19 east, bearing right on 19E to Spruce Pine. Here, take Highway 226 north to Bakersville, then take Highway 261 north to Highway 143 into Roan Mountain State Park, 294 miles. Spruce Pine is 102 miles from Charlotte, 51 miles from Asheville.

ACCOMMODATIONS *Roan Mountain State Park,* 1015 Highway 143, Roan Mountain, TN 37687, 772-0190 or (800) 250-8620, 20 modern cabins, weekly reservations given preference in summer, I–M • *Switzerland Inn,* P.O. Box 399, Little Switzerland, NC 28749, 765-2153 or (800) 654-4026, chalet lodge on a mountain crest, fine views, open May to October, M • *Big Lynn Lodge,* Box 459, Little Switzerland, NC 28749, 765-4527 or (800) 654-5232, upscale motel-style rooms, more scenic vistas, M • *Richmond Inn,* 101 Pine Avenue, Spruce Pine, NC 28777, 765-6993, bed-and-breakfast home overlooking town, I–M, CP • *Pinebridge Inn,* 101 Pinebridge Avenue, Spruce Pine, NC 28777, 765-5543 or (800) 356-5059, former school remodeled into a hotel and conference center, I-E • For Jonesborough, TN, see pages 157–158.

DINING *Chalet Restaurant,* Switzerland Inn (see Accommodations above), Continental fare in a room with a view, M • *Cedarcrest Restaurant,* 311 Locust Avenue, Spruce Pine, 765-6124, casual, family fare, I–M • *High Country Steak and Seafood House,* Highway 226 South, Spruce Pine, 765-8000, the basics, M.

SIGHT-SEEING *Roan Mountain State Park,* Route 1, Box 50, Roan Mountain, TN 37687, 772-3303. Hours: Daily 8 A.M. to 8 P.M. Swimming, picnicking, hiking, tennis, many special programs. Rhododendron gardens in bloom usually late May to late June. Free • *Mineral and Gem Festival,* c/o Mitchell County Area Chamber of Commerce (see below), first weekend in August, gem displays, jewelry-making demonstrations, mine tours. Check current information. $$ • *Mount Mitchell State Park,* Route 128, near Little Switzerland, 675-4611, observation tower, museum, picnicking, restaurant. Hours: Daily in summer 8 A.M. to 8 P.M.; April, May, September to 7 P.M.; rest of year to 6 P.M. Free • *Emerald Village,* P.O. Box 98, Little Switzerland, 765-6463. Hours: Daily in summer 9 A.M. to 6 P.M.; to 5 P.M. spring and fall. From November to April, open by appointment or by chance. $$ • *Penland Gallery,* Penland School of Crafts, Penland, 765-6211. Hours: Tuesday to Saturday 10 A.M. to noon and 1 to 4:30 P.M., Sunday noon to 4:30 P.M. Free • *Museum of North Carolina Minerals,* Blue Ridge Parkway Milepost 226, 765-9483. Hours: May to October, daily 9 A.M. to 5 P.M.; rest of year, Wednesday to Sunday 10 A.M. to 5 P.M. Free.

INFORMATION *Mitchell County Chamber of Commerce,* Route 226 and the Blue Ridge Parkway, Route 1, Box 796, Spruce Pine, NC 28777, 765-9483 or (800) 227-3912; www.mitchell-county.com.

Splendid Summers at the Shoals

The Northwest corner of Alabama is a land of lakes, big bodies of blue formed by mighty dams on the Tennessee River that some have called the "Great Lakes of the South." More than 1,200 miles of shoreline offer infinite possibilities for summer fun.

The "quad cities" of Muscle Shoals, Tuscumbia, Sheffield, and Florence, situated near the banks of the Tennessee, have their own claims to fame, thanks to some special residents, past and present.

The Miracle Worker, the inspiring story of Helen Keller, has thrilled audiences on Broadway and in movie theaters across the country, but nowhere is it quite so moving as when performed at Ivy Green, Keller's birthplace in Tuscumbia, where the real miracle occurred.

It seems appropriate that the Alabama Music Hall of Fame was established near Tuscumbia in 1990, because the area is home to still-active recording studios where the Rolling Stones, Bob Dylan, Aretha

Franklin, and many others have made hit albums. Florence was the birthplace of W. C. Handy, the "father of the blues," who is saluted each August by a spirited festival of jazz and blues.

Between the lakes and the luminaries, this is a refreshing summer getaway. Diverse history has left its legacy, as well, with sight-seeing from Indian mounds to an early 1800s stagecoach tavern, antebellum plantations to a Frank Lloyd Wright home.

Florence, the largest and most interesting of the towns, has many of the sights. The only town on the north side of the river, it was an early Indian settlement and trading post until 1818, when a wealthy group of land developers established a town. The name came from a young Italian who was brought in to lay out the streets.

The city's growth was not thanks to its river, however. The town's site overlooked dangerous rocky shoals and rapids that made the Tennessee impassable for barge traffic. So notorious were these hazards that the entire area became known as Muscle Shoals.

The government tried to build a canal around the shoals in 1836, but it was inoperable within a year. Soon after, the Tuscumbia, Courtland, and Decatur Railroad, the first railroad west of the Virginia mountains, came chugging into town and made river transportation less important. Florence quickly developed into a trading and educational center.

In 1855, Wesleyan University was founded. Yankee General William Sherman used the building as his headquarters in 1865. In 1872, it became part of the first college for teacher training south of the Mason-Dixon line, and the first coeducational college in the South. It is now known as the University of North Alabama.

When President Woodrow Wilson finally began construction of a dam on the Tennessee in 1918, it was not for navigation but as a wartime project intended to generate power to make munitions. Completed in 1925, Wilson Dam—137 feet tall and 4,542 feet wide—was the highest dam in the world. After munitions were no longer needed, the dam would tame the treacherous shoals forever. Wilson became the first of a chain of nine dams built along the Tennessee River from Alabama to Kentucky, improving river navigation and providing hydroelectric power for industry that has greatly aided regional development.

The main navigation lock at Wilson Dam remains one of the highest single-lift locks in the world. When a ship enters the lock, it is raised or lowered as much as 100 feet in order to navigate the river safely. The lock holds 50 million gallons of water, which it can empty in 12 minutes flat. It is fascinating to watch. Visitors can drive across the dam to an overlook on top of the lock.

For a bird's-eye view of the action, take the elevator to the top of Alabama's tallest tourist attraction, the Renaissance Tower, a slim, futuristic shaft rising 500 feet above Pickwick Lake. The Renaissance Grille restaurant offers spectacular views of the dam and the two lakes it formed. Wilson Lake stretches for 15 miles upriver to Wheeler Dam, while Pickwick Lake, fed by the spillwaters below the dam, runs for 52 miles to Pickwick Dam in Tennessee. Exhibits on the main floor of the tower tell more about the work of the Tennessee Valley Authority.

The second floor of the tower features the Alabama Shoals Aquarium and Nature Center, which exhibits some 160 kinds of fish, birds, and animals from around the world. Outside, hundreds of wildflowers grow in a garden maintained by the Alabama Wildflower Society.

Wheeler Dam, named for Confederate General "Fightin' Joe" Wheeler, who later represented the Tennessee Valley in Congress, has formed its own 74-mile lake. Joe Wheeler State Park on 3400 wooded acres around the dam has an attractive lodge with 75 guest rooms, each with a balcony overlooking Wheeler Lake. The park offers tennis, golf, and a marina with boat rentals in season.

All three lakes provide prime fishing. Pickwick, in particular, is famous for smallmouth bass.

When you're not busy with the dam or its lakes, you'll find Florence a city filled with lovely homes, almost 100 included in four Historic Districts. Court Street, the attractive main street of town, has some of the finest dwellings, such as Wakefield, a brick home built in 1825 and patterned after George Washington's ancestral home, and the 1857 Governor O'Neal home, named for the family that produced two Alabama governors.

Courtview, the grand 1855 Greek Revival house at the north end, turned the street into a dead end. The influential builder, George Washington Foster, received special permission from the state legislature to place the house so it would give him an unobstructed river view. Beyond it, farther up the hill, are the handsome columned brick buildings of the University of North Alabama.

One of Florence's oldest structures, Pope's Tavern, is one block from Court on a street that used to be called Military Road because it was the most direct route from Nashville to New Orleans. Andrew Jackson reportedly stopped here in 1814 on his march to battle the British in New Orleans. During the Civil War, the house was used as a hospital for both Union and Confederate soldiers. In 1874, it became a private home, and it remained in one family until it was purchased by the City of Florence in 1965. Now furnished as a tavern once again, it is the site of an annual Frontier Day celebration on the first weekend in June, which includes demonstrations, music, arts and crafts, and storytelling.

Long before Pope's Tavern or the rest of the town existed, this area was inhabited by Native Americans now known as Mound Builders. In many Southern locations huge ceremonial mounds that might once have had temples on their summits are monuments to this ancient past. The mound on South Court Street is the largest in the Tennessee Valley. Tools and artifacts found in and around the mound, some dating back 10,000 years, are displayed at the Indian Mound and Museum.

Two later Florence homes are not to be missed. The Rosenbaum

House is the oldest Frank Lloyd Wright house in the United States still occupied by its original owner. Designed in 1939–40 of cypress, glass, and brick, it is one of only 26 Usonian houses that Wright developed, prototypes for residences that the average American family could afford. It incorporates many Wright innovations—carports, radiant heating, a multilevel cantilevered roof, the use of all natural materials, outside access to every room, and elevations that follow the natural contours of the site. Doors, windows, walls, furnishings, lights, and hardware were all integral parts of the structure in Wright's eyes.

The hand-hewn log cabin where William Christopher Handy was born in 1873 has been restored to tell the story of a remarkable musician, the son and grandson of ministers who left the expected family path to follow his own star. His musical education was part singing classes in Florence's black public school, part listening to the spirituals and melodies he heard along the river. Handy left home at 18, failed at starting a band, worked at a variety of jobs until, at the age of 38, he wrote a campaign song for "Boss" E. H. Crump, mayor of Memphis. It became the classic "Memphis Blues," and the rest is musical history. During his lifetime, Handy wrote over 150 secular and sacred songs, including the universally known "St. Louis Blues." In 1918, he opened a music publishing firm in New York, where he lived until his death in 1958.

Adjoining the cabin is a museum with the most complete collection of Handy's personal papers and artifacts, including his famous trumpet, his personal piano, and handwritten sheet music, including Braille compositions he wrote after losing his sight.

Handy is one of many Alabama-born musicians who are honored at the Alabama Music Hall of Fame, a lavish facility where you can walk through a giant jukebox playing songs by Alabama performers, see wax figures of Nat "King" Cole and Hank Williams Sr., board the tour bus used by the group Alabama, admire costumes worn by Lionel Richie and the Commodores, and hear music from the world's largest guitar. If you want your own hit record as a souvenir, the Music Hall of Fame offers a recording studio complete with taped backup music, and you can take your cassette home with you.

Tuscumbia also offers one of the finest antebellum homes in the state, Belle Mont, built in 1828 as an outstanding example of Palladian architecture, perhaps inspired by Thomas Jefferson's Monticello.

But the most memorable home in Tuscumbia is the far more modest 1820 white clapboard house where Helen Keller was born on June 27, 1880. The healthy child was stricken with a severe illness at 19 months that left her blind and deaf. The miracle wrought by teacher Anne Sullivan, who penetrated Helen's silence to enable her to learn and communicate, revealed a remarkably gifted child. In 1904, with Sullivan still at her side, Helen Keller was graduated cum laude from Radcliffe

College, and went on to become one of history's most courageous and admired women. She dedicated her life to improving conditions for the blind and deaf, writing and lecturing in more than 25 countries on five continents.

The home is still as it was when Helen lived here, as is the cottage that was first a playhouse, then the place where Anne Sullivan tamed and taught the half-wild child. Each is filled with Miss Keller's personal mementos, books, and gifts, including her library and her original Braille typewriter. The well pump where Helen spoke her first word, "wa-wa," remains in its original location as well.

William Gibson's *The Miracle Worker,* telling the story of Anne Sullivan and her miraculous breakthrough, is performed by a talented local cast, who obviously relish their roles. The first performance each year is in June during the Helen Keller Festival, a weeklong event celebrating Tuscumbia's most famous native. A parade, entertainment, arts and crafts, tours of historic sites, puppet shows, and many other special activities take place during the week. It is a unique celebration for a most unique woman—and one more reason to set your sights on Alabama's Shoals.

Area Code: 256

DRIVING DIRECTIONS The quad cities are off Routes 43/17. To reach the Shoals area from Atlanta, take I-20 west to I-65 north, then Highway 20/72A west to Route 43, 232 miles. From Birmingham, take I-65 north and follow directions above, 119 miles; from Nashville, I-65 south, then as above, 177 miles.

ACCOMMODATIONS *Hampton Inn,* 2281 Florence Boulevard, Florence, 35650, 764-8888, M • *Jameson Inn,* 115 Ana Drive, Florence, 35630, 764-5328, I • *Key West Inn,* 1800 Highway 72, Tuscumbia, 35674, 383-0700 or (800) 833-0555, attractive motel complex, I, CP • *Holiday Inn,* 4900 Hatch Boulevard, Sheffield, 35660, 381-4710, lavish indoor pool area, I • *Ramada Inn,* 4205 Hatch Boulevard, Sheffield, 35660, 381-3743, I • *Joe Wheeler State Park Resort Lodge,* 4401 McLean Drive, Rogersville, 35652, off Route 72, 25 miles east of Florence, 247-5461 or (800) 544-5639, reservations, (800) ALA-PARK, lodge or cabins, I. **Bed-and-breakfast inns:** *Wood Avenue Inn,* 658 North Wood Avenue, Florence, 35630, 766-8441, 1880 Victorian home, I–M, CP • *Limestone Manor,* 601 North Wood Avenue, Florence, 35630, 765-0314 or (888) 709-6700, 1915 Georgian Revival home, I–M, CP.

DINING *Dale's Fine Dining,* Mitchell Boulevard, Routes 72 and 43, Florence, 766-4961, steaks are the specialty, I–E • *Renaissance Grille,*

1 Hightower Place, Florence, 766-3200, lunch, dinner, Sunday brunch; unbeatable view, I–M • *Court Street Cafe,* Mobile and Seminary Streets, 767-4300, informal, I • *Ricatoni's Italian Grill,* 107 Court Street, Florence, 718-1002, I • *Louisiana "The Restaurant,"* 406 North Montgomery Avenue, Sheffield, 386-0801, attractive New Orleans decor, Creole menu, M • *George's Steak Pit,* 1206 Jackson Highway, Sheffield, 381-1531, M–E • *Joe Wheeler State Park Restaurant,* 4401 McLean Drive, Rogersville, 247-5466, varied menu, I–M.

SIGHT-SEEING *Ivy Green,* 300 West North Commons, Tuscumbia, 383-4066. Hours: Monday to Saturday 8:30 A.M. to 4 P.M., Sunday 1 P.M. to 4 P.M. $$. *The Miracle Worker,* performed on the grounds six weekends in mid-June to July • *Alabama Music Hall of Fame,* Highway 72 West, Tuscumbia, 381-4417 or (800) 239-AMHF. Hours: Monday to Saturday 10 A.M. to 6 P.M., Sunday 1 P.M. to 5 P.M. $$$ • *Renaissance Tower,* 1 Hightower Place off East Union Street, Florence, 764-5900. Hours: Monday to Saturday 9:30 A.M. to 5:30 P.M., Sunday noon to 5 P.M. • *Alabama Shoals Aquarium,* same hours • *Stanley and Mildred Rosenbaum House,* 601 Riverview Drive, Florence, 764-5274. Hours: Limited; by appointment only. $$$ • *Indian Mound and Museum,* South Court Street, Florence, 760-6379. Hours: Tuesday to Saturday 10 A.M. to 4 P.M. $ • *W. C. Handy Museum,* 620 West College Street, Florence, 760-6434. Hours: Tuesday to Saturday 10 A.M. to 4 P.M. $ • *Pope's Tavern,* 203 Hermitage Drive, Florence, 760-6439. Hours: Tuesday to Saturday 10 A.M. to 4 P.M. $ • *Belle Mont,* 111 Jefferson Avenue, Muscle Shoals, 383-2865. Hours: April to early December, tours Sunday at 2 P.M. and 3 P.M., otherwise by appointment. • *Joe Wheeler State Park,* 201 McLean Drive, Rogersville, off Route 72, 25 miles east of Florence, 247-5466 or (888) 356-8687. Hours: Daylight hours. $.

INFORMATION *Shoals Chamber of Commerce,* 612 South Court Street, Florence, AL 35630, 764-4661 or (877) 764-4661; www.shoalscc.org • *Florence/Lauderdale Tourism,* 1 Hightower Place, Florence, AL 35630, 740-4141; www.flo-tour.org • *Colbert County Tourism and Convention Bureau,* P.O. Box 440, Tuscumbia, AL 35674, 383-0783 or (800) 344-0783; www.colbertcounty.org.

Basking on the Outer Banks

Whether you like your beaches sociable or solitary, you're going to love the Outer Banks of North Carolina. These 120 miles of barrier islands boast the most magnificent shores in the Southeast (if not the nation), and they offer infinite variety in mood. With a little advance guidance, you're sure to find your own place in the sun.

It is true that the location is somewhat remote, and there are no superhighways to make the driving easy, but this is a destination no beach lover should pass by. If you live too far away to drive for a weekend, come for a week—or take a plane.

Most people arriving from the south by car come via US 64 across Roanoke Island, which lies in Roanoke Sound between the mainland and Bodie Island, the central part of the Outer Banks.

Roanoke is the site of a unique bit of history. The British, under Sir Walter Raleigh, established a colony here over 400 years ago, long before the landing at Jamestown, Virginia. But the 116 men, women, and children of the settlement disappeared without explanation. Their story is re-created in the outdoor pageant "The Lost Colony," presented each summer in the town of Manteo. It is the nation's oldest and longest-running outdoor drama.

The theater is located at Fort Raleigh National Historic Site, where the tale of the ill-fated colonists is told in exhibits. The lovely Elizabethan Gardens have been planted here in memory of the lost settlers. Plan to spend time in Manteo when you take a break from the beach. Besides the sights, this is a delightful town on a picturesque marina. Moored at the dock is the *Elizabeth II,* a 69-foot, square-rigged sailing ship representative of the kind that Raleigh might have sailed on in the sixteenth century. And the local branch of the state aquarium is a safe haven on a rainy day. Some of Manteo's lodgings are so inviting, you might even be tempted to stay.

But if you want to be on the beach, continue across the bridge to Bodie Island, arriving in the community of Nags Head. Finding your way on Bodie is simple; there are only two main roads, North Carolina Route 12, known as Beach Road, near the ocean, and US 158, in the center of the island. On the other side of the narrow peninsula, accessible via side roads, is Pamlico Sound, protected waters for sailing, canoeing, and other water sports.

North of Nags Head lie the communities of Kill Devil Hills and Kitty Hawk. Little other than signs differentiate these towns. Shops, restaurants, miniature golf, and other typical beach amusements run nonstop along the center highway, and the beaches are almost completely lined with weathered cottages and low-rise motels. These are fine for families and others who enjoy company at the beach. The motels are standard, with no particular standouts; those listed on page 89 are newer or seem better values.

Two major sights are in this area. The Wright Brothers National Memorial in Kill Devil Hills has a replica of Orville and Wilbur Wright's first successful flying machine, in a museum near the hill where they launched it on December 17, 1903.

They're still launching things at Jockey Ridge State Park in Nags Head, but now it is hang gliders that soar from the highest natural sand dune in the eastern United States. They're great fun to watch, and if you're tempted, Kitty Hawk Kites offers expert instruction, teaching some 2,000 people each year how to fly through the air.

The above-mentioned sand dune is one of eight mammoth dunes in the area formed by shifting winds, a sandscape that looks more like the Sahara than the South. The height of the largest dune varies from 110 to 140 feet, depending on weather conditions. Kids of all ages love climbing these huge sand piles and sliding down.

Though it is convenient to Virginia and the Norfolk airport, the northernmost end of Bodie was the last part to be developed because of its past proximity to Norfolk military bases and bomb testing. Recently this has become the most exclusive preserve on the island, rapidly building up with developments of large, very expensive summer homes, some costing a million dollars or more.

Follow Route 12 north to the town of Duck, and you'll find the area's best shops, particularly in the wooded Scarborough Faire complex. Waterfront Shops, with a walkway on the water, is another attractive enclave.

Continue on Route 12 past the 7,000-acre Audubon preserve and the lineup of developments under construction, and just as the paving ends, look to the left and you'll see the red-brick Corolla Lighthouse, built in 1875. This is one of a set of lighthouses along the Outer Banks dating from the 1870s, built to warn seamen away from the treacherous shoals along the coast. Some are painted in striking black-and-white patterns. Photographs of these landmarks are sold just about everywhere, and visiting camera buffs invariably go out of their way to shoot a set for themselves. The adjoining lightkeeper's house at Corolla has recently been restored.

Signs along the road to the lighthouse mark the Currituck Wild Horse Sanctuary, which has been established to protect the few remaining horses that used to roam here before houses and the highway began usurping their land. The mustangs are descendants of horses brought by the first Spanish settlers in 1583.

Just north of Duck is the pick of Outer Banks lodgings, the Sanderling Inn. Though it was built in 1985, the weathered gray wood and the porches are in the style of summer homes of the 1890s. With an old lifesaving station converted to serve as the dining room, the inn is tastefully at home in its surroundings. Guests here enjoy five miles of private beaches as well as a pool, health club, and spa. Only a true escapist would quibble about the lovely homes spaced among the dunes along the beach.

Such purists are advised to turn south when they arrive on Bodie Island, following North Carolina Route 12 past the horizontally striped Bodie Lighthouse (with a detour for a photo, of course) and the busy marina and fishing center at Oregon Inlet to Hatteras Island. You may want to return to this marina for sportfishing; it is home to the largest fishing fleet on the coast.

Once you cross the bridge over the inlet to Hatteras, you're in the heart of the National Seashore, which has been protected since 1953. Suddenly there's little development in sight, and almost nobody is on the beach. For many people, this is what the Outer Banks are all about. The Seashore stretches for 70 miles across the end of Bodie, the whole length of Hatteras, and on to Ocracoke Island, which can be reached only via ferry.

On Hatteras, you'll first pass Pea Island National Wildlife Refuge, whose nature trails and observation platforms are popular spots with bird and wildlife watchers and wildflower enthusiasts.

Next along the road are a few surviving early U.S. lifesaving stations. The Chicamacomico Station, established in 1874, is one of the oldest. Exhibits remind visitors of the daring rescues that have been made off the treacherous shoals and surf of Hatteras Island, and demonstrations of the old techniques are sometimes given. Check the schedules.

Small villages along the road, such as Rodanthe, Waves, Salvo, Avon, and Hatteras, were allowed to remain because they existed before the National Seashore was declared. Beach worshipers and fishermen occupy most of the widely spaced, low-key motels.

The only thing resembling a crowd on Hatteras is the group usually found taking pictures around the diagonally striped Hatteras Lighthouse, at 208 feet the tallest in the country. It warns ships away from the perils of Diamond Shoals, waters that became known as the "Graveyard of the Atlantic." More than 600 ships have sunk here, victims of shallow shoals, storms, and war.

Heavy storms in 1992 shifted sands and currents, uncovering some of the shipwrecks, which are now visible from shore. Look for the *Laura A. Barnes* at Coquina Beach, three miles north of Oregon Inlet, and the Civil War transport *Oriental,* which can be seen at low tide near the Pea Island National Wildlife Refuge comfort station.

These same storms washed away major portions of the dunes, and some of the huge sandbags used to build a wall against the ocean's surges may still be in evidence. It is a tug-of-war that has gone on for centuries, with storms pulling relentlessly at the exposed shoreline. The Hatteras Lighthouse was recently moved inland to protect it from the water.

At the very end of Hatteras, drive aboard the car ferry for the free 12-mile, 40-minute ride to Ocracoke Island. As soon as you head out to sea and sniff the fresh salt air, the feeling of freedom grows. Ocracoke's 17 miles of beach are the kind of wide, dune-backed, deserted sands that beach lovers dream about. Some areas have lifeguards in attendance, while others are completely deserted, places where there is no one but you, the sun, and the sea.

Ocracoke's deep inlet made it suitable early on as a port for ocean-going vessels. The North Carolina Colonial Assembly recognized the settlement in 1715 and officially proclaimed it a town in 1735.

Not only commercial seamen were attracted here. The secluded location made it a favorite haunt of the infamous pirate Blackbeard, who was killed off Ocracoke in a hand-to-hand battle and then beheaded. Some believe Blackbeard's buried treasure remains on the island.

The ferry pulls into the docks at Silver Lake, a natural harbor on the southern side of the island shared by yachts and fishing boats. The dominant building is a 1942 Coast Guard station. In the distance is the Ocracoke Lighthouse, dating to 1823, one of the oldest still in use on the Atlantic coast.

The entire village is on the National Register of Historic Places and is so picturesque that color sketches of the harbor, painted on weathered boards, are the best-selling island souvenir. Some 100 cottages built between the 1880s and 1930s remain.

A walk around the island yields many discoveries. Stop at the Ocracoke Preservation Society Information Center for a brochure to guide you. Some of the roads are still unpaved. At the end of sandy Howard Lane is Village Craftsmen, the best place to find local crafts. It is owned by Philip Howard, whose island ancestors go back several generations. You'll see the name again in town on Howard's Pub, a popular watering hole known for its original concoction, the Ocracoke Oyster Shooter.

There are over 80 small cemeteries on the island, maintained by families like the Howards, whose ancestors can be traced through the intriguing epitaphs on the headstones.

The British Cemetery, near Northern Pond, is unique. It is the burial ground of four British sailors whose bodies washed ashore, casualties of a battle with a German submarine in 1942. With the Union Jack flying proudly, it is a tiny bit of official British soil in the United States.

Ocracoke's small remaining herd of about two dozen ponies, known as Banker horses, descendants of horses brought by the first English settlers, can be seen on the road near the beach at the Ocracoke Pony Pen, where they have been brought together to be protected and properly fed.

The classic lodging on Ocracoke is the white, balconied Island Inn, a no-frills former 1901 Odd Fellows lodge restored in traditional island style. Berkley Manor is a pleasant alternative, though it lacks water views.

No reservations are needed for the ferry back to reality. Though the schedule says the boats leave every 30 minutes, ferries often run every 15 minutes during peak times, so while there is sometimes a line waiting to board, you'll not have to wait too long.

There's only one problem—you'll never want to leave.

Area Code: 252

DRIVING DIRECTIONS   The Outer Banks are approached via US 64/264 east or via US 158 from the north. Nags Head is about 200 miles from Raleigh-Durham.

PUBLIC TRANSPORTATION   The closest large airports are Raleigh-Durham or Norfolk, Virginia, about a two-hour drive. Dare County Regional Airport, on Roanoke Island, has commuter service from Norfolk; phone 473-2600 for current information. Limousine and van service are also available from Norfolk. From the south, a toll ferry brings motorists from Cedar Island, near Morehead City, to Ocracoke; phone 225-3551 for schedules and rates.

ACCOMMODATIONS   Duck: *Sanderling Inn Resort,* Route 12, S.R. Box 319Y, Duck, 27949, 261-4111 or (800) 701-4111, E–EE, CP.

Nags Head: *The Islander Motel,* Route 12, Nags Head, 27959, 441-6229, small property, pool, all rooms oceanfront, M • *Comfort Inn–Oceanfront South,* Route 12, MP 17, Nags Head, 27959, 441-6315, pool, M–E.

Kill Devil Hills: *Days Inn Oceanfront,* Route 12, MP 8.3, Kill Devil Hills, 27948, 441-7211, attractive lobby, pool, refrigerators, M–E • *Best Western Ocean Reef Suites,* Route 12, MP 8.5, Kill Devil Hills, 27948, 441-1611, cooking facilities, E.

Kitty Hawk: *Holiday Inn Express,* US 158 Bypass, MP 4, Kitty Hawk, 27979, 261-4888, beach, pool, refrigerators, good value, M, CP.

Hatteras Island: *Comfort Inn,* Route 12, Buxton, 27943, 995-6100 or (800) 432-1441, modern, pool, refrigerators, M, CP • *Lighthouse View Motel,* Route 12, Buxton, 27920, 995-5680, overlooking beach, M–E; cottages, weekly only in season, E–EE • *Cape Hatteras Motel,* P.O. Box 939, Buxton, 27920, 995-5611, pool, rooms, and efficiencies, M–E; cottages, E • *Hatteras Harbor Motel,* Route 12, Hatteras, 27920, 986-2565, M–E.

Ocracoke: *Berkley Manor,* Silver Lake Road, P.O. Box 220, Ocracoke, 27960, 928-5911 or (800) 832-1223, warm country-inn feel, pine-paneled walls, no views but nice grounds, easy walk to the harbor, luxury rooms have Jacuzzis, M–E, CP • *Boyette House,* Route 12, P.O. Box 39, Ocracoke, 27960, (800) 928-4261, motel, newer rooms have porches, some Jacuzzis, M–E • *Island Inn,* P.O. Box 9, Ocracoke, 27960, 928-4351, modest rooms, pool, I–M.

Manteo bed-and-breakfast inns: *Tranquil House Inn,* 405 Queen Elizabeth Street, Manteo, 27954, 473-1404 or (800) 458-7069, attractive rooms on the harbor, M–E, CP • *Roanoke Island Inn,* 305 Fernando Street, Manteo, 27954, 473-5511 or (877) 473-5511, wonderful island house, tasteful furnishings, M–E, CP • *White Doe Inn,* 319 Sir Walter Raleigh Street, Manteo, 27954, 473-9851 or (800) 473-6091, E–EE, CP.

Other bed-and-breakfast inns: *First Colony Inn,* US 158, Nags Head, 27959, 441-2343, National Historic Register property, antiques, E–EE, CP • *Cape Hatteras Bed and Breakfast,* Old Lighthouse Road, Buxton, 27920, 995-6004, M, CP • *Seaside Inn,* Route 12, Hatteras, 27920, 986-2700, nicely restored 1928 lodging, M–E.

Cottage rentals: Contact Chamber of Commerce for realtor listings.

DINING   Seafood is the specialty everywhere unless otherwise noted.

Duck: *Blue Point Bar and Grill,* Route 12, The Waterfront Shops, Duck, 261-8090, try the crab cakes, M–E • *Elizabeth's Cafe,* Scarborough Faire, Duck, 261-6145, Nouvelle/country French, E–EE • *Sanderling Inn Resort* (see Accommodations on page 89), M–E.

Nags Head: *Kelly's Restaurant and Tavern,* US 158, Nags Head, 441-4116, M • *Owens' Restaurant,* Beach Road, Nags Head, 441-7309, M • *Penguin Isle,* US 158, Nags Head, 441-2637, M–E • *Malone's at Nags Head,* 4933 South Croatan Highway (US 158), Nags Head, 480-3311, attractive setting with murals, M.

Kill Devil Hills: *Colington Cafe,* 1029 Colington Road, Kill Devil Hills, 480-1123, French accent, M.

Hatteras Island: *Breakwater,* Oden's Dock, Hatteras, 986-2733, overlooking the sound, M–E • *Soundside,* Route 12, Buxton, 995-6200, water views, I–M • *The Froggy Dog,* Route 12, Avon, 995-4106, serves three meals, lively at night, I–M.

Roanoke Island: *Clara's Seafood Grill,* Queen Elizabeth Avenue, Manteo, 473-1727, on the waterfront, M–E • *1587 Restaurant,* Tranquil House Inn (see Accommodations on page 90), sophisticated menu, waterfront views, M–E • *Weeping Radish Brewery and Bavarian Restaurant,* US Highway 64, Manteo, 473-1157, German ambience and menu, brewery tours, I–M • *Queen Anne's Revenge,* Old Wharf Road, Wanchese, Roanoke Island, 473-5466, hidden gem, M–E.

Ocracoke: *Island Inn Dining Room,* Ocracoke (see Accommodations on page 90), I–M • *The Back Porch,* Ocracoke Village, 928-6401, M • *Capt. Ben's Restaurant,* Ocracoke Village, 928-4741, I–M • *Howard's Pub and Raw Bar,* Route 12, 928-4441, ocean view from upper deck, 200 kinds of beer, I–M • *Pony Island Restaurant,* Ocracoke Village, 928-5701, casual, I–M.

SIGHT-SEEING *Cape Hatteras National Seashore,* Route 12, Bodie, Hatteras, and Ocracoke Islands, 473-2111. Visitor centers at Whalebone Junction near US 64, Bodie Island; Oregon Inlet, Bodie Island; and Hatteras Lighthouse, Cape Hatteras. Guided walks, activities, and evening programs held at all locations, mid-June through early September; check current schedules. Hours: Daily 9 A.M. to 5 P.M. Free • *Pea Island National Wildlife Refuge,* Hatteras Island, 987-2394. Hours: Daily dawn to dusk. Visitor-station hours: weekdays 9 A.M. to 4 P.M.; check for times of guided bird walks and children's programs. Free • *Wright Brothers National Memorial,* US 158, Kill Devil Hills, 441-7430. Hours: Daily 9 A.M. to 5 P.M.; in summer, to 6 P.M. $ • *Jockey's Ridge State Park,* off US 158 bypass, Nags Head, 441-7132. Hours: June to August, 8 A.M. to 9 P.M.; April, May, and September, to 8 P.M., rest of year, to 6 P.M. Free • *Cape Hatteras Lighthouse,* North Carolina Route 12, Hatteras Island, 995-4474. Hours: Visitor Center, daily 9 A.M. to 5 P.M.; Lighthouse to 4 P.M. Free • *Hatteras-Ocracoke Ferry,* 928-3841. Hours: Usually on the half hour in season during the day, less frequent in the evening; best to check. Free • *Fort Raleigh National Historic Site,* US 64/264, Roanoke Island, 473-5772. Visitor Center hours: Mid-June to Labor Day, Monday to Friday 9 A.M. to 6 P.M., Saturday 10 A.M. to 5 P.M., Sunday 9 A.M. to 8 P.M.; rest of year, daily 9 A.M. to 5 P.M. Free • *The Lost Colony Drama,* Waterside Theater, 473-3414. Hours: Mid-June to late August, Sunday to Friday 8:30 P.M.; all seats by reservation. $$$$$ • *Elizabethan Gardens,* 473-3234. Hours: June through August, daily 9 A.M. to 7 P.M.; spring and fall, to 5 P.M.; rest of year, to 4 P.M. $$ • *Roanoke Island Festival Park and Elizabeth II,* on the harbor, Manteo, 475-1500, replica of sixteenth-century sailing ship. Hours: June to August, daily 10 A.M. to 6 P.M.; spring and fall, to 5 P.M.; rest of year, 10 A.M. to 4 P.M. $$$$ • *North Carolina Aquarium,* State Road 1116, Airport Road, off US

64/264, Roanoke Island, 473-3493. Hours: Monday to Saturday 9 A.M. to 5 P.M., Sunday from 1 P.M. $$.

SPORTS   *Kitty Hawk Sports,* 441-6800 or (800) 948-0759, six locations, headquarters for watersports such as kayaking, windsurfing, sailing. Phone for information • *Kitty Hawk Kites,* main store, US 158, Kill Devil Hills, across from Jockey's Ridge State Park, 441-4124 or (800) 334-4777; seven other locations including Ocracoke; hang gliding, paragliding instruction, kites, Rollerblade rentals, guided kayak ecotours • *Barrier Island Sailing Center,* Duck, 261-7100, sailboats, catamarans, sailboards • *Waterworks Inc.,* Nags Head Causeway, 441-8875, fishing trips, parasailing, windsurfing lessons, and boat, sailboat, and canoe rentals • *Oregon Inlet Fishing Center,* Oregon Inlet, Bodie, 441-6301, sportfishing trips, boat rentals • *Ocracoke Fishing Center,* Ocracoke, 828-6661.

Bicycle Rentals: *Bike Barn,* Kill Devil Hills, 442-3786; *Duck Village Outfitters,* Duck, 261-7222; *Shore Gear,* Ocracoke, 928-7060.

INFORMATION   *Outer Banks Visitors Bureau,* 704 South Highway 64/264, P.O. Box 399, Manteo, NC 27954, 473-2138 or (800) 446-6262; *Outer Banks Chamber of Commerce,* 10 Town Hall Drive, P.O. Box 1757, Kill Devil Hills, NC 27948, 441-8144; www.outerbanks.org.

On Top of the World in Georgia

When Georgians want to escape the summer heat, they know just where to go. Northeast Georgia is "where spring spends the summer," according to the slogan of Rabun County, one of the counties that shares this big, scenic corner of the state. It's an apt description, since the average temperature in August is 76 degrees.

The state's highest elevations account for the breezes as well as the beauty. Adding to the scenery are four lakes, rushing rivers, waterfalls, and 1,000-foot-deep Tallulah Gorge. Much of the terrain is part of the Chattahoochee National Forest, preserved cool and green forever.

This is great country, whether you want to sit back and admire the scenery or be active outdoors. Hikers, golfers, and fishermen are in their glory. For river rafters, the ultimate challenge is the Chattooga, a National Wild and Scenic River, whose roaring rapids became famous as the location for the movie *Deliverance.* At its toughest, it is the steepest river in the East. Several companies offer guided tours, including calmer stretches for the less adventurous.

Clayton, in the northeast corner, is also a happy hunting ground for crafts and folk art.

The region's Appalachian heritage is celebrated at the annual Georgia Mountain Fair in Hiawassee, and in one of the South's most unique entertainments, the moving musical called *The Reach of Song,* performed in Young Harris. This colorful drama celebrating the history and poetry of the mountains has been declared Georgia's "Official Historic Drama."

The first difficult decision is choosing a home base. One possibility is to stay on the western rim of the region in Towns County. A grand mountain setting is found at the Brasstown Valley Resort in Young Harris, nestled in the hills surrounded by 503 acres of forest. Patterned pine, stone fireplaces, handcrafted twig furniture, and antler chandeliers make this big hotel seem at home in its surroundings. The amenities include golf, tennis, nature trails, fishing, an indoor-outdoor pool—and rocking chairs for savoring the view.

The smaller, modern Fieldstone Inn in Hiawassee is on the shores of Lake Chatuge, a 7,500-acre TVA reservoir and water playground. Guests enjoy a pool, tennis court, fishing dock, and marina, with rental boats right on the premises.

A stay in either resort puts you close to the Fairgrounds as well as Young Harris College, where *The Reach of Song* is performed each night from early June through August. The changes in the mountains, seen through the life and works of native writer and farmer Byron Herbert Reece, form the theme of the musical. The cast is made up of both professionals and enthusiastic local residents, ranging in age from seven to 78.

Later in the summer, the Fairgrounds hosts the big Georgia Mountain Fair, with more than 60 artisans showing off old-time crafts from wood carving and candlemaking to moonshine stilling. Midway rides, mountain heritage booths, and a daily schedule of bluegrass music and country artists keep everyone busy and happy.

The Fred Hamilton Rhododendron Garden adjacent to the Fairgrounds offers a leisurely stroll through more than 2,000 rhododendron and azalea plants.

Hikers will also find this area a handy location. Follow Georgia Route 75 south of Hiawassee and go west on Georgia Route 180 for the turnoff to Brasstown Bald, at 4,784 feet the state's highest mountain. The 360-degree views from the visitor center and observation tower at the summit take in four states. A steep, paved half-mile trail leads from the parking lot to the top. If you'd rather not make the trek, during the summer a shuttle bus will do it for you for a small fee.

To the east in Rabun County, the charming little mountain town of

Clayton, the county seat, offers more variety for dining and lodging and better shopping. The 30-mile drive east on US 76 from Hiawassee to Clayton is one of the loveliest in the state, dipping and curving into even more dramatic mountain scenery.

On this road is Timpson Creek Gallery, overflowing with Southern folk art, painted pieces, handmade twig furniture, and country treasures in a variety of media.

Clayton's Main Street Gallery is well known for its fine folk art and contemporary crafts. Antiquers also will be happy in this area. Shops begin on Main Street and continue north on US 441 for the seven miles through Mountain City and into Dillard.

As you drive north, watch for the small museum of Appalachian artifacts on US 441 that is headquarters for Foxfire, the well-known educational experiment that encourages active learning.

Between Clayton and Dillard, you are in the midst of one of the most beautiful sections of the Georgia mountains. Just off the main highway, in Mountain City, is Black Rock Mountain State Park, cloud-high astride the Eastern Continental Divide at 3,640 feet. Named for its sheer cliffs of dark granite, this is Georgia's highest park. On the right day, you can see 80-mile vistas of the southern Appalachians.

Take one of the side roads off the main highway to savor the loveliness of the region. One highly recommended route is Betty's Creek Road, a left turn after you enter Dillard. Follow this hilly, green, and glorious route for three and a half miles and you can visit the Hambridge Center, a residential center for the creative arts. Founded in 1934, it is a place where artists may come to paint, write, sculpt, compose, and weave in studios surrounded by 600 acres of meadows, streams, and woodlands. Every year the center awards some 70 fellowships, with eight artists in residence at any one time for periods from two weeks to two months. Their art and crafts work can be seen at the Hambridge Gallery, along with work by regional folk artists. The center also offers guided nature walks, workshops, and forums that are open to the public.

Also beckoning throughout this region are prize hiking trails. A complete "Trail Guide to the Chattahoochee-Oconee National Forests," with detailed directions to each trail, is available from the Tallulah Ranger District office in Clayton. The Northeast Georgia Mountain Travel Association publishes a pamphlet detailing where to find waterfalls.

If you're not a hiker, you can get some idea of the Chattooga River's majesty by driving east on US 76. Just after you cross the bridge into South Carolina, there's a parking area and a short trail to outcroppings with fine views of the Bull Sluice Rapids.

The scenery continues to the south on US 441. Right off the highway is Tallulah Falls, the legendary gorge whose waters have been harnessed for hydroelectric power. To take advantage of the lake formed by the Tallulah Falls Dam, the Georgia Power Company and the Georgia Department of Natural Resources have joined forces to create Tallulah Gorge State Park, with a system of trails and overlooks along the north rim to appreciate the awesome 1,000-foot chasm. Georgia Power's adjacent Terrora Park offers a swimming area, sand beach, tennis courts, hiking trails, a playground, and tables for picnicking beside the lake.

Crafts also are still very much part of the picture. The Co-op Craft Store at Tallulah Falls is a showcase for more than 100 members, who produce everything from stained glass to stuffed toys.

The gallery that takes the prize for scenery is the Mark of the Potter, housed in a converted gristmill beside the Soque River on Georgia Route 197, 10 miles north of Clarkesville. The mill is a national historic landmark. Potter Jay Bucek makes and sells his own pottery here, and shows work by 45 other Southeastern craftspeople.

Buy Bucek's book, *Something's Cookin' in the Mountains,* for recipes plus tips on where to find the kind of hidden beauty spots and meet special local people that only a longtime resident can know. Among other places, he will steer you down the road to the Batesville General Store for lunch and their famous biscuits, followed by a browse through the homemade gifts.

Lodgings are choice throughout the region. In Clayton, the Beechwood Inn is a charmer, filled with the kind of tasteful country furnishings you find in magazine spreads.

A few miles north in Mountain City, the York House will also please inn lovers. Tucked away in a valley with mountain views, the expansive 1896 country house is just the place to sit in a rocker on the porch and savor the scenery.

Accommodations at Dillard House are of the standard motel or cottage variety, but facilities include a pool, a tennis court, and stables, and you're just a stroll away from the Southern, family-style, all-you-can-eat meals that have kept folks coming for almost a century. Other members of the Dillard family run various motel accommodations in town. Farther north, at Sky Valley Condominium Resort, 18 holes of golf, a pool, and tennis courts beckon, surrounded by Blue Ridge Mountain peaks. In winter, Sky Valley offers Georgia's only skiing.

More picturesque accommodations await south of Clayton. The Lake Rabun Hotel, a mountain lodge on the banks of the lake, has been a quaint, rustic favorite since 1922. You can see by the walled entrances and iron gates that Lake Rabun was a wealthy estate area earlier in this century. The unspoiled lake has remained quite private, used mainly by those whose homes remain. Rabun Beach provides picnic and swimming areas in a quiet spot amid the mountain laurel.

There's more hiking here, and more of those waterfalls. The Rabun Beach Trail follows and occasionally crosses the waters of Joe Branch. Near the end is Angel Falls, and for those willing to do a little climbing,

Panther Falls awaits upstream. Minnehaha Falls, one of the most beautiful in the area, is reached via the half-mile Fall Branch Trail. To get to the trail, go past the Rabun Beach Recreation Area for a mile, turn left, cross the bridge, and follow Bear Gap Road around the lake for 1.6 miles.

The best known of all the area lodgings is below Lake Rabun, far off the highway on an unpaved road. Glen-Ella Springs, a resort since 1890, is on the National Register of Historic Places. It has been restored with a perfect mix of old-fashioned charm and modern comforts, an effort that won an award from the Georgia Trust for Historic Preservation. A pool and sundeck beckon outside on 17 acres of lawns and meadows, perennial and herb gardens. The dining room is renowned in the region.

If you can't decide where to stay, that may be all to the good. It means you can return for fall color, cozy winter hideaways, and wildflowers in the spring. There's beauty and fun whenever you come to this special section of the mountains.

Area Code: 706

DRIVING DIRECTIONS   Clayton is at the intersection of US 441 and US 76. From Atlanta, take I-85 north to the junction with US 441 north, 116 miles. It is 95 miles from Asheville, 155 miles from Charlotte, 155 miles from Chattanooga, and 56 miles from Greenville, South Carolina. Hiawassee is 30 miles west of Clayton on US 76. To go directly from Atlanta, take I-85 north, branching into I-985 to Gainesville exit 67. Turn left onto US 129 to Cleveland. Go halfway around the square in Cleveland and follow signs for Georgia Route 75. Proceed on Route 75 until it merges with US 76, and continue north.

ACCOMMODATIONS   *Fieldstone Inn,* 3379 US 76, Hiawassee, 30546, 896-2262 or (800) 545-3408, M–E • *Brasstown Valley Resort,* 6321 Highway 76, Young Harris, 30582, 379-9900 or (800) 201-3205, E • *York House,* off US 441, P.O. Box 126, Mountain City, 30562, 746-2068 or (800) 231-YORK, I–M, CP • *Dillard House,* US 441, Dillard, 30537, 746-5348 or (800) 541-0671, motel rooms, I–M; suites, M–E; cottages, M–EE • *Dillard House Chalet Village,* US 441, Dillard, 30537, 746-5348, mountain chalets, M–EE • *Sky Valley Resort,* Sky Valley Way, Dillard, 30537, 746-5301 or (800) 262-8259, range of condominium units, M–EE • *Lake Rabun Hotel,* Lake Rabun Road, P.O. Box 10, Lakemont, 30552, 782-4946, I, CP • *Glen-Ella Springs Inn,* 1789 Bear Gap Road, Clarkesville, 30523, 754-7295 or (888) 455-8896, M–E, CP • For listings of cabins, contact the Rabun County Chamber of Commerce.

DINING   *Castaway Cove,* 3499 US Highway 76 West, Hiawassee, 896-4141, burgers to steaks, I–M • *Julia's Southern Nights,* Highway 441, ½ mile south of Clayton, 782-2052, fresh mountain trout, grilled dishes, best in the area, M. • *Old Clayton Inn,* 60 South Main Street, Clayton, 782-3498, classic old inn with a pleasant dining room, I–M • The *Dillard House* (see Accommodations on page 96), famous family-style feasts, reservations strongly advised, lunch, I; dinner, M • *Glen-Ella Springs* (see see Accommodations on page 96), highly recommended, M, C • *LaPrade's,* Highway 197 North, Lake Burton, Clarkesville, 947-3312, Southern family-style, in business since 1925, open April through November, I–M.

SIGHT-SEEING   *The Reach of Song,* 3379 US Highway 76, Young Harris College, Young Harris, (800) 262-SONG. Hours: Late June through late August, Tuesday to Saturday 8 P.M., general admission. $$$$-$$$$$ • *Georgia Mountain Fair,* P.O. Box 444, Hiawassee, 30546, 896-4191, 12 days, early to mid-August; phone for current dates. $$$ • *Brasstown Bald,* off Route 180 south of Hiawassee, 896-2556. Hours: Memorial Day to October, daily 10 A.M. to 5:30 P.M.; weekends in early spring and November. Free • *Foxfire Appalachian Museum,* US 441, Mountain City, 746-5828. Hours: Monday to Saturday 9 A.M. to 4:30 P.M. Free • *Black Rock Mountain State Park,* US 441, Mountain City, 746-2141. Hours: Daily 7 A.M. to 10 P.M.; office hours, 8 A.M. to 5 P.M. Parking fee, $ • *Moccasin Creek State Park,* Route 197, Clarkesville, 947-3194. Hours: Daily 7 A.M. to 10 P.M.; office hours, 8 A.M. to 5 P.M. Parking fee, $ • *Tallulah Gorge State Park,* US 441 South, Tallulah Falls, 754-7970. Hours: Daily 8 A.M. to dark; Interpretive Center, 8 A.M. to 5 P.M.; Terrora Park area open April through October. Parking fee, $$.

SPORTS   **Hiking information:** Tallulah Ranger District, 809 US Highway 441 South, Clayton, 30525, 782-3320; or contact Forest Supervisor, 508 Oak Street N.W., Gainesville, GA 30501, 536-0541; hiking maps are also available at Rabun Chamber of Commerce • **Whitewater rafting** (phone for information and reservations): *Nantahala Outdoor Center,* (800) 232-7238; *Wildwater Ltd.,* (800) 451-9972; *Southeastern Expeditions,* (800) 868-7238 • **Horseback riding:** *Dillard House Stables,* 746-5348; Smoky Mountain Stables, 782-5836.

INFORMATION   *Northeast Georgia Mountain Travel Association,* P.O. Box 464, Gainesville, 30503, (404) 231-1820; www.ngeorgia.com • *Rabun County Chamber of Commerce,* US 441, Clayton, 30525, 782-4812 • *Towns County Chamber of Commerce,* 1411 Fuller Circle, Young Harris, 30582; 896-4966.

Hitting the High Spots Up Country

Pendleton, South Carolina, is a town with personality.

The village green is picture perfect, and the entire town, which dates to 1790, is on the National Register of Historic Places.

However, the restaurants occupying some of the quaint buildings around the green are the first clue that this community of 3,300 is not your typical, sleepy small Southern town. Take a peek at the menus—Italian, Caribbean, Mennonite, Southern, and Continental.

Now look around town a little. Check out the art deco movie theater, recently renovated to present stage plays by the Clemson Little Theater. Visit the town baker, who hails from England, and the local innkeepers, who moved here from St. Louis. Stop in at the goat farm, whose cheeses are becoming legendary, and call on one of the many talented artisans who have made Pendleton a center for crafts. The spring crafts fair held on the green brings thousands to town.

You're beginning to get the picture. Pendleton is a little bit sophisticated, a little bit offbeat—and a lot of fun to visit. To make things even better, it is just five miles from the campus of Clemson (which accounts for much of the sophistication) and is located in the state's "Up Country," the hilly northwest corner that is home to 11 state parks, five lakes, a wild and scenic river, and a national forest.

One possible plan is to divide Saturday between Pendleton and Clemson, and save Sunday for scenery.

The best place to get your bearings is the Pendleton District Commission, located in the former Hunter's Store, an 1850 brick building across from the village green. A center for the region, it offers scads of brochures, cassette-tape tours, and exhibits of local arts and crafts. The office is open weekdays only, so if you can't get to town on Friday, write ahead for the local walking-tour guide.

You'll learn that this portion of South Carolina belonged to the Cherokee Indians until they chose the wrong side in the American Revolution. The South Carolina militia marched in and wreaked such havoc in Cherokee country that the Indians sued for peace and gave their land to the state. After the war, settlers were attracted by the fertile land, and in 1789, Pendleton County was established, named for a Revolutionary War hero. The next year the town was formed as the county seat. Later the growing district was divided into three counties.

Early farming settlers were soon joined by wealthy, well-educated low-country families who built summer homes in the cooler Up Country. Two of the finer homes are now house museums. Woodburn, circa 1830, was built by prominent South Carolinian Charles Cotesworth

Pinckney. Ashtabula, an 1820s home, was occupied by five respected families over the years.

Farmers Hall, the town's centerpiece, went up on the site of the old courthouse after the district was divided. It was in the second-floor meeting hall that Thomas Green Clemson first advocated the need for a state agricultural college, today's Clemson University. Members of the hall also included Clemson's father-in-law, John C. Calhoun, vice-president of the United States. The ground floor of the hall is now a popular restaurant.

The rest of the town tour takes in the 1819 St. Paul's Episcopal Church and many homes dating from the first half of the nineteenth century, all still privately owned and occupied. Mi Casa, at 430 South Mechanic Street, was the home of Mrs. John C. Calhoun after her husband's death.

Take time for a leisurely stroll on the blocks around the green, looking into the intriguing small antiques, gift, and crafts shops along the way.

It is just a five-minute drive from Pendleton to the campus of Clemson, an unusually interesting campus because of the history associated with the site. The South Carolina Botanical Garden, part of the campus, is also a good reason for the trip. The University Visitors Center offers guided tours and information for touring on your own.

Clemson is located on land that was once the plantation of John C. Calhoun, South Carolina's most eminent early statesman, who spent the last 25 years of his life here. His son-in-law, Thomas Clemson, inherited the Fort Hill house and land after his wife's death. He had long been interested in agriculture, and, in 1888, he bequeathed the 814-acre plantation and a considerable sum of money to establish a scientific and agricultural college.

Clemson College opened formally in 1893 with 4,465 students. It was an all-male military school until 1955, when women were admitted and the focus of the school changed. In 1964 it became a university in recognition of the expanded academic offerings and research pursuits. It would no doubt please Clemson to know that the agricultural, engineering, and architectural schools are highly respected. He might share the pride of the avid fans who root for the Clemson Tigers football team, known for their orange "paw" symbol, which is generously painted around the campus.

The house at Fort Hill was built during the late Federal and early Greek Revival periods, and is characteristic of Up Country South Carolina plantation design. On the grounds are a reconstructed kitchen near the west wing, Calhoun's office, and a restored springhouse on the north lawn. Most of the furnishings are original Calhoun and Clemson family pieces.

Another historic home open for tours is Hanover House, built in 1716 in the low country. It was moved and reconstructed here by the

School of Architecture in the 1940s as a house museum, interpreting the lifestyle of South Carolina's rice, indigo, and cotton planters.

Hanover House is located in the South Carolina Botanical Garden, which got its start in the late 1950s, when a small portion of the Fort Hill estate was set aside to preserve a nineteenth-century camellia collection. It has grown to 270 acres, rich with camellias, native wildflowers, and daffodils, and an arboretum with over 1,000 species of trees. Miles of trails wind through the native woodlands and gardens.

Depending on your time and interests, there are many other worthwhile sights on campus. The Bob Campbell Geology Museum has impressive displays of minerals and gems. Alternatively, you can view the changing art exhibits at the Rudolph E. Lee Gallery or take in a horse or livestock show at the Livestock Arena.

No one should miss a visit to Tiger Treats in the Hendrix Student Center for their famous rich ice cream. Also for sale is delicious Clemson blue cheese and blue-cheese dressing.

The 1840 Liberty Hall Inn in Pendleton is a beautiful yet comfortable antiques-filled home with a wide-railed, two-tiered porch, complete with rockers. The dining room serves some of the best meals in town. Another inn, Rocky Retreat, is a restored 150-year-old home on the National Register of Historic Places, recently turned into a bed-and-breakfast.

If there's no room at the inns, consider a motel in Clemson or lodgings in or near one of the state parks within a half-hour's drive. The Schell Haus, opposite the entrance to Table Rock State Park, is another wonderful bed-and-breakfast choice, beautifully furnished and with grand views from the porch.

Come Sunday, get ready for the best of South Carolina's Up Country. Follow US 76 west and turn north on Route 11, the Cherokee Foothills Scenic Highway, which stretches for nearly 130 miles. Along the way are scenic lookouts and access to many magnificent state parks. The road is flanked by orchards, and in summer, many stands offer fresh-picked peaches from local farms.

One of the newer parks, Devils Fork on Lake Jocassee, opened in 1991 in cooperation with the Duke Power Company. Located three miles from US 11, it is a favorite spot for fishing, boating, and swimming. The 20 cabins overlooking the lake would do credit to a luxury resort. Understandably, they go fast, so plan ahead if you want to try one.

Table Rock State Park is the most striking of the parks, with deep forest set against the massive formation that inspired the name, a slice of granite 3,157 feet high. At the bottom of the mountain is the Table Rock Reservoir, a picturesque lake that provides water for Greenville County. The park offers swimming, rental canoes and boats, carpet golf, and a nature center. The rustic log buildings here, Civilian Conservation Corps projects from the 1930s, include a restaurant that serves up sensational views with lunch and dinner. The cabins are far more basic than those at Devils Fork, but they offer the necessary comforts and supreme privacy.

This park, whose entrance is right on Route 11, affords the best hiking in the region, from easy nature trails to treks to the top of Table Rock and nearby Pinnacle Mountain. The rugged and beautiful Foothills Trail across the ridge of the mountains also passes through the park.

For dramatic views, however, the prize goes to Caesars Head State Park. Take the turnoff north on US 276 and wind your way to the top escarpment, 3,266 feet high, for a truly spectacular panorama, taking in Table Rock and Pinnacle Mountains and many more-distant peaks of the Blue Ridge chain.

You can enjoy this view at the overlook without any effort, but only those energetic enough to tackle a two-mile trail will get to see Raven Cliff Falls, one of the highest waterfalls in the Eastern states.

Those who want to challenge the Chattooga, one of the U.S. Forest Service's system of Wild and Scenic Rivers, will find outfitters happy to oblige.

If the unthinkable happens and it rains, all is not lost. Just take a drive east to Greenville, where there are several art galleries and an attractive small museum in the heart of the nicely refurbished downtown. It's worth the drive just to see the Nippon Center Yagoto, built in the traditional architectural style of early Japan and containing a rock garden that is a replica of a famous garden in Kyoto. The center, which includes an exquisite (albeit expensive) Japanese restaurant, was built by a Japanese businessman as thanks to the community. It hosts classes with Furman University, offering language, cooking, ikebana flower arrangement, and the study of Japanese lifestyle and business practices. Totally unexpected in the hills of South Carolina, the center is one more welcome Up Country surprise.

Area Code: 864

DRIVING DIRECTIONS Pendleton is reached via US 76 off I-85. It is about 120 miles from Atlanta, 118 miles from Charlotte. Clemson is four miles farther north via US 76 or South Carolina Route 187.

ACCOMMODATIONS *Liberty Hall Inn,* 621 South Mechanic Street, Pendleton, 29670, one-half mile south of the green, 646-7500, M, CP • *Rocky Retreat,* 1000 Wilwee Creek Road, Pendleton 29670, 225-3494, M, CP • *Comfort Inn,* 1305 Tiger Boulevard, Clemson, 29631, 653-3600, motel, pool, I • *Lake Hartwell Inn,* 894 Tiger Boulevard, Clemson, 29631, 654-4450, pool, I • *Sunrise Farm Bed and*

Breakfast, 325 Sunrise Drive, Salem, 29676, 944-0121, Victorian country farmhouse and cottages, M, CP • *Schell Haus,* Highway 11, Pickens, 29671, 878-0078, delightful inn, convenient to state parks, M, CP • *Laurel Mountain Motel,* Highway 11, Pickens, 29671, 878-8500, comfortable lodgings, attractive hillside location, I–M • *Devils Fork State Park,* 161 Holcombe Circle, Salem, 29676, 944-2639, luxury cabins, M • *Table Rock State Park,* 246 Table Rock State Park Road, Pickens, 26971, 878-9813, rustic cabins, I–M.

DINING *Farmers Hall Restaurant,* on the green, Pendleton, 646-7014, lunch, I; dinner, M • *Liberty Hall Inn* (see Accommodations on page 101), M–E • *Pendleton House,* 203 East Main Street, Pendleton, 646-7795, warm home setting, M • *Lazy Islander,* across from the green, Pendleton, 646-7672, some Caribbean specialties, I–M • *Country Kettle,* 129 Mechanic Street, 646-3301, bountiful Mennonite buffets, lunch only, I • *Table Rock State Park Restaurant,* East Gate, Table Rock State Park, dinner year-round, I–M; lunches served May through October, I • *Aunt Sue's,* Highway 11, two miles east of Table Rock State Park, 878-4366, April through November, rustic decor, views, part of a small shopping complex, I–M • *Nippon Center Yagoto,* 500 Congaree Road, Greenville, 288-8471, traditional Japanese cuisine, extraordinary setting, M–EE.

SIGHT-SEEING *Ashtabula Plantation,* South Carolina Route 88 East, Pendleton, 646-7249. Hours: April to October, Sunday 2 P.M. to 6 P.M. $$ • *Woodburn Plantation,* US 76 west of town, Pendleton, 646-7249 also. Hours: April to October, Sunday 2 P.M. to 6 P.M. $$ • *Pendleton Playhouse,* 402 South Mechanic Street, Pendleton, 646-8100. Check for current productions • **Clemson University:** *Visitors Center,* 111 Daniel Drive, 656-4789. Hours: Monday to Friday 8 A.M. to 4:30 P.M., Saturday 9 A.M. to 4:30 P.M., Sunday 1 to 4:30 P.M. Guided tours Monday through Saturday 9:45 A.M. and 1:45 P.M., Sunday at 1:45 P.M. • **Campus sights include:** *Fort Hill,* 656-2475. Hours: Monday to Saturday 10 A.M. to noon and 1 to 5 P.M., Sunday 2 to 5 P.M. Donation. • *Hanover House,* 656-2241. Hours: Saturday 10 A.M. to noon and 1 to 5 P.M., Sunday 2 to 5 P.M. Donation. • *Bob Campbell Geology Museum,* 656-4600. Hours: Thursday, Friday, and Sunday 1 to 5 P.M., Saturday 10 A.M. to 5 P.M. Free. • *Rudolph E. Lee Gallery,* Lee Hall (College of Architecture), 656-3883. Hours: Monday to Friday 9 A.M. to 4:30 P.M., Sunday 2 to 5 P.M. Free • *South Carolina Botanical Garden,* 656-3405. Hours: Daily dawn to dusk. Free • *Devils Fork State Park,* 161 Holcombe Circle, Salem, 944-2639. Hours: April to October, daily 7 A.M. to 9 P.M.; rest of year, to 6 P.M.; office, Monday to Friday 9 A.M. to noon and 1 to 5 P.M. Parking fee in season, $ • *Table Rock State Park,* 246 Table Rock State Park Road, Pickens, 878-9813.

Hours: April to October, daily 7 A.M. to 10 P.M.; rest of year, to 9 P.M.; office, Monday to Friday 9 A.M. to 5 P.M. Parking fee in season, $ • *Caesars Head State Park,* 8155 Geer Highway, Cleveland, 836-6115. Hours: April to October, daily 9 A.M. to 9 P.M.; rest of year, to 6 P.M.; office, 9 A.M. to 5 P.M. Parking fee in season, $ • **Whitewater rafting on the Chattooga River:** Phone 800-440-RAFT for information.

INFORMATION *Pendleton District Historical, Recreational and Tourism Commission,* 125 East Queen Street, P.O. Box 565, Pendleton, SC 29670, 646-3782 or 800-862-1795; www.ci.pendleton.sc.us; www.pendleton-district.org • *Discover Upcountry Association,* P.O. Box 3116, Greenville, SC 29602, 800-849-4766; www.upcountry-sc.org.

Blazing Trails Near Cherokee

There's something mystical about the Smoky Mountains. The long, dusky ridges that the Cherokee people called "Place of Blue Smoke" are among the world's oldest mountains, rounded and softened by the ages, and bathed in a perpetual hazy mist that clings to the peaks and fills the valleys.

The tiers roll out into the distance like waves cresting in a lofty ocean, shifting in mood and color with every change in the light. They are equally beautiful outlined by the golden sun or shrouded in wispy fog. No matter how many times you see these mountains, they never look exactly the same.

This is part of the fascination that has made Great Smoky Mountains National Park the most visited of all U.S. national parks, enjoyed by nearly 9 million people each year.

Though it gets crowded in summer, this is the best season for families, with many special activities that children enjoy, including the Junior Ranger program geared to ages five to twelve.

The North Carolina entrance to the park, at Cherokee, adds another dimension to a visit—the chance to learn about the Cherokee Indians, who were the first to live on this land.

It must be said, however, that the modern town of Cherokee has little appeal. It has become overrun with tacky shops selling bogus Indian crafts that have nothing to do with the Cherokees. See the important sights and get out fast.

Far better places to stay are in Maggie Valley, 15 miles to the east, which has its share of touristy attractions but is still a great improvement over Cherokee, or in quieter Bryson City, 10 miles to the west.

The Swag, a superb rustic inn outside of Maggie Valley, is as close as you'll get to a private mountain, set all by itself on a mile-high mountaintop. Guests at Cattaloochee Ranch are also 5,000 feet up, with peerless views and the chance to see the scenery on horseback.

Wherever you stay, spend an evening in Maggie Valley at the Stompin' Ground, where the real flavor of mountain living is provided by the enthusiastic locals who come to clog up a storm every night. The Maggie Valley Opry House is the place to hear bluegrass music. Both are on US 19.

When you are ready for Great Smoky Mountains National Park, head for the Oconaluftee Visitor Center at the Cherokee entrance. Here you can pick up a map and a copy of the *Smokies Guide,* the official park newspaper, which lists all current ranger-guided activities. It will help you plan your day. Among the choices are guided nature walks and hikes to see waterfalls and other scenic areas, storytelling, and talks about many phases of the park, as well as about Cherokee history and culture. Nights bring campfires, slide shows, mountain music, and early-evening nature walks.

Though it includes the highest mountain range in the East and protects the last remnant of the southern Appalachian forest, establishing this 550,000-acre sanctuary was a struggle. The terrain was occupied by hundreds of small farmers and a handful of large timber companies, none of whom were anxious to leave. Congress signed a bill establishing a park in 1926, but since the government was not allowed to buy land for national park use, private money was needed. The states of Tennessee and North Carolina, early competitors to host the park, settled on a location straddling both states, and each contributed $2 million to get things rolling. Private groups and individuals, including many schoolchildren, helped raise another $5 million, and that sum was matched by the Laura Spellman Rockefeller Memorial Fund. Those living on the land were allowed to stay under lifetime leases. Franklin Roosevelt finally dedicated the park in 1934.

Seeing the sights by car is easy but slow, since there is only one main roadway through the park. Newfound Gap Road, running 35 miles from Cherokee to the Tennessee border, provides lookouts with fabulous views all along the way. About midway along the road is the turnoff for the most dramatic vista of all, from Clingmans Dome, where you are atop a ridge 6,642 feet high. Pick a clear day for this visit, since the dome is often enveloped in fog.

To fully appreciate the beauty of the forests, mountains, and streams around you, get out and walk. Though there's plenty of challenge for hardy hikers, you don't have to go far to share the scenery. Watch along the main road, and you'll see signs marking "Quiet Walkways." These are short walks planned as samplers.

There are several easy, self-guiding nature trails as well, under a mile round-trip. The Cove Hardwood Trail, just inside the entrance to the Chimney Tops Picnic Area off Newfound Gap Road, leads to the big trees of a splendid old-growth forest.

In summer, the high-altitude trails off Clingmans Dome Road are rich in wildflowers. One of the best routes is along the Appalachian Trail, where half an hour's stroll in either direction will show you some of the splendid display. Pamphlets with maps, available at the visitor center, detail walks and hikes, and pinpoint waterfalls throughout the park.

Horseback riding is another wonderful way to appreciate the scenery. There are several stables located in the park. On the trails you can see the diverse plant life and may catch a glimpse of some of the animals in these forests.

If you become intrigued with the flora and fauna and want to know more, check the programs at the nonprofit Great Smoky Mountains Institute at Tremont, where there are weekend and three-day field courses in viewing wildlife, forests, streams, and special plants such as mushrooms or ferns. The institute also offers backpacking trips, photo workshops, and family camp programs, all of which include tuition, meals, and lodging at minimal fees.

Some sections of the park will take you back in time to see how early settlers lived. Oconaluftee Pioneer Homestead, adjacent to the visitor center near Cherokee, offers short talks and tours on weekends at 2:30 and 3:30 P.M., focusing on the early days. Often there are living-history demonstrations of old-time skills, and just down the road, at Mingus Mill, you can see corn being ground by a water-powered gristmill.

More perspective on pioneer days can be found at the Cades Cove section of the park in Tennessee, about a 55-mile drive from Cherokee. Traditional chores are demonstrated, such as spinning, weaving, black-smithing, and turning sorghum into molasses, and there are many special events, such as quilt shows. Read more about Cades Cove on pages 143–145.

Be sure to save an afternoon for Cherokee, going past the tacky main street to find the authentic and very worthwhile attractions. A good start is the Museum of the Cherokee Indian, where you'll learn about this once proud and powerful nation. The tribes were forced to abandon their ancestral homeland for the long trek to Oklahoma in 1838, along what has become known as the Trail of Tears. But one band hid in the North Carolina hills, refusing to obey the government edict. They lived as fugitives for many years, but in 1889, by then 1,000 strong, they were given official permission to establish the Qualla Indian Reservation just south of what is now the southern entrance to the national park. Some 4,500 descendants occupy the reservation today.

The Oconaluftee Indian Village is a living-history lesson for children and grownups alike. Cherokees in period dress demonstrate skills passed down through the generations, such as finger weaving, pottery, and basketmaking, and traditional male occupations such as flint chipping, dugout-canoe carving, and blowgun hunting.

The log cabins are typical of what homes here might have been like in the eighteenth century. One of the highlights of the village is the re-created seven-sided council house, where you learn about the age-old culture and rituals that have been handed down.

Another recommended stop in town is the Qualla Arts and Crafts Mutual, an Indian-owned and –operated cooperative primarily responsible for keeping the arts and crafts of the Eastern Band of the Cherokees alive. The offerings, from 300 artisans, range from black pottery to patterned baskets, and from wood carvings to stone sculptures.

You may want to remain into the evening to learn the story of the Cherokee struggle for survival, movingly told in the musical drama *Unto These Hills.* It is performed in an outdoor amphitheater from mid-June to August.

Bryson City offers two more diversions. The Great Smoky Mountains Railroad runs nostalgia trips into the mountains from the 1880s Bryson City depot using diesel or steam locomotives. The most scenic is the four-and-a-half-hour round trip over Nantahala Gorge, with a stop to watch the action (and have an optional lunch) at the Nantahala Outdoor Center, a pioneer rafting company. You can choose a ride-and-raft package or take a rafting trip on your own anytime through the deep, scenic gorge. The pleasant café at the Center is one of the better places to eat in Bryson City.

One last outing that should not be missed is a drive on the Blue Ridge Parkway, which snakes its way heaven-high across the crest of the southern Appalachians for 470 miles, from the Great Smoky Mountains National Park entrance at Cherokee to the Shenandoah National Park in Virginia.

An engineering marvel that took 50 years to complete, the parkway provides an eagle's-eye view of the ridges, away from the crowds found within the park. Driving its winding course is a delight. There's not one commercial sign in sight, only lush greenery and wildflowers. The speed limit is a relaxing 35 miles per hour, and lots of overlooks are perfectly placed to allow you to pull off and gaze at the mountains or take a woodland walk whenever the spirit moves you.

From Cherokee, the parkway leads east to the Balsam Mountain area of the park, and then crosses US 19 at Soco Gap for the turnoff to Maggie Valley. But stay on for a while and you'll come to Waterrock Knob and a fabulous panorama of the Smokies from 5,718 feet.

When you've had enough driving, loop back to your home base, knowing you've just experienced one of the most remarkable roads in the world.

Area Code: 828

DRIVING DIRECTIONS   Cherokee, the North Carolina entrance to Great Smoky Mountains National Park, is located at the intersection of US 19 and US 441. From Atlanta, take I-85 north to the junction with US 441 north, 181 miles. From the east, take I-40 to the US 19 exit, near Waynesville. The park can also be reached via the Blue Ridge Parkway. Cherokee is 162 miles from Charlotte, 50 miles from Asheville.

ACCOMMODATIONS   **Maggie Valley:** *Cataloochee Ranch,* Fie Top Road, Route 1, P.O. Box 500F, Maggie Valley, 28751, 926-1401 or (800) 868-1401, comfortable ranch in a grand setting, tennis, pool, riding, EE, MAP • *The Swag,* Route 2, Box 280A, Waynesville (5 miles from Maggie Valley), 28786, 926-0430, late May through October, superb rustic inn, beautiful country decor, heavenly mountaintop location, EE, AP • *Maggie Valley Resort and Country Club,* Highways 276 and 19, Maggie Valley, 28751, 926-1616 or (800) 438-3861, deluxe resort with golf, tennis, and pool, lodge rooms with balconies, villas, M–E • *Smokey Shadows Lodge,* off Fie Top Road, Maggie Valley, 28751, 926-0001, rustic, informal log lodge, 4,500 feet high, M, CP • *Abbey Inn,* 6735 Soco Road (Highway 19), Maggie Valley, 28751, 926-1188 or (800) 545-5853, motel with a view, some kitchenettes, good bet for families, I–M • *Comfort Inn,* 4324 Soco Road (Highway 19), Maggie Valley, 28751, 926-9106, heated pool, playground, M, CP.

Bryson City: *Hemlock Inn,* off US 19, Bryson City, 28713, 488-3885, open April to October, log lodge, cottages on very attractive hilltop grounds with views, E, MAP • *Fryemont Inn,* Fryemont Road, P.O. Box 459, Bryson City, 28713, 488-2159 or (800) 845-4879, rustic inn on the National Register of Historic Places, chestnut-paneled rooms, views, M, MAP • *Randolph House,* 2283 Fryemont Road, P.O. Box 816, Bryson City, 28713, 488-3472, open April to October, 1895 mansion, also on National Register, E, MAP • *Folkestone Inn,* 767 West Deep Creek Road, Bryson City, 28713, 488-2730 or (888) 828-2730, chalet-style bed-and-breakfast inn, walking distance to Deep Creek Campground entrance of the park and many hiking trails, M, CP.

DINING   *The Swag* (see Accommodations above), by reservation only, exceptional, full dinner, EE • *Maggie Valley Resort and Country Club* (see Accommodations above), Maggie Valley's best, window walls for views, M–E • *J. Arthur's Steakhouse,* 801 Saco Road, Maggie Valley, 926-1817, rambling loft dining room, cozy, known for gorgonzola cheese salad, I–E • *Arf's,* 4352 Soco Road, 926-1566, ribs, seafood, creekside location, I–M • *Smokey Shadows Lodge* (see Accommodations above), by reservation only, full dinner, M • *Relia's Garden,* Nantahala Outdoor Center, US 19, Bryson City, 488-2175, pleasant café for all three meals, I–M.

SIGHT-SEEING *Great Smoky Mountains National Park,* 107 Park Headquarters Road, Gatlinburg, TN 37738, (423) 436-1200; www.nps.gov.grsm. *Oconaluftee Visitor Center,* 150 US 441 North, Cherokee, NC, 497-1900. Hours: In summer, daily 8 A.M. to 7 P.M.; earlier closing rest of year. Free • **Park Horseback Riding:** *Smokemont Riding Stable,* near Smokemont Campground, 497-2373; *McCarter's Riding Stable,* near Tennessee park headquarters on Newfound Gap Road, (423) 436-5354. For other Tennessee stables, ask at nearest park visitor center • *Oconaluftee Indian Village,* US 441 North, Cherokee, 497-2315. Hours: Mid-May to late October, daily 9 A.M. to 5:30 P.M. Guided tours, $$$$ • *Unto These Hills,* Mountainside Theater, US 441 North, Cherokee, 497-2111. Hours: Mid-June to late August, daily 8:30 P.M. $$$$$ • *Museum of the Cherokee Indian,* US 441 North, Cherokee, 497-3481. Hours: Mid-June through August, Monday to Saturday 9 A.M. to 8 P.M., Sunday 9 A.M. to 5 P.M.; rest of year, daily 9 A.M. to 5 P.M. $$$ • *Great Smoky Mountain Railroad,* Bryson City, (800) 872-4681. Trips March to December; phone for current schedules and fees • *Nantahala Outdoor Center,* 13077 Highway 19 West, Bryson City, 488-6900 or (800) 232-7238. Rafting trips daily March to October.

INFORMATION *Maggie Valley Area Chamber of Commerce,* P.O. Box 87, 2487 Soco Road, Maggie Valley, NC 28751, 926-1686 or (800) 785-8259; www.maggie-valley.nc.us; www.visitmaggie.com • *Cherokee Visitor Center,* P.O. Box 460, Cherokee, NC 28719, 497-9195 or (800) 438-1601; www.cherokee-nc.com.

Beach Bounty in Alabama

Are there beaches in Alabama? You betcha. Just west of Florida's better known gulf coast is a 32-mile outpost with the kind of soft sand and balmy breezes beach lovers dream about, and the scene comes complete with sandpipers, starfish, and seashells. Because the sand is 95 percent quartz crystal, it is as fine as powder and a shade of white that positively dazzles in the sunlight.

Though more people every year are discovering L.A. (that's "lower Alabama"), it remains less known than its Florida neighbor, and is, therefore, less crowded and lower key. Pick the kind of beach retreat you prefer, from low-rise motel to comfortable condo, resort hotel to a lodge or cabin in a state park. Families will have their fill of standard beach amusements to keep the kids happy, but couples who prefer peace and solitude can find that, as well. Golfers will find an increasing number of options. And there's interesting territory to explore not far away on the Eastern Shore of Mobile Bay and at historic Fort Morgan to the west.

It isn't surprising that the coast was something of a secret until recently. In 1933, when a canal was cut through to create a section of the Intracoastal Waterway, the beach area actually became an island. The only way in was via barge, ferry, or, eventually, a swing-span bridge. It was not until 1972 that a bridge over the waterway linked the beaches to the rest of the state and families began coming in earnest, building modest vacation cottages on pilings. A bridge also made the connection eastward to Florida.

Then, just as things were looking up, ferocious Hurricane Frederic blew into town in 1979 and the beach was swept clean. The dunes were flattened, along with most of the buildings. The ironic silver lining to the devastation was that Gulf Shores was suddenly in the news, and word was out that Alabama had a coastline. Investors soon arrived, new building began, and the area has prospered ever since, drawing both vacationers and retirees.

Most people these days arrive via Alabama Route 59 from the north, driving past shopping centers and eating places to reach the western end of the community of Gulf Shores, where Route 59 intersects with Route 182, the road paralleling the beaches.

A left turn onto 182 leads past rows of motels, Gulf State Park, Romar Beach, and finally to the second major shoreline community, Orange Beach, the boating center of the coast because of its access to the Gulf of Mexico. At Orange Beach marinas, you can find boat charters, fishing expeditions, and rentals of pontoon boats, Jet Skis, or sailboats.

One unique outing is on the 50-foot sailboat *Daedalus,* which goes out shrimping, often accompanied by an escort of dolphins. Nets are cast as you sail, and as the catch is sorted out, the sweet fresh shrimp are cooked to be enjoyed on the spot.

Fishermen can enjoy a choice of legendary Gulf catches, including bluefish, speckled trout, and Spanish mackerel, or freshwater fishing on 395,000 acres of lakes, back bays, and inlets. Marina docks and bait and tackle shops are the best sources of information on what's biting where.

Most people stay in lodgings right on the beach, but for those who do not, there is a public beach six miles west of Route 59 and parking and swimming are free at the Perdido Point Beach in Orange Beach.

Gulf State Resort Park also has two and a half miles of superb open beach. This 6000-acre playground is a popular convention site and family resort, with tennis courts, an 18-hole golf course, nature and biking trails, and an 825-foot fishing pier for surf casting. The park is booked solid in season, so make plans well ahead of time if you want to stay here.

The park has carefully preserved its marshes and wetlands, but there's even more flora and fauna to be seen at the Bon Secour Wildlife Refuge west of Gulf Shores. Here are nearly four miles of undeveloped beach and 6,200 acres of dunes, wetlands, and pine-oak forests. It is a protected area for indigenous plants and animals, especially endangered species such as loggerhead turtles and American alligators. This is also a bird-watcher's paradise. More than 120 kinds of birds have been spotted during spring and fall migrations.

Families looking for splashier diversions might head for Waterville, USA, a 500,000-gallon wave pool that generates 3-foot waves and provides lots of exciting water slides. The complex also includes miniature golf, go-carts, and other favorites.

The Alabama Gulf Coast Zoo should also please tounsts of all ages. The nicely planted 16-acre park is home to more than 200 exotic animals, from alligators to zebras.

Interesting sight-seeing can be found in several directions. At the western tip of the coast on Route 180, running parallel to Route 182, is Fort Morgan, the 1817 massive star-shaped brick fortress that guarded the entrance to Mobile Bay. It was here in 1864 that Union Admiral David Farragut, annoyed at his fleet's lack of progress against Confederate forces guarding the harbor, was said to have uttered the legendary words "Damn the torpedoes. Full speed ahead." More than 3000 cannonballs were fired in a 19-day siege before the fort finally fell and the last major Confederate gulf defense was lost in one of the key naval battles of the Civil War. A reenactment of the battle takes place every year on the fourth weekend in October.

Visitors are free to climb the steps into the fortress, where cannons still stand at the ready, and to wander through its many arches. The nearby Mobile Bay Light, built in 1885, is one of only three remaining lighthouses along the Alabama coast. The Mobile Bay Ferry leaves from near Fort Morgan on a 30-minute trip to the the Civil War–era Fort Gaines on Dauphin Island, with a nice view of the Gulf en route.

For those who prefer bargains to battles, heading north on Route 59 toward Foley brings you to a shopper's mecca, the Riviera Centre, with over 100 outlet stores. Foley itself will interest antiquers. There are three malls with well over 100 dealers, including the Gas Works where 70 of those dealers are found in a charming art deco building.

Turn west on Route 98 before you get to Foley to explore the many pleasures of the eastern shore of Mobile Bay. The first stop is Point Clear and the Grand Hotel, which has stood on its superb secluded site surrounded by water since 1847. You could easily spend a weekend or more enjoying the facilities of this top-class resort, but for now consider it a choice spot for lunch, and plan your schedule accordingly.

The first 40-room hotel known as the Point Clear was a glittering gathering place for antebellum Southern society. It was christened the

Grand after being rebuilt in 1875 following a fire. The heart pine flooring and framing of that original Grand was used when the hotel was rebuilt in 1941.

Taken over by Marriott in 1981, the main building retains its architecture and charm, the weathered wood and faded brick, the octagonal wood-paneled lobby, and the brick fireplace that soars three stories high. Swimming, boating, riding, tennis, golf—name it and you'll find it here—but nothing tops a simple stroll to Julep Point to gaze out at the water, water everywhere. At night, when there's dancing on this terrace under the stars, it's pure magic.

About a mile south of the Grand Hotel is a place guaranteed to please your sweet tooth. Punta Clara Kitchen is a family-owned business in an 1897 house, a mini-museum of Victoriana where you can watch fudge, pralines, and chocolates being made by hand.

The next stop to the north is the attractive little town of Fairhope, an art colony set on a bluff above the bay. The Eastern Shore Art Center exhibits works in all media in its attractive galleries and holds an outdoor art show during the town's arts and crafts fair, held the third weekend in March each year. More than 200 artists display their work at this major arts event, which celebrates its fiftieth birthday in 2002.

Interesting arts and crafts can be found year-round in the interesting shops within about four blocks on flower-festooned Fairhope Avenue, and the city pier, as the sign says, is "a gathering place for walkers, talkers and fishermen."

Seafood lovers should hurry to Fairhope during Jubilee, which marks a late-summer phenomenon in which a sudden lack of oxygen in the seawater drives bottom-dwelling creatures such as flounder, crab, and shrimp toward the shore. When the word gets out that the catch is coming in, everyone for miles around arrives with buckets and pots in hand.

Fairhope has attractive small bed-and-breakfasts, and is another spot to mark for a return visit.

With so much to recommend it, who knows . . . lower Alabama may one day be as famous as the L.A. on that other coast.

Area Code: 334

DRIVING DIRECTIONS I-10 from east or west and I-65 from the north connect with Route 59 south, which ends in Route 182, the road that parallels the beach area. From Atlanta, take I-85 west to I-65 south, 353 miles. From Birmingham, follow I-65 south, 274 miles.

PUBLIC TRANSPORTATION Gulf Shores is located 34 miles west of Pensacola, Florida, 48 miles east of Mobile. Car rentals are available at both airports.

ACCOMMODATIONS   Rates given are for summer; all are less off-season.

Orange Beach: *Perdido Beach Hilton,* 2720 Perdido Beach Boulevard, 36561, 981-9811, the class of the coast, private beach, four-diamond facilities, and fine dining, many weekend packages, E–EE • *Hilton Beachfront Garden Inn,* 23092 Perdido Beach Boulevard, 36561, 974-1600, on the beach, heated pool, M–E • *Island House Hotel,* 26650 Perdido Beach Boulevard, 36561, 981-6100 or (800) 264-2642, high-rise hotel on a private beach, E • *Hampton Inn,* 22988 Perdido Beach Boulevard, 36561, 974-1598, attractive beachfront motel, M–EE • *Romar House,* 23500 Perdido Beach Boulevard, 36561, 981-6156 or (800) 48-ROMAR, art deco–style bed-and-breakfast inn, no children under 12, M, CP.

Gulf Shores: *Gulf Shores Plantation Resort,* Route 180, P.O. Box 1299, 36542, 540-5000, condo resort with beach, boats, outdoor and indoor pools, tennis, fitness center, M–EE • *Gulf State Park Resort Hotel,* Gulf State Park, 20115 State Highway 135, 36547, 948-4853 or (800) 544-4853, state-operated lodge on beach, resort facilities, rooms, I–M; family suites, M–EE • *East White Sands Resort,* 365 Beach Boulevard, P.O. Box 417, 36547, 662-4853, best of the oceanfront motels, lighted tennis, pool, E–EE • *Quality Inn Beachside,* Highway 182 West, P.O. Box 1013, 36547, 948-6874 or (800) 844-6913, indoor pool, E–EE • *Best Western on the Beach,* 337 East Beach Boulevard, P.O. Box 481, 36542, 948-7047, E–EE.

Point Clear: *Marriott's Grand Hotel,* One Grand Boulevard, 36564, 928-9201 or (800) 544-9933, lavish landmark resort, E–EE.

Fairhope: *Bay Breeze Bed & Breakfast,* 742 South Mobile Street, Box 526, 36533, 928-8976, three rooms, two cottage suites facing Mobile Bay, M, CP • *Church Street Inn,* 51 South Church Street, 36533, 928-8976, pleasant in-town inn, M, CP • *Away at the Bay,* 557 North Mobile Street, P.O. Box 1028, 36533, 928-9725, private beach, suites with kitchens, balconies, M–E • *Magnolia Springs Bed & Breakfast,* 14469 Oak Street, Magnolia Springs, 36555 (between Gulf Shores and Fairhope), 965-7321, 1898 home turned B&B, M–E, CP.

DINING   Orange Beach: *Calypso Fish Grille & Market,* Orange Beach Marina, 981-1415, waterfront dining, seafood, salads, sandwiches, known for hermit crab races, I–M • *Bayside Grill,* Canal Road, Sportsman Marina, 981-4899, Creole, Caribbean, great sunsets, M • *Mango's on the Island,* Orange Beach Marina, 981-1416, fine dining, Cajun and Creole, piano bar, M–E • *Perdido Pass,* 27501 Perdido

Beach Boulevard, 981-6312, on the water, seafood, mesquite grill, M • *Voyagers,* Perdido Beach Hilton (see Accommodations on page 112), Continental, best in the area, E • *Zeke's Landing,* 16619 Perdido Beach Boulevard, 981-4001, on the harbor, seafood, Sunday jazz brunch, M–EE.

Gulf Shores: *Coconut Willies,* Route 59 and 180, 948-7145, local seafood, known for crab claws, great gumbo, I–M • *Hazel's Nook,* corner of Routes 59 and 180, 968-7065, breakfast standout, don't miss the biscuits, also lunch buffets, I • *Kirk Kirkland's Hitching Post,* 3401 Gulf Shores Parkway (Route 59), 968-5041, western ambience, barbecue, steaks, seafood, I–M • *Mikee's Seafood,* 1st Street North and 2nd Avenue East, 948-6452, nautical decor for reasonably priced seafood, I–M • *Original Oyster House,* Highway 59, Bayou Village, 968-2445, the name says it, on the bayou, I–M • *Pink Pony Pub,* Highway 59, 948-6371, burgers and beer, lively local gathering spot on the beach, casual, I–M • *Sea-n-Suds,* Young's by the Sea Motel, East Beach Boulevard, 968-7893, casual restaurant and oyster bar on the pier, I–M • *The View,* 1832 West Beach Boulevard, 948-8888, fine dining with a water view from ninth floor of Gulf Shores Surf and Racquet Club, M–E.

Fairhope: *Fairhope Inn & Restaurant,* 63 South Church Street, 928-6226, elegant dining at fair prices, M • *Jus' Gumbo Bar & Eatery,* 2 South Church Street, 928-4100, just what the name promises, spicy and good, I • *Old Bay Steamer,* 312 Fairhope Avenue, 928-1754, steamed and grilled seafood, fun atmosphere, I–E.

Point Clear: *Wash House,* Route 98, 928-1500, funky old favorite, hidden behind Punta Clara Kitchen shop, M–E • *Marriott's Grand Hotel* (see Accommodations on page 112), Grand Dining Room, formal, Continental menu, E–EE; *Bay View,* more intimate room overlooking Mobile Bay, seafood specialties, M–E.

SIGHT-SEEING *Gulf State Park,* 20115 State Highway 135, Gulf Shores, 948-GULF or (800) 544-GULF. Hours: Daily 8 A.M. to sunset. Entrance free; fees for some activities • *Bon Secour National Wildlife Refuge,* Route 280, Gulf Shores, 540-7720. Hours: Daily, daylight hours; office, Monday to Friday 7:30 A.M. to 4 P.M. Free • *Waterville, USA,* Route 59, Gulf Shores, 948-2106. Hours: Waterpark open Memorial Day to Labor Day, daily 10 A.M. to 6 P.M.; amusement park also open weekends spring and fall, phone for hours. $$$$$ • *Alabama Gulf Coast Zoo,* 1204 Gulf Shores Parkway, Gulf Shores, 968-5731. Hours: Memorial Day to Labor Day, daily 9 A.M. to 4:30 P.M.; rest of year, to 4 P.M. $$$$ • *Fort Morgan State Historical Park,* Route 180, Gulf Shores, 540-7125. Hours: March 1 to October 15, daily 9 A.M. to 6 P.M.;

rest of year, to 5 P.M. $$ • *Eastern Shore Art Center,* 401 Oak Street, Fairhope, 928-2228. Hours: Monday to Saturday 10 A.M. to 4 P.M., Sunday 2 to 5 P.M. Free.

INFORMATION *Alabama Gulf Coast Convention & Visitors Bureau,* Route 59, P.O. Drawer 457, Gulf Shores, AL 36547, 968-7511 or (800) 745-SAND; www.gulfshores.com • *City of Fairhope,* P.O. Drawer 429, Fairhope, AL 36533, 928-2136; www.cofairhope.com.

Making the Most of Monteagle

Monteagle Mountain is part of the lofty Cumberland Plateau that runs across the width of Tennessee like a gentle wall, forming the scenic western boundary of the Tennessee Valley. The hills loom unexpectedly for motorists humming along I-24 between Nashville and Chattanooga, and then disappear. Many speed right by, never suspecting the treasures awaiting atop the mountain.

Pass through the stone gates of the Monteagle Assembly and you've stepped into a storybook Victorian world of quaint wooden cottages with wide porches, lush shrubbery, and flowers. On the heavily wooded grounds are gazebos, narrow winding walking paths, and wooden trestle bridges across scenic ravines.

Five miles to the south are the Gothic stone buildings of the University of the South, an architectural replica of England's Oxford University, in the matching stone town of Sewanee. The campus, some 200 wooded acres, is a place for hiking as well as a picturebook setting for a long-established summer music festival and a rising writer's conference with public lectures by famous authors.

Outdoor lovers who want room to roam will find 12,000 acres of untouched mountain wilderness in the South Cumberland State Recreation Area. This is scenic land, laced with majestic waterfalls tumbling over rocky cliffs, with deep gorges carved into the sandstone by mountain streams. It has been maintained as naturally as possible, so that visitors can enjoy the cascading falls, arches, and stony overlooks just as nature created them.

The first to take advantage of the area's exceptional setting 900 feet above the middle Tennessee basin were Sunday-school workers. The Monteagle Assembly they founded in 1882 was modeled after the Chautauqua Institute in New York, originators of the popular nineteenth-century notion of combining Sunday-school-teacher training with a broader program of education, entertainment, and recreation. The elevation of the plateau made it a perfect escape for families seeking a cool summer retreat.

Soon known as the "Chautauqua of the South," Monteagle's nondenominational program quickly caught on. The first season was essentially a giant tent meeting, with only a restaurant and amphitheater as permanent structures on the grounds. Then boardinghouses, meeting rooms, and private cottages went up to accommodate the thousands who came. Picturesque bridges were built to span the natural gorges and ravines. Eventually there were 162 gingerbread cottages on the 96-acre grounds, as well as dining rooms and indoor meeting facilities. The entire complex is on the National Register of Historic Places.

Over 100 years after its founding, the colony is going strong, with members from 20 states, many of them fifth-generation families who return each summer. The season lasts for eight weeks. While today's program still has a strong religious component, it offers topics as varied as floral design, historic preservation, health, nature, photography, travel, books, and the arts. Tennis tournaments, volleyball, bridge, concerts, and dances are also part of the agenda. A few of the concerts of the Sewanee Summer Music Festival are held on the grounds, and a park ranger from the state recreation area offers guided hikes and talks once a week.

Monteagle used to be strictly for cottage owners and their friends, but that changed in recent years when two inns opened in historic cottages. Their guests are entitled to attend programs and to use the swimming pool and tennis courts. The inns are open year-round and are great getaways when no programs are taking place, offering access to the very private and very scenic grounds.

The Adams Edgeworth Inn, a quaint 1896 Victorian with a railed wraparound porch, is a haven of charm, a combination of period antiques and artful sophistication. Walls are adorned with the owners' impressive collection of more than 100 paintings. Rooms have antique beds, some of them four-posters, with covers that range from fluffy comforters to hand-embroidered Pakistani cashmere blankets. Some have fireplaces.

The inn is full of deft, unexpected contrasts, such as a wood-burning stove beneath a French crystal chandelier and a French rococo vanity with a simple wooden chair made in the nearby crafts village of Bell Buckle.

Rockers on the porch offer a place for peaceful repose, and the library is cozy when the weather is cool. On nice days guests gather for cocktails in the rose garden. Though the inn has no restaurant, guests can arrange in advance to have dinner, not a bad idea since the area is not strong on restaurants.

North Gate Lodge is far more modest, but the former 1890s boardinghouse is pleasant and the rates are quite reasonable.

The University of the South, founded by the Episcopal Church in 1857, is one of the loveliest schools in this or any state. One of the special sights on the Gothic campus is the Du Pont Library collection of rare books and manuscripts. Another is the All Saints' Chapel, a campus landmark, boasting an ivy-covered tower containing the 65-bell Polk Memorial Carillon, one of the largest in the world. Carillon concerts are held most Sunday afternoons.

The chapel is often a setting for all-brass concerts during the Sewanee Summer Music Festival. The highly regarded festival is in its third decade of presenting classical orchestra and chamber concerts in Guerry Hall. Student ensembles also give concerts outdoors on Guerry Garth.

A more recent summer addition is the Sewanee Writers' Conference funded by the estate of the late Tennessee Williams. This series of workshops in fiction, poetry, and playwriting brings outstanding speakers whose lectures are often open to the public. Some noted names in the past were novelist William Styron and poet Richard Wilbur. The last week of the writers' conference often coincides with the music festival concerts, a double helping of the arts.

The campus, which covers 10,000 acres at an elevation of 2,000 feet, is more than architecture—it is a nature lover's delight, with mountain overlooks, hiking trails, waterfalls, and caves. The University View at the end of Tennessee Avenue, marked by a 40-foot marble cross, looks down on the towns of Winchester and Cowan. From the opposite side of the mountain, on the right day you can see as far as 80 miles along the Highland Rim. One of the favorite spots for watching sunsets is Morgan's Steep, a stone shelf on the edge of the Cumberland Plateau.

Two miles south of the campus is Sewanee Natural Bridge, a 25-foot sandstone arch overlooking Lost Cove. Keep driving south and you'll come to the Carter State Natural Area, a 140-acre tract that includes the Lost Cove Caves.

This is one of the nine sections of the South Cumberland State Recreation Area, which is scattered across 100 square miles of south-central Tennessee. Closer to Tracy City on Route 41 is Foster Falls Small Wild Area, featuring 60-foot falls with the largest volume of water of any cascade in the South. The grounds are open for swimming, hiking, and picnicking.

The Fiery Gizzard Hiking Trail winds around the cliffs to connect this area with the Grundy Forest State Natural Area. Features here include Sycamore Falls in the bottom of the Fiery Gizzard Gorge and the unique geological formations known as Chimney Rocks.

According to local legend, Fiery Gizzard got its name when Davy Crockett camped in the area, killed a wild turkey, and was too hungry to wait for the meat to cool, popping the gizzard into his mouth straight from the fire. "That's one fiery gizzard," he is said to have cried.

Great Stone Door near Bersheba Springs is another unusual rock formation, a 150-foot-high crevice at the crest of the Cumberland Plateau above Big Creek Gulf. This section offers panoramic views, hiking, and picnicking.

For more information on the area and maps, stop at the visitors center on Route 41 between Monteagle and Tracy Springs. Drive into Tracy Springs to satisfy your sweet tooth at the Dutch Maid Bakery, Tennessee's oldest bakery, which has been operated by the Baggenstoss family since 1902.

The inspiring surroundings of the region have attracted many craftspeople, whose work can be seen in their own studios or in local shops. Watch for their signs along the highway, and in Sewanee stop at The Lemon Fair for locally made pottery, jewelry, stained glass, and wooden crafts, along with gourmet foods.

One of the favorite events of the year is the Mountain Market on the first weekend in August at the Monteagle Elementary School, a mélange of regional handmade arts and crafts and exhibits by over 200 artists and artisans from 15 states. A big flea market takes place every Saturday and Sunday on I-24 at exit 134.

Restaurants in the area are nothing fancy, but Jim Oliver's rustic Smoke House draws people for miles around for country ham and hickory-smoked bacon. Guests consume more than a million flaky biscuits each year.

There's a different taste awaiting next door at the Monteagle Winery, the largest in the state.

An even more potent lure is found about half an hour's drive to the west in Lynchburg, the home of the man who is arguably the best-known Tennessean. Jasper Newton "Jack" Daniel founded the nation's oldest registered distillery in his hometown in 1866. It is now a historic landmark. Visitors are taken on a tour that includes the seven-story barrelhouse where the aging whiskey is stored and to the charcoal-mellowing vats where the whiskey is filtered for smoothness. A new visitor center was added recently to accommodate the over 300,000 visitors who come to the distillery each year.

If you're going to Lynchburg, be sure to make reservations in advance for the bountiful mid-day family-style dinner at Miss Mary Bobo's Boarding House, a town tradition since 1908. It's another Southern classic.

Area Code: 931

DRIVING DIRECTIONS   Monteagle is off I-24, exit 134. It is 170 miles from Atlanta, 90 miles from Nashville, 50 miles from Chattanooga, and 190 miles from Birmingham.

ACCOMMODATIONS   *Adams Edgeworth Inn,* Monteagle Assembly, Monteagle, 37356, 924-4000 or (877) 352-9466, M–E, CP • *North*

Gate Inn, Monteagle Assembly, Monteagle, 37356, 924-2799, M, CP •
Monteagle Inn, 204 West Main Street, Monteagle, 37356, 924-3869 or
(888) 480-3245, 13-suite bed-and-breakfast inn, M–E, CP • *Best West-*
ern Smoke House Lodge, Routes 64 and 41A, Monteagle, 37356, 924-
2268 or (800) 489-2091, motel and cabins, I–M • *Days Inn,* 742 Dixie
Lee Avenue, Monteagle, 37356, 924-2900 or (800) DAYS-INN, I, CP •
Clouds Rest, 400 Rattlesnake Spring Road, Sewanee, 37375, 598-
0993, bed-and-breakfast near the campus, M, CP.

DINING   *Jim Oliver's Smoke House Restaurant* (see Smoke House
Lodge above), known for smoked meats, homemade jams, country
breakfasts, bountiful buffets, I–M • *High Point,* 224 East Main Street,
Monteagle, 924-4600, steak and seafood in a handsome three-story
home, reservations required, M • *Pearl's Foggy Mountain Cafe,* 14344
Sewanee Highway, Sewanee, 598-9568, eclectic Southern, one of the
area's best, M • *4 Seasons,* Midway Road, Sewanee, 598-5544, catfish,
chicken, and shrimp buffets, Friday and Saturday dinner, Sunday lunch,
I • *Miss Bobo's Boarding House,* Main Street, Lynchburg, 759-7394,
Monday to Saturday, lunch only, 1 P.M., also 11 A.M. in summer, reservations required, M.

SIGHT-SEEING   *Monteagle Assembly,* P.O. Box 307, Monteagle,
37356, 924-2286. Eight weeks of programming each summer, mid-
June to early August. Write for information • *University of the South,*
Sewanee Summer Music Festival, Sewanee Summer Music Center,
University of the South, 735 University Avenue, Sewanee, 598-1225,
concerts from late June to early August; check current schedules •
Sewanee Writer's Conference, 310 Saint Luke's Hall, 598-1141, two
weeks mid-to-late July, check current schedule • *South Cumberland*
Recreation Area, Route 1, Box 2196, Monteagle, 37356, 924-2980.
For maps and information, Visitor Center, Route 41 east, between
Monteagle and Tracy City. Free • *Monteagle Mountain Market,* Mont-
eagle Elementary School, first weekend in August, sponsored by Town
of Monteagle, Monteagle School PTA, and Monteagle Assembly
Woman's Association; check with the Town Hall or the Assembly for
dates • *Monteagle Wine Cellars,* off I-24, exit 134, 924-2120. Hours:
April to October, Monday to Saturday 8 A.M. to dark, Sunday 12 noon
to 5 P.M.; rest of year, noon to 5 P.M. Free • *Jack Daniel Distillery,*
Route 25, Lynchburg (from Monteagle pick up Route 64 and follow off
the mountain to Winchester, continuing to Route 50; take Route 50 to
Route 55 into Lynchburg), 759-6180. Hours: Daily 9 A.M. to 4:30 P.M.
Free.

INFORMATION   *Monteagle Mountain Chamber of Commerce,*
19 College Street, P.O. Box 353, Monteagle, TN 37356, 924-5353;
E-mail: mmtnchamber@blomand.net.

Making the Rounds in Alabama

They've been making tracks in eastern Alabama for a long time. First it was the Creek Indians, then General Andrew Jackson coming through in the early 1800s. Tracks of early settlers can be seen in the photogenic covered bridges of this picturesque wooded region, where you'll also find some of the loveliest wilderness hiking and scenic driving in the state.

Nowadays things are speeding up. Talladega, site of one of the old covered bridges, is also home to the speedway that has gone into the record books as the fastest auto-racing track in the world. The town is also home to many classic Southern homes, some of which are now inviting bed-and-breakfast inns.

It is contrasts like this that make for a wonderful weekend excursion.

Anniston also merits consideration as a base for exploring the region because it boasts a special inn. The Victoria, an 1888 showplace complete with turrets and a wraparound veranda, was occupied by three prominent Anniston families before it was transformed into a country inn and restaurant in 1985. There are three grand period suites in the main building and 44 new units with old-fashioned decor and modern amenities located in an addition across the courtyard. The dining room, done in formal Victorian fashion, is highly recommended, and the pool is a nice refresher on a warm summer day.

You'll see at once that Anniston is an unusually attractive small town. It was born when two industrialists, Samuel Noble and Daniel Tyler, established textile mills and blast furnaces here in 1872, in an effort to bolster the Southern economy after the Civil War. They brought in noted New York architect Stanford White to lay out a model company town, with wide streets and grand churches. It was named "Annie's Town" in honor of Tyler's wife, Annie, and remained a private company town until 1883.

Many of the original churches remain, along the stately divided boulevard called Quintard Avenue and in the Tyler Hill historic district on East Sixth Street, which peaks at a square park surrounded by majestic Victorian homes from the late 1880s.

One interior not to be missed is the St. Michael and All Angels Episcopal Church at the corner of 18th Street and Cobb Avenue. It was built for the foundry workers in 1888 by Noble, who is buried near the entrance. Masons from his native Cornwall were brought to do the outside stonework and the 95-foot altar of white Carrara marble was shipped from Italy. Among the beautiful touches are the alabaster reredos topped with hand-carved angels and glowing stained-glass windows depicting Jesus and the Holy Family, including a Madonna and Child by Louis Comfort Tiffany.

This city's special pride is its Museum of Natural History, a remarkable collection that would do credit to a metropolis many times the size of Anniston. The modern building is divided into halls with varying themes.

The African Hall is home to more than 100 creatures shown in correct habitats, and the Ornithology Hall holds one of the most remarkable bird collections anywhere. Assembled by William Werner, a well-known nineteenth-century naturalist, it includes over 600 kinds of North American birds in their natural habitats, each shown with authentic nests and eggs.

The Underground World exhibit, a replica of an Alabama cave, is complete with cool damp air, pools, stalactites, stalagmites, a travertine dome, and simulated resident bats, snakes, and salamanders.

Nearby is the Berman Museum, another unique find. It contains rare weapons, armor, and an art collection including bronzes by Frederic Remington, all amassed by one man, Farley Berman. One of the notable items is a sixteenth-century Persian scimitar with a handle embedded with rubies, over 1000 diamonds, and a 40-carat emerald.

The Fort McClellan military base that was a mainstay in Anniston for many years has closed, and the city is hoping, in cooperation with the U.S. Fish and Wildlife Service, to turn the property into a wildlife refuge.

Nature and art lovers should pay a visit to the Wren's Nest, a gallery of paintings, prints, and sculptures of wildlife and other subjects by Larry K. Martin. The gallery is located in the refurbished 100-year-old carriage house of the Victoria Inn.

Just south of Anniston is Oxford, where you can see one of the early covered bridges, the Coldwater Bridge in Oxford Lake Park, off Highway 78. This is also a road with several stops for antiquing.

For outstanding scenery, drive south from Anniston on Highway 431 and watch the road wind higher and higher until you reach Cheaha State Park. This peaceful 2,500-acre preserve offers picnicking, boating, and swimming in a mountain lake, and the chance to climb a rustic rock tower for the view from 2,407 feet up, the highest point in the state. The big windows in the park restaurant offer their own sweeping vistas of rolling mountains and forest.

The park is within the Talladega National Forest and opens to the Cheaha Wilderness Area, the southernmost extension of the Appalachians and a glorious place for a hike. The Pinjote Trail System traverses the highest terrain in the state for nearly 100 miles. It is a prize route along the edge of rock bluffs, through forested coves, and beside rocky streams. There are several entry points—in the park, at the Coleman Lake Recreation Area to the north, and in the Friendship community to the south.

One of the state's best auto routes, the Talladega Scenic Drive, begins one mile southwest of Cheaha and ends on Highway 78 near Heflin. There are many magnificent vistas such as the rocky escarpment off Sherman Cliff. Remember this drive during foliage season; it is heavenly from mid-October through November.

Cheaha offers a lodge, chalets and cabins, and is a fine place for a weekend stay among the tall trees—if you can reserve early enough to get one of the popular accommodations.

Another option is Talladega, where you can choose from several fine inns. In the town's historic district are Oakwood, a columned showplace built in 1847 by the town's first mayor, and Somerset House, a charming turn-of-the-century home. The Governor's House, a columned mansion built in 1850 by former governor Lewis Parson, has been moved to a farm overlooking Logan Martin Lake, renovated, and filled with antiques. Orangevale, another antiques-filled beauty, is a Greek Revival–style plantation home in the country on farmland, with log cabins, the old kitchen, well house, and smokehouse. Families will enjoy seeing the horses, cattle, and sheep.

Talladega was officially founded in 1834, but the local history goes back even further. The site was part of the Jackson Trace, the first wagon road through the Creek Indian nation, built by Andrew Jackson and his army of Tennessee volunteers. A monument located a block from Courthouse Square marks the Big Spring where the Indian village of Talladega was defeated by Jackson in the Creek Indian War of 1813. The city grew up later around this same spring.

Though the town square is no longer the thriving trading center of the past, the historic 1836 brick courthouse, the oldest in continuous use in Alabama, stands proud, and there are many other historic structures in town. The Silk Stocking Historic District south of the square includes many homes dating to the 1820s. Watch for the small markers on the lawns giving the owners and dates of the most significant houses. East South Street is especially fine.

Another important local site is Talladega College, founded in 1867 by two former slaves. Still predominantly black, it was the first college in the state open to all races and has many fine landmark buildings along the oak-lined campus.

Another school of interest is the Alabama Institute for the Deaf and Blind, one of the country's most comprehensive institutions of its kind. Two buildings, Grace Hall and Jemison House, are over 100 years old, and Manning Hall, the administration building, dates to 1850.

Talladega boasts one of the state's oldest covered bridges, the Waldo Bridge, six miles south of town on Highway 77. This truss-type bridge dates from around 1858. The surrounding area is now a pioneer park, including Riddle's Grist Mill and a log cabin about the same vintage as the bridge.

To see how the pace of life has picked up since horse-and-buggy days, head for the Talladega Superspeedway. Built in the late 1960s, this is the site of the state's two largest sport events, the Winston 500 Race, held in late April, and the DieHard 500, the final major NASCAR Winston Cup stock-car competition of the season, usually held the last Saturday in July. Qualifying rounds begin on the Thursday before the big races.

Both events are nationally televised and regularly sell out the 83,000-seat stadium. Tickets go on sale many weeks in advance, and hotel rooms are sold out for miles around.

Whenever you visit Talladega, you can relive some of the great races at the International Motorsports Hall of Fame. It is filled with famous stock cars, Indy cars, and drag racers. Exhibits range from the 1935 Bluebird brought from England by Sir Malcolm Campbell to triumph at Daytona Beach, to the 1985 Ford Thunderbird driven by Bill Elliot when he established the record for the fastest 500-mile race ever run— 186.288 miles per hour. Many of the cars were loaned or donated by top-name racers.

The track has also inspired a modern downtown addition, the Talladega-Texaco Walk of Fame, created as a memorial to the late driver Davey Allison. Built along a wall in an oval echoing the Talladega track, the walk holds raised plaques saluting the driver voted by fans each year as their favorite. Balloting takes place at the track in April, and an induction ceremony is held in July.

From Talladega, head south on Highway 21 and connect with Highway 76 to reach a unique eastern-Alabama attraction, De Soto Caverns Park.

The park's vast onyx cave has a long and colorful history. It was discovered in 1540 by Spanish explorer Hernando de Soto, who camped nearby during his quest for the Fountain of Youth. The Creek Indians considered it a holy place, the birthplace of their ancestors. It became the first officially recorded cave in the United States in 1796, when Benjamin Hawkins, the superintendent of Indian tribes in the region, wrote to President George Washington describing its beauty.

The cave was used by the Confederates to mine saltpeter for gunpowder during the Civil War, and was notorious during Prohibition as a speakeasy well out of sight of the authorities.

Today it is a major state tourist attraction. The history is told in an entertaining way by the pleasant guides, who also point out the eerie formations created by the dripping of mineral-rich waters. The grand finale is a sound-and-light show complete with leaping waters, presented inside the cave's best-known feature, the great onyx cathedral, a space higher than a 12-story building.

In the park outside the cave await such family amusements as a playground, a maze in the form of a wooden stockade, and the chance to pan for gemstones and gold.

On the way to the cave, you will pass the Kymulga covered bridge spanning Talladega Creek. It was one of four under construction at the start of the Civil War and the only one to escape burning by the Union army. It is on the National Register of Historic Places.

The adjoining three-and-a-half-story mill was built in the 1860s by slave labor and restored in 1988. On a guided tour, you can watch corn being ground. The mill and bridge are part of a 78-acre park with the largest stand of white oak trees east of the Mississippi and a giant sugarberry tree. It's yet another place where history and scenery meet in eastern Alabama.

Area Code: 256

DRIVING DIRECTIONS   Anniston is on Highway 431 just north of I-20. From Atlanta, follow I-20 west, 87 miles; from Birmingham, take I-20 east, 66 miles. Talladega is 24 miles south via Highway 21.

ACCOMMODATIONS   *The Victoria,* 1604 Quintard Avenue, Anniston, 36201, 236-0503, M–E, CP • *Somerset House,* 701 North Street East, Talladega, 35160, 761-9251, M, CP • *Oakwood Bed and Breakfast,* 715 East North Street, Talladega, 35160, 362-0662, 1847 Federal home near courthouse square, I, CP • *The Governor's House,* 500 Meadowlake Lane, Talladega, 35160, 763-2186, I, CP • *Orangevale,* 1400 Whiting Road, Talladega, 35160, 362-3052, M, CP • *Cheaha Mountain Lodge,* Cheaha State Park, Highway 281, 2141 Bunker Loop, Delta, 36258, 488-5115 or (800) ALA-PARK, lodge, I–M; rustic cottages, I; modern chalets, M.

DINING   *The Victoria* (see Accommodations above), M • *Top O' the River,* 3220 McClellan Boulevard, Anniston, 238-0097, corn bread, catfish, and nice old photos on the walls, I–M • *Betty's Bar-B-Q,* 401 South Quintard, Anniston, 237-1411, old Southern favorite, I • *Le Mama's,* Walnut Street, Anniston, 237-5500, in the old railroad station, lunch only, I • *Cheaha Mountain Lodge* (see Accommodations above), go for the views, I–M • *Cafe Royal,* 110 Court Square East, Talladega, 362-3186, soup and sandwiches, I • *Old Mill Restaurant,* Highway 77, Waldo (south of Talladega), 761-0043, actually an old mill, good food, varied menu, known for catfish, dinner Friday, all day Saturday and Sunday, I–E.

SIGHT-SEEING   *Cheaha State Park,* 19644 Highway 281, Delta, 488-5111 or (800) 846-2654. Hours: Daily, daylight hours. Parking fee, $ • *Anniston Museum of Natural History,* 4301 McClellan Boulevard, Anniston, 237-6766. Hours: Monday to Saturday 10 A.M. to 5 P.M., Sunday 1 to 5 P.M. $$ • *Berman Museum,* 840 Museum Drive, 237-6261. Hours: Monday to Saturday 10 A.M. to 5 P.M., Sunday 1 to 5 P.M. $$ • *Church of St. Michael and All Angels,* 1000 West 18th Street,

Anniston, 237-4011. Hours: Daily 9 A.M. to 4 P.M. Free • *International Motorsports Hall of Fame,* 3198 Speedway Boulevard off I-20, exit 173, Talladega, 362-5002. Hours: Daily 8:30 A.M. to 5 P.M. $$$$ • *Talladega Superspeedway,* 3366 Speedway Boulevard, P.O. Box 777, Talladega, 35160, off I-20 exit 173. Ticket office, 362-7223. Check for current schedules and ticket information • *De Soto Caverns Park,* De Soto Caverns Parkway off Highway 21, Childersburg, 378-7252. Hours: April to September, Monday to Saturday 9 A.M. to 5:30 P.M., Sunday 1 to 5:30 P.M.; rest of year, to 4:30 P.M. $$$$; cave plus other attractions, $$$$$.

INFORMATION *Calhoun County Chamber of Commerce,* 1330 Quintard Avenue, P.O. Box 1087, Anniston, AL 36202, 237-3536 • *Greater Talladega Chamber of Commerce,* 210 East Street South, P.O. Drawer A, Talladega, AL 35160, 362-9075; www.talladega.com.

Heaven High in Highlands

Highlands, North Carolina, is the closest to heaven you can get without leaving this world behind.

The highest town east of the Mississippi River, perched at an altitude of over 4,118 feet at the southern tip of the Blue Ridge Mountains, this pinch of paradise is a world apart, surrounded by more than a million acres of the Nantahala National Forest. In every direction, roads wind toward stunning views, mirror lakes, and walking paths on trails lined with rhododendron and pine. More than 200 waterfalls tumble through these hills.

Cool and green in summer, Highlands and the whole region become an autumn fantasy when the nights grow cool and the foliage turns to gorgeous gold, orange, and russet red.

Oddly enough, a resort town was not what the Northern founding fathers, Samuel Truman Kelsey and Clinton Carter Hutchinson, had in mind when they bought up property in 1875. Fresh from completing the town of Hutchinson, Kansas, they were looking to the Southeast for a business center. When they checked out the topography, however, they had to settle for a mountain retreat instead. By 1883 they had cut 40 miles of road out of the native forest, incorporated a town of 300 residents, and were advertising Highlands across the Southeast as a health retreat whose climate and fresh air had rejuvenating powers.

Highlands quickly became a favorite hideaway for wealthy Southerners, as it has remained for well over a century. Many have summer homes on the grounds of the exclusive Highlands Country Club, founded in 1929 around a Donald Ross golf course. Their support has helped spawn many activities, including a summer playhouse now well past its fiftieth season, a chamber music festival, and a forum on international affairs.

Lately the town has also become a popular retirement community and has been attracting tourists, along with Floridians escaping the heat, swelling the population of 2,000 to 20,000 in summer. But compared to most places, the two-block Main Street is still delightfully unspoiled—no fast food, no gewgaw souvenirs, no bright lights. And the encircling mountains ensure that Highlands will never grow too large.

There are plenty of shops, to be sure, but they are upscale emporiums where browsing is a joy. Downtown remains so compact that none of the Main Street shops even bother about storefront numbers. Their wares range from English antiques to Japanese porcelains to Appalachian quilts, all in the best of taste. Southern Hands carries as fine an assemblage of regional crafts as you'll see anywhere.

There's just a smattering of sight-seeing in town. The Bascom-Louise Gallery, inside the Hudson Library, showcases regional artists, and there's a botanical garden right behind the local nature center.

The Scottish heritage of this region is also reflected in an annual Scottish Tartans Festival in mid-September and in the Wee Shoppe at the edge of town, on US 64, which sells all kinds of British Isles imports, from tartans to teas.

You can easily find a place to stay right on Main Street, within easy range of all the shopping. Two old-timers, the 1880 Highlands Inn and its sister across the street, the 1878 Old Edwards Inn, have been nicely restored and refurbished.

Since mountain views are what Highlands is all about, an even better bet is just a few blocks up the hill. Colonial Pines is a delightful bed-and-breakfast inn, cozy and welcoming, with a big wide porch affording nonstop mountain views. The requisite rockers are waiting for you.

One of the most spectacular views around is from the Skyline Lodge, on a mountaintop four miles from town. The 1920s lodge, designed by Frank Lloyd Wright, is made of native granite and has enormous windows to take in the mind-boggling vistas. Rooms here are less unusual—in fact, they're downright motelish. But there's a pool and tennis courts, and the panoramas from the ceiling-high dining-room windows are dazzling.

It's necessary to get out and about to appreciate the beauty that can be seen only on a drive or a walk outside of town.

Begin by driving to the end of East Main Street as it turns into Horse Cove Road. If you feel like taking a 20-minute hike, stop at the Highlands Nature Center on Horse Cove Road and take the path to Sunset Rock, overlooking the town.

Come back to the road, and you'll wind around some 37 curves

before you come to the cove itself. A very short detour onto Wilson Gap
Road will give you a view of Highlands' venerable Giant Poplar, said to
be one of the three largest poplars in the nation. Then continue on
Horse Cove Road until you come to a fork. On the right will be Bull
Pen Road, a gravel road leading to an outlook on the Chattooga, a
national wild and scenic river. Go left on Whiteside Cove Road, and
you'll pass the world's smallest post office, Grimshaw's. There are
magnificent views along this drive of Whiteside Mountain, striking for
its steep sheer cliffs.

You can double back the way you came and enjoy the scenery from
a different perspective or continue on Whiteside Cove Road to North
Carolina Route 107 south of Cashiers, turning left onto US 64 west to
get back to Highlands.

Another scenic drive awaits on North Carolina Route 106 south from
Highlands toward Dillard, Georgia. Look for a turnoff in about three
miles to the dirt road leading to Glen Falls, a series of three large falls,
each dropping 60 feet into the Overflow Creek in Blue Valley. About a
half-mile farther on Route 106 is the Blue Valley Overlook, a spot
where the mountains seem to go on forever.

Just a half-mile farther on is a picturesque shopping stop, the Lick
Log Mill Store, an 1851 log cabin in a lavish garden setting, filled with
folk art and other nice country things.

For a veritable feast of waterfalls, head west from Highlands on US
64/28 toward Franklin along the Cullasaja River Gorge. You'll be riding
beside a river that ripples over rapids and cascades into a series of dramatic falls, all within sight of the road. Among these are Bridal Veil
Falls, which you can drive under in your car, and Dry Falls, so named
because you can walk behind the falls without getting wet.

Before you get to Franklin, watch for Buck Creek Road on the right,
connecting US 64 west with 64 east toward Cashiers. The Buck Creek
community is in a basin surrounded by hardwoods, a brilliant sight in
the fall. The road continues east in a series of sharp curves between
thickly wooded hillsides until the trees open again at Cowee Gap for an
awe-inspiring view of Whiteside Mountain.

The drive from Highlands to Cashiers is ten miles, and if you arrive
in time for lunch, both the Market Basket and Cornucopia will serve
you nicely or prepare takeout picnics to allow you to continue your
scenic drive.

The next stop is Whitewater Falls, the highest waterfall in the East,
about 20 minutes from Cashiers. Take North Carolina Route 107 south
for about 13 miles, and at the Whitewater Falls sign, turn left onto
South Carolina Route 130 into South Carolina; continue to the stop
sign and turn left onto Whitewater Road, Route 1171, for one mile.
When you see the Whitewater Falls sign, turn right into the parking
area and take an easy walk of five to ten minutes to an overlook and

view of the two-level, 411-foot falls, spuming as they crash onto the rocks. The energetic will find trails to the top and bottom of the falls. For more national forest hiking trails, ask for a brochure at the information center in either Highlands or Cashiers.

The shops of Cashiers are scattered along the sides of the highway. The town lacks the quaint main street or the surrounding mountains of Highlands, but there is no shortage of exceptional lodgings nearby.

High Hampton Inn and Country Club, set on 1,400 acres, 3,600 feet high amid the mountains, is a determinedly old-fashioned resort with rockers on the porch and huge, four-sided fireplaces inside, where guests gather to enjoy hot soup at noon or afternoon tea. Rooms in the main house or in the 19 cottages around the grounds are simply furnished with mountain pine pieces made on the premises, chenille bedspreads, and rag rugs.

This remains the kind of place where guests play croquet and lawn bowling, and where they swim in the lake, not a pool. It is also the site of a spectacular golf course with Chimney Top and Rock Mountain standing guard. The eighth green, beneath Rock Mountain, is a classic. Seven tennis courts, boating, sailing, fly-fishing and instruction, and guided walks to scenic areas are among the multitude of activities. Considering the amenities and the three bountiful meals plus afternoon tea, rates here are surprisingly reasonable.

Those who prefer a more intimate setting will appreciate the Millstone Inn, a rustic shingled home built in the 1930s atop a shady knoll some 3,500 feet high. Views of Whiteside Mountain can be seen from many of the pine-paneled bedrooms as well as from the picture window of the commodious, beamed living room, which takes up most of one of the two wings of the house. The autumn views are so spectacular that some people book a year in advance.

A few miles away is the Innisfree Inn on Lake Glenville, a new "old Victorian," built in classic style in 1989. The most popular room here is Victoria's Suite, where the whirlpool for two is surrounded by windows with a mountain view.

Whether you take your views from the whirlpool or a car window, a front porch or a hiking trail, you'll surely agree that Highlands and its neighbors are heavenly places to be.

Area Code: 828

DRIVING DIRECTIONS   Highlands is at the intersection of US 64 and North Carolina Routes 28 and 106. It is 140 miles from Atlanta, 65 miles from Asheville, 180 miles from Columbia, South Carolina, 150 miles from Knoxville, and 160 miles from Charlotte. From Atlanta, take I-85 north, exit at I-985 Gainesville, which becomes Georgia Route 365. Continue to US 23/441 north to Dillard, then follow

Georgia Route 246, which becomes North Carolina Route 106 at the North Carolina state line, and continue to Highlands.

ACCOMMODATIONS *Highlands Inn,* 4th and Main Street, Highlands, 28741, 526-9380 or (800) 694-6955, old-timer on Main Street, M–E, CP • *Colonial Pines Inn,* 541 Hickory Street, Highlands, 28741, 526-2060, convenient, charming, private, great mountain views from the big porch, M–E, CP • *Toad Hall,* 61 Sequoyah Point Way, Highlands, 28741, 526-3889 or (888) 891-3889, one-time lakefront estate, special, M–E, CP • *4½ Street Inn,* 55 4½ Street, Highlands, 28741, 526-4464, pleasant small inn, M–E, CP • *Highlands Suite Hotel,* 205 Main Street, Highlands, 28741, 526-4502, all the amenities, E–EE, CP • *Chandler Inn,* Highway 64 and Martha's Lane, Highlands, 28741, 526-5992 or (888) 378-6300, surrounded by greenery, rockers on the porch, fireplace suites, I–E, CP • *Skyline Lodge,* Flat Mountain Road, P.O. Box 630, Highlands, 28741, 526-2121 or (800) 575-9546, 50 acres on a secluded mountaintop, stunning lodge, motel-style rooms, pool, M.

Cashiers area: *Millstone Inn,* Highway 64 West, P.O. Box 949, Cashiers, 28717, 743-2737, M–E, CP • *High Hampton Inn and Country Club,* 640 Hampton Road (State Route 107 S.), Box 338, Cashiers, 28717, 743-2411 or (800) 334-2551, superb resort, rustic lodge, all sports, open April through November, E, AP • *Innisfree Inn,* 7 Lakeside Knoll, P.O. Box 469, Glenville, 28736, 743-2946, romantic Victorian ambience, E, CP.

DINING *On the Verandah,* Highway 64 West, Highlands, 526-2338, scenic spot overlooking Lake Sequoyah, talented chef-owner, best in town, M–E; also Sunday champagne brunch with jazz, M–EE • *Wolfgang's on Main,* East Main Street, Highlands, 526-3807, mix of New Orleans and Bavaria and it somehow works, M–E • *Lakeside Restaurant,* Smallwood Avenue, Highlands, 526-9419, casual, popular, featuring seafood, M–E • *Central House,* country decor, many seafood specialties, M–E • *Paoletti's,* Main Street, Highlands, 526-4906, Italian, Old World ambience, M–E • *Jack's at Skyline,* Skyline Lodge (see Accommodations above), go for lunch and the view, I–M; dinner, M–E • *Cafe of the Arts,* Main Street, Highlands, 526-5166, French cafe, M–E • *Cornucopia,* Highway 107 South, Cashiers, 743-3750, quaint 1892 building, sandwiches for lunch, gourmet fare for dinner, I–M • *Market Basket,* Highway 107 South, Cashiers, 743-2216, informal lunch and takeout by day, fine dining at night, M–E • *Carolina Smokehouse,* Highway 64 West, Cashiers, 743-3200, best pit barbecue around, I.

SIGHT-SEEING *Bascom-Louise Gallery,* East Main Street (Horse Cove Road), 526-4949. Hours: Tuesday to Saturday 10 A.M. to 4 P.M. Free.

INFORMATION *Highlands Chamber of Commerce,* Town Hall, P.O. Box 404, Highlands, NC 28741, 526-2112; www.highlands-chamber.com • *Cashiers Chamber of Commerce,* P.O. Box 238, Cashiers, NC 28717, 743-5191; www.cashiers-nc.com.

A Golden Glow in Georgia

When the sun casts its glow on the sands and the marshes, it is easy to understand why Georgia's offshore islands have been dubbed "the Golden Isles."

Located about an hour south of Savannah, these beautiful barrier islands are a perfect escape, offering sports and beaches galore, set among unspoiled marshes and woodlands of moss-hung live oaks, pines, and palmettos.

But there is a lure here beyond recreation, a special mystique from the golden glow and dreamy feel imparted by the ever-present marshes and the romance of the past. Jekyll and St. Simons, the two most visited islands, have equal charm but very distinct personalities shaped by their histories. Whichever you choose, make time to visit the other.

Jekyll Island was once the very private province of some of America's most prominent families. For many years this remained plantation country, with Sea Island cotton as the major crop. But the Civil War ended the plantation era, and the island's canny owners conceived the idea of selling it as a hunting retreat for wealthy Northerners.

In 1887 the Jekyll Island Club was formed, with a limit of 100 shares of stock. Members purchased the island for the then-exorbitant amount of $125,000. For the next 55 years it was the exclusive domain of millionaires. Families such as the Goulds, Astors, Rockefellers, Morgans, and Pulitzers were among the first to build 20-room summer "cottages," arriving by yacht and taking their meals together in the ornate Victorian clubhouse, where some members also preferred to stay. Their homes were deliberately kept simple, but life was not without its comforts. The club was a Victorian vision with a five-story turreted tower, a gourmet kitchen, a wine cellar, and a croquet lawn. Armies of servants were boated ashore.

In the early years, club activities included hunting, horseback and carriage rides, and picnics. In later years, golf and tennis were added.

Members and their guests not only played here, but made a bit of history. President William McKinley planned his reelection campaign on the island in 1899. In 1910, J. P. Morgan assembled the nabobs of the banking industry for a secret meeting that plotted the Federal Reserve Act. The first transcontinental telephone call was made from Jekyll when Theodore Vail, a Bell executive and later president of AT&T, made simultaneous contact with Woodrow Wilson at the White House, Alexander Graham Bell in New York, and one of Bell's aides in San Francisco.

Although the Depression and World War II took their toll on this way of life, it can still be seen and experienced. In 1946 the state of Georgia took possession of Jekyll Island, connecting it to the rest of the world by a causeway and opening its beaches, woodlands, and marshes as a tranquil refuge for all. The grand Victorian clubhouse has been restored to the tune of $20 million as the Jekyll Island Club Hotel, and you can still play indoor tennis on the court that J. P. Morgan built for himself in 1929.

The entire 240-acre Jekyll Island Club preserve has been declared a National Historic Landmark. The Jekyll Island Museum, which maintains 25 of the original buildings, offers trolley tours of the complex, as well as visits inside the remaining grand cottages and Faith Chapel, the small church that was adorned with two stained-glass windows by Louis Comfort Tiffany. Goodyear Cottage includes a gallery of Southern art and a museum shop.

The guest rooms at the Jekyll Island Club are beautifully furnished in reproduction antiques, and some rooms have fireplaces and balconies. Those who prefer to be on the beach will find a lineup of hotel-motels along the 10-mile strand at the other side of the island. Things are much livelier here, with such child-pleasing diversions as miniature golf, a water park with a wave pool, and a soccer complex.

The first golf course, constructed in 1898, now has company. With 63 holes of golf, Jekyll Island is Georgia's largest public golf resort. The Oleander course, known for its bunkers, is the toughest. Also available are a 13-court tennis complex and a fitness center. Where millionaires' yachts used to dock, you can now board boats for deep-sea fishing or scuba diving.

Not to worry, however, if you want to get away from all this activity. Since only one-third of the island is allowed to be developed, much of the center remains pristine, reserved for quiet outings on the 20 miles of biking and walking paths that meander among twisted live oaks trailing wispy scarves of moss.

St. Simons Island, with its charming Colonial village, is becoming a popular art colony and upscale retirement haven as well as a resort town. Although it is more built up than Jekyll Island, it still has managed to retain open spaces and its own romantic history.

It was in 1736 that 4,477 men and 72 women and children arrived from Savannah to build a fort to protect the new colony of Georgia. Known as Fort Frederica, it was here that Spanish invaders from Florida were ousted for good at the Battle of Bloody Marsh in 1742. The fort is now maintained by the National Park Service, and the foundations of many of the original dwellings have been excavated.

Lovely Christ Church, erected in 1886 to replace an earlier structure destroyed by British troops, housed the congregation originally founded by John and Charles Wesley, Anglican missionaries who came to Georgia with Governor Oglethorpe and subsequently returned to England to found the Methodist Church. Christ Church was built by the Reverend Anson G. P. Dodge Jr. as a memorial to his wife, Ellen, who died during their honeymoon trip. Their tale is one of the romantic St. Simons Island legends retold in the books of the late novelist Eugenia Price, who lived on the island.

Wandering around town, shoppers will find treasures in the boutiques and galleries along Frederica Road and in the village. At the end of Mallery Street in the village are a fishing pier and a waterfront park, pleasant places to linger. It is exactly 129 steps to the top of the nearby 1872 lighthouse, a climb that yields sweeping views of the islands. This lighthouse replaced one of America's oldest, destroyed by Union troops in the Civil War. The old lightkeeper's cottage now houses the Museum of Coastal History.

St. Simons Island has many championship golf courses, including some on the grounds of former plantations, with picturesque ruins as unexpected hazards. Sea Palms Golf and Tennis Resort offers access to 37 holes of golf and 12 tennis courts, and guests have beach access to the Beach Club on the island. The King and Prince Beach Resort is for those who prefer to be directly on the water. Guests here have privileges at the Hampton Club golf course.

Two of the best courses are among the famed 54 holes of golf that belong to The Cloister, the well-known resort located on Sea Island, across a causeway from St. Simons Island. Developed in the 1920s, The Cloister remains a genteel world apart, a moss-draped Spanish-style retreat with the best of everything. It is one of the most outstanding resorts in the South.

Many miles of St. Simons Island's beaches are open to the public. The surrounding wetlands that inspired poet Sidney Lanier to write about "The Marshes of Glynn" in the 1870s remain untouched. Guided nature walks and salt-marsh boat tours are available.

The marshes are protected by law because of their ecological importance as a buffer preventing erosion, as a nesting ground for all manner of seabirds, and as a rich spawning ground for the delicious shrimp found on island menus.

For those who can afford the tab, Little St. Simons Island, reached via a short boat ride from St. Simons Island, is a fabulous, very private getaway. Read more about it on page 280.

One of the best excursions from the Golden Isles is a trip to the deep, dark, and mysterious waters of Okefenokee Swamp. The closest gateway is the less-visited east entrance to the Wildlife Refuge at Folkston. Facilities here include hiking trails for swamp viewing, a wildlife drive, a 50-foot observation tower overlooking the Okefenokee, and a 4,000-

foot boardwalk into the swamp. The best fun is actually getting out on the water. Suwannee Canal Recreational Concession offers rental canoes or guided boat trips for gliding among the cypress trees, a wonderful chance to pay your respects to the gators lazing in the sun or floating along like logs with gleaming eyes. You'll also get close-up views of the open "prairies" dotted with floating vegetation so massed it almost seems solid. Great blue herons and other magnificent birds love these habitats; bring your binoculars and a camera and be forewarned—no matter how much film you bring, it probably won't be enough.

Area Code: 912

DRIVING DIRECTIONS   St. Simons Island, Sea Island, and Jekyll Island are situated off Georgia's southeast Atlantic coast. From north or south, they can be reached via US 17, the Golden Isles Parkway, off I-95, or drivers coming from Savannah can follow the more scenic US 17 all the way, 70 miles. From Atlanta, follow I-75 south to Macon, then I-16 east toward Savannah and I-95 south to Brunswick. Signs point the way to Jekyll Island and St. Simons Island, about 300 miles.

PUBLIC TRANSPORTATION   The closest airports are Savannah, about 75 miles north, and Jacksonville, Florida, 65 miles south, and there is a connector service to Brunswick.

ACCOMMODATIONS   **Jekyll Island:** *Jekyll Island Club Hotel,* 371 Riverview Drive, 31527, 635-2600 or (800) 535-9547, M–EE • *Clarion Resort Buccaneer,* 85 South Beachview Drive, 31527, 635-2261 or (800) 253-5955, oceanfront, M–EE • *Comfort Inn Island Suites,* 711 North Beachview Drive, 31527, 635-2211 or (800) 204-0202, M–E • *Villas by the Sea,* 1175 North Beachview Drive, 31527, 635-2521 or (800) 841-6262, condominium hotel with 1- to 3-bedroom apartments, M–EE.

St. Simons Island: *Sea Palms Golf & Tennis Resort,* 5445 Frederica Road, 31522, 638-3351 or (800) 841-6268, rooms and condos, M–EE • *The King and Prince Beach Resort,* 201 Arnold Road, 31522, 638-3631 or (800) 342-0212, M–EE • *Sea Gate Inn,* 1014 Ocean Boulevard, 31522, 638-8661 or (800) 562-8812, motel with waterfront section, I–E • *Hampton Inn,* 2204 Demere Road, 634-2204 or (800) HAMPTON, pool, M • *Days Inn,* 411 Longview Plaza, Frederica Road, 31522, 634-0660 or (800) 870-3736, good value, I–M, CP.

Sea Island: *The Cloister,* 31561, 368-3611 or (800) SEA-ISLAND, EE, AP.

Little St. Simons Island: *The Lodge on Little St. Simons Island,* P.O. Box 21078, 31522, 638-7472 or (888) 733-5774, EE, AP.

DINING   Jekyll Island: *Grand Dining Room,* Jekyll Island Club (see Accommodations on page 132), wonderful setting, good food, M –EE • *Blackbeard's,* 200 North Beachview Drive, 635-3522, seafood, ocean views, outdoor dining, I–M • *Latitude 31,* 1 Pier Road, 635-2531, seafood is the specialty, outdoor dining on the pier, I–M.

St. Simons Island: *Blanche's Courtyard,* 440 Kings Way, 638-3030, Victoriana and gaslights, M • *J. Mac's Island Restaurant and Jazz Bar,* 407 Mallery Street, 634-0403, bistro ambience, fine seafood, crab cakes, M–EE • *Crab Trap,* 1209 Ocean Boulevard, 638-2047, very informal, I–M • *Frederica House,* 3611 Frederica Road, 638-6789, family dining, lots of seafood, I–M.

Sea Island: *The Cloister* (see Accommodations on page 132), elegant, jackets required, EE prix fixe.

SIGHT-SEEING *Jekyll Island Historic District Tours,* from Museum Orientation Center, Stable Road, 635-2762. Hours: Daily tours on the hour, 10 A.M. to 3 P.M. $$$$ • *Fort Frederica National Monument,* Frederica Road, St. Simons Island, 638-3639. Hours: Daily 9 A.M. to 5 P.M. $ • *Christ Church,* off Frederica Road near the fort, St. Simons Island, 638-8683. Hours: Daily 2 to 5 P.M.; Donation • *St. Simons Island Lighthouse Museum,* 101 12th Street, St. Simons, 638-4666. Hours: Monday to Saturday 10 A.M. to 5 P.M.; Sunday from 1:30 P.M. $$ • *Okefenokee National Wildlife Refuge,* east entrance, Route 121, 8 miles south of Folkston, 496-7836. $$$$. *Suwannee Canal Recreational Concession, Inc.,* 496-3331. Guided boat tours in Okefenokee, 30, 60, and 120 minutes, combined ticket with refuge entrance fee, $$$$$. Also canoe and bicycle rentals.

ACTIVITIES *Summer Waves Water Park,* 210 South Riverview Drive, Jekyll Island, 635-2074. Hours: Late May to early September, Sunday to Thursday 10 A.M. to 6 P.M., Friday and Saturday to 8 P.M.; July, Saturdays to 9 P.M. $$$ • **Sailboats:** *Barry's Beach Service,* St. Simons, 638-8053; *Weadore Sailing,* Jekyll Island, 223-4419 • **Kayak tours/rentals:** *Jekyll Wharf Marina,* 635-3152; *Ocean Motion Surf Company,* St. Simons, 638-5226; *Southeast Adventure Outfitters,* St. Simons Island, 638-6732 • **Deep Sea Fishing:** Many options; contact the Visitors Bureau for a full list.

NATURE ACTIVITIES *Jekyll Island Nature Walks:* held year-round, led by docents of the University of Georgia Marine Extension

Service; phone 635-9102 for current schedules • *Marsh Hen Boat Tours,* St. Simons Island, 638-9354, birding, shelling, and marsh excursions • *Coastal Encounters,* Jekyll Island, 635-9102, marine science programs including kayaking, marsh, beach, and maritime forest studies, birding trips.

INFORMATION *Brunswick & The Golden Isles Visitors Bureau,* 4 Glynn Avenue, Brunswick, GA 31520, 265-0620 or (800) 933-2627; www.bgivb.com • *Jekyll Island Welcome Center,* 45 South Beachview Drive, Jekyll Island, GA 31527, 635-3636 or (800) 841-6586 • *St. Simons Island Visitors Center,* 530B Beachview Drive, St. Simons Island, GA 31522, 638-9014.

Fall

Overleaf: Price Lake, near Blowing Rock. Photo courtesy of North Carolina Travel and Tourism Div.

Lolling About the Low Country

If you arrive in the low country for the first time and somehow feel you've been there before, that's not unusual. Beaufort, South Carolina, is familiar to anyone who has seen the movies filmed here, such as *The Big Chill, Forrest Gump,* or Pat Conroy's *The Great Santini* and *The Prince of Tides.* The small town where Pat Conroy grew up and taught is quintessential low country—ancient oaks overhung with moss, a river meandering by, inlets and boats everywhere.

Though it is tranquil today, Beaufort (pronounced "Bew-fort") has had an active history. Seven flags have flown there since the first Spanish explorers came in 1520. The town was officially founded in 1711, and by the nineteenth century was described as the queen of the Sea Islands, the wealthiest, most aristocratic and cultivated city of its size in America. The streets are lined with the gracious homes once occupied by plantation owners who grew rich growing indigo, Sea Island cotton, and rice, and built fine residences in town with wraparound porches and wide balconies facing the river.

The town endured four years of Northern occupation during the Civil War, but while many homes were confiscated, few were destroyed. Prosperity returned in this century. The United States Marine base at Parris Island was established nearby during World War I, and in 1958 a major shipping terminal was opened. Tourists began coming as early as the 1960s, and the movies still being filmed here have greatly increased their numbers.

There's very good reason to come. The whole center of Beaufort is a historic district, still looking much as it did in the nineteenth century. There are 90 historic homes and buildings, some dating from the early 1700s beneath shady, towering, moss-hung oak trees.

Check into one of the fine homes now serving as an inn and take a stroll. Guided walking tours are offered, as well as tours by bus, by boat, and in horse-drawn carriages, which seem right at home on Beaufort's streets. But the town is small, and it's easy enough to wander on your own, at a slow pace in keeping with the languid aura of the town and allowing the time to admire the homes and gardens. Walking tour leaflets are available at the visitor center.

Bay is the main street, running parallel to the Intracoastal Waterway and rimmed by a seven-acre waterfront park. Several local restaurants open to the park and face the waterway, which runs into the Beaufort River.

They treasure tradition there even in cuisine, which features traditional low-country specialties such as she-crab soup, shrimp and grits, oyster stew, and red rice. One of the lovely local inns, the Beaufort Inn, is among the prime places to sample the best local fare.

You'll find some intriguing small shops on Bay Street, along with some of the town's numerous antiques shops. More antiques are found on the 900 block of Port Republic Street, and a printed guide to all the shops is available in many shops or at the visitor center.

The Federal-style John Mark Verdier House on Bay Street gives a glimpse of gracious low-country living in the early days. Built by a wealthy merchant in 1790, it has been restored and furnished in keeping with that period and is open to the public. The Marquis de Lafayette was entertained there in 1825. Less welcome were the Union forces who occupied the home from 1861 to 1865.

Continue right to the end of Bay Street, turn left on New Street, and you'll come to the 1717 Thomas Hepworth House, the oldest in town. Go right on Craven, left on East, and right again on Federal to Pinckney Street and the Old Point section, facing the river.

The finest homes are on the Point, on Pinckney, Hancock, and Short Streets. Tidalholm, at the very end of Hancock, is the house that was featured in both *The Big Chill* and *The Great Santini*. Built in 1850 by James Fripp, it was one of the many homes sold at auction by the federal government during the 1860s. In this case, the house was bought by a sympathetic Frenchman who returned it to the Fripp family.

One of the oldest homes is the 1720 Hext House, known as Riverview, on Pinckney between Hancock and Baynard.

These are private homes, but if you plan your visit for mid-October, when the Historic Beaufort Foundation sponsors its Fall Tour of Homes and Plantations, you'll be able to go inside for an intriguing look at the hospitality of today and yesterday.

Come back toward the water on Carteret Street, and at the corner of Craven Street you'll see the Arsenal. Built of brick and tabby (a type of cement that contains oyster shells) in 1795 and rebuilt in 1852, it housed the Beaufort Volunteer Artillery, one of the oldest military units in America. It is now a museum whose exhibits are donated or loaned by local citizens. They cover a wide range, from Indian arrowheads and tools to costumes of the 1800s and Civil War weapons.

At the corner of Craven and Church Streets is the Milton Maxey House, known as "Secession House," built around 1813 on a tabby foundation dating from 1724. It belonged to the prominent Rhett family, and it was there that the first Ordinance of Secession, taking South Carolina out of the Union, was drawn up.

Turn right on Church to St. Helena Episcopal Church, dating from 1724. This was a Civil War hospital, and churchyard gravestones were brought inside to be used as operating tables. Docents are usually on hand Monday to Friday for tours or questions.

Owing to the large number of war casualties, Abraham Lincoln established a national cemetery outside Beaufort in 1863 as a resting place for Union soldiers. Located on US 21, it includes the graves of 9,000 Union soldiers and 122 Confederates.

Turn left on King Street for three blocks, then left on Monson, and left again toward the water to see a final cluster of fine early homes at the other end of Bay Street. These include the 1785 Edward Barnwell House, used as Union headquarters; the 1811 James Joyner Smith House, the residence used by the Union's commanding general; Leverett House, a pre-Revolutionary home moved to this location from St. Helena Island around 1850; the 1786 Thomas Fuller House, also known as Tabby Manse; and the William Elliott House, called the Anchorage, another pre-Revolutionary home now extensively remodeled as a restaurant.

Beaufort is located on Port Royal Island and is surrounded by dozens of other islands, large and small. One of the best ways to see them is by boat on the Beaufort River. You'll also get a sense of the terrain when you drive on US 21, known as Sea Island Parkway, across the bridge to Lady's Island and past a series of inlets and islets, some so small you hardly know you've gone from one island to another.

Lady's Island is of interest mainly for its seafood restaurants on the water. Next comes St. Helena Island, and fascinating bits of history at Penn Center and Frogmore.

This was plantation country, but the planters of St. Helena abandoned their property and fled inland as Union troops neared. A group of abolitionists inaugurated the Port Royal experiment for the benefit of the 10,000 blacks who remained, providing newly freed slaves with opportunities for education and self-sufficiency. In 1862, two female missionaries from the North established the first local school for black children in a building shipped from Philadelphia that was dubbed the Penn School. The school continued to operate for nearly a century, graduating its last class in 1953. It was then renamed Penn Center and dedicated to a new purpose—to provide services related to health care and community enrichment for the islanders. Martin Luther King Jr. and other black leaders met there to plan their 1963 march on Washington and their 1965 march in Selma, Alabama. It is now a national historic landmark.

You can see the original buildings as well as the brick church just across the road, built in 1855, with steep stairs to a balcony where slaves were relegated. The church became the spiritual center for the Penn School and is still in use. The York W. Bailey Museum has an exhibit on the unique native black history and culture of the area. It was named for a Penn School student who became the first African-American to practice medicine on St. Helena.

In these communities, where boats were the only means of transportation in early days, residents remained isolated, and many old traditions are preserved. The Gullah dialect, spoken by slaves from Africa, can be heard today among their descendants. Old superstitions, such as buying charms and amulets from witch doctors to ward off evil spirits, also remain.

Traditionally the center of black magic was Frogmore, the tiny community on US 21 just past the turnoff to Penn Center. This was the home turf of Dr. Buzzard, the king of the witch doctors. Frogmore also has its own famous dish, Frogmore stew, an old island recipe combining sausage, shrimp, potatoes, and corn boiled in beer. Visitors come to hear Gullah spoken, to sample the stew—and, who knows, maybe to banish hexes. The Gullah Festival, usually held around Memorial Day weekend in Beaufort, celebrates the old heritage with crafts, dancing, singing, storytelling, and games. November brings an annual heritage festival at the Penn Center.

If you are intrigued with St. Helena, you can sign on for a Gullah-N-Geechie Mahn tour of the area conducted by Gullah-speaking guides.

Beyond St. Helena, a bridge leads to Hunting Island, the largest of a group of islands that once were hunting preserves for wealthy planters. The island is now a state park, with a lighthouse whose steep spiral stairs lead to a dazzling view. The park offers wildlife "browsing areas" for spotting animals, boardwalks over the salt marshes, and four miles of beach.

Across the next bridge is Fripp Island, now entirely a privately owned resort, where homes and villas can be rented to enjoy the uncrowded beach, golf course, and tennis courts.

Returning on US 21, make a left turn onto South Carolina Route 802 across the McTeer Memorial Bridge and you're on the way to Parris Island, the base where recruits are toughened into U.S. Marines. Some 20,000 men and 2,000 women complete their rigorous training there each year. Curious visitors arrive at the rate of 100,000 a year, and they are welcome; just ask at the gate to be directed to the visitors' center. If you come on Friday morning, you can see the weekly raising of the colors and recruit graduation.

If you are expecting a stark boot camp, think again. Like most of the low-country islands, Parris offers history spanning 450 years, natural beauty, water views, and beaches. When complimented on the beauty of the island, however, the marine on duty at the visitors' center smiled and said, "Yeah, visitors call it paradise. We call it hell."

The reason becomes clear when you see the recruits drilling on the parade grounds or tackling the "confidence course," a formidable obstacle course of logs, cables, pipe, and rope that makes for a supreme test of coordination and endurance. The most challenging of the 11 obstacles are known as the "dirty name" and the "slide for life."

The printed driving tour, available at the gate, leads to all the major sights on a 15-mile loop past historic buildings, barracks, training grounds, and the section where women have been quartered since becoming part of the corps in 1949. Down the palmetto-lined main road are two famous statues. "Iron Mike," erected in 1924 to honor marines who lost their lives in World War I, has become the symbol of the marines. A replica of the Iwo Jima Monument in Arlington, Virginia, commemorates the heroic flag-raising on Mount Suribachi in 1945. It is an enduring symbol of the U.S. victory in World War II.

In the Parris Island Museum are displays on island and Marine Corps history, vintage Marine Corps uniforms and weapons, and a display explaining the training process, including a model of the infamous confidence course.

Despite the trials they may have endured here, many ex-marines return to retire in the low country. That's not really too surprising. This is an area that is hard to resist.

Area Code: 843

DRIVING DIRECTIONS Beaufort is between Charleston and Hilton Head, a short drive off I-95. It is 266 miles from Atlanta, 262 miles from Charlotte. Approaching on I-95 from the north, take exit 8 and South Carolina Route 170; from the south, take exit 33 and US 21. US 17 is the scenic route from Charleston, 69 miles; South Carolina Route 70 leads to Hilton Head, 43 miles.

ACCOMMODATIONS *Rhett House,* 1009 Craven Street, Beaufort, 29901, 524-9030 or (888) 480-9530, elegant antebellum home, antiques, gardens, best in town, E, CP • *Beaufort Inn,* 809 Port Republic Street, Beaufort, 29902, 521-9000, 1907 Victorian, attractively furnished rooms, M–E, CP • *Two Suns Inn,* 1705 Bay Street, Beaufort, 29901, 522-1122 or (800) 532-4244, comfortable inn in a 1912 home, M–E, CP • *Old Point Inn,* 212 New Street, Beaufort, 29901, 524-3177, an 1898 Victorian in a historic district, I–M, CP • *Cuthbert House,* 1203 Bay Street, Beaufort, 29902, 521-1315 or (800) 327-9275, restored 1790 home on the National Register, fine river views, spacious suites, E–EE, CP • *Hunting Island State Park,* 1775 Sea Island Parkway, St. Helena, 19920, 838-2011, rustic cabins, some with fireplaces, some oceanfront, I–M.

DINING *Beaufort Inn* (see Accommodations above), excellent, eclectic menu, best in town, M–E • *Bistro de Jong,* 205 West Street, Beaufort, 524-4994, modern Southern cuisine in pleasant atmosphere, M • *The Bank Waterfront Grill,* 926 Bay Street, Beaufort, 522-8831, in the old bank, casual, I–M • *Ultimate Eating,* 761 Sea Island Parkway, Beaufort, 838-1314, the place to sample traditional low-country dishes, I–M • *Emily's Restaurant and Tapas Bar,* 906 Port Republic Street, Beaufort, 522-1866, classic menu, E, and wide selection of tapas, each $ • *Plum's,* 904½ Bay Street, Beaufort, 525-1946, informal, porch facing the river, excellent sandwiches for lunch, I; eclectic international menu for dinner, M • *Whitehall Plantation Inn,* Whitehall Drive,

Lady's Island (just across the bridge from Beaufort), 521-1700, early plantation house on the water, great sunset-watching, M–E • *Pelican's Perch,* 1413 Sea Island Parkway, Beaufort, 838-5936, informal place for seafood, I–M • *11th Street Dockside,* 11th Street West, Port Royal, 524-7433, fresh seafood at the shrimp boat docks, I–E.

SIGHT-SEEING *Fall Tour of Homes,* annual weekend in October. Information from Historic Beaufort Foundation, P.O. Box 11, Beaufort, 29901, 524-6334 • *Beaufort Museum (The Arsenal),* 713 Craven Street, 525-7471. Hours: Daily, except Wednesday and Sunday, 10 A.M. to 5 P.M. $ • *John Mark Verdier House,* 801 Bay Street, Beaufort, 524-6334. Hours: Tuesday to Saturday 11 A.M. to 4 P.M. $$ • *St. Helena's Episcopal Church,* Church and North Streets, Beaufort, 522-1712. Hours: Monday to Friday 10 A.M. to 4 P.M. Donation • *Penn Center, York W. Bailey Museum,* Martin Luther King Jr. Drive, St. Helena Island, 838-2432. Hours: Monday to Friday 10 A.M. to 4 P.M. $ • *Hunting Island State Park,* 1775 Sea Island Parkway, St. Helena Island, 838-2011. Hours: Daily 6 A.M. to 9 P.M. Parking fee, $$ • *Parris Island Marine Corps Recruit Depot,* off South Carolina Route 802; visitors' center, 525-3659; museum, 525-2951; bus tour information, 525-3650. Hours: Daily 10 A.M. to 4:30 P.M. Free.

Tours: Check for current hours and rates: *Spirit of Old Beaufort Walking Tours,* 103 West Street Extension, 525-0459; *Carriage and Van Tours:* Several leave from the Visitor Center; *Gullah-N-Geechie Mahn Tour,* St. Helena Island, 838-7516; *Islander,* 524-4000, 1¾-hour tour of Beaufort River from downtown Marina; *ACE Nature tours,* One Coosaw River Avenue, Beaufort, 521-3099, pontoon boat tours into marshes and around islands to see marine and shore birds, alligators, dolphins.

INFORMATION *Greater Beaufort Chamber of Commerce and Visitor Center,* 1106 Carteret Street, P.O. Box 910, Beaufort, SC 29901, 524-3163 or (800) 638-3525; www.beaufortsc.org.; www. southcarolinalowcountry.com.

On the Peaceful Side of the Smokies

For those who love the beauty of the Smokies but not the crowds and commercialism, Townsend, Tennessee, is a tonic. Though it is one of the three main entrances to Great Smoky Mountains National Park, this town, population under 350, is anything but touristy—no wall-to-wall gift shops, no chain restaurants, nary a discount outlet.

One reason that Townsend has escaped buildup is that the gateway there doesn't lead into the heavily trafficked main park road. So Townsend makes it easy enough to get to the park for a visit but is convenient to beautiful areas that many visitors miss—for example, the 4,000-acre, mountain-rimmed valley called Cades Cove and the Little River Gorge. You can also find scenic drives and hiking trails guaranteed to be traffic-free even at the height of fall color season.

US 321, the main artery through Townsend, links with heavily wooded Scenic Highway 73 into the park. Bear right at the intersection and you'll soon spy the green meadows of Cades Cove. In early Appalachian days, *cove* was another word for *valley,* and this one is ringed by surrounding mountains.

This was frontier country in 1820, when it was acquired by the state of Tennessee from the Cherokee Indians. In 1850, the population of settlers peaked at 685, comprising 137 families, each an almost self-contained economic unit.

The population began to dwindle as families eventually moved farther west in search of newer and more fertile frontiers. Many members of the community moved out when the national park was established in the late 1920s, leaving their homes, churches, and mill behind.

The 11-mile driving tour of the cove on a one-way loop shows the original lifestyle in the valley. The historic structures include a working gristmill, a variety of barns, three churches, and a wonderful collection of log homes. There are 17 stops on the driving loop; only the visitors' center and blacksmith shop are not historic structures. All the other buildings were assembled there after removal from other places in the park.

The Gregg-Cable House, built in 1879, may have been the first frame house in the community. It served as a store, boardinghouse, and private residence, and remained in the family until Aunt Becky Cable died in 1940.

The cantilever barn, a building style that originated centuries ago in Europe, was used frequently in eastern Tennessee. The loft could hold several tons of hay, and the large overhead protected many head of cattle plus farm equipment. There were no posts to get in the way.

Half-hour walking tours of the historic community are given by park rangers, and there are living-history demonstrations at the gristmill area. Special programs at the homes and churches tell about how the first settlers lived and worshipped.

Cades Cove makes for an excellent bicycle tour, with time to savor the scenery, and bike rentals are available in the park. Horseback riding is offered from the Cades Cove Riding Stables, which also gives hayrides in the Cove in season.

The favorite hike from the Loop Road is to Abrams Falls, one of the largest waterfalls in the park, reached via a moderate five-mile round-trip trek.

For trails outside the park in the Townsend area, ask for the hiking brochure at the town's visitors' center. The center also offers a guide to bicycle trails, both in and out of the park.

If you turn left instead of right at the junction near the park entrance, you will be taking a scenic drive along the Little River Gorge and looking upstream at the rapids. The gorge road was constructed on the bed of railroad tracks once used in the logging operations that built the town of Townsend early in this century. It takes about 45 minutes from Townsend along this road to reach the Sugarlands Visitor Center, south of Gatlinburg.

Along the way you will see Indian Head, also known as Great Stone Face, a large rock overhanging the highway that seems to have been carved by some celestial sculptor into the likeness of the face of an Indian. Meigs Falls is also visible from the highway, across from the spot where Meigs Creek empties into the river. Take a break to see Laurel Falls, one of the most visited in the park, reached via an easy, paved 1.25-mile walk.

East of Fighting Gap Creek, watch for Maloney Point and an excellent view of the Sugarlands Valley and 6,593-foot Mount LeConte, the highest peak in Tennessee.

Past the Sugarlands Visitor Center, Little River Road feeds into the Roaring Fork Motor Nature Trail, a pleasant, albeit steep and curvy, drive through five miles of young forest and past aging pioneer structures. You can pick up a self-guiding booklet at the road entrance. Much of the drive follows the rapid descent of the creek. Water cascades down the moss-covered rocks in a noisy froth that tells you why the falls were named "roaring."

From there you can turn north on US 441 to check out the shops in Gatlinburg, or join the rest of the leaf-lookers on Newfound Gap Road, the main park road.

If you prefer more private drives to admire the foliage, there are two prime routes off the Cades Cove Loop Road. About a third of the way along the 11-mile loop, a sharp right turn takes you onto Rich Mountain Road, a well-maintained, one-way gravel road. It presents panoramic views of Cades Cove and is a favorite spot for photographers. If you are energetic, it is a moderate 8.5-mile round-trip hike to the top and back.

The road leads to the Dry Valley area near Tuckaleechee Caverns, and to US 321 in Townsend. Take a break underground to visit the cavern, a mile-long walk along an underground stream with lots of stalactites and stalagmites in eerie shapes on all sides.

A longer detour from the Loop Road is the right turn just past the Cable Mill area to Parsons Branch Road, another gravel road, which follows the Little Tennessee River on its route to the North Carolina state line. You'll have a close-up view of the trees in their autumn finery on the way to Calderwood Lake and Dam, where there are fine vistas of Shuckstack, a 4,000-foot peak at the southern end of the park. The road descends to US 129, where a right turn takes you to the Chilhowee Dam and Lake, with easy access for fishing and boating.

Highway 129 continues across the mouth of Abrams Creek—at 857 feet, the lowest point in Great Smoky Mountains National Park.

To complete your foliage route, at Chilhowee, turn right again to the Foothills Parkway. Eventually this parkway will stretch for 72 miles north, ending at I-40, and will offer dramatic Smokies vistas. The plan for the parkway, approved by Congress in 1944, has been slow to be realized, but the 17-mile section from US 129 to US 321 at Walland is complete, and it is noted for its autumn views.

When you turn right, back to Townsend, on US 321 at Walland, you are at the turnoff to West Millers Cove Road and the most elegant lodging on the Tennessee side of the Smokies, Blackberry Farm. It is hard to imagine a more scenic view than the ridges of the mountains seen across the green lawns from the inn's terrace. The rambling stone-and-shingle house is on 1,100 secluded acres offering mountain trails and trout streams to please hikers, joggers, cyclists, and anglers. Tennis, swimming, and lawn games complete the picture.

The inn's sitting room has the ambience of an English country house, and the 25 guest rooms are decorated with rich English florals and antiques. Rates include three sumptuous meals.

If you prefer something a bit more modest, there's an equally delightful choice high on a ridge in Townsend, with equally spectacular views of Rich Mountain. The Richmont Inn is built in the shape of a classic cantilever barn and is furnished simply and tastefully, with an appreciation of the area and its history. Each room is named for a prominent Appalachian settler and is decorated appropriately. Most have fireplaces, some have spa tubs, and several offer private balconies for savoring the view. The inn offers many packages.

Richmont's Cove Cafe serves one of the best and most unusual dinner choices in Townsend, a Swiss fondue dinner featuring a cheese fondue appetizer, salad, steak, shrimp-and-chicken fondue entree, and fruit dipped in Swiss dark chocolate for dessert.

The inn is in the Laurel Valley Vacation Home Development, which includes a golf course with lovely views. Homes and condos may be rented in the development for a weekend or a week. At the top of the hill is a restaurant with its own view. Townsend dining reflects the town—no frills, but plenty of variety.

An excellent option for families is Pioneer Cabins and Guest Farm, vacation log cabins with full kitchens, set on 41 secluded acres. The grounds include a pond for fishing and boating, hiking trails, a petting farm, and a pick-it-yourself vegetable garden.

There are many other cabin colonies in the area, and particularly pleasant motels in town, with lovely garden landscaping. In fact, Townsend offers everything you might expect for a fall mountain outing—except the crowds.

Area Code: 865

DRIVING DIRECTIONS   Townsend is located on US 321, about 32 miles south of Knoxville. From I-40 at Knoxville, take US 441 south to US 321. From southern points, Townsend can be reached on a scenic route via US 411 to US 129 to US 321 south, or by taking I-75 past Chattanooga to the Lenoir City exit to US 321 south. It is 213 miles from Atlanta, 197 miles from Nashville.

PUBLIC TRANSPORTATION   Townsend is about a 45-minute drive from Knoxville's McGee Tyson Airport.

ACCOMMODATIONS   *Blackberry Farm,* 1471 West Millers Cove, Walland, 37886, 380-2260 or (800) 862-7610, EE, AP • *Richmont Inn,* 220 Winterberry Lane, Townsend, 37882, 448-6751, M–E, CP • *Best Western Valley View Lodge,* Highway 321, P.O. Box 148, Townsend, 37882, 448-2237 or (800) 292-4844, motel, I • *Highland Manor Motel,* Highway 321, P.O. Box 242, Townsend, 37882, 448-2211 or (800) 213-9462, I–M, CP • *Pioneer Cabins and Guest Farm,* 253 Boat Gunnel Road, P.O. Box 207, Townsend, 37882, 448-6100 or (800) 621-9751, M • *Laurel Valley Rentals,* c/o White Oak Realty, P.O. Box 247, Townsend, 37882, 448-6697 or (877) 448-2040, private homes, villas, cabins, one to five bedrooms, M–EE. There are many additional cabin and cottage rentals; contact chamber of commerce for complete list.

DINING   Cove Cafe, Richmont Inn (see Accommodations above), featuring Swiss fondue dinners, reservations required, E for full dinner • *Laurel Valley Restaurant,* Laurel Valley Resort, 448-9534, informal ambience, lovely setting and views, M • *Carriage House,* 8310 State Highway 73, Townsend, 448-2263, country cooking, I–M • *Hearth and Kettle,* Highway 321, Townsend, 448-6059, more country cooking, I • *Timbers,* 8123 Lamar Alexander Parkway (US 321), 448-6838, prime ribs are the specialty, I–M.

SIGHT-SEEING *Great Smoky Mountains National Park,* 107 Park Headquarters Road, Gatlinburg, 436-1200. Hours: Cades Cove Visitor Center, in summer, daily 9 A.M. to 7 P.M.; to 6 P.M. in spring and fall; rest of year, 8:30 A.M. to 4:30 P.M. Hours may vary, so it's best to check. Free • *Tuckaleechee Caverns,* off US 321, Townsend, 448-2274. Hours: April 1 to October 31, daily 9 A.M. to 6 P.M.; late March and early November, 10 A.M. to 5 P.M.; closed rest of year. $$$$.

SPORTS **Bicycle rentals:** *Cades Cove Bike Shop,* Cades Cove, 448-9034 • **Golf:** *Laurel Valley Golf Course,* 720 Country Club Drive, 448-6690, phone for fees and tee times • **Horseback riding and hayrides:** *Cades Cove Stables,* 4035 Lamar Alexander Parkway, Townsend, 448-6286; *Davy Crockett Riding Stables,* Highway 73, Townsend, 448-6411.

INFORMATION *Smoky Mountain Visitors Bureau,* c/o Townsend Visitors Center, 7906 East Lamar Alexander Parkway (US 321), Townsend, TN 37882, 448-6134; www.smokymountains.org.

Making History in Georgia

The peaceful villages and rural farmland in southwestern Georgia don't seem to be places where historic events would take place—but sometimes looks are deceiving.

Andersonville, just a dot on the map, became the site of the most notorious Confederate prison of the Civil War era, a place where more than 12,000 Union prisoners perished.

Plains is a town to restore your faith in the American dream. Who could have predicted that this isolated hamlet, population 650, would have produced the first president to come from the South since the Civil War? Or that it would become a tourist attraction that draws thousands of visitors each year?

Near the little town of Lumpkin, the 1850 village of Westville, a remarkably realistic re-creation of a nineteenth-century village, is unique in Georgia. Much of the town's charm is lively history that will keep you entertained as you learn.

While you're in the neighborhood, you can take a look at Providence Canyon, Georgia's own wondrous "Little Grand Canyon." And you might wind things up in Columbus, a city that has nicely preserved its past.

The proper headquarters for your historic weekend is the lavishly restored 1892 Windsor Hotel in Americus, less than ten miles from Plains to the southwest and Andersonville to the northeast. If you prefer cozier quarters, there are several bed-and-breakfast inns in town and nearby.

Founded in 1832 as the county seat, Americus prospered both before and after the Civil War from the abundant surrounding cotton fields and from its position as a railroad center. The town has preserved many of the best of its antebellum and turn-of-the-century buildings. Pick up a local driving tour and admire the Victorian homes on Church Street and Rees Park, the earlier structures on Taylor Street, and the mix of periods on Lee and College Streets.

Downtown, a major building boom occurred in the prosperous 1880s and 1890s. The old wooden buildings were replaced with grand brick structures such as the Glover Opera House and the courthouse, with its imposing clock tower.

The queen of them all was the Windsor Hotel, known as the crown jewel of southern Georgia in the days when it hosted elaborate balls. When the Windsor reopened in 1991, with the brick towers and turrets, golden oak woodwork, and soaring atrium lobby as grand as ever, it sparked the further downtown revitalization now taking place.

Jimmy Carter, a young politician from neighboring Plains, got his political start representing Americus and Sumter County in the Georgia legislature. Carter celebrated his seventy-fifth birthday in 1999 at the Rylander Theatre, a 1921 landmark fresh from restoration that is once again home to live entertainment.

The restored Rylander Building is now headquarters for a project Carter has done much to support, Habitat for Humanity International. Dedicated to building homes for the poor, it was founded by a local man, Millard Fuller, who received a Presidential Medal of Freedom for his efforts. The headquarters offers tours of Habitat houses built over the past 20 years, an international village of houses like those built by Habitat overseas, and also a tour of Fuller's former law office—where it all began. If you stop in the gift shop, Our House, your purchase will help to further the organization's work.

When you've had a look around Americus, take the short drive to Andersonville. It is a sobering experience to tour the grounds of what was officially known as Camp Sumter and realize the harsh reality of this place, now a serene field of green. The short slide program at the visitors' center will help you understand what took place there.

Stone columns mark the line once formed by stockade posts at this largest of the Confederate military prisons, built in 1864. During the prison's 14 months of existence, more than 45,000 Union soldiers were crowded into these inadequate stockades, without trees for shade and with no shelter except their own clothing, scraps of tenting, and loose lumber.

Food was scarce for both captors and captured. Thousands died from disease, malnutrition, polluted water, and exposure. Photos of the bone-thin prisoners released at the end of the war remind one of the concentration camp survivors of World War II. The commander of the camp, Henry Wirz, was tried and executed after the war.

The Andersonville National Historic Site, which includes a national cemetery where soldiers from both sides are buried, today serves as a memorial to all Americans ever held as prisoners of war. The museum, the National POW Museum, explains the role of prisoner-of-war camps in history and commemorates the sacrifice of Americans who lost their lives in such camps.

The five-acre town at the terminal where prisoners arrived by train is now known as Andersonville Civil War Village. The old depot has become a welcome center and museum for the village, which includes picnic areas, a restored log church, and a restored pioneer farm area. Civil War buffs will want to investigate the remarkable collection of memorabilia at the Drummer Boy Museum, which is open by appointment only. The Andersonville Guild, the group responsible for much of the restoration, sponsors a historic fair the first full week-end in October, including mock skirmishes between Confederate and Union troops.

If you go back to Americus for the night, the best bet for dinner is the Windsor Hotel's handsome dining room. Or, if you're up for a drive of about 25 miles, head for Lake Blackshear and the Daphne Lodge, specializing in game dishes and good ol' catfish dinners. The biscuits there are famous.

When you make your way to Plains, you'll find a town as unpretentious as its most famous resident. The Jimmy Carter National Historic Site, administered by the National Park Service, is headquartered in the Plains High School, which is both a Welcome Center and a museum of Carter memorabilia. Films trace Carter's rise to national prominence and offer a picture tour of his Plains home. The film tour is narrated by none other than Jimmy and Rosalynn Carter, both attired in blue jeans. The former president sounds like any proud do-it-yourselfer when he points out the shelves and bed he built for his daughter, Amy.

You can buy a self-guided tour booklet or rent a cassette to take you around town to other sites. An important one is the Plains Depot, now a museum of the 1976 campaign. This is where Carter made his home-town headquarters, where he was greeted by crowds of neighbors whenever he came home, no matter what the hour. It was there that he returned after his election as the nation's thirty-ninth president, bringing tears to the eyes of his friends and shedding a few tears himself. Other places on the tour are Carter's boyhood farm, the public housing unit that was Jimmy and Rosalynn's first apartment, and the Plains United Methodist Church, where they were married in 1946.

The present family home is not open to visitors, but anyone is welcome to the Maranatha Baptist Church, where Carter still delivers

Sunday-school lessons at 10 A.M. when he is in town. After the 11 A.M. worship service, the Carters are happy to shake hands with visitors and pose for photos.

Plains is small—you can see everything in less than two hours—but you won't soon forget it.

From Plains, it's about a 26-mile drive to Lumpkin, a pretty little town boasting a classic square. Stop for a look at the Singer Company, Georgia's oldest hardware store, established in 1838 by Johann George Singer, a German immigrant, and still operated by his great-great-grandson. Dr. Hatchett's Drug Store Museum and Soda Fountain, on the square, will serve an old-fashioned milk shake or a cherry Coke along with sandwiches and salads, and you can admire displays of patent medicines, medical equipment, and other drugstore items as they were 100 years ago.

Nearby is Westville, an outdoor museum on 58 acres that re-creates a village straight out of the 1850s. The buildings are authentic, from farmhouse to town house, from church to carriage shelter; they were all brought from nearby areas and reassembled as a town.

The residents in each house or strolling along the unpaved paths of the village wear properly old-fashioned clothing, including ruffled bonnets and broad-brimmed hats to keep off the sun. As you walk around, you'll likely see an elderly craftsman making baskets, hear the clang of the blacksmith's hammer, and smell the gingerbread and biscuits cooking on the stove and in the fireplace.

It's only seven miles west of Lumpkin on Georgia Route 39C to Providence Canyon State Conservation Park, where multicolored layers of soil form Georgia's "Little Grand Canyon." The chasm is vast, the colors are fantastic, and the wild azaleas and wildflowers growing in the protected canyon make for a scene of rare natural beauty. The park provides picnic grounds and three miles of hiking trails if you want to stay awhile.

A fine way to wind up the weekend is to come back east to Lumpkin and take Georgia Route 27/US 280 north about 31 miles to Columbus.

Columbus was a planned city, established in 1828 on the banks of the Chattahoochee River. The home of many mills and the Columbus Iron Works, which manufactured cannons and gunboats during the Civil War, the city has preserved many of its early buildings in a 26-block National Register Historic District, which can be seen in a short, pleasant drive.

For some award-winning examples of preservation, go along the river to see the old iron works, now the striking Convention and Trade Center, and over to Front Avenue, on the edge of the historic district, where an abandoned mill has been converted into a most unusual Hilton hotel.

Ride along Broadway to view the city's attractively restored Victorian homes. Don't miss the Springer Opera House on Tenth Street at

First Avenue, an 1871 beauty that has been restored to its Victorian splendor and is once again presenting plays on its stage. It is now the official state theater of Georgia.

If you have the time, the Historic Columbus Foundation offers guided walking tours of several historic properties. Military buffs may want to make a stop at the Confederate Naval Museum, the only one of its kind, where remains of two warships are on display, or take in the National Infantry Museum at Fort Benning, a march across time with the American infantry from the 1750s to the present.

If children are along, you'll want to look into the Space Science Center sponsored by Coca-Cola at Columbus College. The interactive programs are limited to school groups, but everyone is welcome to view planetarium and laser shows and to visit the observatory for stargazing.

A short visit to the handsome Columbus Museum will tell you more about the development of the entire Chattahoochee valley. The museum's excellent film about the city boasts about the barbecue that is Columbus's pride. Taste a sample at one of the locations of Country's Barbecue, and you'll see why.

Or perhaps you'd rather wind up a weekend of history with another bit of the past, at Bludau's at the 1839 Goetchius House. Thanks to philanthropist J. W. Woodruff (one of the Coca-Cola Woodruffs), the New Orleans–style mansion was saved and moved to a new site in the Lower Broadway Historic District. The elegantly restored interior is now a series of dining rooms with an equally elegant Continental menu.

Area Code: Plains, Americus, Westville, 912; Columbus, 706

DRIVING DIRECTIONS   Americus is at the intersection of US 19 and US 280/Georgia Route 27, about 28 miles west of I-75. From Atlanta, the most direct route is south on US 19, or take I-75 and turn west on US 280, 130 miles. From Americus to Plains, drive 9 miles west on Georgia Route 27; continue on Georgia Route 27 another 26 miles to Lumpkin. From Lumpkin to Columbus, follow US 27/Georgia Route 1 north into US 280 north, 31 miles. Returning from Columbus to Atlanta, take I-185 into I-85 north, 123 miles. Birmingham is 114 miles from Columbus via US 280; it's about another 66 miles to Americus.

ACCOMMODATIONS   *Windsor Hotel,* 125 West Lamar Street, Americus, 31709, 924-1555 or (888) 297-9567, M–E, CP • *1906 Pathway Inn,* 501 South Lee Street, Americus, 31709, 928-2078 or (800) 889-1466, 1906 home in historic district with circular veranda, stained glass, M, CP • *Rees Park Garden Inn,* 504 Reese Park, Americus, 31709, 931-0122, 1847 antebellum home facing a park, I–M, CP • *Cottage Inn,* Highway 40 North, Americus, 31709, 931-0609, antebellum raised cottage, I, CP • *Morris Manor,* 425 Timberlane Drive, Americus,

31709, 924-4884, Georgian Colonial, rural setting, I, CP • *A Place Away Cottage,* 110 Oglethorpe Street, Andersonville, 31711, 924-1044, quaint private cottage, I, CP • *Plains Bed & Breakfast Inn,* 100 West Church Street, Plains, 31780, 824-7252, comfortable modest Victorian home, I, CP • *Historic Columbus Hilton,* 800 Front Avenue, Columbus, 31901, (706) 324-1800, restored nineteenth-century mill, pool, M–E.

DINING *Windsor Hotel Grand Dining Room* (see Accommodations above), M–E • *Forsyth 1889 Bar and Grill,* 124 Forsyth Street, Americus, 924-8193, pine-paneled and hearty family-style food, I • *Sheppard House,* 1610 Vienna Highway, Americus, 924-8756, come for lunch buffet and barbecue, closes at 5:30 P.M., I • *Daphne Lodge,* Highway 280, Lake Blackshear (25 miles east of Americus), 273-2596, country lodge serving quail, rabbit, fried catfish, I–M • *Andersonville Restaurant,* 213 West Church Street, Andersonville, 928-8888, rustic setting for Southern-style buffet lunches and weekend dinners, with peach cobbler for dessert, I.

Columbus: *Bludau's Goetchius House,* 405 Broadway, Columbus, 324-4863, 1839 antebellum mansion, Continental menu, M–E • *Minnie's Uptown Restaurant,* 100 South 8th Street, 322-2766, traditional Southern lunch buffets, open Monday to Friday, I • *Country's Barbecue* (three locations, all with delicious barbecue): 329 Broadway, 596-8910; 313 Mercury Drive, 563-7604; Main Street Village, Hamilton Road at Weems Road, 660-1415, all I.

SIGHT-SEEING *Habitat for Humanity International,* 322 West Lamar Street, Americus, 924-6935 or (800) 422-4828. Hours: Guided tours Monday to Friday 8 A.M., 10 A.M., 1 P.M., 3 P.M., or by appointment. Free • *Andersonville National Historic Site,* Georgia Route 49, Andersonville, 924-0343. Hours: Park, daily 8:30 A.M. to 5 P.M.; *National Prisoner of War Museum,* daily 8:30 A.M. to 5 P.M. Free • *Andersonville Civil War Village,* State Road 49, 924-2558. Hours: Daily 9 A.M. to 5 P.M. Free. *Historic Fair,* c/o Andersonville Guild, P.O. Box 6, Andersonville, 31711, 924-2558. Crafts demonstrations, music, dancing, and mock Civil War battles; held first weekend in October; check for current information • *Jimmy Carter National Historic Site,* headquarters in the old high school, 300 Bond Street, Plains, 824-4104. Hours: Daily 9 A.M. to 5 P.M. Free • *Providence Canyon State Park,* Georgia Route 39C, Lumpkin, 838-6202. Hours: Mid-April to mid-September, daily 7 A.M. to 9 P.M.; rest of year, to 6 P.M.; visitor center, open daily 8 A.M. to 5 P.M. Parking fee, $; free Wednesday • *Westville Village,* Martin Luther King Drive, off Georgia Route 27, Westville, 838-6310. Hours: Tuesday to Saturday 10 A.M. to 5 P.M., Sunday 1 to 5 P.M. $$$$.

Columbus: *Columbus Museum,* 1251 Wynnton Road, 649-0713. Hours: Tuesday to Saturday 10 A.M. to 5 P.M., Sunday 1 to 5 P.M. Free • *Heritage Corner Walking Tours,* Historic Columbus Foundation, 700 Broadway, Columbus, 322-3181. Hours: Tours given Monday to Friday 11 A.M. and 3 P.M., Saturday and Sunday at 2 P.M. $$ • *Woodruff Museum of Civil War and Naval History,* 202 Fourth Victory Drive, Columbus, 327-9798. Hours: Tuesday to Friday 10 A.M. to 5 P.M., Saturday and Sunday 1 to 5 P.M. Donation • *National Infantry Museum,* Building 396, Baltzell Avenue, Fort Benning, 545-2958. Hours: Tuesday to Friday 10 A.M. to 5 P.M., Saturday and Sunday 1 to 5 P.M. Donation • *Coca-Cola Space Science Center,* Columbus College, 4225 University Avenue, Columbus, 649-1470. Check for hours. Planetarium, $$; laser light shows, $$$; observatory, free.

INFORMATION *Americus-Sumter County Chamber of Commerce,* 400 West Lamar Street, P.O. Box 724, Americus, GA 31709, 924-2646; www.americus.net~chamber • *Columbus Convention and Visitors Bureau,* 1000 Bay Avenue, P.O. Box 2768, Columbus, GA 31901, (706) 322-1613.

Telling Tales in Jonesborough

Storytellers are spellbinders. The skill of an actor, the wit of a comedian, and warmth that either might envy, these are the tools of the trade of a talented teller, who knows how to stir the imagination, how to send you into gales of laughter—and how to move you to tears.

If you have not experienced the joy of a tale told by a master, make haste next October to Jonesborough, Tennessee, where the nation's best tellers gather for the National Storytelling Festival, a nonstop marathon of verbal treasure.

As the oldest town in Tennessee and the first in the state to be listed on the National Register of Historic Places, tiny Jonesborough, population 3,100, is the perfect setting. The new National Storytelling Center makes Jonesborough a mecca for those who love the art. Even when nothing special is happening, a storytelling session takes place every Tuesday night at the Dilworth Diner on Main Street.

Storytellers have been with us as long as there have been children to plead "Tell me a story," but the art waned after the invention of the printing press and was almost lost in the pat scripts and canned laughter of the television age.

A Jonesborough journalist, Jimmy Neil Smith, was inspired when he heard someone telling tales on the radio one fateful day over 20 years ago. The storytelling festival he first put together in 1973 in the high school gym and on a hay wagon in front of the Jonesborough courthouse was the first full-fledged gathering of its kind. Today the festival attracts more than 8,000 visitors for over 100 hours of storytelling and has spearheaded a national revival of storytelling.

You'll find giant tents set up around the town, each one big enough to hold about 1,000 people. One is devoted entirely to family programs, making this a great weekend with the kids.

Begin your visit with the purchase of a ticket at the visitors' center and a look at the schedule. During the day, three tellers perform per hour in each tent, followed by a half-hour break. In the evening, eight or nine tellers take turns. There's also an extra ghost-story session in Mill Spring Park on Friday and Saturday nights lit by spooky lantern light. One ticket gives admittance to all the tents, so you can take your tales in small or massive doses, as you please.

All of the 20-plus performers are stars of the storytelling circuit, but there are superstars among them, so if the names are not familiar to you, talk to people around you to discover the standouts. You can also check the resource sales tent to see which names have the most tapes and books to their credit.

In any event, you'll want to spend some time in the resource tent. The big selection of books, records, and tapes gathered there from many sources is unmatched, and it is a major lure for many people who come to the festival. The sales tent, like the festival, is sponsored by the International Storytelling Foundation, an organization based in Jonesborough and dedicated to fostering storytelling in classrooms, in libraries, and at local gatherings. The foundation recently became an affiliate of the Smithsonian Institution.

When you've zeroed in on a few tellers you want to hear, find them on the schedule and take a seat in the tent where they will perform. Do this long before the appointed hour to be sure of getting a seat; if you wait until the session begins, you'll be left standing in the rear. The pleasure you'll reap from those who perform while you are waiting makes the time go fast. Young or old, mountain man or city sophisticate, each brings something unique and personal to the art, leaving listeners enriched. The advance-ticket order form highlights the featured tellers each year.

If you see that Donald Davis is appearing, grab a seat in a hurry. A native of the southern Appalachians and a retired minister, Davis spins wonderful tales of the trials of growing up, of imperious grandmothers and mischievous but well-meaning boys, stories that never fail to spark recognition and warm laughter.

Bearded Jay O'Callahan of Marshfield, Massachusetts, is another extraordinary teller who livens his performances with sound, rhythm, and movement. He has performed on National Public Radio and has won awards for his recordings.

The possibilities go on and on. Waddie Mitchell spins cowboy yarns. Kathryn Windham not only collects and tells ghost stories but is said to have a resident ghost in her home in Selma, Alabama. Mary Hamilton will surely enchant you with her hilarious tall tales, told with such conviction you can't quite be sure whether they are too tall to be true. Ray Hicks, a western North Carolina potato farmer and jack-of-all-mountain-trades, is considered the patriarch of traditional storytelling in America. Don Keding accompanies his tales with music on guitar, banjo, and spoons.

The scheduling allows plenty of time to wander around Jonesborough. If this town's buildings could speak, they would tell marvelous stories of their own. The town came within two votes of becoming the capital of America's fourteenth state, which would have been known as Franklin.

This was the frontier country of legends. Daniel Boone helped open up the territory, and Davy Crockett was born down the road. In 1779 the first township was staked out in what was then part of North Carolina and was named in honor of a state assemblyman, Willie Jones. Later, North Carolina ceded its western land, including Jonesborough, to the new federal government. Congress did not respond immediately, so the people set up their own government, forming the state of Franklin, with Jonesborough as capital and John Sevier as governor.

Franklin was expected to be officially named the first new state since the original 13 colonies, but it received only seven of the needed nine votes, supposedly because two delegates known to favor admission were absent when the vote was taken. So Franklin disappeared into Tennessee, which, in 1796, finally became the nation's sixteenth state.

Jonesborough prospered anyway as a major stopping place for pioneers moving westward. The citizens built railroads and published newspapers, including the nation's first antislavery periodicals. Andrew Jackson lived there for a time, practicing law and presiding in the courthouse. Andrew Johnson was a neighbor. Frontiersmen often came into town to pay their taxes in beaver skins.

But recent events had not been kind to the town. When Interstate 81 ignored Jonesborough, and malls in Johnson City began to hurt business on Main Street, stores began to close and buildings fell into disrepair. Realizing that their best hope for the future lay in the past, town leaders developed a plan to restore historic Main Street, hoping to build an economy based on tourism.

Special events such as Historic Jonesborough Days, held annually around the Fourth of July holiday, began to draw people. But it was the National Storytelling Festival that put Jonesborough firmly on the map. The large, modern visitors' center on the edge of town is a sign of the new prosperity. This is where you can pick up a printed walking tour to guide you around the tiny town. The building also includes a museum chronicling the local history.

Most of the sights are right on Main Street. Cradled between hills, the four-block heart of town is paved with brick and cobblestone and crammed with history. The look is still very much nineteenth century. Electric wires have been buried, and streetlights resemble old-fashioned gas lamps. The architecture, which might be called "frontier Colonial," is a mix of brick, clapboard, and hand-hewn logs.

The Chester Inn, dating from the 1790s, is the oldest frame structure in town, an integral part of the past as well as the future for Jonesborough. It has hosted Presidents Jackson, Polk, and Johnson, and it was nearby that Jackson once helped fight a fire while wearing only his nightshirt. The building is now one of three that make up the National Storytelling Center. The center, which spans three acres, includes the offices of the International Storytelling Foundation, a library, a shop, and an educational and interpretive building where a storyteller can often be heard in action.

The Christopher Taylor House, a circa-1778 two-story log house, was rescued from a lonely field outside town and became the keystone of the town's restoration effort. Andrew Jackson boarded there during his stay in town. It was in Jonesborough that Jackson was admitted to the bar and later presided as a judge. In 1913 an imposing new towered courthouse with a massive clock was built on the site of the town's original 1779 courthouse.

The Greek Revival Presbyterian Church, built in the 1840s, retains its original pulpit, pews, and slave gallery. Many homes from the 1830s and 1840s are also pointed out on the tour.

Behind many old façades are galleries and gift shops. Increasingly, Jonesborough is becoming a center for art and crafts. The Keene Gallery features art by eastern Tennessee artists in a restored 1879 wooden commercial building. Other worthwhile stops are the Jonesborough Art Glass Gallery, Jonesborough Designer Craftsmen, Tennessee Quilts, and the Artisan Studio Gallery.

For gifts and geegaws, Old Town Hall houses some 30 merchants selling antiques, crafts, clothing, and toys. The Salt House, where salt was rationed in the 1840s, holds specialty shops. The Jonesborough Antique Mart brims with collectibles in 50 minishops.

During the festival, food is served at outdoor stands, but otherwise options are limited in Jonesborough. There is, however, one exceptional choice. The Parson's Table, housed in the soaring spaces of an 1874 Gothic church, is filled with Victoriana and charm. The menu is French, and the Sunday buffet brings crowds from miles around.

If you take the time for an afternoon's drive, more history beckons all around the area. About 15 minutes west, off US 11E, is the Davy Crockett Birthplace State Historic Park on the Nolichuckey River, with a restoration of the cabin where the famed frontiersman was born. Another 15 minutes farther west, in Greeneville, is the home of Andrew Johnson, a national historic site, as well as the quaint stone buildings of

Tusculom, Tennessee's oldest college, and the state's oldest jail, dating to 1804.

Head north to Rogersville to see the oldest original courthouse still in use in Tennessee, dating from 1836, and the oldest continuously operating hotel in the state, the 1824 Hale Springs Inn.

Like Jonesborough, Greeneville and Rogersville are towns that have beautifully preserved the look of the past. They supply pictures; the words of the storytellers bring them to life.

<u>Area Code: 423</u>

DRIVING DIRECTIONS   Jonesborough is located on US 11E in eastern Tennessee, about 95 miles east of Knoxville and 6 miles southwest of Johnson City. It is reached via I-81. From Atlanta, take I-75 north to I-40 east, which merges into I-81. Continue to exit 23, US 11E, at Bulls Gap, about 325 miles.

PUBLIC TRANSPORTATION   Tri-City Regional Airport, serving Johnson City, is 25 minutes from Jonesborough.

ACCOMMODATIONS   (Jonesborough bed-and-breakfast homes are small and fill up far in advance for the Storytelling Festival, when rates may be slightly higher than usual. Alternatives are the motels and hotels in Johnson City, where early reservations are also advised.) *Hawley House,* 114 East Woodrow Avenue, Jonesborough, 37659, 753-8869 or (800) 733-8869, quaint eighteenth-century log-and-frame home, folk art, best in town, M–E, CP • *May-Ledbetter House,* 130 West Main Street, Jonesborough, 37659, 753-7568, nicely restored 1904 Victorian, M, CP • *Franklin House,* 116 Franklin Avenue, Jonesborough, 37659, 753-3810, reconstructed 1840 home, Jonesborough, 37659, I–M, CP • *Bugaboo Bed and Breakfast,* 211 Semore Drive, Jonesborough, 37659, 753-9345, very pleasant country home one mile from town, I–M, CP • More inns are opening all the time; write to the visitor center for a complete list.

Inns outside Jonesborough: *Big Spring Inn,* 315 North Main Street, Greeneville, 37743, 638-2917, lovely old home and gardens, M–E, CP • *Hale Springs Inn,* 110 West Main Street, Rogersville, 37857, 272-5171, state's oldest inn, M, CP • *Jam 'n' Jelly Inn Bed and Breakfast,* 1310 Indian Ridge Road, Johnson City, 37604, 929-0039, M, CP.

Johnson City Hotels and Motels: *Garden Plaza Hotel,* 211 Mockingbird Lane, Johnson City, 37604, 929-2000, M • *Comfort Inn,* 1900 South Roan Street, Johnson City, 37604, 928-6000, motor hotel, I–E • *Comfort Suites,* 3118 Brownsmill Road, Johnson City, 37604, 610-0010, M • *Hampton Inn,* 508 North State of Franklin Road, Johnson City, 37604, 929-8000, I–M • *Holiday Inn,* 101 West Springbrook

Drive, Johnson City, 37604, 282-4611, M • *Fairfield Inn by Marriott,* 207 East Mountcastle, Johnson City, 37601, 282-3335, motel, I • *Super 8 Motel,* 108 Wesley, Johnson City, 37601, 282-1818, I.

DINING   *The Parson's Table,* 100 West Woodrow Avenue, Jonesborough, 753-8002, delightful setting in a nineteenth-century church, French fare, lunch, I; dinner, M–E • *Main Street Café,* 117 West Main Street, Jonesborough, 753-2460, in-town spot for lunch or early dinner, I • *Peerless Steak House,* 2531 North Roan Street, Johnson City, 282-2351, seafood and steaks, I–M • *Galloway's,* 807 North Roan Street, Johnson City, 926-1166, pleasant atmosphere, Continental menu, M–E • *Firehouse,* 327 West Walnut, Johnson City, 929-7377, converted 1930s firehouse, ribs are the specialty, I–M.

SIGHT-SEEING   *National Storytelling Festival,* three-day event held the first weekend in October. Phone for current information from *Storytelling Foundation International,* 116 West Main Street, Jonesborough, 753-2171 or (800) 952-8392. Ask also about hours and programming for the new National Storytelling Center opening in 2001 • *Jonesborough-Washington County History Museum,* 117 Boone Street, 753-1015. Hours: Monday to Friday 8 A.M. to 5 P.M., Saturday and Sunday 10 A.M. to 5 P.M. $ • *Davy Crockett Birthplace State Park,* off US 11E, Limestone, 257-2167. Hours: Museum and visitor center, Monday to Friday 8 A.M. to noon and 1 to 4:30 P.M. Free • *Andrew Johnson National Historic Site,* visitor center, Depot and College Streets, Greeneville, 638-3551. Hours: Daily 9 A.M. to 5 P.M. Visitor center, free; homestead, $.

INFORMATION   *Historic Jonesborough Visitors Center,* 117 Boone Street, P.O. Box 375-E, Jonesborough, TN 37659, 753-1010 or (800) 400-4221; www.jonesborough.tricno.net.

Autumn Leafing in Alabama

Mention Lookout Mountain and many people think of Tennessee, but in Alabama they know better. The peak known by this name may rise above Chattanooga; the range may touch on Georgia; but most of this 100-mile-long mountain ridge lies squarely in Alabama's northeastern corner, where it provides one of the Southeast's most spectacular fall foliage routes.

Surely one of the most scenic interstates in the country is I-59 north of Gadsden, running across the crests of the southern Appalachian foothills with autumn color in full glory on all sides. The Lookout Mountain Parkway, between Gadsden and Mentone, is a parallel route, not really a parkway and not as high as the interstate, but a lovely fall drive for those who prefer country back roads. It runs right through DeSoto State Park, one of the most beautiful in Alabama, and into Mentone, a delightful mountain town.

If you plan a leaf-watching tour, you can also take in a variety of sights and pleasures along the way. Natural wonders beckon, ranging from waterfalls to underground lakes to dramatic canyons. Country music fans can visit the hometown and museum of the group Alabama; golfers can tee off on a mountaintop course in the clouds; riders can visit a scenic dude ranch; and shoppers can go wild at the state's biggest flea market and largest outlet mall.

The southern end of the parkway begins in Gadsden, where you can start things off nicely with a ride on the riverboat *Alabama Princess* along the scenic Coosa River. Special fall color cruises are scheduled in late October and early November.

Gadsden's pride is Noccalula Falls, cascading 90 feet down into a beautiful ravine. According to legend, an Indian princess, heartbroken because her father disapproved of the man she loved, plunged to her death there on her wedding day rather than go through with a dreaded arranged marriage. Her bereaved father named the falls in her memory. A statue of the young girl stands near the waterfall.

The falls are just one part of a town park that includes botanical gardens with over 25,000 azaleas, a pioneer village, miniature train rides, picnic areas, hiking trails, miniature golf, and a children's playground.

Though the best lodgings and scenery await farther north, shoppers might choose to stay in Gadsden on Friday night in order to beat the crowds headed for Boaz, 19 miles north via US 431. This is one of the South's largest outlet centers, with more than 140 stores. The crowds have spawned a number of antiques malls, as well.

If you're more intrigued with the kind of bargains to be found at a giant flea market, you can join the hunt about 20 miles north of Gadsden in Collinsville, where Trade Day brings out 1,000 vendors selling crafts, clothing, furniture, fresh produce, plants, animals, and—you name it. This Saturday outdoor event has been a tradition since the early 1900s.

Should you be in this area on Sunday, the Mountain Top Flea Market goes into action in Attalla, on US 278 just outside Gadsden. A little bit of everything is for sale on this 970-acre site. It's the state's biggest flea market event.

If you're looking for beauty rather than bargains, head north on the Lookout Mountain Parkway, which begins as Tabor Road, off Noccalula Road just past Noccalula Falls Park. The road changes numbers as it wends its way north, becoming Alabama 176 and then County Road 89.

Turn right off the parkway on Alabama 176 at Dogtown for an awe-inspiring sight, the Little River Canyon, one of the deepest gorges in the eastern United States. A 22-mile paved drive follows the steep, wooded wall of the canyon north to the river's source, with many overlooks for marveling at the sheer drop below.

Little River is the only river in America that flows almost its entire length on top of a mountain. Branches of the river formed in northwest Georgia and northeast Alabama come together to make one stream running down the middle of Lookout Mountain. At the intersection of the rim road and Alabama 35, the stream feeds into 60-foot Little River Falls. Farther south, the river eventually leaves the mountain at Little River Canyon Mouth Park and flows into Weiss Lake.

If you want to take time to add a touch of town to your country, follow Alabama 35 west at this point to Fort Payne, best known as the home of the wildly successful country music group Alabama. Three of the four members of the group are natives, and the band was born there, so it is for sentimental reasons that the Alabama Fan Club and Museum is located nearby. An audiovisual presentation tells the story of the group, and giant photos, awards, and lots of memorabilia trace the members' careers.

Fort Payne's other attractions include the 1891 stone train depot, richly adorned with turrets and arches. It is now a museum filled with local history exhibits. The Fort Payne Opera House, built in 1889, was described then as "the most convenient and handsome opera house in the state." Nicely restored, it is the oldest theater in Alabama still in use.

Come back east on Route 35 and continue north again on County Road 89 into DeSoto State Park. Part of a protected 15,000-acre federal preserve that includes Little River Canyon, this 5,000-acre park is a wonderful place to stay or to visit. The grounds offer scenic lookouts, miles of hiking trails, tennis courts, a pool, and lawn games. The 25-room lodge of native stone and rock has a good restaurant and a big country porch complete with rockers. Accommodations are available in the lodge, in rustic cabins on the grounds, or in 22 chalets with fireplaces for cool fall evenings.

Continue past the park on County Road 89 toward Mentone and you'll see the turnoff for DeSoto Falls. Formed by the west fork of the Little River, the falls have an impressive 100-foot drop. A historic dam there created a beautiful mountain lake, ideal for fishing and boating.

When you see the final stop on the Alabama portion of the Lookout Mountain Parkway, you may well want to settle in and stay awhile. The tiny, totally charming town of Mentone, perched on the mountain rim 1,000 feet above the valley, is in lush, wooded terrain that has made it a longtime favorite area for summer camps. Tucked away in scenic surroundings are several very appealing small bed-and-breakfast inns.

Interesting shops now fill some of Mentone's weathered buildings. In the old Hitching Post, where square dances used to be held upstairs, you'll find Gourdies, which sells imaginative gourd dolls, and Crow's Nest Antiques. This is the unofficial town welcome center, with information about what's going on. The little downtown is enjoying a bit of a rejuvenation, including the sprucing up of the old Mentone Springs Hotel, a dominant presence on Main Street.

Mentone has also developed into a center for crafts. The town is filled with artisans showing their wares during the Mentone Fall Colorfest, the third week in October, timed for the peak fall color.

Mentone has two other unexpected attractions, both owned by the same family. Above town is the Cloudmont Ski and Golf Resort—that's right, "ski." When the weather is cold enough for snowmaking, this is Alabama's one and only ski area. In balmier seasons you can play golf there in the clouds, teeing off from a formation of rocks.

The latest adjunct to Cloudmont is the Shady Grove Dude and Guest Ranch, set on 1,000 acres with 100 miles of trails and many miles of rivers and wilderness for other adventures. Guests enjoy horseback and wagon rides and western-style square dancing. Accommodations are strictly on the rustic side, but you needn't stay here to ride, and it's a great place to visit.

This region has its share of scenery underground as well as above. Sequoyah Caverns, west of I-59 above Valley Head, is renowned for its "Looking Glass Lakes," reflecting the otherworldly cave formations for a double measure of eerie beauty. Outdoor attractions at the cave include deer, peacocks, streams full of rainbow trout, and a herd of American bison.

Cave lovers may want to make the drive farther north, close to the northern state line, for another cave that is now a national monument. Excavations show that Stone Age men took shelter in Russell Cave some 9,000 years ago. The site, a limestone chamber 210 feet long and 107 feet wide, was discovered in 1953, and archaeologists have found records of continuous human habitation from 7000 B.C. to about A.D. 1000. After a self-guided tour of the shelter, you can stop at the visitors' center to see prehistoric tools and artifacts found during excavation.

From Mentone, it's an easy drive to the end of the parkway through Georgia (where you can detour for spectacular scenery at Cloudland Canyon State Park) and into Chattanooga, or you can hurry things along on I-59 and still have scenery galore. Or, having now seen the beauty of Alabama's portion of Lookout Mountain, you may just want to turn around and do it all again.

Area Code: 256

DRIVING DIRECTIONS Gadsden, the start of this suggested route, is at the intersection of I-759 and US 411, 3 miles off I-59, exit 188. From Birmingham, follow I-59 north, 60 miles. From Atlanta, follow I-20 west to I-59, 112 miles. Gadsden is 90 miles south of Chattanooga via I-59, or about 100 miles on the Lookout Mountain Parkway.

ACCOMMODATIONS *De Soto State Park Lodge,* 256 County Road 951, Fort Payne, 35967, 845-5380 or (800) ALA-PARK, lodge, I; cabins and chalets, I–M • *Mentone Inn,* Highway 117, P.O. Box 290, Mentone, 35984, 634-4836 or (800) 455-7470, unassuming old-fashioned stone-and-wood 1927 lodge in town, pine paneling, big porches, I, CP • *Valhalla,* 672 County Road 626, Mentone, 35984, 634-4006, cottages on 20 acres bordering De Soto State Park, M • *the secret,* 2536 Highway 68 West, Leesburg, 35983, 523-3825, dramatic hideaway, vaulted-ceiling guest rooms with decks, rooftop deck and pool, M, CP • *The Lodge on Gorham's Bluff,* 101 Gorham Drive, Box 160, Pisgah, 35765, 451-3435, lodge with verandas atop a 700-foot bluff overlooking the Tennessee River, elegant guest rooms, M, CP.

Bed-and-breakfast inns: *Winston Place,* 353 Railroad Street, Valley Head, 35989, 635-6381 or (888) 494-6786, antebellum mansion, M, CP • *Raven Haven,* Highway 117, County Road 639, Mentone, 35984, 634-4310, hideaway stone house, themed rooms, M, CP • *Mountain Laurel Inn,* 624 County Road 948, Box 443, Mentone, 35984, 634-4673 or (800) 889-4244, on Little River Canyon, M, CP • *Cove Creek Bed & Breakfast,* 5595 US Highway 278 East, Hokes Bluff (near Gadsden), 35903, 494-0094, lavish columned home on 139 acres, with riding stable, lake, pool, M, CP.

DINING *The Dish,* 6081 Highway 117, Mentone, 634-3669, simple menu in small, charming setting, I • *The Bistro,* 1630 Highway 117, south of Mentone, 634-8200, wide menu, good reports, I • *Cragsmere Manna,* De Soto Parkway South (Route 89), Mentone, 634-4677, nineteenth-century home on the mountain's rim, varied menu, by reservation weekends only, I–M • *Log Cabin Restaurant and Deli,* 6080 Highway 17, Mentone, 634-4560, quaint, popular, oldest building in town, sandwiches, salads, lunch and dinner, I • *Little River Cafe,* 4608 De Soto Parkway N.E., Fort Payne, 997-0707, popular home-based restaurant with owner who plays piano and sings folk music, I • *Mountain Inn Restaurant,* De Soto State Park (see Accommodations above), good food, views, generous Sunday buffet, I–M • *Top O' the River,* 1606 Rainbow Drive, Gadsden, 547-9817, family-style, catfish, cornbread, and all the fixings, I • (To see where the mountain folks gather, have breakfast at the *Tiger Inn* in Valley Head.)

SIGHT-SEEING *Noccalula Falls Park,* 1500 Noccalula Road, Gadsden, 549-4663. Hours: Daily 9 A.M. to dusk. $$ • *Alabama Princess Riverboat,* Highway 411, P.O. Box 1892, Gadsden, 549-1111. Check for current schedules, rates. • *De Soto State Park,* 13883 County

Road 89, Fort Payne, 845-5380. Hours: Daily 7 A.M. to dusk. $ •
Alabama Fan Club and Museum, 101 Glenn Boulevard South, Fort
Payne, 845-1646. Hours: Monday to Saturday 8 A.M. to 4 P.M., Sunday
noon to 4 P.M. $ • *Depot Museum,* 105 Fifth Street Northeast, Fort
Payne, 845-5714. Hours: Monday, Wednesday, and Friday 10 A.M. to
4 P.M., Sunday 2 to 4 P.M. Donation • *Sequoyah Caverns,* Route 1, off I-
59, 6 miles north of Valley Head, 635-0024. Hours: March 1 to Novem-
ber, daily 8:30 A.M. to 5 P.M.; rest of year, weekends only. $$$ • *Russell
Cave National Monument,* 3729 County Road 98, Bridgeport, 495-
2672. Hours: Daily 8 A.M. to 5 P.M.; earlier in winter. Free • *Cloudmont
Ski and Golf Resort,* Box 435, County Road 89, Mentone, 634-4344,
18-hole golf course, tennis, fishing, hiking, swimming, skiing in winter.
Check current fees • *Shady Grove Ranch,* off Highway 117, Mentone,
c/o Cloudmont, 634-4344, guided trail rides and wagon rides. Check
current schedules and rates.

INFORMATION *Alabama Mountain Lakes Association,* 25062
North Street, P.O. Box 1075, Moorsville, AL 35649, 350-3500 or
(800) 648-5381; www.almtlakes.org • *DeKalb County Tourist Asso-
ciation,* P.O. Box 681165, Fort Payne, AL 35968, 845-3957;
www.hsv.tis.net/~dekbtour • *Gadsden-Etowah Chamber of Com-
merce,* P.O. Box 185, Gadsden, AL 35902, 543-3472 or (800) 320-
1692; www.gadsdenchamber.com.

A Taste of Fall in Ellijay

Ellijay, Georgia, is a small town, but in autumn it takes on a big title:
Apple Capital of Georgia.

Some 600,000 bushels of apples—a large percentage of the state's
crop—are grown in the Ellijay/Gilmer County region.

In autumn, both roadside stands and the big "apple houses" overflow
with a dozen different varieties of fresh-picked fruit, not to mention
cider, apple butter, apple fritters, apple turnovers, apple pies, and just
about every good thing you can think of made from fall's favorite crop.

Of course, there's an apple festival, held on the second and third
weekends of October. By nice coincidence, that overlaps the Columbus
Day weekend date of the big, lively Praters Mill Country Fair, located
not too many miles away in Dalton, a town also known for its carpet
bargains. Other towns worth visiting in the neighborhood are Jasper,
where the famous Georgia marble is mined, and Blue Ridge, for scenic
railway rides and lots of outdoor activities. Add a backdrop of lakes,

rivers, and misty mountains aglow in autumn hues, and you can pack a peck of pleasures into the long weekend.

Make your first stop the Gilmer County Chamber of Commerce in East Ellijay, where you can pick up a driving-tour map of the apple orchards. Ellijay's town square makes for rewarding browsing through antiques and gift shops. Gilmer County's imposing 1900 courthouse is worth a tour, and the Gilmer Arts and Heritage Association, housed in a historic home on Broad Street, often has interesting art exhibits.

If you come for the Apple Festival, head for the fairgrounds south of town on old US 5, where you'll find apple exhibits, arts and crafts, and lots of good home cooking.

Golfers will be glad to know that Ellijay offers an 18-hole scenic golf course, the Whitepath Golf Club, with a resort lodge adjacent if you want to stay near the links. One of the problems in conquering the mountain topography was figuring out how golf carts would climb the hills, a dilemma that was solved by cutting tunnels into the mountainside so that golfers could move from hole to hole.

A dozen of the 20 or so orchards in the area are clustered along Georgia Route 52 east of Ellijay. Route 515 south of town has more choices, including Panorama Orchards, one of the biggest and most complete of the apple houses. It is one of many orchards where you are welcome to pick your own apples.

Like most of the orchards, this one has been family owned and operated for generations; the Stembridge family established the business in 1927. The apple selection includes not only familiar varieties like Delicious and McIntosh, but many that never make it to the ordinary grocery store, apples with names like Yates and Arkansas Black, about 20 varieties in all. Free samples in the apple house help you pick your favorites.

In the apple house, a viewing window lets you watch the bakers at work in the kitchen—and just wait until you taste their fried apple pies! A unique feature at Panorama is an observation window that lets you see some of the packing operations and cider making that go on behind the scenes.

When you've loaded your goodies into the car, head north to Blue Ridge and you've moved into Fannin County. National forest makes up more than 40 percent of the land in this county, making it a great place for hiking along the Appalachian Trail and other well-known paths such as Duncan Ridge and Rich Mountain.

The visitors' center in the town depot will provide you with detailed scenic driving tours into the mountains and countryside around town. Ask for Tour One, a one- to two-hour back road circuit that runs partway along the Toccoa River and includes views of Deep Gap, the Lake Blue Ridge Recreation Area, and Springer Mountain. The route passes not only scenery but bits of history, such as old gristmills and pioneer log homes.

Besides scenery, Blue Ridge is known for its mountain music concerts. The Sugar Creek Music Park has country music and dancing every weekend, and Bluegrass Festivals in spring and fall complete with cloggers, square dancers, and fiddlers.

A highly recommended short detour from Blue Ridge is Forge Mill Crossing, a shopping and dining complex in Morganton, on Georgia Route 60 six miles east of town. The shops are intriguing and the restaurant is one of the best in this part of Georgia. Patrons line up there for the mountain trout and lemon chess pie.

To the north, just across the Tennessee border, is the Ocoee River, site of the 1996 Olympic canoe and kayak competitions. The river flows alongside the road as you make the drive, so you can watch the rapids and the many international whitewater races held there—you might even decide to experience a rafting trip for yourself.

One way to see the action on the river is to board the vintage steam trains of the Blue Ridge Scenic Railway, which makes a 13.5-mile run to the Tennessee border. The trip takes an hour and a half, with a layover in the Ocoee riverside towns of McCaysville and Copperhill.

Drive over to Dalton for a bit of history that is Georgia's own. Just before the turn of the century, a young Dalton girl named Catherine Evans saw a hand-tufted bedspread she liked and copied it, selling her work for $2.50. It was much admired, and she began teaching other ladies in town how to tuft. Soon a cottage industry was booming. Highway 41, from Chattanooga to Atlanta, became known as "Peacock Alley" for the rows of colorful spreads hanging on clotheslines along the route, many adorned with a colorful peacock with its feathers displayed across the spread.

The story of this unique cottage industry is told in a fascinating little museum run by the local historical society in an 1890 building called Crown Gardens and Archives. The structure was once the office of the Crown Cotton Mills, the town's first textile manufacturer. Some of the early spreads are displayed there. There's also a room devoted to Robert Loveman, who wrote the lyrics to the Georgia state song as well as a poem familiar to many: "It is not raining rain to me, it's raining daffodils."

The tufting techniques used for the spreads were eventually applied to carpets, and the rest is history. Dalton produces more than 200 miles of carpet every day, more than half of the world's supply and a $5 billion business.

Those who come to Dalton to shop for carpeting can save 30 to 70 percent off retail prices at the many mill outlets. If you plan to buy carpets, it's a good idea to learn something about how to shop and what measurements you need before you make the trip. Beckler's, one of the larger outlets, offers a comprehensive free guide to buying carpet. Write to P.O. Box 9, Dalton, GA 30722, or phone (800) BECKLER.

Carpet or not, it is definitely worth a trip to Dalton for the Prater's

Mill Country Fair, an event now past its twenty-fifth anniversary. The fairgrounds adjoins a three-story gristmill built in 1855 and operated continuously until after the Civil War. It still grinds cornmeal on special occasions such as the spring and fall country fairs, when the original mill store is also open for fairgoers. These events draw over 150 artists and craftsmen to town to demonstrate their techniques and sell their wares. The festivities include mountain music and mounds of traditional Southern foods.

The story of another Georgia industry and a family dynasty founded on marble unfolds in Jasper and the neighboring hamlet of Tate. A stonecutter named Henry Fitzsimmons, who was passing through the valley in 1835, is credited with being the first to spot and mine a vein of rich marble.

The land belonged to Samuel Tate, whose family would acquire legendary wealth from the mines when Samuel's son Stephen persuaded the railroad to come into Pickens County so that the marble could be shipped out easily. For over 100 years, Georgia marble has been used for famous buildings, statues, and monuments all over the world. The incredible supply in the area is, in fact, estimated to be large enough to supply the world's building needs for 3,000 years.

In this area, still dominated by the quarries of the Georgia Marble Company, you'll find homes with marble steps, flower beds with marble borders, and marble sidewalks. In Jasper, the high school and even the old Pickens County Jail are made of blocks of marble. Once a year, on the first weekend in October, you can visit the quarries during the annual Marble Festival.

But you can see one of the most elaborate results of the Tate fortune anytime—and even stay there if you like. Colonel Sam Tate, the eldest of Stephen's 19 children, became president of the Georgia Marble Company in 1905, and by 1924 his fortune was estimated at $165 billion. He used some of the rare Etowah pink marble from the quarry to construct a marble mansion in 1923, but he lived in his pink palace for only 12 years before he died at age 78, leaving no heirs. Nicely restored and grand once again, the Tate House is now a palatial bed-and-breakfast inn and restaurant.

Jasper also offers a far more rustic but no less appealing lodging at the Woodbridge Inn, a simple 12-room lodge overlooking the mountains. It adjoins the restaurant, whose chef is considered among the best in the mountains.

If you want to include some truly magnificent scenery in your trip, consider staying at the lodge at Amicalola State Park, 20 miles east of Ellijay. The mountain views from these modestly priced rooms are unmatched.

One final option for lodging near Ellijay is Carter Lake, a big body of blue water 11 miles long, with 62 miles of shoreline amid the mountains. The lake was created when Carters Dam was constructed to generate hydroelectric power. The only development that has been allowed on the pristine shoreline is one small marina with motel rooms and lakeside cabins, including new octagonal-design cabins with vaulted ceilings, full kitchens, fireplaces, covered porches, and oversize TVs. Or, for the ultimate view of the surrounding mountain foliage, you can rent a 60-foot houseboat that sleeps up to eight, leaving the rest of the world behind and waking up to glorious views reflected in the water.

At the least, come down and rent a pontoon boat for a while. The lake is one of the loveliest of the many pleasures of the northwest Georgia mountains. And if you bring along a picnic, those tasty Ellijay apples make a perfect dessert.

Area Code: 706

DRIVING DIRECTIONS   Ellijay is located on Georgia Route 515, a continuation of I-575. Blue Ridge is to the north, Jasper to the south on the same road. Dalton is to the west, reached via Georgia Route 52. From Atlanta, take I-75 north into I-575. Near Jasper, the road changes to Georgia Route 515. Stay on this road and proceed north to Ellijay, a total trip of about 55 miles. Ellijay is about 75 miles from Chattanooga.

ACCOMMODATIONS   *Whitepath Lodge,* 987 Shenandoah Drive, Ellijay, 30540, 276-7199 or (888) 271-7199, pool, tennis, adjoining golf course, M–E • *Stratford Motor Inn,* East Ellijay, 30539, 726-1080 or (800) 526-1258, golf packages offered, I • *Cohutta Lodge,* 500 Cochise Trail, Chatsworth, 30705, 695-9601, valley view rooms are prime, M • *Tate House,* Highway 53, Tate, 30177, 735-3122 or (800) 342-7515, M–E; also, cabins with hot tubs and fireplaces, E • *Woodbridge Inn Lodge,* 44 Chambers Street, Jasper, 30143, 692-6293, I–M • *Carters Lake Marina and Resort,* 575 Marina Road, Chatsworth, 30705, 276-4891, rooms and cabins, I–M; houseboats, EE • *Amicalola Falls State Park,* off Georgia Route 52, Dawsonville, 30534, 265-8888, lodge rooms, suites, cabins, I–M; new luxury cabins, E; houseboats, 3 nights and up, E • *Blue Ridge Mountain Cabins,* Blue Ridge, 632-8999, M • There are dozens of additional cabin rental choices; contact the Fannin County Chamber of Commerce (see below) for a full list.

Bed-and-Breakfasts: *Cobb House on the River,* 193 River Street, Ellijay, 30540, 635-1833, M, CP • *Elderberry Inn,* 75 Dalton Street, Ellijay, 30540, 635-2218, I, CP • *Hearthstone Hall,* 2755 Highway 282, Chatsworth, 30705, 695-6535, M, CP.

DINING   Ellijay: *Calico Cupboard Restaurant,* North Main Street, Ellijay, 635-7575, Southern specialties, pies and cobblers, I • *Forge Mill Crossing Restaurant,* Forge Mill Road at Highway 76, Morganton (6 miles east of Blue Ridge), 374-5771, a regional favorite, I–M •

Toccoa Riverside Restaurant, Aska Road, Blue Ridge, 632-7891, casual, country cooking, scenic setting, outdoor deck on the river, I–M • *Fannin Inn,* Highway 76, south of Blue Ridge, 632-2005, known for pot pies, peanut soup, I • *Woodbridge Inn* (see Accommodations on page 167), a top choice, M–E • *Jasper Family Restaurant,* 65 Cove Road, Jasper, 692-6897, all-you-can-eat buffets, I • *Countryside Cafe,* Steve Tate Highway, Marble Hill, (770) 893-3389, a cut above, M • *Amicalola Falls State Park,* (see Accommodations on page 167), pleasant surroundings, reasonable prices, I–M • **Barbecue:** *The Pink Pig,* Old Highway 5 North, Ellijay, 632-2403, barbecue and good garlicky salad dressing, I • *Poole's Barbecue,* Craig Street, East Ellijay, 635-4100, I.

SIGHT-SEEING *Prater's Mill Country Fair,* Dalton, c/o Prater's Mill Foundation, P.O. Drawer H, Varnell, GA 30756, 694-MILL, held twice annually, on Mother's Day and Columbus Day weekends in Dalton. Phone for current hours and admission costs • *Georgia Apple Festival,* Ellijay, second and third weekends in October; contact Gilmer County Chamber of Commerce (see below) for information • *Sugar Creek Music Park,* Highway 5 northwest of Blue Ridge, 632-2560. Phone for current offerings • *Crown Gardens and Archives, Whitfield-Murray Historical Society,* 725 Chattanooga Avenue, Dalton, 278-0217. Hours: Tuesday to Friday 10 A.M. to 5 P.M.; Saturday 10 A.M. to 1 P.M. Free • *Blue Ridge Scenic Railway,* Blue Ridge Depot, 632-9833 or (800) 934-1898. Hours: June to October, Saturday 9 A.M. and 2 P.M., Sunday 2 P.M. $$$$.

SPORTS **Bicycle rentals:** *Cartecay River Bicycle Shop,* Ellijay, 635-2453 • **Horseback riding:** *Old Orchard Stables,* Ellijay, 635-2998; *Double D Trail Rides,* Blue Ridge, 632-6975 • **Whitewater rafting:** *Ocoee River Whitewater Rafting,* (800) 899-MTNS; *Wildwater Rafting,* (800) 451-9972; *Southeastern Expeditions,* (800) 868-7238 • **Golf:** *Whitepath Golf Club,* Ellijay, 270-3080 • **Canoe and kayak:** *Mountaintown Outside Expeditions,* Ellijay, 635-2524; *RiverRight,* Ellijay, 273-7075 • **Boating and Fishing:** *Carters Lake Marina,* off Georgia Route 136 (between US 411 and Georgia Route 515), Chatsworth, 334-2248; *Lake Blue Ridge Marina,* Blue Ridge, 632-2618.

INFORMATION *Gilmer County Chamber of Commerce,* 368 Craig Street, East Ellijay, GA 30539, 635-7400; www.gilmer county.com • *Fannin County Chamber of Commerce,* P.O. Box 875, Blue Ridge, GA 30513, 632-5680 or (800) 899-6867; www.blue ridgemountains.com.

Hunting Ghosts
Near Georgetown

According to the last count, Georgetown County, South Carolina, has a population of about 49,000—plus a number of ghostly characters who show up often, though rarely for the census. This low-country land, known as the Tidelands, is also said to be the most haunted place in the South. People here not only believe in ghosts, they swear by them.

Join the local residents paying their respects at the annual doings the week before Halloween and you, too, may meet some of the interesting characters who haunt the county. The daily Swamp Fox tram tours turn into ghost-story sessions, some of the inns feature ghost stories, and there are other ghostly events that change from year to year, each replete with scary histories, strange noises, and the promise of a ghostly presence or two.

At the very least, you'll learn a lot about ghosts while discovering the charming old port town of Georgetown and some of the loveliest, least-crowded beaches on the South Carolina coast at Litchfield and Pawley's Island. A magnificent sculpture garden is another local lure.

Anybody can tell you about the best-known of Georgetown's spectral visitors. Among the favorites is Alice Flagg, known as "the Little White Lady of the Hermitage" (the Hermitage is a plantation at Murrells Inlet, north of Georgetown).

Alice secretly wore on a chain around her neck a ring given to her by a forbidden lover, until her brother spied the ring and hid it away, unmoved by his sister's tears. Though she turned the house upside down searching, Alice never found her ring. Not long after, she fell ill with typhoid and died. She has often been sighted in the Hermitage garden and in her former bedroom. More than once, later owners of the house have entered a room to find it a wreck, with drawers opened and their contents scattered.

There are various theories about the identity of the man dressed all in gray, known as "the Gray Man of Pawleys Island," but there is unanimous agreement that he appears to give warning before a storm or tragedy occurs. He was sighted before the great storms of 1893 and 1916, and preceding Hurricane Hazel in 1954 and Hugo in 1989.

Georgetown also has its own resident in-town ghosts. There's the British soldier who once tripped on an uneven step in the house at the corner of Duke and Screven Streets and tumbled to his death. Lots of people have tripped since, but none have fallen; they say that an invisible pair of gentle hands steadies them.

The state's third-oldest city, Georgetown has an interesting unhaunted past, as well. Though located at the southern end of the

Grand Strand, 35 miles from Myrtle Beach, the flavor and history there are entirely different.

This area could well have been the site of the first European settlement in the United States if the Spanish colony established in 1526 had succeeded, but the settlement was ravaged by disease and the colonists perished within a year.

Two centuries later, English settlers formed Prince George Parish, and in 1730 they laid out the plans for Georgetown. The five surrounding rivers and their marshlands were ideal for growing first indigo and then rice. The rich plantation culture rivaled that of Charleston. By 1840 it produced nearly half of the total rice crop of the United States. Planters used some of their fortunes to build summer cottages along the beach at Pawleys Island, creating one of the first resorts on the Atlantic coast.

The Rice Museum, upstairs in the historic Old Market Building in Georgetown, tells about the crop that accounted for the town's early glory. Some of the original plantations south of town remain to recall even more vividly the flavor of the past. The building itself, known to locals as the Town Clock, is Georgetown's equivalent to Big Ben. It is surrounded by LaFayette Park, an oasis of flowers and greenery tended by a local garden club.

Hopsewee Plantation, built in 1740, was the birthplace of Thomas Lynch Jr., a signer of the Declaration of Independence. This is a typical low-country plantation house, with four rooms opening to a wide center hall on each floor. Special features are the graceful staircase and the hand-carved moldings in every room.

Hampton Plantation, now a state park, was built in 1735 and hosted President Washington in 1791. Its owners have included some of South Carolina's most prominent families. The rice fields and magnificent old oaks remain. The big plantation house, a two-and-a-half-story mansion, is left unfurnished in order to show the architectural detail. Walls have cutaway sections to reveal construction techniques.

Not far from Hampton is St. James Santee Church, an Episcopal church dating from 1768. The red-brick structure still boasts the original brick columns on the portico and box pews inside.

Many more plantations still stand along the rivers where they once flourished, hidden from view except from the water. Several boat excursions go past the plantations, along sleepy waterways that have hardly been altered since the end of the plantation system after the Civil War. Boat cruises also include shelling expeditions to offshore islands. Check the operators listed in the sight-seeing section, page 174, for current offerings.

A more recent estate is now the Bellefield Nature Center. The home was owned by presidential adviser and Wall Street wizard Bernard Baruch, who entertained many notables there, including Franklin Roosevelt and Winston Churchill. Baruch's daughter Belle left the property to the state for research in forestry and salt-marsh ecosystems. The center offers nature exhibits and films.

In this century, Georgetown's livelihood comes from its busy port, now dedicated to bulk cargo handling, and from the paper mill that is a none-too-scenic presence just outside town.

The town itself retains its early charm and looks better than ever since a recent renovation restored Front Street and built a Harbor Walk along the Sampit River. The historic district, roughly seven blocks long and three blocks deep, makes for a wonderful stroll past some 50 significant sites, including many homes from the 1700s.

Of special note is the Prince George Winyah Episcopal Church, circa 1750, whose congregation was first established in 1721. It retains its Colonial gated pews.

The oldest house in town, the Blythe Tavern House, dates from 1737. Following its use as a tavern, it became the residence first of a surgeon in the Revolutionary War, then later of South Carolina governor Robert F. W. Allston. The eighteenth-century windows remain.

The 1740 Heriot House has several legends, from stories of resident ghosts to tales of blockade-runners and bootleggers who were guided to shore by a light in the dormer windows.

The 1769 Harold Kaminski House is now open to visitors as a museum, with an outstanding collection of antiques. A few of Georgetown's other picturesque homes are now bed-and-breakfast inns.

The prize lodging in this area is farther north, at Litchfield Plantation, one of the major early producers of rice. The grounds have been used for a residential development, but the original 1750 "big house" has been restored as an elegant inn, with four bedrooms decorated with exquisite taste. The entry is an allée of moss-hung, centuries-old live oaks; the patio overlooks the rice fields. You can breakfast outside on mild mornings to bird songs, and return in the evening to watch sensational sunsets. The inn maintains a private beach club for guests on Pawleys Island. Staying there is as close as most of us will ever get to having our own plantation.

The nearby Litchfield Beach and Golf Resort is also on former plantation grounds, but the old buildings are gone. The new resort, with its seven-mile private beach, three golf courses, and the largest tennis complex on the Grand Strand, is one of the choicest lodgings in the area, with the bonus of many indoor facilities when the weather is uncooperative.

Pawleys Island, the oldest beach resort between North Carolina and Charleston, retains many of its eighteenth- and nineteenth-century cottages, including the Pelican Inn, the reputed home of the famous Gray Man. The narrow island is small and wonderfully private. There is only one rambling, rustic old wooden inn, so most people rent cottages to enjoy the beautiful beaches.

Pawleys Island is best known to many people for its hammocks. In the 1800s, a riverboat pilot named Joshua John Ward created a cotton-rope hammock woven without knots and renowned for its perfect comfort and coolness. They are still handwoven, just as in the past, and are now available in natural cotton or soft-spun polyester. You can watch the weaving at the Hammock Shop, which is now part of a charming shopping and dining complex of nicely landscaped cottages under ancient oaks.

Farther north on US 17 is Brookgreen Gardens, famous for its statuary set amid beautiful plantings. The largest showcase for outdoor sculpture in the world and a national historic landmark, the gardens exhibit 500 sculptures, including works by artists such as Daniel Chester French, Gaston Lachaise, and Augustus Saint-Gaudens.

Brookgreen was the idea of Archer Huntington, heir to a railroad and shipbuilding fortune, and his wife, Anna, a gifted sculptor. They bought several South Carolina plantations, comprising some 6,635 acres, to preserve the native plants and animals and to exhibit Anna Huntington's work. The idea expanded to include other artists who produced the representative sculpture the Huntingtons favored. No abstracts are allowed.

Anna Huntington's graceful *Diana of the Chase,* posed in the middle of a tranquil pool, is a stunning welcome to the ten-acre sculpture gardens. Though the original plantation house burned, a magnificent allée of 200-year-old live oaks, draped with silvery moss, remains. It has become a focal point for a series of interconnected gardens with pools, ponds, and fountains, forming a butterfly-shaped background for the sculptures. Strategic plantings ensure year-round displays.

Across the road, in Huntington Beach State Park, is the brick castle Atalaya, built in the 1930s by the Huntingtons. The park itself offers beach access and nature trails.

Georgetown County ends at Murrells Inlet, a picturesque fishing village founded in the early eighteenth century. Capt. Dick's Marina at Murrells Inlet is headquarters for deep-sea-fishing expeditions as well as for nature cruises into the salt marshes. A marine biologist accompanies these educational tours, where marsh plants and animals are collected and brought on board to be seen, touched, and discussed.

The inlet has its full share of ghost stories and legends, including the tale of the famous Alice. The narrow channels were also a favorite hideout for pirates. The story of Drunken Jack is part of the pirate lore. Jack was a crewman who came ashore with his pirate captain, Blackbeard, to bury a stash of hijacked rum. Jack missed the boat while sleeping off a hangover, and when the crew returned for him some two years later, legend has it that all they found were 32 empty rum casks and Jack's bleached bones.

A restaurant named in Jack's honor is one of a slew of eating places along the inlet, making Georgetown County the seafood capital, as well as the ghost capital, of South Carolina.

<u>Area Code: 843</u>

DRIVING DIRECTIONS   Georgetown is at the intersection of US 17 and US 701 north/south and US 521 from the west. It is 35 miles south of Myrtle Beach, 322 miles from Atlanta, 178 miles from Charlotte, 123 miles from Columbia. From I-95, take US 521 east.

PUBLIC TRANSPORTATION   Myrtle Beach Airport is 18 miles north of Georgetown; Charleston is 60 miles south.

ACCOMMODATIONS   **Georgetown:** *1790 House,* 630 Highmarket Street, 29440, 546-4821 or (800) 890-7432, in the historic district, M, CP • *Shaw House,* 613 Cypress Street, 29440, 546-9663, pleasant home with marsh views, I, CP • *Alexandra's Inn,* 620 Prince Street, 29440, 527-0233 or (888) 557-0233, restored home, some Jacuzzis, M, CP • *Harbor House,* 15 Cannon Street, 29440, 546-6532 or (877) 511-0101, on the harbor, M–E, CP • *Mansfield Plantation,* 1776 Mansfield Road, 29440, 546-6961 or (800) 355-3223, antebellum plantation house and guest houses on 900 scenic acres, M, CP • *Hampton Inn Georgetown Marina,* 420 Marina Drive, 29440, 545-5000, I–M • *Carolinian Inn,* 706 Church Street, 29440, 546-5191, in-town motel, pool, I, CP.

Pawleys Island: *Litchfield Plantation,* P.O. Box 290, 29585, 237-9121 or (800) 869-1410, original 1750 plantation home, elegant and exceptional, EE, CP; Guest House, E–EE, CP • *Litchfield Beach and Golf Resort,* P.O. Box 320, Highway 17 North, 29585, 237-3000 or (800) 344-5590, beach, golf, tennis, spa, and health club, rooms, I–M • *Sea View Inn,* P.O. Box 216, 29585, 237-4253, rambling beachside guest house with ocean and marsh views, E–EE, AP • *Hampton Inn Pawleys,* 150 Willbrook Boulevard (Highway 17), 29585, 235-2000, motel on a golf course, I–M.

Beach rentals: *Pawleys Island Realty,* 237-2431 or (800) 937-7352 • *Dunes Realty,* 237-4473 or (800) 779-3947 • *The Dieter Company,* 237-2813 or (800) 950-6232 • Chamber of Commerce has additional listings.

DINING   *River Room,* 801 Front Street, Georgetown, 527-4110, waterfront views, charbroiled seafood specialties, I–M • *Rice Paddy Restaurant,* 819 Front Street, Georgetown, 546-2021, waterfront spot for low-country cuisine, M–E • *Carriage House Club at Litchfield Plantation* (see Accommodations above), 237-9322, international cuisine in handsome setting, E • *Frank's Restaurant and Bar,* Highway 17, Pawleys Island, 237-3030, popular local gathering place, M–E • *The Litchfield Mayor's House,* Litchfield Village Shops, 2614 S. Highway 17, Pawleys Island, 237-9082, eclectic upscale menu, E–EE •

Community House Restaurant, Highway 17, Pawleys Island, 237-8353, Italian in a converted schoolhouse, M • *Litchfield Beach Fish House,* Highway 17, Litchfield Beach, 237-3949, no-frills fresh fish, M.

Murrells Inlet (all have water views, seafood specialties): *Bovine's,* Business Highway 17, 651-2888, open wood-fired grill, very popular, M–E • *Captain Dave's Dockside,* Business Highway 17, 651-5850, low-country dishes, M–E • *Drunken Jack's,* Business Highway 17, 651-2044, informal, I–M.

SIGHT-SEEING *Rice Museum,* 633 Front Street, Georgetown, 546-7423. Hours: Monday to Saturday 9:30 A.M. to 4:30 P.M. $$ • *Kaminski House Museum,* 1003 Front Street, Georgetown, 546-7706. Hours: Tours on the hour Monday to Saturday 10 A.M. to 4 P.M., Sunday 1 to 4 P.M. $$ • *Hopsewee Plantation,* US 17, 12 miles south of Georgetown, 546-7891. Hours: March through October, house tours Tuesday to Friday 10 A.M. to 4 P.M., $$; grounds (open daily), $ • *Hampton Plantation State Park,* 1950 Rutledge Road, off US 17, 20 miles south, McClellanville, 546-9361. Hours: Thursday to Monday 9 A.M. to 6 P.M.; office hours, 11 A.M. to noon. No park admission. Mansion hours: Memorial Day to Labor Day, Thursday to Sunday 11 A.M. to 4 P.M.; rest of year, 1 to 4 P.M. $ • *Brookgreen Gardens,* US 17, Murrells Inlet, 237-4218 or (800) 849-1931. Hours: Daily 9:30 A.M. to 5:30 P.M. $$$$ • *Huntington Beach State Park,* US 17, 17 miles north, 237-4440. Hours: Daily 6 A.M. to 6 P.M.; April to September, to 10 P.M. Admission March to November, $$; rest of year, free. Grounds include Atalaya mansion; tours June through August, 9 A.M. to 5 P.M. $. **Boat tours** (phone for current schedules and rates): *Rover Marine,* end of Broad Street, Georgetown, 546-8822, barrier island shelling and lighthouse tours on the cruiser *Carolina Rover* or *Tall Ship Jolly Rover,* also Pirate Adventure cruises • *Cap'n Rod's Lowcountry Plantation Tours,* 711 Front Street, Georgetown, 477-0287, plantation, lighthouse, harbor, and shell tours • *Capt. Dick's Marina,* Highway 17, Murrells Inlet, 651-3676 or (800) 344-FISH, naturalist educational cruises, scenic cruises, and deep-sea fishing excursions. **Tours:** *Swamp Fox Tours II,* 527-6469, tram tours from Visitors' Center, 1001 Front Street, hourly Monday to Friday 10 A.M. to 4 P.M.; check for Ghost Story schedules and events the last week of October. • *Georgetown Tour Company,* 546-6827, tram tours on the half hour, 10:30 A.M. to 2:30 P.M. $$$ • *Miss Nell's Tours,* walking tours from Mark Twain Bookstore, 723 Broad Street, Georgetown, 546-3975.

INFORMATION *Georgetown County Chamber of Commerce,* P.O. Box 1776, Georgetown, SC 29442, 546-8436 or (800) 777-7705; www.georgetownsc.com.

Fishing for Fun in Chattanooga

Want to hear a fish story? A real whopper? Check into what's happening along the Tennessee River in Chattanooga, Tennessee.

Time was when people passing through Chattanooga, lured by the ads on the highway, might drive up Lookout Mountain for the view and see Rock City and Ruby Falls. Downtown Chattanooga was rarely on anybody's list.

All of that changed in 1992, when derelict industrial buildings along the river were replaced by parkland and the sensational Tennessee Aquarium. The 9,000 finny residents attract nearly a million visitors each year, and the aquarium was only the centerpiece of a plan that is transforming the riverfront, with more family attractions each year.

One thing hasn't changed. By land or by sea, October is fabulous along the scenic Tennessee River, when the wooded shore bursts into a blaze of fiery autumn hues. River cruises and train rides specially planned to see the foliage are longtime local traditions. There's even a major folk and country music festival at the scenic point of the river known as "the Grand Canyon of the Tennessee." You can get there via a riverboat ride from Chattanooga.

There couldn't be a better time to discover the changes that have made Chattanooga an increasingly popular weekend destination. The challenge is how to fit everything into one weekend. Here's a plan, with a city overview the first day and foliage forays the second, that might work. But be forewarned, a day is not enough to fully appreciate the city's sights.

Start at the waterfront and be prepared to fall hook, line, and sinker, for this is the largest aquarium in the world devoted to freshwater life. Wait until you see the excitement they've created in this dazzling $45 million, 12-story complex, one of the most technologically advanced aquariums in the country. It's all the more meaningful since the river you are learning about is right outside the door.

Escalators take you to the top, beneath the pyramid-shaped glass roof, to a mountain cove forest like those where many of the tributaries of the river originate. This realistic scene comes complete with mountain mist, a waterfall, a woodland pool, and native plants and animals.

Begin your descent along the canyon, and you'll soon be looking below the surface of the water to watch the fish that live in re-creations of three natural habitats—a mountain stream, an otter pool, and a mountain sink pond—the last of these providing an especially intriguing view for fishermen, who can discover where the trout like to hang out.

The Tennessee River Gallery traces the river's history—from the days when the waters ran wild to modern times, after the TVA controlled flooding and provided power with its system of 35 dams. Nickajack Lake represents underwater life in the body of water created by a dam, and Reelfoot Lake duplicates the waters of Tennessee's largest natural lake.

The final leg of the river's journey is the Mississippi Delta, a re-created cypress swamp whose denizens include alligators, turtles, toads, and snakes.

In a special section devoted to the Gulf of Mexico, you'll see stingrays gliding between bonnethead sharks and colorful ocean fish swimming through the tangled roots of mangrove trees.

The aquarium is enlightening and entertaining from top to bottom. The only problem with the facility may be its popularity. To avoid overcrowding, only a certain number of people are admitted at one time, so come early or be prepared to be given a later entry time—not so terrible, since it will leave you time to explore some of the nearby city.

You won't have to look far to see the most dramatic changes in Chattanooga. Ross's Landing, the park that surrounds the aquarium, has replaced the industrial clutter that once separated the city from its river. The unique design, alternating bands of colored stone and waterways, traces the stages of local history, brought to life with quotations and artifacts embedded in the walls and the pathways. The objects form a kind of treasure hunt for the kids, who can spy everything from Civil War cannonballs to arrowheads.

The city's visitors' center has moved to the landing, so it is easy to get a map and brochures to guide you farther afield. Two major nearby attractions will help you pass the time quite happily. Kids (and their families) will love the brightly colored, three-story interactive optics tower seen through the big glass wall of the Creative Discovery Museum. The imaginatively designed museum allows visitors to create a computerized self-portrait, tune in to instruments from around the world and create original music, dig for dinosaur bones, build a robot, and use their creativity in the Inventor's Workshop. Some of the unique features include a two-story water sculpture and a "Little Yellow House" just for preschoolers.

Another very popular diversion is the IMAX 3-D theater, opened under the auspices of the aquarium in 1996.

To see more of the newly pristine riverfront, walk out on the recently restored, century-old Walnut Street Bridge spanning the water; it's touted as the world's longest pedestrian bridge. Ross's Park is the start of a riverside path that will eventually run for 22 miles, offering recreation and beauty. You can see some of the results to date at the segment called Tennessee Riverpark, on the outskirts of town near Chickamauga Lake. A popular rowing center has also grown up on the river.

Across the bridge, a formerly neglected area on the north side of the river is beginning to bloom with shops, restaurants, and a park with an old-fashioned carousel.

From Ross's Park, it's a short walk uphill to the the 1905 mansion that was once the home of Coca-Cola magnate and philanthropist George Thomas Hunter. Now the Hunter Museum of American Art, it holds a collection most impressive for a city this size, and it is still growing; a large modern wing was added to the mansion in the 1970s. The art includes works by Mary Cassatt, John Singer Sargent, Winslow Homer, and many others. A sculpture garden outside offers a fine view of the Tennessee River.

Across the street is a quirky museum, the collection of Anna Safely Houston, who never met a piece of antique glass she didn't like. Her home displays the glassware Houston found irresistible, including 15,000 pitchers, many of which had to be hung from the ceiling to fit into the house.

Beyond the museums is the Bluff View Art District, with the spacious and excellent River Gallery, which includes a sculpture garden on the river. This area also offers eating places, a coffeehouse, and the handsome Bluff View Inn in a restored Colonial Revival mansion. The Back Inn Café, behind the inn, is one of the most popular spots in town, especially on balmy days, when you can view the river from the outdoor café.

The free downtown shuttle that stops in front of Ross's Park travels about 14 blocks inland to what was long Chattanooga's best-known symbol, the Chattanooga Choo Choo. The city's grand 1909 Victorian Terminal Station has been redone as a hotel complex that is now operated by Holiday Inn. The ticket windows and passenger waiting area, beneath a lavish 85-foot dome, serve as the hotel's lobby and front desk. Beyond are tracks with old trains, some of them converted into narrow but nicely furnished sleeping rooms.

Even if you stay elsewhere, you can have dinner in the diner, visit a display of model trains, or board the Downtown Arrow for a train ride to the Tennessee Valley Railroad Museum, where railroad memorabilia and vintage locomotives and cars are displayed. The railroad runs its own excursions into the countryside.

On the way to the Choo Choo, you'll pass Warehouse Row, a renovation that converted turn-of-the-century railroad warehouses into a growing complex of outlet stores.

If you can tear yourself away from downtown, on the afternoon agenda is a ride up the Lookout Mountain Incline Railway, the world's steepest passenger railway, with a grade of 72.7 percent. The mile-long ride up the mountain takes just 10 minutes, and it emerges near Point Park, one of the two sections of Chickamauga and Chattanooga National Military Park.

The visitors' center at the park's entrance gate offers information about the area and an eight-minute slide orientation about the battle for

Chattanooga and its importance in determining the outcome of the Civil War. Also on display is James Walker's huge 13-by-30-foot painting *The Battle Above the Clouds.*

Afterward, walk to the edge of the mountain and marvel at the view, an eagle's-eye perspective on city, countryside, and Moccasin Bend, a turn in the winding Tennessee River, just below. The Ochs Museum, named for onetime Chattanooga resident Adolph S. Ochs, owner-publisher of *The New York Times,* tells more about the battle that sealed the fate of the Confederacy.

When you descend from the mountain and pick up your car, you can drive across the Georgia line to the main Chickamauga Battlefield section of the park, one of the first national military parks, established by Congress in 1888. The attractive visitors' center offers an excellent multimedia presentation portraying the fierce battle.

Take the seven-mile self-guided drive around the battlefield. It is maintained as close as possible to its 1863 appearance, with monuments marking troop positions. The beauty of the setting, now meadows and woodland, is a dramatic contrast to the battlefields where blood ran so freely that Confederate general William Bates called Chickamauga "a river of death." The Chickamauga campaign cost more than 18,000 of the 66,000 Confederate troops involved; Federal losses were 16,000 out of 58,000.

Civil War buffs may also want to visit the Battles for Chattanooga Museum, with a three-dimensional electric map reproducing the historic terrain with more than 5,000 miniature soldiers in place. Guns flash and cannons puff real smoke as the battle action is traced.

Inn lovers will find more choices in the Lookout Mountain area, including the Chanticleer Inn, a hideaway of mountain stone cottages. Two highly recommended stops are just across the Georgia border. The Gordon-Lee Mansion, an 1847 antebellum house, is a national historic site and so elegant it is open for tours. Captain's Quarters, an early 1900s home, will delight lovers of cozy Victoriana.

Back to sight-seeing: If you still have time and energy, you can consider the well-advertised attractions on Lookout Mountain. Rock City is quite an amazing series of rock formations, literally a two-acre "city of rocks." The up-and-down trail, sometimes through narrow passages, is fun to follow, and the views from "Lover's Leap" are spectacular, even if they do make things corny with a Mother Goose Village and characters like Rocky the Elf.

Ruby Falls is another matter. Getting to the falls involves a long trek to the end of the cave along a narrow underground catwalk, after which the lights are dimmed and a spotlight finally hits the falls. To this visitor, the narrow stream, albeit 145 feet high, was unimpressive and not worth the long walk. The crowds don't help.

Raccoon Mountain Cave, outside the city, has no waterfall, but the tour through its Hall of Dreams and the Crystal Palace takes you to far more beautiful and unusual underground formations. If you make the trip to Raccoon Mountain, you'll find child-pleasing amusements such as a water slide, horseback riding, and a mini–Grand Prix racetrack where you can take a turn in a racing car. The TVA maintains a storage lake at the top of the mountain, where the visitor center provides a lovely view of the Tennessee River Gorge.

Having seen as many sights as you can fit into one day, you can turn your attention to foliage tours. The main event is the annual Fall Color Cruise and Folk Festival, held at the Tennessee River Nickajack Reservation on the edge of Nickajack Lake (the real one), at the heart of the Grand Canyon of the Tennessee River. Celebrating its thirtieth birthday in 1998, the festival is one of the Southeast's largest outdoor musical events and a Who's Who of country music superstars; there are also cloggers and dance teams on hand. In addition, there's plenty of good food. Crafts demonstrations and contests, including musical compositions, add to the fun, which in recent years has spilled over to the riverfront downtown.

Buses make the trip to Nickajack Lake from Chattanooga, but it's more fun to come via the *Southern Belle* riverboat, which has entertainment on board.

If you prefer to see the countryside by land, board the Tennessee Steam Excursions run by the Tennessee Valley Railroad, a tradition as old as the festival itself. The choice of rides includes a daylong roundtrip into scenic northwestern Georgia.

Train or cruise boat, Chattanooga is the place to make the most of autumn—and to wave a fin at the fish at the same time.

Area Code: 423

DRIVING DIRECTIONS   Chattanooga is at the intersection of I-24 and I-75. From Atlanta, follow I-75 north, about 116 miles. From Birmingham take I-59 north into I-24, 149 miles. From Nashville, follow I-24 south, 134 miles.

ACCOMMODATIONS   Inns: *Bluff View Inn,* 411 East Second Street, Chattanooga, 37403, 265-5033, beautifully decorated mansion on the river, best in town, M–EE, CP • *Adams Hilborne Inn,* 801 Vine Street, Chattanooga, 37403, 265-5000, Victorian home in historic Fort Wood neighborhood, a short drive from downtown, E–EE, CP • **Downtown hotels:** *Chattanooga Choo Choo Holiday Inn,* 1400 Market Street, Chattanooga, 37402, 266-5000, I–E • *Chattanooga Clarion Hotel,* 407 Chestnut Street, Chattanooga, 37402, 756-5150 or (800) 221-2222, within walking distance of the aquarium, M, CP • *Chattanooga Marriott,* 2 Carter Plaza, Chattanooga, 37402, 756-0002 or (800) 841-1674, adjoining the city convention center, M–EE • *Radisson Read House,* 827 Broad Street, Chattanooga, 37402, 266-4121, historic downtown hotel, M–E • *Days Inn Rivergate,* 901 Carter Street, Chattanooga, 37402, 266-7331 or (800) 511-3326, walking distance to downtown, free shuttle service, I–M • **Lookout Mountain area:** *Alford House,* 5515 Alford Hill Drive, Chattanooga, 37419, 821-7625, I–M, CP; bridal suite, E, CP • *Chanticleer Inn,* 1300 Mockingbird Lane, Lookout Mountain, GA 37350, (706) 820-2015, I–M, CP • *Gordon-Lee Mansion,* 217 Cove Road, Chickamauga, GA 30707, (706) 375-4728, M, CP • *Captain's Quarters,* 13 Barnhardt Circle, Fort Oglethorpe, GA 30742, (706) 858-0624 or (800) 710-6816, three-course breakfast, M–E, CP • Chattanooga has many motels; write to the Convention and Visitors' Bureau for a complete list.

DINING   *212 Market,* 212 Market Street, 265-1212, contemporary decor and menu, convenient to the aquarium, lunch, I–M; dinner, M–EE • *Back Inn Café,* behind Bluff View Inn (see Accommodations on page 179), informal, popular outdoor café area, M • *Tony's Pasta Shop and Trattoria,* 212 High Street, 265-5033, Italian, I–M • *The Loft,* 328 Cherokee Boulevard, Chattanooga, 266-3601, best steaks in town, M–EE • *Mount Vernon,* 3509 Broad Street, 266-6591, longtime local standby, Southern dishes, M • *Big River Grille and Brewing Company,* 222 Broad Street, 267-2739, lively setting near aquarium in former trolley barn, freshly brewed beers and homemade sodas, wide menu, I–M.

SIGHT-SEEING   *Tennessee Aquarium,* 1 Broad Street, 265-0695 or (800) 262-0695. Hours: Tickets sold daily 10 A.M. to 6 P.M.; May 1 to Labor Day, Friday, Saturday, and Sunday to 8 P.M. Adults, $$$$$; children, $$$ • *Aquarium IMAX Theater,* Chestnut and Second Streets, same phone as aquarium. Hours: Shows begin hourly, Sunday to Wednesday 10 A.M. to 7 P.M., Thursday to Saturday 10 A.M. to 9 P.M. Adults, $$$; children, $$ (combination tickets with aquarium are available) • *Creative Discovery Museum,* 321 Chestnut Street, 756-2738. Hours: May to August, daily 10 A.M. to 6 P.M.; September to April, to 5 P.M. and closed Monday. Adults, $$$; children, $$ • *Hunter Museum of American Art,* 10 Bluff View at Third Street, 267-0968. Hours: Tuesday to Saturday 10 A.M. to 4:30 P.M., Sunday 1 to 4:30 P.M. $$ • *Houston Museum of Decorative Arts,* 201 High Street, 267-7176. Hours: Memorial Day to Labor Day, Monday to Saturday 9:30 A.M. to 4:30 P.M., Sunday noon to 4:30 P.M.; rest of year, closed Sunday. $$ • *Lookout Mountain Incline Railway,* 827 East Brow Road, Lookout Mountain, 821-4224. Hours: Daily 8:30 A.M. to 6 P.M.; Memorial Day to Labor Day, to 9 P.M. $$$ • *Chickamauga and Chattanooga National Military Park,* Chickamauga Visitors' Center, US 27, nine miles south of Chattanooga at Chickamauga, Georgia, (706) 866-9241. Visitors' center hours: Memorial Day to Labor Day, daily 8 A.M. to 5:45 P.M.; rest of year, 8 A.M. to 4:45 P.M. Visitors' center, free; multimedia presentation, $$ • *Point Park Visitors' Center,* Lookout Mountain, Chattanooga.

Hours: Daily 9 A.M. to dusk; visitor center, Memorial Day to Labor Day, daily 8 A.M. to 5:45 P.M.; rest of year, 8 A.M. to 4:45 P.M. $ • *Battles for Chattanooga Museum,* 3742 Tennessee Avenue, 821-2812. Hours: Memorial Day to Labor Day, daily 9:30 A.M. to 6 P.M.; rest of year, 10 A.M. to 5 P.M. $$ • *Rock City Gardens,* 1400 Patten Road, Lookout Mountain, Georgia, (706) 820-2531. Hours: Memorial Day to Labor Day, daily 8:30 A.M. to 8 P.M.; rest of year, 9 P.M. to dusk. $$$ • *Ruby Falls–Lookout Mountain Caverns,* Lookout Mountain Scenic Highway, Chattanooga, 821-2544. Hours: Memorial Day to Labor Day, daily 8 A.M. to 9 P.M.; spring and fall, to 8 P.M.; rest of year, to 6 P.M. $$$$ • *Tennessee Valley Railroad,* 4119 Cromwell Road or 2200 North Chamberlain Avenue, East Chattanooga, 894-8028. Hours: June through August, Monday to Saturday 10 A.M. to 5 P.M., Sunday noon to 5 P.M.; April, May, September through November, Monday to Friday 10 A.M. to 1:30 P.M., Saturday 10 A.M. to 5 P.M., Sunday 11:30 A.M. to 5 P.M. Trains leave from both stations, phone for current schedules. $$$$$ • *Raccoon Mountain Crystal Caverns,* 319 West Hills Drive, Route 4, Chattanooga, 821-9403. Hours: Daily 9 A.M. to 5 P.M.; in summer, 9 A.M. to 9 P.M. $$$$ • *Chattanooga Riverboat Company,* Southern Belle River Cruises, 201 Riverfront Parkway, Pier 2, 266-4488 or (800) 766-2784, sight-seeing, lunch, dinner, Dixieland and moonlight cruises; check current schedules and rates.

Fall foliage events (check for current dates, events, and rates): *Fall Color Cruise and Folk Festival,* (706) 275-8778. Bus or boat transportation from Chattanooga via the riverboat *Southern Belle* 266-4488 or (800) 766-2784 • *Tennessee Autumn Trains,* Tennessee Valley Railroad, 894-8028.

INFORMATION *Chattanooga Area Convention and Visitors' Bureau,* 1001 Market Street, P.O. Box 111, Chattanooga, TN 37401, 756-8687 or (800) 322-3344; www.chattanoogafun.com.

Striking Gold in Dahlonega

The year was 1828, over two decades before anybody ever dreamed of heading to a place called California. It started with a deer hunter named Benjamin Parks who stubbed his toe on a gold-laden hunk of rock. Before you could say "Get rich quick," the word was out, the prospectors came running, and America's first gold rush was on in northeast Georgia.

In 1833 the boomtown of Dahlonega was established as the seat of

Lumpkin County. The town's name came from the Cherokee word *dala-nigei-i,* meaning "yellow," the color of the precious stuff that brought the town to life.

People are still coming to Dahlonega in droves, but they are after different treasures nowadays. They come to bone up on an unusual bit of history, to browse crafts shops in nineteenth-century buildings around one of the prettiest squares in the state, and to stay in country inns or cozy mountain cabins.

Those who come during the third week in October get a feel for the past as the town celebrates Gold Rush Days with a pioneer parade, a beard-growing contest, and other high jinks. More than 300 arts and crafts exhibitors gather for the occasion in the public square and the historic district.

Far from least, folks come to enjoy the wooded countryside surrounding Dahlonega, the thousands of acres of the Chattahoochee National Forest comprising a wilderness world of hills and valleys, lakes and streams, and towering waterfalls. Whether you hike the start of the Appalachian Trail, float down a lazy river, or take a scenic drive, this is one of the state's most beautiful areas in autumn—and anytime.

There's more sight-seeing nearby, as well as the shops of the alpine village of Helen, and on the way you can drop into the town of Cleveland, famous for its Babyland General Hospital, where the dolls known as Cabbage Patch Kids are born.

You'll learn all about the golden past at the Dahlonega Gold Museum, now occupying the columned courthouse that was built in the center of the square in the boom times of 1836. This is the oldest public building in northern Georgia and the state's second-most-visited historic site. Exhibits and a film show the history of the county and how the gold was mined and processed. Also displayed are some of the larger nuggets found, as well as coins minted locally from the gold.

By 1837, Dahlonega had its own branch of the U.S. Mint. For the next 23 years, some 1.3 million gold coins, amounting to over $6 million, were produced, with the identifying letter *D.*

The operation was closed by the Confederate States Treasury Department in 1861, when gold coinage was deemed too expensive to meet the needs of a wartime economy. According to records, the last $25,000 worth of bullion and coins were sent to Charleston to help the Confederate cause. After the war, the building and surrounding property were turned over to the school that is now North Georgia College.

The mint was destroyed by fire in 1878. The following year, Price Memorial Hall was built on the old foundation on a hill above the town. The building's tall gold steeple is the most visible site on the North Georgia campus and a town landmark; it is covered with 23 ounces of Dahlonega gold. The building houses a collection of rare Dahlonega-minted coins.

One of the most interesting ways to relive the old days is to take a tour of the Consolidated Gold Mines, through the tunnels and past the "glory hole" of the largest and most advanced gold mine ever established east of the Mississippi River. The 7,000-acre mine contained about 200 tunnels and a 120-stamp mill to pulverize the gold ore.

The Consolidated went out of business in 1907 and was abandoned until 1980, when an award-winning restoration removed over 4,000 tons of dirt and debris from the massive tunnel network that had been blasted out of solid rock over 100 years before. The knowledgeable guides who conduct the 40-minute tours are the miners who helped resurrect the mine.

When you've had your tour, you can try your own hand at panning for gold and gemstones, either at Consolidated or at the old Crisson Mine, where you can also see demonstrations of a 112-year-old stamp mill once used to crush quartz so that the gold within it could be extracted. This is only one of two such working mills in the eastern United States. It is said that there's still gold to be found—just not enough to merit the expense of commercial mining.

Incidentally, according to one Georgia guidebook, a famous phrase was coined in the area when Matthew Stephenson, assayer of the Dahlonega Mint, stood on the balcony of the courthouse in 1849 urging miners not to rush off to California, pointing to the ridge in front of him and promising, "There's millions in it." Supposedly, Mark Twain paraphrased Stephenson's words in his book *The Gilded Age,* writing, "There's gold in them thar hills."

You can buy a sample of Dahlonega gold fashioned into jewelry at the Gold Shop, on the square. Gold-dipped leaves and dogwood blossoms make unusual and inexpensive souvenirs, or you can purchase a locket filled with Dahlonega gold dust.

This is just one of many interesting shops around the square, where the arcaded sidewalks and vintage buildings may remind visitors of mining towns in the Old West.

A popular coffeehouse serves sandwiches and desserts on the square, and the Fudge Factory will tempt you with a dozen kinds of treats. But don't spoil your appetite before you visit the Smith House, an old-fashioned mountain hotel that has been serving bountiful, family-style Southern feasts of fried chicken, country ham, and all the fixings ever since Mrs. Smith began cooking for a 22-seat dining room in 1922.

Dahlonega offers several small cafés in town, and some appealing small inns. One of the prize lodgings is Mountain Top Lodge, outside of town on 40 acres among the oaks and pines, with soaring hilltop views. The rambling house is filled with warmth and wonderful country decor, antiques, and crafts.

One recommended detour from town for flower lovers is Antique

Rose Emporium, where display gardens are planted with hundreds of varieties of antique roses. The shop here will definitely please gardeners. Walk upstairs in the farmhouse for a beautiful view of mountains and gardens.

When you are ready for a closer inspection of the autumn leaves, one excellent way to take in the splendor of this region is from the serene seat of a canoe. Appalachian Outfitters in Dahlonega offers rental canoes, kayaks, and tubes for excursions on the Chestatee and Etowah Rivers—and guided trips, as well. The Amicalola is another beautiful stream, with steep, dramatic rock faces rising from the water's edge.

If you prefer to see the area by car, you won't have to drive far from Dahlonega for scenic vistas. Turn at the town traffic light and follow Georgia Route 60 north about 13 miles to the Chestatee Overlook. A little farther north you can take in another fine view—the Yahoola Valley—from Woody's Gap, a picnic area beneath the tall trees. The Appalachian Trail passes here, in case you want to take a walk.

Keep heading north to Suches and Woody's Lake, a mountain lake in a wonderfully picturesque setting. If you continue driving, you'll come to Lake Winfield Scott, in the heart of the Chattahoochee National Forest, go through Sosebee Cave Scenic Area, and finally arrive at Vogel State Park, one of the oldest state parks and still one of the loveliest. You can hike, fish, picnic, or play a round of miniature golf there.

Waterfalls are plentiful in this region, but none of the others match Amicalola Falls, in the state park, 18 miles west of Dahlonega on Georgia Route 52. Cascading down from 729 feet, this is the highest waterfall in the eastern United States. The park's 1,020 acres include three and a half miles of nature trails. For the hardy, an eight-mile approach trail leads to Springer Mountain and the southern terminus of the Appalachian Trail, which runs north from there to Maine for 2,150 miles.

The Amicalola Park Lodge is another extraordinary place to stay. Ceiling-high picture windows in the main lobby take in the views; the mountain vistas from the bargain-priced guest rooms would cost a fortune in a resort hotel.

In fall, a must stop at the entrance to the park is Burt's Pumpkin Farm, where you can take a scenic hayride past the pumpkin fields and pick out a big orange beauty to take home.

More waterfalls are in store if you head northeast from Dahlonega on US 19. Continue on US 19 as it merges into US 129, a drive of about another 11.5 miles, to reach the De Soto Falls Recreation Area and five more waterfalls. De Soto Falls is the giant here. It cascades in three tiers, beginning on high with a 200-foot drop down a granite rock incline. You can get a fine view right from US 129 bordering the area.

Keep driving east on US 129 and you'll soon be in Cleveland, where the Babyland General Hospital must be seen to be believed. The "nurses," dressed in spotless white, take quite seriously their job of giving life to the latest creations of Xavier Roberts, who conceived the idea of the dolls known as Cabbage Patch Kids. One of the newborns "delivered" from the cabbage patch before your eyes will likely be named for you. Needless to say, they hope you'll want to adopt the doll, or one of the dozens of others waiting in the gift shop, hoping for new homes.

Turn north on Georgia Route 75 to visit another unusual mountain attraction, the old lumber town of Helen, now transformed into a Tyrolian village. The Bavarian steeples and architecture seem far from home in Georgia, but that doesn't appear to bother the swarms of tourists who eat in the German restaurants, play in the Alpine Amusement Park, and shop, shop, shop in some 200 gift shops and outlet stores. You need no guide here—you can't miss the stores.

All of this part of northeastern Georgia is becoming a center for wineries, with several available for visits around Dahlonega (see Sightseeing listings below), but visiting the Habersham Winery tasting room, south of Helen, has a major added attraction. It is near to Naccochee Village, a complex offering horseback riding, canoeing, fishing, an antiques mall, and the chance to visit historic Nora Mill, where the water-powered millstones have been grinding grain for over 100 years. The whole-grain grits they label "Georgia Ice Cream" are truly gourmet fare.

Visit Helen from September to early October for another unique attraction down south, an old-country Bavarian Oktoberfest, with oompah bands, polkas, lederhosen, and plenty of *bier.*

There's a total change of scene if you follow Georgia Route 17 south of Helen and continue on Georgia Route 255 into the placid Sautee and Nacoochee Valley area. Here are more authentic Georgia country inns, such as the 1837 Stovall House, with wonderful views from the big wraparound porch and an excellent dining room. Closer to Cleveland, Gourdcraft Originals, off Georgia Route 255, is worth seeking out for the whimsical toys and decorative pieces created from gourds.

Get your camera ready for another waterfall wonder when you head for Anna Ruby Falls, off Georgia Route 356, north of Helen. This is a double falls created by the joining of the Curtis and York Creeks off Tray Mountain. An easy paved path of less than half a mile leads to the falls and a visitors' center.

A 4.8-mile hiking trail connects this area to Unicoi State Park, also reached via Georgia Route 356. This is one of Georgia's most complete resort parks, comprising over 1,000 acres, with a handsome 100-room lodge and a restaurant. Swimming, fishing, and boating on a 53-acre lake, forest trails, four lighted tennis courts, and a gift shop loaded with local crafts are among the attractions.

It's just more proof that you can still strike weekend gold in the magnificent mountains of Georgia.

Area Code: 706

DRIVING DIRECTIONS Dahlonega is at the intersection of Georgia Route 60 and US 19, off Georgia Route 400. From Atlanta, follow Georgia Route 400 north to Route 60, about 71 miles.

ACCOMMODATIONS *Mountain Top Lodge,* Route 7, P.O. Box 150, Dahlonega, 30533, 864-5257 or (800) 526-9754, great location, good value, I–M, CP • *Black Mountain Lodge,* Black Mountain Road, Box 540, Dahlonega, 30533, 864-5542 or (800) 923-5530, contemporary mountaintop inn with soaring common spaces, E, MAP • *Worley Homestead Inn,* 168 Main Street West, Dahlonega, 30533, 864-7002, 1845 home on National Historic Register, M, CP • *Royal Guard Inn,* 203 South Park Street, Dahlonega, 30533, 864-1713, Scandinavian style B&B, I–M, CP • *Blueberry Inn and Gardens,* 400 Blueberry Hill, Dahlonega, 30533, 219-4024 or (877) 219-4024, new farmhouse-style inn about 10 miles from town on 50 acres with pond and mountain views, M, CP • *The Smith House,* 202 South Chestatee Street, Dahlonega, 30533, 867-7000, classic old inn, comfortable but simple rooms, I–E • *Mountain Laurel Inn,* 135 Forrest Hills Road, Dahlonega, 30533, 864-6456 or (800) 654-6313, lavish luxury complex with cabins, contemporary inn, and lodges, built for 1996 Olympics, E–EE • *Stovall House,* Highway 255 North, Sautee Valley, 30571, 878-3355, M, CP.

State parks (statewide reservation number, (800) 864-PARK): *Amicalola Falls State Park,* Highway 52, Dawsonville, 30534, 265-8888 or (800) 869-8420, spectacular views, lodge rooms, suites, and cabins, I–M • *Unicoi State Park,* Highway 356, P.O. Box 849, Helen, 30545, 878-2824 or (800) 869-8420, lodge and cabins, I–M.

Log cabins: *Hatfield's Hideaway Cabins,* 864-6743 • *Bend of the River Cabins and Chalets,* 219-2040 • *Cavendar Creek Cabins,* 864-7221 • Many more cabin listings are available; check with the chamber of commerce.

DINING *The Smith House* (see Accommodations above), bountiful Southern family-style meals, a local landmark, I • *Renee's Café,* 135 North Chestatee Street, Dahlonega, 864-6829, simple setting for some of the best food in town, I–M • *Rick's,* 47 South Park Street, Dahlonega, 867-9422, a former partner at Renee's serves highly rated fare, I–M • *Caruso's,* 19B East Main Street, Dahlonega, 864-4664, popular Italian, I • *Wylie's,* 19 North Chestatee Street, Dahlonega, 867-6324, pub with light fare, live music Thursday to Saturday, I • *Hofbrauhaus,* 1 Main Street, Helen, 878-2248, German-Austrian, attractive decor, nice location on the river, M–E • *Stovall House* (see Accommodations above), I–M • *Amicalola Falls State Park Restau-*

rant, (see Accommodations on page 186), I • *Unicoi Restaurant,* Unicoi State Park (see Accommodations on page 186), I.

SIGHT-SEEING *Dahlonega Gold Museum,* Public Square, Dahlonega, 864-2257. Hours: Monday to Saturday 9 A.M. to 5 P.M., Sunday 10 A.M. to 5 P.M. $ • *Consolidated Gold Mine,* Highway 19 connector, Dahlonega, 864-8473. Hours: Daily 10 A.M. to 4 P.M.; to 5 P.M. mid-June to mid-August. $$$$ • *Babyland General Hospital,* 19 Underwood Street, Cleveland, 865-2171. Hours: Monday to Saturday 9 A.M. to 5 P.M., Sunday 1 to 5 P.M. Free • *Amicalola Falls State Park,* Highway 52, Dawsonville, 265-8888. Hours: Daily 7 A.M. to 10 P.M.; office hours, 8 A.M. to 5 P.M. Parking, $ • *Unicoi State Park,* Highway 356, Helen, 878-2824. Hours: Daily 7 A.M. to 10 P.M.; office hours, 8 A.M. to 5 P.M. Parking, $ • **Gold panning:** *Crisson Gold Mine,* Highway 19 connector, Dahlonega, 864-6363; *Consolidated Gold Mine* (see above) • **Canoe trips and rentals:** *Appalachian Outfitters,* Highway 60 South, Dahlonega, 864-7117 or (800) 426-7117 • **Horseback riding:** *Sunny Farms North,* Long Branch Road, Dahlonega, 867-9167 • **Vineyards:** *Blackstock Vineyards,* 5452 Towns Creek Road, Dahlonega, 983-1371; *Frogtown Cellars,* 3300 Damascus Church Road, Dahlonega, 865-0687; *Wolf Mountain Vineyards,* Dahlonega, 992-9922; *Three Sisters Vineyards,* Vineyard Way, P.O. Box 849, Dahlonega, 865-0359; *Habersham Winery tasting room,* Alpine Village Outlet Mall, Helen, 878-WINE.

INFORMATION *Dahlonega-Lumpkin Chamber of Commerce and Welcome Center,* 13 South Park Street, Dahlonega, GA 30533, 864-3711 or (800) 231-5543; www.dahlonega.org.

A Capital Trip to Columbia

State capitals are generally good places to visit, offering historic sites and museums, plus good restaurants catering to the bigwigs who come to break bread with legislators.

College towns have different charms—scenic campuses, sports, theater groups, concerts, and a spirit of perpetual youth, evidenced in the shops, cafés, and clubs frequented by the students.

Seldom do the twain meet—except in Columbia, South Carolina. Columbia is the only Southeastern city that is home to both the state's government and its largest university. Add an exceptional zoo and the Colonial attractions of nearby Camden, including a fabled steeplechase race, and you have more than ample ingredients for a capital weekend.

One of the first planned communities in the country, Columbia was established in 1786 as a carefully chosen site for the state capital, a centrally located compromise between low country and Up Country factions. Though the city has spread in all directions, the wide boulevards of the original plan are still evident in the heart of town, the site of both the 1855 statehouse and the college founded in 1801.

Since most city attractions are downtown, and the straight grid pattern makes it easy to find your way around, this is the best place to stay. The most unusual lodging and best choice is Claussen's Inn, a 1928 brick building, formerly a bakery, now converted to offer oversize and very attractive rooms. It is in the Five Points district, near the university, where the streets are lined with interesting shops, galleries, and restaurants. Bed-and-breakfast homes in the historic district are also excellent choices.

Though Columbia's history goes back a long way, many of the original buildings were burned in 1865 when General Sherman's troops occupied the city, destroying an area of 84 blocks and more than 1,300 buildings. Only the university, the unfinished new statehouse, and the home of the French consul were spared. Most of today's stately buildings and the modern city, with its population of 112,000, have risen since that time.

A good place to begin sight-seeing is at the oldest remaining site, the lovely original campus of the University of South Carolina, known as the Horseshoe. It is entered on Sumter Street between Greene and Pendleton Streets. You can pick up a campus-walking-tour brochure at the admissions office in Lieber College, the first building on the right as you face the Horseshoe. Information is also available at the University Visitor Center, in Carolina Plaza at the corner of Assembly and Pendleton Streets.

The buildings on either side of the oak-and-magnolia-rimmed green date from 1805 to 1855; all are listed on the National Register of Historic Places. A major ten-year restoration project has returned the exteriors to their 1850 appearance while modernizing the interiors for contemporary needs. Many are now used as residence halls for honor students.

The center monument, honoring Jonathan Maxcy, the first president of the college, was designed by South Carolinian Robert Mills, the first prominent native-born American architect, best known for his design of the Washington Monument. Mills was instrumental in the architectural development of the college until 1840.

Among the buildings you will pass on a stroll around the Horseshoe are the beautiful 1810 Regency-style home of the president of the university and Rutledge College, which was the only building when South Carolina College first opened its doors in 1805. Rutledge served as dorm, lecture hall, chapel, and library for the 29 students. Today's campus enrollment tops 26,000, and there are some 127 campus buildings.

At the head of the Horseshoe stands the stately, columned McKis-sick Museum, a relatively new addition, built as a library in 1940. Southern folk art, the Howard Gemstone Collection, and the Bernard Baruch Collection of Silver are among the reasons a visit to the museum is well advised.

The rest of the campus is modern, but it makes for a pleasant hour's stroll. Two buildings that are farther away, on Assembly Street, but that you may possibly want to visit later in your stay, are the Carolina Coliseum, where USC Gamecock basketball games are played, and the Koger Center for the Arts, where entertainment ranging from ballet to bluegrass to Broadway shows is presented. If you come in football season, you may want to be among the avid Gamecock fans who fill the stadium.

It is a short walk from the campus to the official state buildings. If you want to do more than admire them as you walk by, you'll have to come on a weekday; since most are closed on weekends. The exception is the South Carolina State House, which is definitely worth a stop. It is one of the most beautiful of all state capitols, faced with Corinthian columns of blue granite outside and graced with palmettos, the official state tree, within. Begun in 1855, the domed building was still only a shell when General Sherman's men attacked the city. Metal stars on the west and southwest walls mark places that were struck by artillery shells. Inside you can watch the proceedings of the legislature from brass-railed balconies or stroll the historic halls.

Across the street from the State House is Trinity Cathedral, a small-scale replica of England's Yorkminster Cathedral. Prominent South Carolinians, including six governors, are buried in the churchyard.

The governor's mansion was originally built as officers' quarters for Arsenal Academy. After Sherman's visit, it was the only building left on the academy grounds. It was renovated and declared the official governor's residence in 1867. Two other fine homes that were moved to adjacent sites are used for official guests and for state occasions.

The mansion is located in the residential Arsenal Hill Historic District of Columbia, a section considered desirable since the antebellum era for its elevation and city views. Finlay Park, a good place to see those views, was restored in 1990 on the site of a park that had been destroyed by turn-of-the-century industrialization.

More fine homes can be seen by driving along Blanding and Richland Streets, areas that escaped Sherman's flames. If you must choose only one of Columbia's four historic homes, make it the Robert Mills Historic House and Park. Planned by Mills in 1823 for a prominent Columbia merchant, the columned home has an elegant main floor with curved walls, matching drawing rooms, and decorative niches typical of Mills's style.

The other museum houses include the Hampton-Preston Mansion and Garden, built from 1818 to 1835, which was the home of two prominent South Carolina families, and the more modest 1872 home where President Woodrow Wilson lived during the four years his father was a minister in Columbia. The 1850 Mann-Simons Cottage is of interest because it shows how free blacks lived during Columbia's antebellum period.

Allow plenty of time when you move on to the South Carolina Museum, housed in what was the world's first all-electric textile mill. The restored four-story structure is huge and holds displays covering every facet of the Palmetto State—artistic, scientific, and historic. In the natural-history section you can touch a 30-million-year-old tooth from a giant white shark and see replicas of creatures from the Ice Age; in the history galleries you will relive the beginning of the Civil War and visit a one-room schoolhouse and a vintage country store.

The South Carolina State Museum is located on Gervais Street, the center of an old warehouse district known as Congaree Vista—or, more commonly, just "the Vista." It is rapidly reviving with interesting galleries, antiques shops, and restaurants.

The Columbia Museum of Art may surprise you with its fine Renaissance art and contemporary graphics collections. It is in a striking modern facility downtown that includes a children's gallery and a trompe l'oeil secret garden orientation gallery.

If you can manage to fit enough of the above into one day, you can start fresh the next morning at the multi-award-winning Riverbanks Zoo and Garden, the favorite public attraction in South Carolina, with nearly a million visitors a year. There's good reason for this popularity. The complex uses the latest in naturalistic exhibit techniques, such as simulated African plains where giraffes, zebras, black rhinos, and ostriches can feel at home, and a realistic re-creation of the rain forests of South America.

The real showplace is the Aquarium Reptile Complex, added in 1989, home to thousands of fish and reptiles, amphibians and invertebrates, from all over the world.

The newest addition to the zoo complex is a 70-acre botanical garden with both formal gardens and woodland trails for wandering.

Having visited with the animals and flowers at the zoo, save the rest of the afternoon to hobnob with the horsey set in Camden, 30 miles to the east via I-20, the town that calls itself the Steeplechase Capital of the World.

The oldest inland town in the state, dating from 1733, Camden played a vital role in the American Revolution when Lord Cornwallis took the town in 1780 and moved with his officers into the Kershaw Mansion, the finest home in town. Camden became one of the main garrisons maintained by the British in South Carolina.

A reconstruction of the Kershaw Mansion is part of Historic Camden, a Colonial village to which authentic Revolutionary War–era

houses have been moved to be preserved. The complex includes archae-
ological findings of the old town walls and forts used during the British
occupation in 1780–81. On the first weekend in November, cannons
roar and muskets pop as the battle between the British and the Americans is reenacted during the annual Revolutionary War Field Days and
Heritage Days Crafts Fair.

Pick up the guide to historic sites at the Historic Camden gift shop. It
will guide you to more early homes along Broad Street, the main street
of town, and on other avenues such as Laurens and Chewning Streets,
around Monument Square.

By 1802, Camden was already holding horse races. In this century,
wealthy families such as the Buckleys, du Ponts, and Firestones settled
into the fine nineteenth-century estates along wooded and secluded
byways in the Kirkwood section—streets such as Lyttleton and Greene
and Kirkwood Lane—where they raised, rode, and prepared to race
their thoroughbred horses. The big, graceful, 1854 home on Kirkwood
called Kamschatka, for example, was bought and renovated by the late
William F. Buckley Sr. Kirkwood is one of many lanes that remain
unpaved, to be easier on the horses' hooves.

Springdale Race Course, developed in the late 1920s, quickly
became famous for its premier steeplechase-training facilities. In 1970,
local resident Marion du Pont Scott underwrote the first Colonial Cup
International Steeplechase, with the first $100,000 purse ever offered in
a steeplechase racing event. Mrs. Scott willed the track to the state in
1983, along with a $1 million endowment for its upkeep. It is the set-
ting for two prestigious steeplechase events each year, the very social
Carolina Cup, in March, and the continuation of the Colonial Cup, in
mid-November. The fall event is less crowded and less formal than the
spring race, but no less fun. Time your visit correctly, and you can join
the spectators enjoying an elegant lunch alfresco while they watch the
top thoroughbred 'chasers in the world running for the prized gold cup.
The winner of the Colonial Cup must lead the pack around a marathon
course that includes 17 fences.

If you can't make the race, you can visit the National Steeplechase
Museum at the Springdale Race Course or watch horse shows and riding competitions at Westfall Arena almost every weekend. The polo
ponies, too, are in action almost any Saturday at 2 P.M. at the Camden
Polo Field. It will give you a feeling for the equestrian life that still
reigns supreme in Colonial Camden.

Area Code: 803

DRIVING DIRECTIONS   Columbia is at the junction of I-20, I-26,
and I-77. From Atlanta, follow I-20 east, 215 miles. From Charlotte,
take I-77 south, 92 miles.

PUBLIC TRANSPORTATION Columbia is served by most major airlines as well as by Amtrak trains and Greyhound buses.

ACCOMMODATIONS *Claussen's Inn,* 2003 Greene Street, Columbia, 29205, 765-0440 or (800) 622-3382, M–E, CP • *Richland Street Bed & Breakfast,* 1425 Richland Street, Columbia, 29201, 779-7001, a Victorian charmer, M, CP • *Chesnut Cottage,* 1718 Hampton Street, Columbia, 29201, 256-1718, historic cottage, E, CP • *Whitney Hotel,* Devine and Woodrow Streets, Columbia, 29205, 252-0845, all suites, near Five Points, E • **Downtown hotels:** *Governor's House Hotel and Suites,* 1301 Main Street, Columbia, 29201, 779-7790, I–M • *Adam's Mark,* 1200 Hampton Street, Columbia, 29201, 771-7000, M–E • *Holiday Inn Coliseum at USC,* 630 Assembly Street, Columbia, 29201, 799-7800, M • *Clarion Town House,* 1615 Gervais Street, Columbia, 29201, 771-8711, M • **Camden:** *Greenleaf Inn,* 1308-10 Broad Street, Camden, 29020, 425-1806 or (800) 437-5874, two nineteenth-century homes, I, CP • *The Carriage House,* 1413 Lyttleton Street, Camden, 29020, 432-2430, delightful little 1840 raised cottage with antiques and an English garden, I, CP.

DINING Columbia: *Lavecchia's Seafood Grille,* 1734 Main Street, 376-8888, artful presentation of excellent food, especially seafood, M–E • *Garibaldi's,* 2013 Greene Street, Five Points, Columbia, 771-8888, art deco decor, excellent Italian, I–E • *Mangia, Mangia,* 100 State Street, West Columbia, 791-3443, another Italian winner with Tuscan specialties, I–M • *Al's Upstairs Italian Restaurant,* 304 Meeting Street, West Columbia, 794-7404, intimate dining rooms, popular, reservations advised, M–E • *Diane's on Divine,* 2400 Devine Street, Columbia, 254-3535, Continental, music on Friday and Saturday, M–E • *Motor Supply Co. Bistro,* 920 Gervais Street, Columbia, 256-6687, eclectic menu changes daily, M • *Hennessy's Restaurant,* Main and Blanding Streets, Columbia, 799-8280, varied menu, Cajun to crab cakes, longtime local favorite, M–E • *Key West Grill and Raw Bar,* 1736 Bush River Road (at I-20), Columbia, 772-0000, tropical decor, seafood and light fare, I–M • *New Orleans Riverfront,* 121 Alexander Road, West Columbia, French Quarter ambience, on the river overlooking downtown, M–E • For hearty, inexpensive Southern country cooking, look for *Lizard's Thicket,* with 14 locations all around town • **Camden:** *The Paddock House,* 514 Rutledge Street, 432-3222, renovated livery stable, pub and formal dining room, lunch, I; dinner, M.

SIGHT-SEEING *South Carolina State Museum,* 301 Gervais Street, Columbia, 898-4921. Hours: Monday to Saturday 10 A.M. to 5 P.M., Sunday 1 to 5 P.M. $$ • *South Carolina State House,* Main and Gervais Streets, Columbia, 734-2430. Hours: Monday to Friday 9 A.M. to 5 P.M., Saturday 10 A.M. to 5 P.M., and the first Sunday each month

1 to 5 P.M. Free • *University of South Carolina,* Visitors' Center, Pendleton and Assembly Streets, 777-0169. Information is also available from the admissions office of Lieber College, the Horseshoe, Sumter Street between Greene and Pendleton Streets, 777-7700. Hours: Monday to Friday 8:30 A.M. to 5 P.M., Saturday 9:30 A.M. to 2 P.M. Free campus tours offered Monday to Friday at 10 A.M. and 2 P.M.; reservations preferred • *McKissick Museum,* University of South Carolina Horseshoe, Columbia, 777-7251. Hours: Monday to Friday 9 A.M. to 4 P.M., Saturday and Sunday 1 to 5 P.M. Free • *Historic Columbia Foundation,* 252-1770, operates four historic houses; hours for all are Tuesday to Saturday 10:15 A.M. to 3:15 P.M., Sunday 1:15 to 4:15 P.M. Tickets for all are at Mill House, each $$. *Robert Mills House,* 1616 Blanding Street; *Hampton-Preston Mansion and Garden,* 1615 Blanding Street; *Woodrow Wilson Boyhood Home,* 1705 Hampton Street; *Mann-Simons Cottage,* 1403 Richland Street • *Columbia Museum of Art,* Main at Hampton Street, Columbia, 799-2810. Hours: Tuesday to Saturday 10 A.M. to 5 P.M., Sunday 1 to 5 P.M. $$ • *South Carolina Confederate Relic Room and Museum,* 920 Sumter Street at Pendleton, Columbia, 734-9813. (The museum is scheduled to move to new quarters, so check the location.) Hours: Monday to Friday 8:30 A.M. to 5 P.M., first and third Saturday each month 10 A.M. to 5 P.M. Free • *Riverbanks Zoo and Garden,* off I-126, west of downtown, Greystone Boulevard exit, P.O. Box 1060, Columbia, 779-8717. Hours: Monday to Friday 9 A.M. to 4 P.M., Saturday 9 A.M. to 5 P.M. $$$ • *Koger Center for the Arts,* University of South Carolina, 701 Assembly and Greene Streets, 777-7500. Wide variety of performances; check current schedules • *Historic Camden Revolutionary War Site,* US 521, Camden, 432-9841. Hours: Monday to Saturday 10 A.M. to 5 P.M., Sunday 1 to 5 P.M. $$ • **Steeplechase races:** *Springdale Course,* 200 Knights Hill Road, Camden, 432-6513. Phone for dates of future Carolina and Colonial Cup events and for hours of National Steeplechase Museum.

INFORMATION *Metropolitan Columbia Convention and Visitors' Bureau,* P.O. Box 15, Columbia, SC 29202, 254-0479 or (800) 264-4884 • *Columbia Visitors' Center,* 1012 Gervais Street. Hours: Monday to Friday 10 A.M. to 5 P.M., Saturday 10 A.M. to 4 P.M.; open seasonally on Sunday; www.columbiasc.net • *Kershaw County Chamber of Commerce,* 724 South Broad Street, Camden, SC 29020, 432-2525 or (800) 968-4037; www.camden-sc.org.

Rounding the Triangle in North Carolina

North Carolina's Research Triangle may be best known for business, but it holds a triple helping of treats for visitors. Raleigh, Durham, and Chapel Hill, the points of the triangle, are only minutes apart and share the thickly wooded, green countryside of the state's rolling central Piedmont. Yet each town has a distinct history and personality.

Each boasts a major university, making the three towns sports rivals, especially on the basketball court. The great Michael Jordan polished his skills at Chapel Hill, and Duke's Blue Devils play to sellout crowds in Durham from November to March.

Although each city alone could pleasantly occupy a weekend, because of their proximity many visitors try to combine them in a single trip. At the least, schedule a long weekend; you won't regret the time.

The first decision is where to stay. Each city offers an abundance of lodgings, but this vote goes to the lively ambience of Chapel Hill, a small, sophisticated community dominated by the campus of the University of North Carolina.

If you can afford the tab, the prime place in the entire triangle is eight miles south of town. The Fearrington House, a member of the prestigious Relais & Chateau group, is adjacent to the shopping village of a posh residential community. It offers elegantly furnished rooms and suites, a charming garden, and a dining room whose prix fixe dinners get raves.

Chapel Hill's chief attraction is the 700-acre campus of the oldest state university in the country. It runs along Franklin Street, the city's main thoroughfare.

Established in 1793 and enrolling students since 1795, UNC was the only public institution in the U.S. granting college degrees in the eighteenth century. Among many distinguished graduates is President James Polk. The UNC visitors' center, in the west entrance of the Morehead Building, offers maps and information about the university, including tours. Some limited metered parking is available next to the building, but safer bets are the town lots at the intersections of Rosemary and Columbia or Rosemary and Franklin Streets.

To explore on your own, ask at the visitors' center for a self-guided tour brochure or, on weekdays, check out one of the prerecorded narrated walking-tour tapes and a Walkman. Within Morehead, be sure to step into the domed and columned rotunda. It contains an impressive art collection, including Rembrandt Peale portraits of George and Martha Washington. The adjoining planetarium offers science exhibits as well as planetarium shows.

The printed tour will lead you around the old campus and some of its landmarks. These include Old East, the first campus building, still used as a residence hall; the Morehead-Patterson Bell Tower, which chimes to call students to class ten minutes before each hour; and the Old Well, where students once dipped water from an oaken bucket. Virtually the only source of water for over a century, the well is now encased by columns and a dome, and is an unofficial symbol of the university.

Allow time for the Wilson Library, whose gracious reading rooms and ornately carved ceilings have been nicely restored. Another recommended stop is the Ackland Art Museum, whose holdings include paintings by Delacroix, Rubens, and Degas, and rare Oriental art.

The campus includes an arboretum, its best-known feature a 200-foot wisteria arbor. The North Carolina Botanical Garden is another fine place for a change of pace on a pleasant day.

When you are ready for worldly diversions, the low brick buildings along Franklin Street are filled with shops, and the restored Carr Mill in Carrboro, just west of town, along Greensboro Street, offers a variety of tempting stores and restaurants. Check at the arts center in Carrboro for theater and concert performances.

Quite a different scene awaits in Raleigh. A modern city of 285,000 that celebrated its two-hundredth birthday in 1992, Raleigh has managed to keep intact most of the green squares from the original city plan. Stop at the Capital Area Visitors' Center for a free map pointing out city sights.

A tour of Raleigh almost has to begin with the stately Greek Revival–style 1840 state capitol building. Except for the offices of the governor and lieutenant governor, the work of government is now carried on elsewhere, but the original state senate and house chambers have been restored to their appearance from 1840 to 1865, complete to the desks and chairs, created originally by William Thompson, a Raleigh cabinetmaker.

Also in the neighborhood are two major state collections. The North Carolina Museum of History reflects progress from the Stone Age to the Space Age. A wide variety of displays, ranging from native plants and animals to fossils and the skeleton of a 55-foot whale, fill the North Carolina State Museum of Natural Sciences, now ensconced in a $60 million new home that makes it the largest natural-history museum in the Southeast. The seven-story facilty's highlights include the dinosaur exhibit and nearly 3,500 live animals, birds, and insects from hummingbirds to a two-toed sloth. Live exhibits include a re-created dry tropical forest and an arthropod zoo of venomous spiders and scuttling centipedes.

The nearby Governor's Mansion is an 1891 Queen Anne Victorian beauty with a magnificent ornate interior that rates a tour if you are in town when the building is open to the public. The mansion adjoins Oakwood, one of the city's oldest neighborhoods, a nice place for a walk to admire more Victorian homes.

Another neighborhood highly recommended for a visit is Raleigh's revitalized City Market, a 1914 produce district of cobbled streets and tin-roofed buildings that has been transformed into the city's arts district, with boutiques, cafés, and several small galleries. Artspace, a strikingly renovated onetime Ford showroom at the corner of Blount and Davie, includes a gallery and 30 studios and workshops where artists both create and sell their work.

Raleigh's historic highlight is Mordecai House, a columned home dating back to 1785 and occupied by the same prominent family for five generations. Their original furnishings, including a fascinating library, remain. The grounds boast an herb garden and the tiny frame cabin that was the birthplace of Carolina-born President Andrew Johnson, moved here from its original site on Fayetteville Street.

A new attraction in the historic section of town is Exploris, an interactive museum with a special mission, to encourage youth to make connections with other people in the world.

The highway known as the Beltline divides downtown and its older neighborhoods from the city's newer suburban areas. Beyond the Beltline lies a major attraction, the North Carolina Museum of Art. The $15 million contemporary showplace, designed by Edward Durell Stone, is beautifully set on 140 parklike acres. European paintings from 1300 to 1800, including 71 paintings from the important Samuel H. Kress collection; American nineteenth-century art; and an exceptional gallery of Jewish ceremonial art are strengths of the museum.

There's a pleasant sense of calm in Durham, where the downtown loop and Main Street are lined with vintage buildings dating from the 1890s to the 1930s. The whole area has been declared a historic district.

The sign at the city limits, "Welcome to Durham, City of Medicine," tells you that this is a place known for its many hospitals, the extensive facilities of the Duke Medical Center, and the presence of more than 300 medical- and health-related companies in the community.

But you can't be in town for long without being aware of another industry that formed the city—the processing of tobacco. Civil War troops were the first to discover the excellent properties of North Carolina "brightleaf" tobacco, an acquired taste that remained with them after the war. Tobacco factories, past and present, are very much in evidence around town, marked by their many brick chimneys. One former factory has been converted into a popular center for dining and shopping known as Brightleaf Square.

"Bull Durham," also the title of a popular movie a few years ago, became the city's nickname thanks to the Blackwell Tobacco Company, the first factory in town, whose symbol was inspired by the bull on the Colman's mustard jar. The original Bull Durham Factory still stands at 201 West Pettigrew Street.

By the time James B. Duke founded the American Tobacco Company in 1890, incorporating Blackwell and four other large producers, the bull was one of the best-known trademarks in the world, spawning the term "bull pen" and the expression "shooting the bull," inspired by the habits of those who chewed tobacco.

Durham residents, incidentally, are great fans of the Durham Bulls, the Class-A baseball team featured in the movie. The team has a new downtown stadium since the movie was made, and draws more than 300,000 fans each year. The snorting bull mascot seen in the film is ensconced in the new ballpark.

It's fun to start Durham sight-seeing by visiting the original Duke homestead, where you can see the humble 1852 farm where Washington Duke first grew and packed pouches of tobacco. A small museum traces the growth of the now-controversial industry.

Then head for Durham's proudest sight, the magnificent campus that resulted from tobacco profits. The original East Campus, established in 1892 as Trinity College, acquired many of its red-brick Georgian buildings and the grassy quadrangle when it was rebuilt and renamed Duke University in 1924.

Duke came into its full glory when the Gothic Revival West Campus was built between 1924 and 1938, emerging as one of the most beautiful American colleges thanks to a generous endowment from James B. Duke, Washington's son.

A statue of James Duke stands in front of the magnificent chapel that he specified to be the dominant feature of the campus. The chapel, which seats 1,470, is rich with statuary and stained glass and boasts a 120-foot bell tower. The 50-bell carillon can be heard at the end of each day. A concert on the 5,000-pipe Benjamin N. Duke Memorial Organ is held every weekday at 12:30 P.M. Free concerts and performances are also sometimes held in the 55-acre Sarah P. Duke Gardens, a beautiful blending of formal terraced landscaping and woodland surroundings. Four miles of allées, walks, and pathways lead past lawns, native wildflowers, an Asiatic arboretum, and formal plantings. The new Doris Duke Center is a handsome orientation to the gardens.

The Duke Museum of Art will soon have a fine new home. Construction began in 2000 on a new museum that will include sculpture gardens. It will bear the name of its benefactor, philanthropist Raymond D. Nasher, a Duke alumnus.

The 6,800-acre Research Triangle Park, set in the pine groves on the edge of Durham, is a unique partnership between business and academia that merits a driving tour. The Glaxo Wellcome Building, designed by Paul Rudolph, is the acknowledged architectural showpiece of the vast complex, but the park includes many other innovative designs. The breakthroughs resulting from Triangle research run the gamut from AstroTurf to AZT.

A bit of history for Civil War buffs is the Bennett Place State Historic Site, where the war ended in 1865 when Confederate general Johnston surrendered to Union general Sherman 17 days after Lee's surrender at Appomattox. The site includes a reconstructed farmhouse, outbuildings, an interpretive center, and a museum.

If children are along, Durham has some special attractions, including the hands-on exhibits at the expanding North Carolina Museum of Life and Science, where recent additions include the West Point on the Eno Park. The park offers a reconstructed working gristmill circa 1778, a nineteenth-century blacksmith shop, the Hugh Mangum Museum of Photography, and opportunities for picnicking, hiking, rafting, and canoeing.

Whatever your age and interests, you'll find plenty of pleasures in the Triangle, distinct diversions almost equally divided among the towns.

Area Code: 919

DRIVING DIRECTIONS The Research Triangle cities are reached via I-40 from east and west, I-85 and I-70 from north and south. From Atlanta or Charlotte to Chapel Hill, the southwest corner of the triangle, follow I-85 north to I-40 southeast and turn south on US 15/501; it is 356 miles from Atlanta, and 135 miles from Charlotte. Continue past the Chapel Hill exit on I-40 into US 64 for exits to Raleigh, the southeast corner. For Durham, the top of the triangle, stay on I-85 and watch for exits. Distances between triangle cities: Chapel Hill is 12 miles from Durham, 28 miles from Raleigh; the distance from Raleigh to Durham is 23 miles.

PUBLIC TRANSPORTATION Raleigh-Durham airport, 13 miles from Chapel Hill, is served by many major carriers. The Triangle area is also served by Amtrak.

ACCOMMODATIONS Chapel Hill: *Fearrington House,* 2000 Fearrington Village Center, Pittsboro (eight miles south of Chapel Hill), 28312, 542-2121, E–EE, CP • *The Inn at Bingham School,* 6720 Mebane Oaks Road, Box 267, Chapel Hill, 27514, 563-5583 or (800) 566-5583, former headmaster's home now an inn in the country, M, CP • *Hillsborough House,* 209 East Tryon Street, Hillsborough, 27278, 644-1600 or (800) 616-1660, imposing home in the historic district, M, CP • *Carolina Inn,* 211 Pittsboro Street, Chapel Hill, 27514, 333-2001 or (800) 962-8519, old standby, close to campus, E • *Siena Hotel,* 1505 East Franklin Street, Chapel Hill, 27514, 929-4000 or (800) 223-7379, luxury hotel, E • *Sheraton Chapel Hill Hotel,* 1 Europa Drive, Chapel Hill, 27514, 968-4900, hotel with tennis, health club, M • *Best Western University Inn,* Highway 54, Chapel Hill, 27514, 932-3000, upscale motel adjoining golf course, golf and tennis privileges, M.

Raleigh: *Oakwood Inn,* 411 North Bloodworth Street, Raleigh, 27604, 832-9712, bed-and-breakfast inn in historic neighborhood, M, CP • *William Thomas House,* 530 North Blount Street, Raleigh, 27604, 755-3966 or (800) OLDE-INN, 1881 Victorian bed-and-breakfast, M–E, CP • *Cameron Park Inn,* 211 Groveland Avenue, Raleigh, 27602, 828-1448, recently renovated bed-and-breakfast inn, M, CP • *Sheraton Capital Center Hotel,* 421 South Salisbury Street, Raleigh, 27601, 834-9900, convenient in-town location, M–E • *Holiday Inn State Capital,* 320 Hillsborough Street, Raleigh, 27603, 832-0501, M.

Durham: *Washington Duke Inn and Golf Club,* 3001 Cameron Boulevard, Durham, 27706, 490-0999 or (800) 443-3853, adjoining Duke campus, best in town, E–EE • *Durham Hilton,* 3800 Hillsborough Road, Durham, 27705, 383-8033 or (800) HILTONS, pool, attractive landscaping, M • *Durham Marriott at the Civic Center,* 201 Foster Street, Durham, 27701, 768-6000 central location, M • *Arrowhead Inn,* 106 Mason Road, Durham, 27712, 477-8430, 1775 colonial home just outside town, M–E, CP.

For lists of many other area hotels and motels, write to respective visitors' bureaus.

DINING   Chapel Hill: *Fearrington House* (see Accommodations on page 198), elegant, EE, prix fixe • *Crook's Corner,* 610 West Franklin Street, 929-7643, casual, delicious, and creative Southern cuisine, I–M • *La Residence,* 202 West Rosemary Street, 967-2506, charming decor, French/American menu, M–E • *Carolina Crossroads,* Carolina Inn (see Accommodations on page 198), contemporary Southern, M–E • *Pyewacket,* 431 West Franklin Street, 929-0297, varied menu, Mediterranean to Southwest, veranda, M • *411 West,* 411 West Franklin Street, 967-2782, cozy Italian café, I–M • *Il Palio,* Siena Hotel (see Accommodations on page 198), gourmet Italian, M–E • *Mama Cip's Kitchen,* 498 Rosemary Street, 942-5837, traditional Southern, I–M.

Raleigh: *Angus Barn,* Highway 70 West at Airport Road, 787-3505, rustic ambience, thick steaks, prize-winning wine list, M–EE • *Forty-Second Street Oyster Bar and Seafood Grill,* 508 West Jones Street, 831-2811, seafood, M–E • *Lucky 32,* 832 Spring Forest Road, 876-9932, eclectic menu changes monthly, popular, M • *Irregardless Cafe,* 901 West Morgan Street, 833-9920, healthy eclectic menu, jazz nightly, M • *Big Ed's City Market Restaurant,* 220 Wolfe Street, 836-9909, down-home Southern cooking for breakfast, lunch, and dinner Thursday to Saturday, I • *518 West Italian Cafe,* 518 West Jones Street, 829-2518, "California-Italian," M • *The Warehouse,* 427 Dawson Street, 836-9966, lots of tapas plus extensive menu; complex includes two nightclubs, I–M • *Cooper's Barbecue,* 109 East Davie Street, City Market, 832-7614, a local landmark since the 1920s, I.

Durham: *The Fairview,* Washington Duke Inn and Golf Club (see Accommodations on page 199), elegant dining overlooking the golf course, E–EE • *Magnolia Grill,* 1002 Ninth Street, Durham, 286-3609, creative sauces and presentations, top-rated chef, M–E • *Taverna Nikos,* Brightleaf Square, 682-0043, good Greek food in attractive, airy surroundings, I–M • *Brightleaf 905,* 905 West Naub Street, 680-8848, national praise for creative cuisine, M–E • *Cafe Parizade,* Erwin Square, 2200 West Main Street, 286-9712, colorful decor, excellent Mediterranean food, M–E • *Another Thyme,* 109 North Gregson Street, 682-5225, sophisticated multicultural cuisine, M • *George's Garage,* 737 Ninth Street, 286-4131, former supermarket turned lively restaurant, seafood and pastas, swing dancing on Friday nights, M • *The Galeria Restaurant,* Radisson Governors Inn, I-40 at Davis Drive, Research Triangle Park, 549-8631, skylight, greenery, live jazz on weekends, lunch buffet, I; dinner, M–E • *Bullock's Bar-B-Que,* 3330 Quebec Drive, 383-3211, no-frills, great barbecue, lunch or very early dinner—it closes at 7 P.M., I.

SIGHT-SEEING   Chapel Hill: *University of North Carolina at Chapel Hill,* UNC Visitor Center, 250 East Franklin Street, West Lobby, 962-1630. Hours: Monday to Friday 10 A.M. to 5 P.M., Saturday 10 A.M. to 2 P.M.; phone to check hours • *Ackland Art Museum,* Columbia Street at Franklin, UNC campus, 966-5736. Hours: Wednesday to Saturday 10 A.M. to 5 P.M., Sunday 1 to 5 P.M. Free • *Morehead Planetarium,* 250 East Franklin Street, UNC campus, 962-1236. Hours: Art and science exhibits, Sunday to Tuesday 12:30 to 5 P.M., Wednesday to Friday 12:30 to 5 P.M. and 7 to 9:30 P.M., Saturday 10 A.M. to 5 P.M. and 7 to 9:30 P.M. Free. Planetarium shows, check current schedules at 549-6863. $$ • *North Carolina Botanical Garden,* Old Mason Farm Road off US 15/501 Bypass, 962-0522. Hours: Monday to Friday 8 A.M. to 5 P.M., Saturday 9 A.M. to 6 P.M., Sunday 1 to 6 P.M. Free • *ArtsCenter,* 300G East Main Street, Carrboro, 929-2787. Check for current programs.

Raleigh: *North Carolina Museum of Art,* 2110 Blue Ridge Road, 839-6262. Hours: Tuesday to Saturday 9 A.M. to 5 P.M., Sunday noon to 5 P.M.; guided tours daily at 1:30 P.M. Free • *North Carolina State Capitol,* Capitol Square, 733-4994. Hours: Monday to Friday 8 A.M. to 5 P.M., Saturday 9 A.M. to 5 P.M., Sunday 1 to 5 P.M. Free • *Mordecai Historic Park,* 1 Mimosa Street, 834-4844. Hours: Monday and Wednesday to Saturday 10 A.M. to 3 P.M., Sunday 1 to 3 P.M. Guided tours on the hour. $$ • *North Carolina Museum of History,* 1 East Edenton Street, 715-0200. Hours: Tuesday to Saturday 9 A.M. to 5 P.M.,

Sunday noon to 5 P.M. Free • *North Carolina State Museum of Natural Sciences,* Bicentennial Plaza, 11 West Jones Street, 733-7450. Hours: Monday to Saturday 9 A.M. to 5 P.M., Sunday 1 to 5 P.M. Free • *Exploris,* 201 East Hargett Street, 834-4040. Hours: Tuesday to Saturday 9 A.M. to 5 P.M., Sunday noon to 5 P.M. $$$.

Durham: *Duke University,* 684-8111. East Campus, entrance on Main Street just past Buchanan Boulevard; West Campus, entrance on Chapel Drive off Duke University Road. Tours for prospective students leave from Undergraduate Admissions, 2138 Campus Drive, West Campus; check current schedule, 684-3214 • *Duke University Chapel,* West Campus, 684-2572. Hours: Daily 8 A.M. to 5 P.M. Free • *Sarah Duke Gardens,* West Campus, 684-3698. Hours: Daily 8 A.M. to dusk. Free • *Duke University Museum of Art,* East Campus, 684-5135. Hours: Tuesday to Friday 10 A.M. to 5 P.M., Saturday 11 A.M. to 2 P.M., Sunday 2 to 5 P.M. Free (Note that a new museum is being built; check for opening.) • *Duke Homestead State Historic Site and Tobacco Museum,* 2828 Duke Homestead Road, 477-5498. Hours: April to October, Monday to Saturday 9 A.M. to 5 P.M., Sunday 1 to 5 P.M.; rest of year, to 4 P.M. Free • *North Carolina Museum of Life and Science,* 433 Murray Avenue, 220-5429. Hours: Monday to Saturday 10 A.M. to 5 P.M., Sunday 1 to 5 P.M.; Memorial Day to Labor Day, to 6 P.M. $$$$ • *West Point on the Eno,* 5101 North Roxboro Road, 471-1623. Hours: Park open daily 8 A.M. to dusk. Tours given March to December, Saturday and Sunday 1 to 5 P.M. Free • *Bennett Place State Historic Site,* 4409 Bennett Memorial Road, 383-4345. Hours: April to October, Monday to Saturday 9 A.M. to 5 P.M., Sunday 1 to 5 P.M.; rest of year, to 4 P.M. Free.

INFORMATION *Chapel Hill/Orange County Visitors Bureau,* 501 West Franklin Street, Suite 104, Chapel Hill, NC 17516, 968-2060 or (888) 968-2060; www.chocvb.org • *Greater Raleigh Convention and Visitors' Bureau,* One Hanover Square, 421 Fayetteville Street Mall, Suite 1505, P.O. Box 1879, Raleigh, NC 27602, 834-5900 or (800) 849-8400; www.raleighcvb.org • *Durham Convention and Visitors' Bureau,* 101 East Morgan Street, Durham, NC 27701, 687-0288 or (800) 446-8604; www.durham-nc.com.

Counting Columns Near Athens

Though it is best known as the home of the University of Georgia, Athens, Georgia, has another claim to fame. Set on a hill beside the Oconee River, lush with towering oaks and leafy magnolias and filled with fine homes, Athens is the first stop on Georgia's Antebellum Trail, a swath of land missed by Yankee troops who devastated so much of the state. Stately columned mansions welcome visitors to the gracious past all the way from Athens to Macon. When you've seen one set of columns, you haven't quite seen them all, because each stop has a different personality.

Athens and its school are the perfect starting points for exploring the northern end of the trail, offering history, art, a growing slate of top entertainment, the state botanical garden, and a sports hall to delight Georgia Bulldog fans. Not far away are two unique detours, places to watch crafts in the making and a state park that can add golf and boating to the agenda. And little Madison, the final antebellum stop on this tour, is a contender for the title of "prettiest town in Georgia."

The picturesque campus that is the centerpiece of Athens was one of the country's first chartered state universities. It was established on this site in 1801, the same year Athens was founded. Many well-to-do families moved to town early in the nineteenth century to send their sons to the university, accounting for the handsome homes that abound today. A number of these homes are now occupied by campus fraternities and sororities, but whatever may go on behind the stately columns, the appearance is still classic Old South.

So is the old campus. Walk through the nineteenth-century arch at Broad Street and College Avenue to the quadrangle of the Old North Campus and feel the tradition all around you. Circling the green are venerable buildings that include the Old College (1805), Waddel Hall (1821), and Demosthenian Hall (1824). The 1832 chapel and Phi Kappa Hall, built in 1834, are beautiful examples of Greek Revival architecture.

The Founders Memorial Garden on the campus was planned as a memorial to the founders of the Athens Ladies Garden Club, the oldest garden club in the nation, formed in 1891. With its meandering flagstone walkways, slate walls, trickling fountain, and precision-cut boxwood garden, it makes for a delightful stroll. A camellia garden surrounds an 1857 brick home that is the former headquarters for the Garden Club.

You'll need your car to reach the East Campus, a major recent addition on the last undeveloped segment of the original 40,000 acres ceded by the legislature for the college. It is located between East Campus

Road and River Road, near the Athens Perimeter Road College Station Road exit.

This is where you will find the new greatly expanded Performing and Visual Arts complex, with the music school and four major performance halls, including the 1,100-seat Hodgson Hall, where major concerts and events take place. The enlarged, modern three-story Georgia Museum of Art now has ample space for its fine collection, which for years was stored belowground due to lack of space. The museum café has glass walls looking out on a central plaza.

East Campus also includes the state-of-the-art Ramsey Student Center for Physical Activities, which includes the Gabrielsen Natatorium, host to the 1997 SEC swimming and diving championships. The UGA Visitors' Center is located here in the building known as the Four Towers, at the junction of College Station Road and River Road. The greatly expanded facilities offer free campus maps and information, and interactive video displays about the university. Free campus tours leaving from the site are the best way to get a full picture of the expanse of the school.

Sports fans won't want to miss Butts-Mehre Heritage Hall, farther out to the west past the Coliseum, where they can relive the greatest moments in Georgia sports history. The polished red-granite and glass building was built with private donations and named for two past coaching greats, Wally Butts and Harry Mehre. The third and fourth floors are a salute to Georgia sports, especially the "Dawgs." There are national championship trophies and tributes to stars of yesterday, including Heisman trophy winners from Frankie Sinkwich to Herschel Walker. Videos replay memorable moments from the past.

Downtown Athens begins on Broad Street just opposite the campus gate and has its full quota of lively cafés filled with students. The central area has been declared a historic district and has its own interesting structures, such as the 1855 First Presbyterian Church, the art deco Georgia Theater, and the 1904 City Hall, a Beaux Arts building set on the highest point in town.

In front of City Hall is what is believed to be the world's only double-barreled cannon, one of the more curious relics of the War Between the States. It was invented in 1863, but unfortunately failed to fulfill its mission of firing two balls simultaneously.

The other curiosity invariably pointed out to visitors is the oak tree that stands in a square at Dearing and Finley Streets, known as "the tree that owns itself." In appreciation of the tree's beauty and sheltering shade, the owner deeded the huge tree possession of itself and all the land within eight feet around it. When the tree was destroyed by a storm in 1942, one of its acorns was planted, and the descendant of the original planting now stands in the same space.

Like its university, Athens is growing. The Classic Center downtown is a new venue for meetings and includes spaces that can hold up to

4,000 for rock concerts or 2,250 for plays, musicals, and concerts. This makes it possible for traveling Broadway shows and many other top attractions to visit the city.

Another addition is the Morton Theatre, which opened in 1910 as a vaudeville showcase for black performers, including greats like Duke Ellington, Bessie Smith, and Cab Calloway. The historic theater has been beautifully renovated and now stages a variety of events in atmospheric surroundings.

The dining scene is increasingly sophisticated as well, with everything from Spanish tapas to Creole crab dishes to Old South barbecue on the menu.

Rock music fans should plan at least one night in Athens to sample the local music scene. As home to such nationally known groups as R.E.M. and the B-52s, the city has gained a national reputation as an innovator of "new wave" rock, and there are more than a dozen places where you can hear live music. Find out who is playing where in *The Flagpole*, the free tabloid paper found in local restaurants and hotels.

With all these changes, Athens's chief attractions for many continues to be its traditional avenues of lovely white-columned Greek Revival homes. For a sampling, just drive along Prince Avenue. Lumpkin House, at number 248, is an 1843 Greek Revival mansion that belonged to the first chief justice of the supreme court of Georgia. At 570 is the home of the president of the university, guarded by 14 Corinthian columns on the front and sides and facing a five-acre garden.

The Taylor-Grady House, number 634, was built in the 1840s. A later occupant was Henry W. Grady, an Athens native who graduated from the university in 1868 and went on to become managing editor of the *Atlanta Constitution* and a leading spokesman for the New South following the Civil War. The house has been restored and is open to visitors on weekdays.

Another historic home, the Church-Waddel-Brumby House on Dougherty Street, was built in 1820. Also beautifully restored, it serves as both a house museum and the Athens Welcome Center.

On a fine fall day, one of the nicest places to be in Athens is the State Botanical Garden of Georgia. Located two miles from the campus, the 313-acre preserve is set in a forest along the Middle Oconee River. Five miles of walking paths take in dramatic ravines, spring-fed streams, and a variety of specialty gardens that include roses, dahlias, herbs, perennials, rhododendrons, azaleas, and daffodils. No matter what the weather, tropical displays surrounded by flowing streams and ponds await in the conservatory. The café there is a pleasant stop for lunch.

This beautiful spot and the campus gardens are highlights, but they have plenty of blooming company as Athens has one of the most diverse collections of gardens and specialty nurseries in the Southeast. The Athens Welcome Center has a free brochure that points the way to these treasures, the *North Georgia Garden and Nursery Trail.*

A couple of detours from Athens are rewarding. Those who favor the contemporary should definitely consider the Rivendell Bed and Breakfast Inn, eight miles away in Watkinsville. A new home built in English country style, it has striking contemporary touches such as lofty beamed ceilings, picture windows, and big stone fireplaces, and is filled with antiques and art. Another local find is Ashford Manor, a charming Victorian inn.

Watkinsville, the center of Oconee County, is another stop on the Antebellum Trail, with a historic district containing some 38 structures representing nineteenth- and twentieth-century architectural styles. Eagle Tavern, built in the late 1700s when Watkinsville was a frontier town and used for years as a stagecoach stop, is now a museum and the county welcome center. Visitors can see examples of handcrafted furniture and artifacts typical of the early days. The Elder Mill Covered Bridge is another reminder of olden days, located off Highway 15, south of Watkinsville.

A haven for many artists and craftsmen, the county is the scene of an annual juried exhibition each spring known as the Southworks Arts Festival, held at the Oconee Cultural Arts Foundation Art Center on School Street. The center also hosts ongoing exhibits, classes, and theatrical productions. The local welcome center has a guide to the studios and gift shops of area artists.

Oconee County is also a center for U-pick farms—strawberries in spring, peaches in summer, pumpkins in the fall. The welcome center can guide you to seasonal locations. Heritage Park is a nice stop for hiking and biking trails and a 10-acre lake, and the Oconee National Forest offers canoeing and hiking.

An interesting drive on a country road south of Watkinsville takes you to Happy Valley Pottery and the chance to see a thriving crafts business housed in what were once chicken coops. Jerry and Kathy Chappelle started making pottery as a sideline while he was teaching art at the University of Georgia. The venture has been so successful that they now have assistants helping to turn out the colorful decorative wares, which can be found in craft shops nationwide. Visitors are welcome to watch the potters in action, and there's a gift shop where you can see their finished work as well as work by other artisans. Phone for driving directions if you want to make the trip.

Wind your way farther south to Rutledge for another local crafts team. The Barn Raising is run by master craftsman Paul Jones and his wife, Pam, an accomplished quilter. Though the name remains, the business has outgrown its original barn quarters. Now there is a shop on the main street selling country crafts and quilts, and a workshop across the way where Paul and his staff finish wood furniture by hand, applying the patina of age to reproduction pine cabinets, tables, and chairs.

"Downtown" Rutledge runs for only a couple of blocks, but it is an interesting example of a community determined to upgrade. Notice the names on the 2,000 engraved bricks on the new sidewalks, each one bought by a resident for $30 to help with the repaving. Other craft and antiques shops are joining old-timers like the 75-year-old hardware store. The Yesterday Café, a converted turn-of-the-century drugstore, is highly recommended for a break at the sundae bar or for a meal in an old-fashioned setting that includes many vintage town photos.

From Rutledge, you are only a few miles from Madison and back on the Antebellum Trail. Madison prospered early in the nineteenth century as the county seat, where many wealthy cotton planters chose to build their fine town houses. The domed courthouse, a 1905 beauty, was once featured as the centerfold in a *Life* magazine article on courthouses of the South. More than 100 antebellum and Victorian homes remain in the town's historic district. The house tours held in May and December are always sellouts.

A walking-tour brochure and a taped guide to help you identify and date the houses are available at both the Chamber of Commerce Welcome Center and the town cultural center. As this is a small town of 3,500, a short drive or an amble are sufficient for a good sampling of the town's beauty. You can see the finest of the homes on Main Street, the Old Post Road, and Academy Street.

Worth noting is the Cornelius Vason House, at 549 Old Post Road, one of the oldest structures in town and now a private residence. It was used as a stagecoach inn on the route between Charleston and New Orleans during the period when Madison was considered the wealthiest and most aristocratic town between the two cities.

One beautiful home open to visitors is Heritage Hall, a pillared 1835 Empire-style mansion that now belongs to the Madison County Historical Society. The high ceilings, fireplaces, and typical four-over-four floor plan epitomize the antebellum era. The home is furnished with pieces from the 1830–1870 period.

Another building that can be visited is the restored 1895 Romanesque Revival–style school, now serving as the town cultural center, offering history displays, and changing art exhibits.

The Presbyterian Church, constructed in 1842 in Old English style, has a Tiffany window and a silver communion service with an interesting history. It was stolen during the Civil War and later returned by federal order. The wrought-iron chandeliers of the 1842 Advent Episcopal Church are even older than the building. The church still has its slave gallery, now quarters for the organ and choir.

When you've counted enough columns, you may want to head for Hard Labor Creek State Park, near Rutledge. The name comes from the stream running through the park; there's disagreement over whether it was bestowed by the slaves who tilled nearby fields or by Indians who found the stream difficult to ford. Be assured that the only hard labor these days is chasing lost golf balls; the 18-hole course is known for its challenge. The park also offers hiking trails, horseback riding, and a lake with a swimming beach, plus pedal boats and canoes for hire.

If the "Dawgs" aren't playing well, here's the perfect place to work off your frustration.

Area Code: 706

DRIVING DIRECTIONS   Athens is at the intersection of US 78 and US 441. From Atlanta, take I-85 north to Route 316, 66 miles.

ACCOMMODATIONS   Bed-and-breakfast inns: *Magnolia Terrace,* 277 Hill Street, Athens, 30601, 548-3860 or (800) 891-1912, comfortable accommodations in a 1912 home, spacious porch for relaxing, closest bed-and-breakfast to downtown, M, CP • *Nicholson House,* 6295 Jefferson Road, Athens, 30607, 353-2200, Colonial Revival home built around 1820, hand-hewn log house, on five acres, five miles from downtown, M, CP • *Rivendell Bed and Breakfast,* 3581 South Barnett Shoals Road, Watkinsville, 30677, 769-4522, striking contemporary home, I, CP • *Ashford Manor,* 3 Harden Hill Road, Watkinsville, 30677, 769-2633, 1893 Victorian on five acres, gardens and swimming pool, M, CP • *Burnett Place,* 317 Old Post Road, Madison, 30650, 342-4034, an 1830 Federal home, M, CP • *Brady Inn,* 250 North Second Street, Madison, 30650, 342-4400, Victorian cottage, M, CP • *Southern Cross Guest Ranch,* 1670 Bethany Church Road, Madison, 30650, 342-8027, working horse ranch offering horseback riding and full meals and/or bed-and-breakfast, M, CP.

Athens motels: *Holiday Inn,* 197 East Broad Street, 30603, 549-4433 or (800) 465-4329, indoor pool, nearest to campus, M • *Athens Courtyard by Marriott,* 166 Finley Street, 30601, 369-7000 or (800) 321-2211, I–M • *Best Western Colonial Inn,* 170 North Milledge Avenue, 30601, 546-7311 or (800) 528-1234, good value, I, CP.

DINING   Athens: *East West Bistro,* 351 East Broad Street, 546-9378, dishes from around the world, new menu each week upstairs, huge eclectic menu downstairs, M • *The Basil Press,* 104 East Washington Street, 227-8926, Mediterranean with a Southern twist, M • *Harry Bissett's New Orleans Cafe and Oyster Bar,* 279 East Broad Street, 353-7065, Cajun and Creole, I–M • *Last Resort Grill,* 174-184 West Clayton Street, 549-0810, imaginative, eclectic menu, I–M • *Broad Street Bar & Grill,* 311 East Broad Street, 548-5187, sports motifs, burgers to steaks, I–M • *The Grill,* 171 College Avenue, 543-4770, classic diner, campus favorite for burgers, etc., open 24 hours, I • *Wilson's Soul Food,* 351 North Hull Street, 353-7289, local landmark for good home cooking, I • *Bluebird Cafe,* 493 South Clayton Street,

549-3663, vegetarians' mecca serving Indian and Mediterranean fare, I
• *DePalma's,* 401 East Broad Street, 354-6966, old favorite for pizza
pasta and Italian dishes, I–M • *Charlie Williams' Pine Crest Lodge,* off
Whitehall Road, 353-2606, country setting, rustic buildings, water-
wheel, all-you-can-eat buffet at family-style tables, a local tradition,
Friday and Saturday nights only, M.

Other locations: *The Spaghetti Store,,* 24 Greensboro Highway,
Watkinsville, 769-9330, I–M • *Yesterday Café,* 120 Fairplay Street,
Rutledge, 557-9337, I • *Gautreau's Cajun Cafe,* 24 Greensboro Highway, Watkinsville, 769-9330, I–M • *Olde Colonial Restaurant,* 108
Washington Street, Madison, 342-2211, a local standby for nearly 50
years, I–M • *Blue Willow Inn,* 294 N. Cherokee Road (Georgia Highway 11), Social Circle (15 miles west of Madison), 602-2606, elegant
country inn with classic Southern fare, voted best small-town restaurant
in the South, M.

SIGHT-SEEING *University of Georgia Welcome Center,* Four Towers Building, 542-0842. Hours: Monday to Friday 8 A.M. to 5 P.M., Sat-
urday 9 A.M. to 5 P.M., Sunday 1 to 5 P.M. Check current schedule of free
guided tours • *Georgia Museum of Art,* University of Georgia, East
Campus, 542-4662. Hours: Tuesday to Saturday 10 A.M. to 5 P.M.,
Wednesday to 9 P.M., Sunday 1 to 5 P.M. Free • *Butts-Mehre Heritage
Hall,* Pinecrest Drive and Lumpkin Street, University of Georgia, 542-
9094. Hours: Monday to Friday 8 A.M. to 5 P.M. Free • *Founders
Memorial Garden,* 325 South Lumpkin Street, Athens, 542-3631.
Hours: Garden open daily, daylight hours. Free • *Taylor-Grady House,*
634 Prince Avenue, Athens, 549-8688. Hours: Monday to Friday
10 A.M. to 1 P.M. and 2:30 to 4 P.M. $$ • *Church-Waddel-Brumby
House/Athens Welcome Center,* 280 East Dougherty Street, Athens,
353-1820. Hours: Monday to Saturday 10 A.M. to 6 P.M., Sunday 2 to
6 P.M. Free • *State Botanical Garden of Georgia,* 2450 South Milledge
Avenue, Athens, 542-1244. Hours: Garden, daily 8 A.M. to dusk; Visi-
tors' Center/Conservatory, Tuesday to Saturday 9 A.M. to 4:30 P.M.,
Sunday 11:30 A.M. to 4:30 P.M. Free.

Watkinsville area: *Happy Valley Pottery,* Carson-Graves Road,
Watkinsville (phone for driving directions), 769-5922. Hours: Monday
to Friday 10 A.M. to 5 P.M., Saturday 9 A.M. to 5 P.M. • *Mockingbird
Forge,* US 441 at Farmington, 769-7147. Hours: Variable; it's best to
phone ahead.

Madison: *Heritage Hall,* 277 South Main Street, 342-9627. Hours:
Monday to Saturday 10 A.M. to 4:30 P.M., Sunday from 1:30 P.M. $ •
Madison-Morgan Cultural Center, 434 South Main Street, 342-4743.
Hours: Tuesday to Saturday 10 A.M. to 4:30 P.M., Sunday 2 to 5 P.M. $ •

Hard Labor Creek State Park, off I-20 west of Madison, 557-3001. Hours: Park, 7 A.M. to 10 P.M.; office, 8 A.M. to 5 p.m.

INFORMATION *Athens Convention and Visitors Bureau,* 300 North Thomas Street, Athens, GA 30601, 357-4430 or (800) 653-0603; www.visitathensga.com • *Oconee County Visitor Bureau,* Eagle Tavern, P.O. Box 959, Watkinsville, GA 30677, 769-5197 • *Madison Convention and Visitors Bureau*, P.O. Box 826, 115 East Jefferson Street, Madison, GA 30650, 342-4454 or (800) 709-7406.

Winter

Overleaf: Gingerbread House, Savannah. Photo courtesy of Tourist Div.,
Georgia Department of Industry and Trade

Getting the Spirit in Gatlinburg

Set in a valley ringed by high mountains, with a national park at its front door, Gatlinburg, Tennessee, has everything going for it—and sometimes a little too much. In peak season, as many as 30,000 visitors per night can invade this town of 3,500. The main street of town, often clogged with traffic, is wall-to-wall with 400 shops vying for the tourist trade.

That's why December is a wonderful time to come to town. The crowds are small and the town is aglow with its annual Smoky Mountain Lights show for the entire month. The main street is crowned by 20 glittering archways of light. All around are animated displays of lights reaching anywhere from 20 to 60 feet into the sky. They personalize the show by creating local scenes—a 40-foot log cabin commemorating the first houses in Gatlinburg, for example, or the town mascot, the Gatlinbear, shown fishing on the river or making moonshine at his still.

Sure, the jack-in-the-box popping up and the fireworks blasting off around the American flag are a little flashy, but it's Christmas, after all, and it's easy to get into the spirit.

You can enjoy the outdoors there even in winter. Ober Gatlinburg, a recreational complex at the top of Mount Harrison, just outside town, offers skiing in winter and a year-round weatherproof indoor ice arena. The road up by car is steep and windy, but an aerial tramway runs from town for 2.2 miles to the top of the mountain, providing fabulous views of the Smokies on the way.

Gatlinburg's Sky Lift cable chair travels from the main street up the steep incline of 2,300-foot Crocket Mountain, a further opportunity for glorious vistas of the area.

There's another good reason for a visit to Gatlinburg during the Christmas season: shopping. There's no better place to look for one-of-a-kind handcrafted gifts, and just down the road is Pigeon Forge, packed with outlet store bargains.

The crafts tradition is strong in Gatlinburg. Founded in the 1790s and named for a nineteenth-century merchant, Radford Gatlin, the early mountain town was so isolated that residents made their own baskets and pottery and did their own weaving out of necessity. In 1912, Pi Beta Phi, a national sorority for women, opened the Settlement School in town, where many mountain children received their first real education. The school began to teach local craftspeople how to supplement their living through a cottage-crafts industry. To provide an outlet for their wares, as well as to help support the school, the Arrowcraft Shop was subsequently established.

Now known as the Arrowmont School of Arts and Crafts, the school is still a highly respected teaching center located in the heart of Gatlinburg. The Arrowcraft Shop remains, filled with quality crafts, perfect for holiday giving.

The opening of Great Smoky Mountains National Park in 1934, with Gatlinburg as a gateway, brought more visitors and gave a real boost to the crafts movement. The largest group of independent artisans in North America now lives in the scenic hills outside town. Turn east on US 321 for about eight miles and you'll come to the Great Smoky Arts and Crafts Community, an eight-mile loop including over 70 working studios and galleries in quaint quarters.

In many studios you can meet the artists. Turn left and follow Glades Road up the hill, looping back down on Buckhorn Road. Along the way, drop in on someone like Jeff Pullium, who fashions practical and beautiful things out of pewter, silver, and copper, or Ross Markley, who turns out beautiful wooden pieces of burl and native woods and also sells Nantucket baskets and gemstone jewelry at his shop, the Woodturner. Stop into Ogle's Broom Shop, where the one-of-a-kind brooms and walking sticks made by Tammie and David Ogle have surprisingly low price tags. It's hard to imagine a pleasanter, more personal way to shop.

If you prefer to see a variety of crafts in one place, the Arts and Crafts Community comes together for an annual Great Smoky Arts and Crafts Christmas Show in early December at the Gatlinburg Convention Center. Craft shows are held at the same location in summer and mid-October, as well.

This is also the part of Gatlinburg where you'll find three extraordinary inns, each tucked away in a secluded spot with wide-screen mountain views. Until you've awakened in the morning and watched the mist melt off the mountaintops, you haven't really appreciated the full beauty of the Smokies.

Buckhorn Inn, in operation since 1938, is the picture of a cozy mountain escape. The big living room has beams, a massive stone fireplace, a grand piano, shelves filled with books, and large picture windows opening to a Smokies panorama. The inn offers dinner, with a changing and quite sophisticated menu; nonguests are welcome by reservation.

Hippensteal Inn has equally stunning views but quite a different feel. The owner is noted local artist Vern Hippensteal, and the first floor is a gallery of his work. Not surprisingly, one of his favorite subjects is the mountains. The recently built inn has Victorian-style furnishings and broad verandas across each of the three floors for mountain gazing.

The third inn, the Colonel's Lady, is a rustic and romantic hideaway with an English hostess who tells about the furnishings, which evoke the charm of an English country inn. Afternoon tea is served in the library.

Inn choices in other locations that provide quiet and mountain views are listed in the Accommodations section that follows.

Just in case you haven't checked off everyone on your Christmas list in Gatlinburg, follow Glades Road north into Bird's Creek Road, drive north through the scenic hills, and turn left at Upper Middle Creek Road toward Pigeon Forge, where there are more manufacturers' outlets than you've ever imagined in one place. They offer everything from cowboy boots and clothing to sheets and towels.

Another enjoyable stop north of town is the Apple Barn Cider Mill and General Store, where you can peek into the kitchen through a viewing window and watch apple treats in the making. The general store sells apple butter, applewood-smoked country ham and bacon, and lots of other gifts that may please someone you know.

If there's somebody really special on that list, you may want to drive a few miles farther north on US 441 toward Sevierville and the Five Oaks Factory Stores, where you'll encounter such upscale names as Brooks Brothers, Lenox China, and Magnavox.

If you want to pick an inn closer to the bargains, Blue Mountain Mist Country Inn is just the place. Set in farm country between Pigeon Forge and Sevierville, this recently built farmhouse feels as if it has been there forever—until you see the Jacuzzis in some of the rooms.

Pigeon Forge is more shopping mall and motel strip than town, but there's a lot happening here. Dollywood, the entertainment park owned by singer Dolly Parton, gets all dolled up for the season, with millions of twinkling lights outlining every village building and adorning festive trees. Even the park's triple-loop roller coaster, the Tennessee Tornado, is lit up for the occasion.

During the Smoky Mountain Christmas celebration, usually mid-November until late December, Santa is on hand in his workshop to greet children and take special orders before the holiday, and the whole family can climb aboard the Fantasy Express for a melody-filled train ride. The entertainment—a year-round feature—goes full tilt during holiday season, and Dolly herself may be on hand performing concerts with proceeds going to her Dollywood Foundation.

Dolly also has a hand in the second major attraction in Pigeon Forge, the Dixie Stampede, a four-hour show that is part rodeo, part Deep South, featuring 32 precision-trained horses and a bevy of hoop-skirted Southern belles. A four-course dinner comes with the show. From Thanksgiving through New Year's, Christmas in Dixie is the theme.

These are the biggest and best-known of half a dozen Pigeon Forge entertainment spots with names like Smoky Mountain Jubilee and Music Mountain Theatre, and other well-known performers can be heard at the Louise Mandrell Theater and the Anita Bryant Music Mansion. You'll see why the town advertises itself as "action packed."

Dolly Parton's interest in this area is no accident. She grew up in Sevierville, right up the road from Pigeon Forge, a pleasant small mountain town that is the marketing center for the surrounding farms. They've placed a handsome statue of their favorite daughter in front of the town courthouse.

Winter or no, you'll not want to visit this area without a drive into the Great Smoky Mountains National Park. In the still of winter, with the throngs and the traffic gone, you can contemplate the beauty of this great park and gain new appreciation for the mountains it preserves. On a crisp, sunny winter day, there's little fog and the vistas are even wider without foliage to block the views. It makes it easy to understand why this is the most visited of all the national parks.

Area Code: 865

DRIVING DIRECTIONS Gatlinburg is on US 441/321 at the gateway to Great Smoky Mountain National Park, 39 miles south of Knoxville. From I-40 at Knoxville, take US 441 south. From southern points, take I-75, which merges into I-40, and turn south from I-40 at US 441. It is 137 miles from Chattanooga, about 250 miles from Atlanta, 223 miles from Nashville.

ACCOMMODATIONS *Buckhorn Inn,* 2140 Tudor Mountain Road, Gatlinburg, 37738, 436-4668, M–E, CP • *Hippensteal Inn,* Grassy Branch Road, P.O. Box 707, Gatlinburg, 37738, 436-5761 or (800) 527-8110, M–E, CP • *The Colonel's Lady,* 1120 Tanrac Trail, Gatlinburg, 37738, 436-5432 or (800) 515-5432, M–E, CP • *Eight Gables Inn,* 219 North Mountain Trail, Gatlinburg, 37738, 430-3344 or (800) 279-5716, M–E, CP • *Butcher House in the Mountains,* 1520 Garrett Lane, Gatlinburg, 37738, 436-9457, M–E, CP • *Blue Mountain Mist Country Inn,* 1811 Pullen Road, Sevierville, 37862, 428-2335 or (800) 497-2335, M, CP • *Von Bryan Inn,* 2402 Hatcher Mountain Road, Sevierville, 37862, 453-9832, M–E, CP.

DINING Gatlinburg: *Buckhorn Inn* (see Accommodations above), full dinner, set menu, by reservation only, E • *The Peddler,* 820 River Road, 436-5794, cabin on the river, steak is the specialty, M–EE • *The Burning Bush,* 1151 Parkway, near the park entrance, 436-4669, varied menu, M–E • *Maxwell's,* 1103 Parkway, 436-3738, pasta to prime rib, M–E • *The Wild Plum Tea Room,* 555 Buckhorn Road, 436-3808, charming log house serving lunch only; specialties include wild plum tea and plum muffins, I • *Bennetts Pit Bar-B-Que* (two locations), 714 River Road, Gatlinburg, 436-2400; 2910 Parkway, Pigeon Forge, 429-2200; saucy ribs and sandwiches, I • **Sevierville:** *Applewood Farmhouse Restaurant,* off US 441, 425-1222, pleasant ambience, apple fritters, country ham, fried chicken, M • *Five Oaks Inn,* 1103 Parkway (US 441), 453-5994, elegant Continental menu, one of the area's best, M–E.

SIGHT-SEEING   *Great Smoky Arts and Crafts Community,* P.O. Box 807, Gatlinburg, 37738, 671-3600, www.smokymtns-crafts.com; ask for a free guide to more than 70 artists and craftsmen • *Ober Gatlinburg,* top of Mount Harrison, accessible via steep winding road off US 441; aerial tramway leaves from 1101 Parkway, 436-5423. Hours: Daily; ski area, December to mid-March; ice-skating arena and aerial tramway, year-round; usually 10 A.M. to dusk, but it's best to check. $$$ • *Sky Lift,* South end of US 441, 436-4307. Hours: Daily; winter hours vary, best to check. $$$ • *Dollywood,* US 441 at Dollywood Lane, Pigeon Forge, 428-9488 or (800) DOLLYWOOD; phone for special Smoky Mountain Christmas dates and hours. $$$$$ • *Dixie Stampede,* US 441, Pigeon Forge, 453-4400 or (800) 356-1676; phone for "Christmas in Dixie" schedules. $$$$$.

INFORMATION   *Gatlinburg Chamber of Commerce Visitors and Convention Bureau,* 446 Brookside Village Way, Suite 8, Gatlinburg, TN 37738, (800) 568-4748; www.gatlinburg.com • *Pigeon Forge Department of Tourism,* 2450 Parkway (US 441), P.O. Box 1390, Pigeon Forge, TN 37868, 453-8574 or (800) 251-9100; www.pigeon-forge.tn.us.

Savoring Christmas in Savannah

In the jazz clubs, they may sing about "Hard-hearted Hannah, the Vamp of Savannah"—but she's nowhere to be found in this sweet Southern city.

Savannah is a soft-spoken lady, her welcome warm and genuine, and cordial hospitality is as natural a part of things as the Spanish moss draping the live oaks in the town's green squares.

This hospitality can be sampled at its very best in December, when a beautiful city decks its halls and opens the doors to many of its finest private homes, each dressed in Christmas finery.

Savannah also has some unique celebrations marking the Christmas 1864 arrival of General William Sherman and his 60,000 Union soldiers. Even this infamous Yankee succumbed to Savannah's charms, and he spared the city from the burning that had accompanied much of his march. He sent a now-famous telegram to President Lincoln reading, "I beg to present to you as a Christmas gift the city of Savannah . . ."

Soldiers in authentic uniforms re-create the event at Old Fort Jack-

son, portraying the final hours prior to the troops' coming. The city had
no choice but to surrender after a coastal blockade had brought cotton
trading to a halt.

Much of Savannah still looks as it did in the 1800s, for the heart of
the town is one of America's largest urban historic districts. There are
more than 2,000 buildings of historic or architectural interest, many of
them graceful beauties adorned with wrought-iron balconies and stairs.
The buildings are all the lovelier for the greenery surrounding them, 21
landscaped squares that turn the old city into an urban garden.

It was James Oglethorpe, Georgia's founder, who, in 1733, laid out
this ingenious grid for America's first planned city—broad, straight
avenues dotted with green squares. Today the squares function almost
as outdoor living rooms for the families who live around them, places
for friendly chats, neighborhood gatherings, and sometimes even a
wedding.

A good place to get your bearings is the visitors' center in the old
railroad station. It includes the Savannah History Museum, with films
and exhibits that bring the city's past to life and mark some landmarks
with displays, such as the park bench used in the film *Forrest Gump* and
the "Bird Girl," the bronze statue pictured on the cover of the best-
selling story of Savannah's most notorious murder case, *Midnight in
the Garden of Good and Evil.*

You'll find information at the visitors' center about guided tours of
the city, most of which depart just outside. One option is a tour of the
sites in *Midnight;* all of the tours pass the beautiful Mercer mansion in
Monterey Square, the scene of the crime. There's even the "Savannah
Map of Good & Evil" for admirers of the book who want to cover all
its sites.

Since the old city is compact, walking tours are especially recommended when the weather is fine, which it usually is. Though nights are
cold, the average December daytime high is 62 degrees. Gray Line
offers the official tours of the Historic Savannah Foundation. If you
prefer a self-guided tour, pick up "Sojourn in Savannah," the official
guidebook.

However you tour, you'll learn that the earliest settlement, high on a
bluff overlooking the Savannah River, was intended as a defensive
buffer between the English port at Charleston and the Spanish settlement in Florida. But the location, just 18 miles from the Atlantic Ocean,
soon made Savannah a prominent port in its own right. The grandest
homes were the mansions of cotton barons in the halcyon days before
the Civil War, when bales of cotton from Georgia plantations were
known as "white gold."

The stately brick Federal-style Davenport House, known for its delicate plasterwork and elliptical staircase, was the inspiration for the
city's first restoration efforts. The threat to tear it down prompted a

protest by local residents and the birth in 1955 of Historic Savannah, which raised money to save the home.

Historic Savannah continues to acquire properties and hold them until preservation-minded buyers can be found. It has extended its efforts to the Victorian homes in an area beyond the original historic districts, with another 800 buildings designated as national landmarks; the results so far are less impressive than those in the original old city.

The foundation's houses are only the start of lovely homes that are open for tours. The Owens-Thomas House and Museum is an urban villa, circa 1816, said to be one of the outstanding examples of Regency architecture in the United States. The Green-Meldrim House, now the parish house for St. John's Episcopal Church, was constructed in the early 1850s and served as headquarters for General Sherman during the occupation. His troops camped in the city's Colonial Park Cemetery.

The Telfair Mansion and Museum includes opulent period rooms restored to their 1819 appearance and showing the lifestyle of a prominent family of the nineteenth century. The mansion is now part of the oldest public art museum in the South, with American, French, and German Impressionist paintings and changing exhibits in the handsomest of settings.

The classical 1848 residence of Andrew Low also has a special place in history as the site where Juliette Gordon Low founded the Girl Scouts of America in 1912. The Regency town house where Low was born has been restored and serves as the Juliette Low Center, a national program center for the Girl Scouts. Each December it joins the Owens-Thomas House in hosting a Victorian family holiday party, with caroling, parlor games, dancing, crafts, and all the trappings of Christmas past.

The 1819 Scarbrough House, a Regency–style mansion, now houses the Ships of the Sea Museum, with maritime models, antiques, and exhibits that include a replica of the *Savannah,* the first steamship to cross the Atlantic, and of the sinking *Titanic.*

The King-Tisdale Cottage has become a museum devoted to the history of African-Americans in Savannah and the Sea Islands. The Ralph Mark Gilbert Civil Rights Museum takes the saga forward into the city's struggle during that turbulent period in American history, with 15 display areas and a moving video in which Savannah natives recall their roles at that time.

As the historic preservation movement gained momentum in Savannah, the empty brick warehouses that once stored cargo along the river were transformed into shops and restaurants. Cobblestoned River Street has plenty of gift shops, and there are interesting crafts to be seen on the First Saturday festivals held outdoors on the Rousakis Waterfront Plaza from March through December. This is also the place to board a riverboat cruise on the Savannah River.

The area called City Market includes shops, restaurants, and an arts center with more than a dozen studio/art galleries where you can watch work in progress. The city specializes in antiques shops, with dozens in the historic district alone.

Savannah dining focuses on Southern-style seafood, including gumbos, deviled crab, and oyster stews, often accompanied by hush puppies and Savannah red rice. That low country favorite, shrimp and grits, is also on many menus. The number of sophisticated restaurants in the city continues to grow, especially around Market Square. Almost everyone, natives and tourists alike, visits Mrs. Wilke's Boarding House, Savannah's best-known eating place. Lunch consists of a 20-dish all-you-can-eat extravaganza. No reservations taken here—just join the line.

Among Savannah's delights are the beautiful historic homes now serving as inns where you can come home to polished silver at afternoon tea, cordials or dessert in the evening, and perhaps a praline on your pillow at night.

There are dozens of appealing choices, but two old-timers of special note for their elaborate decor are the Gastonian, comprising two 1868 town houses filled with Empire and Regency antiques, and the Ballastone, an 1835 home with the city's characteristic curved wrought-iron staircase and balconies.

Whichever inn you choose, you'll be in the heart of old Savannah—and the best of the Old South.

Area Code: 912

DRIVING DIRECTIONS   Savannah is on the Georgia–South Carolina border, 18 miles inland from the Atlantic, off I-95, exit I-16 east, or I-16 coming from the west. From Atlanta, follow I-75 south to I-16 east, about 250 miles. It is 110 miles south of Charleston.

PUBLIC TRANSPORTATION   The big modern airport outside Savannah is served by several major airlines. Limo service and cabs are available from the airport, and no car is needed to get around the historic district. Amtrak and Greyhound also have terminals in the city.

ACCOMMODATIONS   (Zip code: 31401) *Ballastone Inn,* 14 East Oglethorpe Avenue, 236-1484 or (800) 822-4553, E–EE, CP • *Foley House Inn,* 14 West Hull Street, 232-6622 or (800) 647-3708, E–EE, CP • *The Gastonian,* 220 East Gaston Street, 232-2869 or (800) 322-6603, E–EE, CP • *The Granite Steps,* 126 East Gaston Street, 233-5380, EE, CP • *Hamilton-Turner Inn,* 330 Abercorn Street, 233-1833 or (888) 448-8849, E–EE, CP • *Magnolia Place Inn,* 503 Whitaker Street, 236-7674 or (800) 238-7674, E–EE, CP • *President's Quarters,* 225 East President Street, 233-1600 or (800) 233-1776, E, CP • *Eliza*

Thompson House, 5 West Jones Street, 236-3620 or (800) 348-9378, M–E, CP • *Gaston Gallery,* 211 East Gaston Street, 238-3294, M–EE • *Bed and Breakfast Inn,* 117 West Gordon Street, 238-0518, best budget choice, M, CP • Savannah inns may be booked through a central reservations service: *Historic Reservations,* (800) 791-9393.

Small hotels with charm in the historic district: *The Marshall House,* 123 East Broughton Street, 644-7896, M–EE• *River Street Inn,* 115 East River Street, 234-6400 or (800) 253-4229, M–E • *Mulberry Inn,* 601 East Bay Street, 238-1200 or (800) 554-5544, E.

DINING *Elizabeth on 37th,* 105 East 37th Street, 236-5547, turn-of-the-century mansion, innovative Southern cuisine, tops, EE • *The Olde Pink House,* 23 Abercorn Street, 232-4286, fine dining in an eighteenth-century mansion, M–E • *17 Hundred 90 Inn,* 307 East President Street, 236-7122, Continental, rack of lamb a specialty, M–E • *River House,* 125 West River Street, 234-1900, former waterfront warehouse, casual nautical decor, M–E • *Mrs. Wilke's Boarding House,* 107 West Jones Street, 232-5997, local legend, a must for breakfast or lunch, I • *Nita's Place,* 140 Abercorn Street, 238-8233, Southern soul food, lunch only, I.

City Market area: *Bistro Savannah,* 309 West Congress Street, 233-6266, interesting Southern seafood dishes, highly recommended, M • *Garibadi's Café,* 315 West Congress Street, 232-7118, Italian, I–M • *Sapphire Grill,* 110 West Congress Street, 443-9962, creative contemporary menu, M • *The Lady & Sons,* 311 West Congress Street, 233-2600, home-style Southern • *Seasons in Savannah,* 313 West St. Julian Street, 233-2626, updated Southern, M–E • *City Market Café,* 224 West St. Julian Street, 236-7333, I–M.

SIGHT-SEEING *Christmas in Savannah.* Dozens of events beginning in late November and extending through December. Write to the Visitors' Bureau (see Information, below) for a full list • *Andrew Low House,* 329 Abercorn Street, 233-6854. Hours: Monday, Wednesday, Friday, and Saturday 10:30 A.M. to 4 P.M., Sunday noon to 4 P.M. $$ • *Davenport House Museum,* 324 East State Street, 236-8097. Hours: Monday to Saturday 10 A.M. to 4 P.M., Sunday 1 to 4 P.M. $$ • *Green-Meldrim Home,* 1 West Macon Street, 232-1251. Hours: Tuesday, Thursday, and Friday, 10 A.M. to 4 P.M., Saturday, 10 A.M. to 4 P.M. $$ • *Juliette Gordon Low Girl Scout National Center,* 142 Bull Street, 233-4501. Hours: Monday, Tuesday, and Thursday to Saturday 10 A.M. to 4 P.M., Sunday 12:30 to 4 P.M. $$$ • *King-Tisdale Foundation and Cottage,* 514 Huntingdon Street, 234-8000. Tours by appointment • *Owens-Thomas House,* 124 Abercorn Street, 233-9743. Hours: Tuesday to Saturday 10 A.M. to 5 P.M., Sunday 2 to 5 P.M. Monday noon to

5 P.M. $$$ • *Ralph Mark Gilbert Civil Rights Museum,* 460 Martin Luther King Jr. Boulevard, 231-8900. Hours: Monday to Saturday 9 A.M. to 5 P.M. $$ • *Savannah History Museum,* 303 Martin Luther King Jr. Boulevard, 238-1779. Hours: Daily 8:30 A.M. to 5 P.M. $$ • *Ships of the Sea Maritime Museum,* 41 Martin Luther King Jr. Boulevard, 232-1511. Hours: Tuesday to Sunday 10 A.M. to 5 P.M. $$ • *Telfair Mansion and Art Museum,* 121 Barnard Street, 232-1177. Hours: Tuesday to Saturday 10 A.M. to 5 P.M., Sunday 1 to 5 P.M. $$$ • *Tybee Island Lighthouse,* US 80, 18 miles east of Savannah, 786-5801. Hours: April to Labor Day, daily, except Tuesday, 9 A.M. to 6 P.M.; October to March, Monday, Thursday, and Friday noon to 4 P.M., Wednesday, Saturday, and Sunday from 10 A.M. $$.

Historic military sites: *Fort McAllister State Historic Park,* Spur 144 off US 144, 22 miles south of Savannah. Hours: Monday to Saturday 9 A.M. to 5 P.M., Sunday 2 to 5:30 P.M. $ • *Fort Pulaski National Monument,* US 89, 15 miles east of Savannah, 786-5787. Hours: Daily 8:30 A.M. to 5:15 P.M.; to 6:45 P.M. Memorial Day to Labor Day. $ • *Old Fort Jackson,* 1 Fort Jackson Road, 232-3945. Hours: Daily 9 A.M. to 5 P.M. $$.

Riverboat cruises: *Savannah River Queen,* 9 East River Street, 232-6404 or (800) 786-6404. Phone for schedules and reservations.

Walking Tours: *Savannah Walks,* 123 East Congress Street, 238-WALK or (888) SAV-WALK; *Historic Walking Tours of Savannah,* 135 Bull Street, 233-0119; *Ghost Talk/Ghost Walk,* 127 East Congress Street, 233-3896. **Other tours:** Many narrated bus, carriage, and trolley tours leave from the Visitor Center; check current offerings there.

INFORMATION *Savannah Area Convention and Visitors' Bureau,* P.O. Box 1628, Savannah, GA 31402, 236-0407 or (877) 728-2662 • *Savannah Visitor Center,* 303 Martin Luther King Boulevard, 944-0455; www.savannahvisit.com.

Season's Greetings in Asheville

It was love at first sight for George Washington Vanderbilt. The grandson of famed financier Commodore Cornelius Vanderbilt was a 25-year-old bachelor when he became enchanted with the mountain views around Asheville, North Carolina. Far from his family's palaces in Newport and points east, Vanderbilt bought up 125,000 acres surrounding Mount Pisgah and, in 1890, began to build his 255-room estate, Biltmore, still the largest private home ever constructed in the United States.

Today Biltmore is a tourist attraction that greets nearly 800,000 visitors each year. The crowds are biggest when the house is lavishly decorated for one of this country's most extraordinary Christmas tours. The tours are the star attraction of a six-week celebration throughout Asheville, which ends with a citywide First Night festival of arts on December 31 to welcome the new year.

Not the least of Asheville's holiday lures is a host of sophisticated galleries and shops that will surely inspire your Christmas giving. The city is well known as a crafts center.

Now the largest town in western North Carolina, with a county-wide population of over 190,000, Asheville was settled by Scotch-Irish immigrants whose Appalachian culture is still evident in the regional music and crafts. But when the railroad arrived in the 1880s, Asheville was discovered by the affluent. They came to spend the summer amid the beautiful mountain surroundings and helped the town develop an unusual sophistication, as evidenced by the art films, galleries, French pastries, chocolate truffles, and fine cuisine available around town. Visitors enjoy all this while still taking advantage of hiking, white-water rafting, and the Blue Ridge Parkway, just minutes away.

Biltmore remains the city's biggest attraction. When Vanderbilt decided to build his dream house, he called on Richard Morris Hunt, one of the most prestigious architects of the day, and Frederick Law Olmsted, the father of American landscape architecture.

Hunt modeled his design on the great Renaissance châteaux of the Loire Valley, using tons of Italian marble and carloads of Indiana limestone. The house required five years and an army of stonecutters and artisans to complete.

Hunt also traveled through Europe with Vanderbilt, selecting most of the 50,000 art objects that remain today. These include artworks by Renoir, Sargent, and Whistler; furniture by Sheraton and Chippendale; a chess set and gaming table that belonged to Napoleon; fifty Persian and Oriental rugs; and eight sixteenth-century Flemish tapestries.

The house was also considered one of the most advanced of its day, as it included some of Thomas Edison's first lightbulbs, central heating, a fire alarm system, elevators, indoor plumbing for all 35 bedrooms, and a newfangled gadget called the telephone.

Olmsted's contributions to this, his last project, were a great arboretum and park, a blend of European pastoral designs and his own naturalistic style. Formal gardens, a grand three-mile approach road, and a tree-lined esplanade leading to the entrance of Biltmore House were part of the plan.

George Vanderbilt did not live long to enjoy his mansion. After his death, in 1914, a large portion of the original estate was obtained by the US government, forming the nucleus for the Pisgah National Forest—a fitting development, since Vanderbilt had started the nation's first school of forestry on this land in 1898.

Biltmore Estate was inaugurated on Christmas Eve in 1895 with a lavish celebration for 200. The present-day Christmas celebrations feature re-creations of the Victorian decor of that first holiday, with the addition of lavish touches that George Vanderbilt would surely have admired.

The decorations, which the floral staff begins preparing in July, include more than 10,000 feet of evergreen roping, 1,500 poinsettias, topiary deer, 450 red velvet bows, and 130 wreaths. Rooms are aglow with 35 Christmas trees, requiring some 5,000 ornaments.

Christmas tours can be taken in the daytime or in the evening, by enchanting candlelight. Tickets can be validated for a free next-day return visit for a look at the grounds. Given the size of the house and the myriad furnishings worth a closer look, a return call is a good idea anyway.

The Biltmore has made some additions over the years. The former dairy complex is now a winery producing wines from the estate's own vineyards. The winery includes a bistro that is a fine place for lunch or dinner. The newest addition to the property is an impressive new inn with 213 rooms and suites, allowing visitors to stay on the estate.

When you've finished your tour, Biltmore Village awaits at the entrance to the estate, with a variety of upscale shops, including the exceptional New Morning Gallery, a showcase for the best of contemporary crafts.

In addition to housing for estate workers, the picturesque village, constructed from a plan by Olmsted, has a train station and the Gothic-style All Souls Episcopal Church, the latter designed by Richard Hunt in 1896.

Asheville's second noted attraction is far more modest. It is the boyhood home of author Thomas Wolfe. The boardinghouse known as the Old Kentucky Home, run by his mother, was immortalized by Wolfe in his novel *Look Homeward, Angel*. Wolfe stayed away from his home for eight years after outraging everyone with his portrait of the town. Now he is the city's favorite native, honored with an annual celebration on his birthday in early October. The home, owned by the state, has been kept exactly as it was when Wolfe lived here, and it gives interesting insight into the author's life and work. Since a recent fire, the house has been closed for restoration, but informative guided tours continue around the perimeter, and the Visitor Center is open with an exhibit on Wolfe and a slide show depicting his life.

Two other homes made festive for the holidays are the Vance Birthplace, home of Zebulon Vance, North Carolina's Civil War–era governor, and the Smith-McDowell House, an 1840 home where daytime tours and candlelight tours with music are offered.

The Grove Park Inn, the next stop for holiday touring, is another wonderful part of Asheville history. Constructed in 1913 on 140 acres atop Sunset Mountain, the building is now listed on the National Register of Historic Places and has hosted many famous guests, from Woodrow Wilson to Will Rogers. The roster includes nine US presidents. The hotel boasts one of the nation's outstanding collections of furnishings from the Arts and Crafts Movement, pioneered by furniture makers such as Roycrofters and Charles Stickley, and architects like Frank Lloyd Wright.

The building is a mountain masterpiece, built of rough-cut stones with natural slate floors and with a scalloped red-tile roof that gives the look of a rustic fairy-tale castle. The stone-walled Great Hall is stunning, with huge wooden columns, hammered-copper light fixtures, and two ceiling-high fireplaces.

Though some of the original furniture was lost as subsequent owners sought to modernize, new owners in 1955 recognized the importance of the original inn and have carefully restored and preserved what was left. Now expanded with two new wings in harmony with the original building, Grove Park is a full-scale, four-star resort. The most recent addition is a full-service spa.

The inn really gets into the spirit of things at Christmas, with its own yards of garlands and beautiful floral displays. The public is invited into the Great Hall at noon Monday through Friday to join in caroling with an enthusiastic employee chorus, cheerily clad in red and capped with Santa hats. Saturdays bring visits from Santa himself and craft demonstrations by regional artists. Evening piano concerts, candlelight caroling, and a gingerbread village and electric train display are other holiday highlights.

Grove Park is only the first of many choice lodgings in Asheville. Richmond Hill is the very picture of an elegant 1897 Queen Anne manor house, with native oak paneling, 12-foot ceilings, and a splendid staircase with hand-turned spindles as a dramatic entry to the upper floor.

More modest but no less appealing are bed-and-breakfast homes such as Cedar Crest, an 1890 Victorian not far from the Biltmore Estate, and several fine Victorian homes in the Montford Historic District, an in-town neighborhood now being rediscovered and restored. The contemporary Cairn Brae and the luxurious Inn at Wintersun will appeal to those who want a retreat in the nearby mountains surrounding Asheville. For visitors who prefer being downtown, the Haywood Park Hotel offers oversized rooms in a novel setting—a renovated department store.

When you take time to explore downtown, you'll find a surprising juxtaposition of buildings, the old mixed with the new, jarring in spots but on the whole a good sign of the rejuvenation of the city center. The city claims that it has more art deco architecture from the 1920s and 1930s than any other Southeastern city except Miami Beach. The pink-roofed City Building, at 70 Court Plaza, is the prime example.

An I. M. Pei–designed tinted-glass office building seems out of place, but the Pack Place Arts and Science Center is an important and attractive addition to downtown, providing a home for the Asheville Art Museum, a gem and mineral museum, a hands-on health museum for children, and a theater.

Asheville's most famous crafts group is the Southern Highland Handicraft Guild, which operates the Folk Art Center and a crafts shop on the Blue Ridge Parkway just outside town. A visit also gives the chance for a drive along the scenic parkway. The guild also has a gallery on US 70 in Asheville.

More galleries and interesting small shops can be found along Biltmore Avenue, Haywood Street, and the other angled lanes that make for interesting browsing downtown. Antiquers may also want to make a foray east on I-40 to Black Mountain, where Cherry Street is loaded with shops.

You might want to note that the Chocolate Fetish, in the Haywood Park Hotel Promenade, was rated by the *Los Angeles Times* as the nation's best maker of chocolate truffles. It's a sweet idea for someone special on your shopping list.

Area Code: 828

DRIVING DIRECTIONS   Asheville is in the mountains of western North Carolina, reached via I-40, I-26, or the Blue Ridge Parkway. From Atlanta, take I-85 north past Greenville, South Carolina, to I-26 north, about 208 miles. Asheville is 113 miles from Charlotte via I-77 north to I-40 west, 110 miles from Knoxville via I-40 east.

PUBLIC TRANSPORTATION   The Asheville Regional Airport is served by several major airlines.

ACCOMMODATIONS *Haywood Park Hotel,* One Battery Park Avenue, Asheville, 28801, 252-2522 or (800) 228-2522, E, CP • *Renaissance Asheville Hotel,* One Thomas Wolfe Place, Asheville, 28801, 252-8211, newly refurbished luxury hotel, many rooms with mountain views, E–EE • *Grove Park Inn Resort,* 290 Macon Avenue, Asheville, 28804, 252-2711 or (800) 438-5800, E–EE • *Inn on Biltmore Estate,* c/o the Biltmore Company, One North Park Square, Asheville, 28801, (800) 858-4130, E–EE • *Richmond Hill Inn,* 87 Richmond Hill Drive, Asheville, 28806, 252-7313 or (888) 742-4549, E–EE, CP • *Cedar Crest Victorian Inn,* 674 Biltmore Avenue, Asheville, 28803, 252-1389, M–E • *Albemarle Inn,* 86 Edgemont Road, Asheville, 28801, 255-0027, handsome columned early 1900s home, M–EE, CP • *Cairn Brae,* 217 Patton Mountain Road, Asheville, 28804, 252-9219, mountain retreat, M–E, CP • *Inn at Wintersun,* One Winterson Lane, Fairview, 28730, 628-7899 or (888) 628-1628, luxury estate on 80 acres, 15 minutes from Asheville, E–EE, CP.

Montford neighborhood: *Wright Inn and Carriage House,* 235 Pearson Drive, Asheville, 28801, 251-0789 or (800) 552-5724, M–EE, CP • *The Colby House,* 230 Pearson Drive, Asheville, 28801, 253-5644 or (800) 982-2118, M–E, CP • *The Lion and the Rose,* 276 Montford Avenue, Asheville, 28801, 255-ROSE or (800) 546-6988, E, CP • *Flint Street Inns,* 116 Flint Street, Asheville, 28802, 253-6723 or (800) 234-8172, M, CP.

Motels near Biltmore Estate: *Quality Inn Biltmore,* 115 Hendersonville Road, Asheville, 28803, 274-1800, M–E • *Forest Manor Inn,* 866 Hendersonville Road, Asheville, 28893, 274-3531, pleasant wooded grounds, I–E, CP • *Howard Johnson–Biltmore,* 190 Hendersonville Road, Asheville, 28803, 274-2300, I–E • There are many additional motels; write for a full list.

DINING *23 Page,* Haywood Park Hotel (see Accommodations above), stylish, sophisticated menu, M–E • *Gabrielle's,* Richmond Hill Inn (see Accommodations above), lovely Victorian setting, EE, prix fixe • *Horizons,* Grove Park Inn (see Accommodations above), elegant, E–EE • *Vicenzo's,* 10 North Market Street, 254-4698, art deco dining room, upscale Italian, M–E • *Biltmore Winery Bistro,* Biltmore Estate, 274-6341, convenient for sightseers, pizza to full meals, I–M • *Possum Trot Grill,* 8 Wall Street, 253-0062, Cajun, I–M • *Windmill European Grill,* 85 Tunnel Road, 253-5285, German and many other Continental cuisines, M • *The Market Place,* 20 Wall Street, 252-4162, high ceilings, pleasant ambience, fine dining, M–EE • *Café on the Square,* 1 Biltmore Avenue, Pack Place, 251-5565, American, California accent, I–M • *Barley's Tap Room,* 42 Biltmore Avenue, 255-0504, young and lively, good pizza and 24 kinds of beer on tap, live music, I • *The Laughing Seed,* 40 Wall Street, 252-3445, innovative vegetarian menu, popular, I–M • *Blue Moon Bakery,* 60 Biltmore Avenue, Asheville, 252-6063, boulangerie/patisserie with bistro tables for breakfast and lunch, delicious pastries, I • *Mountain Smokehouse,* 820 Fairview Road, 298-8121, chopped pork and fried chicken, bluegrass band and clogging, I.

SIGHT-SEEING *Biltmore Estate,* just north of I-40, exit 50 or 50B, Asheville; request information from One North Park Square, Asheville, 28801, 274-6333 or (800) 242-6480; www.biltmore.com. Hours: Daily 9 A.M. to 5 P.M. $$$$$ • *Christmas at Biltmore,* from early November to January 1. Daily daytime and candlelight evening tours, reservations required, available after July 1 by calling (800) 289-1895. $$$$$ • *Light Up Your Holidays Festival,* mid-November to December 31, includes concerts, caroling, tours, parade, exhibits, and First Night community-wide New Year's Eve celebration; for complete schedule, contact Asheville Convention and Visitors Bureau (see Information, below) • *Thomas Wolfe Memorial State Historic Site,* 48 Spruce Street, 253-8304. Hours: April to October, Monday to Saturday 9 A.M. to 5 P.M., Sunday 1 to 5 P.M.; rest of year, Tuesday to Saturday 10 A.M. to 4 P.M., Sunday 1 to 4 P.M. $ • *Zebulon Vance Birthplace State Historic Site,* Reems Creek Road off US 25 north, near Weaverville, 645-6706. Hours: November to March, Tuesday to Saturday 10 A.M. to 4 P.M., Sunday 1 to 4 P.M.; rest of year, Monday to Saturday 9 A.M. to 5 P.M., Sunday 1 to 5 P.M. Donation • *Smith-McDowell House,* 283 Victoria Road, 253-9231. Hours: April to December, Tuesday to Saturday 10 A.M. to 4 P.M., Sunday 1 to 4 P.M.; rest of year, closed Sunday. $$ • *Pack Place,* 2 South Pack Square, 252-3866. Hours: Tuesday to Saturday 10 A.M. to 5 P.M, Sunday 1 to 5 P.M. One ticket admits to *Asheville Art Museum, Colburn Gem and Mineral Museum, Health Adventure,* and *YMI Cultural Center,* $$$; or individual museums. $$ • *Folk Art Center,* Blue Ridge Parkway, Milepost 382, 298-7928. Hours: April to December, daily 9 A.M. to 6 P.M.; rest of year, to 5 P.M. Donation • *Biltmore Homespun Shops,* Grovewood Road near Grove Park Inn, 253-7651. Hours: April to December, Monday to Saturday 10 A.M. to 6 P.M.; rest of year, Monday to Saturday 9 A.M. to 6 P.M. Includes North Carolina Homespun Museum and Antique Auto Museum. Free.

INFORMATION *Asheville Convention and Visitors Bureau,* P.O. Box 1010, Asheville, NC 28802, 258-6102 or (800) 280-0005; www.ashevillechamber.org.

Having a Blast in Huntsville

Where would you go to see the Saturn V rocket that took the first Americans to the moon . . . to find out how it feels to experience the "g" forces astronauts encounter on launch and reentry . . . to buckle up for a let's-pretend mission aboard a space shuttle?

The answer is Huntsville, Alabama, the birthplace and showplace of America's space program. More than 1,500 pieces of rocket and space hardware and over 60 hands-on exhibits are part of Huntsville's out-of-this-world US Space and Rocket Center.

A visit brings back the exciting days when America was making its first forays into space and reminds the visitor of Huntsville's leading role in that drama. It's also an opportunity to get acquainted with one of Alabama's most interesting cities, past, present, and future. Uncrowded March is an excellent time for a visit, especially on a weekend warm enough to take advantage of the parks and recreation that abound in and around town.

The state of Alabama was actually born in Huntsville. John Hunt, a pioneer from Tennessee, was the first to settle there, moving his family to a log home near a spring in 1805. Later, when the Huntsville land office became the place where most of the public lands in the northern part of the Alabama Territory were offered for sale, people from all over flocked there to buy parcels in the fertile Tennessee Valley. By 1818 it seemed natural to make this the temporary capital, where the first constitution for the twenty-second state was drafted in 1819 and the first governor was inaugurated.

The capital was moved to a more central location, but Huntsville continued to prosper as the processing center for cotton raised in the surrounding countryside. It flourished until the Civil War, continuing to furnish political leadership for the state. One of the largest collections of fine antebellum homes in Alabama survived the war with little harm because Huntsville became headquarters for the troops in the area and the town was spared.

It was almost a century later that this textile town of 16,000 began to change dramatically. The army needed a place to manufacture chemical weapons at the start of World War II, and 39,000 acres of cotton fields near Huntsville became the Redstone Arsenal. In 1950, Wernher von Braun and 117 other German rocket scientists were sent to Redstone to do rocket research, and the Space Age was born. The Redstone, America's first rocket providing the capability to launch an artificial satellite, was developed there. The Redstone Arsenal was responsible for *Explorer I,* sent into orbit in 1959.

In 1960, the Marshall Space Flight Center was created when space exploration was transferred from the military to the National Aeronautics and Space Administration (NASA). The sixties were the glory years when John Glenn made his historic orbit around the earth and Neil Armstrong stepped onto the moon. Von Braun had gone back to Washington by 1972, but Huntsville was still in the forefront, developing the Skylab space station. It is currently building portions of the International Space Station and designing next-generation rockets.

The US Space and Rocket Center, the world's largest space science museum, is spectacular. The space program is traced there in a lively way that invites visitors to get involved. Allow at least half a day for a visit.

You might want to start in the Spacedome Theater, where the IMAX movies feature breathtaking photography shot from hundreds of miles above the earth's surface by the crews of space shuttle missions. Viewers share this ride around the earth and into the stars, with the sensation of being suspended in space.

Having sensed some of the excitement of space travel, you are ready to see what it took to launch those astronauts. Floor guides in orange space suits are strategically placed to give information and answer your questions.

Among many highlights in the big museum is the space shuttle orbiter mock-up, built in 1977 and used to test equipment and procedures for the first shuttle launch, and Rocket City Legacy, which utilizes artifacts, video, and exhibits to depict Huntsville's role in the space program,

Much of the fun in the museum comes from participatory exhibits that allow you to sit in an Apollo capsule mock-up, perform tasks with a robotic arm, and land the space shuttle. The G Force Accelerator takes 45 people at a time on an introduction to astronaut training, the multi-g forces of launch and reentry. The Mars Mission simulator is a make-believe voyage to the red planet.

The Space Shot gives new meaning to the word *liftoff.* The $1.3 million thrill ride simulates a 45-mile-per-hour trip straight up a 180-foot tower. You even experience two or three seconds of weightlessness at the top of the ride.

The four-acre Rocket Park outside the building is the world's most comprehensive collection of rockets, including the first Saturn V built for NASA and now a national historic landmark. A full-size upright replica of the Saturn V can be seen for miles, towering above the space center.

Also outside is the $200 million Lockheed SR-71/A-12 Blackbird, the air force spy plane that set many speed and altitude records before being retired in 1990. The Blackbird is capable of flying 2,200 miles per hour, three times the speed of sound.

If you would like to tour some of the current NASA facilities where rockets are developed and where a space station is being built, you can sign up for bus tours at the ticket desk in the main lobby.

If you really want to get involved in space, you can enroll in the U.S. Space Camp, a firsthand introduction to the space program that includes a simulated mission to Mars. There are weeklong and weekend camps for adults and for schoolchildren, and a weekend parent-child camp that is the ultimate in Space Age togetherness.

Needless to say, all of this activity has brought huge changes to Huntsville, where a quarter of the jobs are with the army or NASA. The Cummings Research Park has headquarters for many major companies working with the space programs, resulting in another 16,000 high-tech employees. The population of Huntsville has increased tenfold, and the city now boasts one of the South's highest median incomes.

The downtown is a pleasant mix of gracious old and striking new. The 1860 depot has been nicely restored and offers an audiovisual presentation on the history of Huntsville, with lifelike animated figures discussing the good old days. Displays include vintage trains and a delightful operating scale model of the depot yards and its steam trains as they looked in the mid-1860s.

Downtown still centers around the old Courthouse Square, where there is history on all sides. On the west side stands the last of the original buildings of early Huntsville, the 1835 Greek Revival First Alabama Bank, which has been in continuous service since it was built. It is now known as the Regions Bank.

On the east side is the 1845 Schiffman Building, one of several remaining antebellum commercial structures. The actress Tallulah Bankhead was born in a second-floor apartment there in 1902.

To the south, the Harrison Brothers Hardware Store has been in business since 1879 and remains the picture of an early mercantile establishment. It has been nicely preserved and is now operated by the Historic Huntsville Foundation. Purchases are still wrapped in brown paper and tied with string.

Constitution Village, commemorating Alabama's entry into the Union at the 1819 Constitutional Convention, is just south of the square on Gates Avenue. Four major buildings of the period from 1805 to 1819 have been reconstructed here. Costumed interpreters bring back the days of 1819 as they take you through Constitution Hall, the Clay Building, the Boardman complex, and the Neal Residence and Kitchen.

It is interesting to note that the 44 men who shaped the state's future met in a carpenter's shop. From this group would come six Alabama governors and half a dozen United States senators. Today there is a young carpenter on hand to demonstrate the woodworking skills employed in the shop before and after its brief role in history.

A recent addition near the Constitution Center is the EarlyWorks Children's Museum, dramatizing the city's history. This hands-on two-story learning center showcases nineteenth-century Alabama's natural resources, lifestyles, and occupations in a lively and entertaining way. Exhibits include tales told by a talking tree, an old-time cabinet shop, a robotic telegrapher, and demonstrations of early hearth cooking. The experience is truly hands-on—you have the chance to try on old-fashioned clothing, board a floating 46-foot keelboat, and play instruments on an interactive bandstand.

The city's two historic districts also begin just off the square. The Twickenham District, to the southeast, is where you can see more than 60 antebellum homes in a three-mile radius. Descendants of original owners still live in many of these homes, some of which are open for touring during the Huntsville Pilgrimage in spring and on the Christmas Holiday House Tour, held the second Saturday of December.

The 1819 Weeden House Museum, a superb example of Federal architecture, is always open to the public. It was the home of nineteenth-century poet and artist Maria Howard Weeden, and it exhibits many of her paintings. This is the oldest building in Alabama open to the public.

The Old Town District, to the northeast, consists mainly of residences built between 1870 and 1930, forming an attractive neighborhood of closely spaced, ornate Victorian homes. Free printed tours of both this and the Twickenham District are available at the town information center.

The sleek new Huntsville can be seen at the Big Spring International Park, on the west side of the square. It includes the site of the spring where John Hunt founded the city in 1805. This spring is big, indeed. Its fresh water, flowing at the rate of 24 million gallons a day, comes from beneath the rocky bluff dominated by the Regions Bank and flows into a lagoon surrounded by the handsome park. The landscaping includes many gifts from foreign countries, the most dramatic being the red sculptured "friendship bridge" from Japan that spans the lagoon. The recently built Huntsville Museum of Art in the park offers seven galleries to show its own collections and touring exhibits.

Across the lagoon is the attractive Wernher von Braun Civic Center, the town's cultural hub, which houses an auditorium seating 10,000, exhibit halls, and the tourist information center.

One of the newer attractions in Huntsville is Sci-Quest, the North Alabama Science Center, a chance to explore and experience science. Exhibits cover topics such as aerodynamics, electricity, light and optics, mechanics and motion. Hands-on exhibits such as a flight simulator and bubble tanks engage visitors young and old.

For a change of pace, the Huntsville Botanical Gardens, near the Space and Rocket Center, is a pleasant getaway, with 112 acres of woodland paths and dogwood trails and seasonal floral displays. A butterfly house is open from May into October, and the garden is transformed with colorful holiday lights from Thanksgiving until New Year's Day.

There's more nature to be found if you follow US 431 east of town four miles to the top of Monte Sano, where Monte Sano State Park covers 2,140 acres, offering an abundance of trees, scenery, and scenic overlooks.

The Burritt Museum and Park, also set atop the mountain, provides its own scenic views and the chance to tour a 14-room mansion built by a prominent Huntsville physician. Historic structures there include log cabins, a blacksmith shop, a smokehouse, and a wooden church. Picnic tables and wooded trails beckon visitors.

The Madison County Nature Trail, 12 miles from downtown on Green Mountain, is another outdoor sanctuary offering wooded paths, a 16-acre lake, a covered bridge, and a wildlife sanctuary. More recreation awaits at the Madison County Lake, 105 acres including boat rentals and picnic facilities. Ditto Landing Marina, south of town, is the area's major access to the nearby Tennessee River.

Golfers seeking an outing need look no farther than Hampton Cove, off US 431 south, where there are 54 holes of championship golf designed by Robert Trent Jones. This is the start of Alabama's Robert Trent Jones Golf Trail and is a top-notch public golf facility in a mountain setting.

All of which goes to show that Huntsville is state-of-the-art on earth as well as in space.

Area Code: 256

DRIVING DIRECTIONS Huntsville is on US 72, reached via I-565 off I-65. It is 101 miles north of Birmingham via I-65 north to I-565. From Atlanta, take I-20 west to I-65 north, 180 miles. From Nashville, follow I-65 south, 103 miles.

PUBLIC TRANSPORTATION Several major airlines serve Huntsville International Airport.

ACCOMMODATIONS *New Country Inn and Suites,* 4880 University Drive, Huntsville, 35816, 837-4070 or (800) 456-1578, attractive grounds, M • *Radisson Suite Hotel,* 6000 South Memorial Parkway, Huntsville, 35802, 882-9400, near Space Flight Center, M • *Huntsville Marriott,* 5 Tranquility Base at Space Center, Huntsville, 35805, 830-2222, indoor/outdoor pool, M • *Hilton Huntsville,* 401 Williams Avenue, Huntsville, 35801, 533-1400, good downtown location, M • *Holiday Inn Express,* 3808 University Drive, Huntsville, 35816, 721-1000, I • *Courtyard by Marriott,* 4804 University Drive, Huntsville, 35816, 837-1400, I–M • *Days Inn North,* 2201 North Memorial Parkway, Huntsville, 35810, 536-7441 or (800) 329-7466, I • All hotels listed above have outdoor pools.

DINING *Green Bottle,* 975 Airport Road SW, 882-0459, fine regional cooking, one of the best in the area, M–E • *Ol' Heidelberg*

Café, 6125 University Drive, HQ Shopping Center, 922-0556, German decor and food, longtime standby, I–M • *Fogcutter Restaurant,* 3805 University Drive Northwest, 539-2121, steaks and seafood, salad bar, business lunch favorite, I–M • *Green Hills Grille,* 5100 Sanderson Road, 837-8282, Southwestern, I–M • **Downtown choices:** *Jazz Factory,* 109 North Courthouse Square, 539-1919, San Francisco cuisine, M • *Bubba's,* 109 Washington, 534-3133, ribs and burgers, business crowd by day, lively sports bar at night, I–M; *Bubba's BBQ,* 101 Washington Street, 534-9888, I • *Eunice's Country Kitchen,* 1004 Andrew Jackson Way, 534-9550, the place for a hearty Southern breakfast or lunch, famous biscuits, I.

SIGHT-SEEING *US Space and Rocket Center,* One Tranquility Base, just off I-565/US 72A, 837-3400. Hours: Daily 9 A.M. to 5 P.M. $$$$$ • *Alabama Constitution Village,* 109 Gates Avenue, 535-6565. Hours: Monday to Saturday 9 A.M. to 5 P.M. $$$ • *EarlyWorks Children's Museum,* 404 Madison Street, (800) 678-1819. Hours: Monday to Saturday 9 A.M. to 5 P.M. $$$$ • *Historic Huntsville Depot,* 320 Church Street, 554-8100. Hours: Monday to Saturday 9 A.M. to 5 P.M. $$$; Trolley tours. $ • *Huntsville Museum of Art,* 320 Church Street, 535-4350. Hours: Tuesday to Saturday 10 A.M. to 5 P.M., Thursday to 9 P.M., Sunday 1 to 5 P.M. Donation • *Weeden House Museum,* 300 Gates Avenue, 536-7718. Hours: March to December, Tuesday to Saturday 1 to 4 P.M. $ • *Sci-Quest, the North Alabama Science Center,* 102D Wynn Drive, off I-565, 837-0606. Hours: Tuesday to Friday 9 A.M. to 6 P.M., Saturday noon to 6 P.M., Sunday 1 to 6 P.M. $$ • *Burritt Museum and Park,* 3101 Burritt Drive, off US 431 east, 536-2882. Hours: Park grounds open daily 7 A.M. to 7 P.M. $$; mansion open March to mid-December, Tuesday to Saturday 10 A.M. to 4 P.M., Sunday noon to 4 P.M. Free with park admission • *Huntsville Botanical Garden,* 4747 Bob Wallace Avenue, 830-4447. Hours: May to October, Monday to Saturday 8 A.M. to 6:30 P.M., Sunday 1 to 5 P.M.; rest of year, Monday to Saturday 9 A.M. to 5 P.M., Sunday 1 to 5 P.M. $$ • *Madison County Nature Trail,* South Shawdee Road, Green Mountain, 883-9501. Hours: Daylight hours. Parking fee, $ • *Monte Sano State Park,* 5105 Nolen Avenue, off US 431 east, 534-3757. Hours: Daylight hours. Parking fee, $ • *Ditto Landing Marina,* Hobbs Island Road off US 231, north of the river, 883-9420 or (800) 552-8769, picnic facilities on the Tennessee River. Hours: Daylight hours. Free • *Hampton Cove Golf Course,* US 431 south, 551-1818, phone for golfing information, tee times.

INFORMATION *Huntsville Convention and Visitors Bureau,* 700 Monroe Street, Huntsville, AL 35801, 551-2230 or (800) 772-2348; www.huntsville.org

Under the Spell in Charleston

You'll need no photographs to remember a visit to Charleston. This seductive charmer casts a spell that lingers long in the memory.

On the streets of the old city, it could still be the eighteenth century. Church spires remain the tallest points in the Charleston skyline. No city in America has done a better job of preserving its original homes—block after block of them, tempting visitors out to walk, to admire the graceful tiered piazzas, to peek in at the hidden gardens.

Spring is considered the prime season in Charleston, but it is also the most crowded. Since temperatures are mild most of the year, those who plan a late-winter trip will get the lowest rates at inns and have the city almost to themselves.

Simply exploring the streets of this beguiling city would make for a memorable visit, but an eventful 350-year history has left a rich sight-seeing legacy, from plantations and formal gardens to museums and magnificent churches. Antiquing is choice, and water and beaches beckon on all sides. In fact, the only problem in Charleston is finding time for all the possibilities.

A carriage ride from the City Market through the historic district and along the waterfront is the traditional way to get the lay of the land and learn a bit of local lore. You'll discover that Charleston's first English settlers, who arrived in 1670, were joined the next year by pioneers from Barbados, accounting for the pastel colors and semitropical feel the city retains to this day. The lineup known as Rainbow Row, along the waterfront battery, is a favorite subject for local artists.

Charleston quickly prospered as a seaport. Ships sailed out carrying first furs and lumber, then rice, indigo, and cotton. They returned with fine goods from around the world, giving Charleston the reputation of a cultured "little London" in the wilds of the New World, the richest city in the South, with maritime traffic that surpassed that of Boston. America's first municipal college, museum, and formal garden were established in Charleston in the 1700s.

This was also one of the first planned towns in the colonies, laid out with two "great streets," Market and Broad, intersecting at Market Square. The gracious plan still stands.

Churches are plentiful, as part of the city's early sophistication resulted from its attitude of religious tolerance, which attracted a host of settlers to the "Holy City." By the end of the eighteenth century, the first Baptist church in the South and the nation's second-oldest synagogue had been established, and there were churches for French Huguenots, Congregationalists, Scotch Presbyterians, Lutherans, Methodists, and Roman Catholics.

The lovely Colonial-style St. Michael's Episcopal Church, dating to 1761, is one of the few city churches in America that retains its original design. It was there that George Washington and Robert E. Lee worshipped while in Charleston. The steeple, now beautifully restored, was one of the most prominent victims of Hurricane Hugo in 1989.

Charleston has been a sunnier place since Hurricane Hugo paid its unwelcome call and claimed some of the ancient, moss-draped live oaks that once formed a shady canopy. But some say this only makes it easier to see the beauty that has remained in full measure. And the tour guides remind visitors that the city has recovered from worse disasters over the years—fire, plague, other hurricanes, and occupation in both the Revolutionary War and the Civil War.

The Civil War started at Fort Sumter, off Charleston Harbor, and bombardment during the war was so heavy that by the time Union troops came in, they were greeted only by vacant houses, deserted warehouses, gardens gone to seed, and grass growing in the streets. No sooner had reconstruction gotten under way than an earthquake shook things up further in 1886. Metal earthquake rods installed in surviving homes to fortify them in case of future catastrophes are still obvious.

All this misfortune proved a blessing in disguise. Charleston was too poor to "modernize," so her historic homes remained, shabby but unchanged, while other cities remodeled to suit the gingerbread styles of the Victorian era. Saving this irreplaceable architecture was the goal when the Preservation Society of Charleston was formed in 1920. This is the oldest community-based preservation organization in the nation. In 1931 Charleston enacted the first historic district ordinance in the United States, and preservation fever spread.

The Festival of Houses and Gardens, held in April, and the House and Garden candlelight tours of private homes each fall, offer an inside view of some of the wonderful results.

After gaining an overview of the city via carriage, it's time to get out on foot, the only way to fully appreciate Charleston's color and charm. You can do it yourself with a printed guide, available from the visitors' center, or sign up for any of several guided walking tours.

One simple route to follow on your own is to begin at the City Market, following Meeting Street to the water, then come back on Church Street, passing many of the city's most important sites along the way. The Market, established in 1788, was the main trading mart for the town in early days. It is now filled with shops, many quite touristy, but among the open-air vendors are ladies at work weaving the sweetgrass baskets that are a Charleston tradition, brought by the first arrivals from Africa.

Take time to stop in at the fine Gibbes Museum of Art on Meeting Street to see the work of Charleston artists like Alice Ravenel Huger Smith, whose watercolors so beautifully depict the rice plantations that produced the city's early wealth. The museum also has interesting collections of Oriental art and of miniature portraits from the eighteenth and nineteenth centuries.

In the Council Chamber of the 1801 City Hall, at the corner of Meeting and Broad streets, are many exceptional early portraits, including a Trumbull portrait of George Washington. In the shade of the post office and the federal court on the opposite corner are more ladies creating those unique baskets and wreaths.

At number 51 is one of the grandest of the homes maintained by the Historic Charleston Foundation, the Nathaniel Russell House, built in 1808 and famed for its "flying staircase," spiraling upward for three floors with no visible means of support.

Quaint Tradd Street is one of many lanes that extend from river to river, lined all the way with lovely homes. Detour there or on almost any side street to admire the piazzas and the almost hidden gardens beyond. A few of the streets still have their original cobblestone paving.

At the end of Meeting Street are the mansions of the Battery and a park and promenade along the water. The Greek Revival–style Edmonston-Alston House, at 21 East Battery, is one of the more ornate homes open for touring.

The waterfront, continuing east of the old city walls opposite Fort Sumter, long a center for wharves and warehouses, has given way to Waterfront Park, which won the 1992 Federal Design Achievement Award.

Heading back on Church Street takes you past another home worth looking into, the 1770 Heyward-Washington House, once owned by a signer of the Declaration of Independence. The walk also leads past the venerable Dock Street Theater, which opened back in 1736 when the street was known as Dock Street, and finally to St. Philip's, whose cemeteries include the graves of many distinguished early South Carolinians. The greatest of them all, John Calhoun, a vice president of the United States, was relegated to the west side of the street, unable to be buried in the yard next to the church because he was not a Charleston native.

Rebuilt in 1835 following a fire, St. Philip's was long known as the Lighthouse Church for the light in the steeple that once guided ships into port.

If time allows, visit the northern part of the city for the Charleston Museum, America's oldest, now in a $6 million complex loaded with clothing, furniture, silver, photos, and other memorabilia from Colonial times through the Civil War. Two fine restored period homes are under museum supervision, the 1803 Joseph Manigault House and the 1772 Heyward-Washington House. Combination tour tickets are available.

The museum is part of the revival of this part of town, along with the big, handsome Visitors' Reception and Transportation Center, in the former train depot.

The newest attraction in Charleston, the South Carolina Aquarium on Charleston harbor, invites a visit to appreciate its bounty of colorful exhibits.

A drive north on South Carolina Route 61 to the plantations along the Ashley River is not to be missed, but the plantations easily merit a weekend on their own. If you do want to combine them with Charleston, see "Plantation Pleasures Near Charleston," starting on page 60.

The first choice in lodgings for many visitors is one of the historic homes that have been converted to charming bed-and-breakfast inns. Among these, Two Meeting Street Inn is prime, a spacious and gracious 1890 Victorian mansion with Tiffany glass, elegant furnishings, and an unbeatable location facing the water. A more historic choice is the exquisite 1763 John Rutledge House Inn, one of only 15 surviving homes belonging to signers of the Constitution. Good value is the Phoebe Pember House, a fine home with elaborate plasterwork and detailing and a walled garden; the Carriage House there is the closest you can come to having your own historic Charleston home. Those who want to be convenient to town shopping will find some attractively furnished small hotels a few doors apart on King Street. Charleston Place is the choice for those who want a centrally located luxury hotel; it adjoins the city's main shopping complex and is opposite the city's newest shopping addition, Saks Fifth Avenue. Several appealing new smaller hotels have opened on the street called Vendue Range, near the water.

Dining measures up to everything else in this exceptional city. Sample some low-country specialties such as Charleston's own creamy she-crab soup, best when served with a dollop of sherry, and the surprisingly delicious combination of shrimp and grits.

What to do with any remaining time in Charleston? A dozen antiques stores beckon on King Street, along with scores of other shops. A boat ride to Fort Sumter, where the Civil War began, offers a tour of Charleston Harbor as a bonus. Public beachfront parks await to the north on Isle of Palms and to the south at Folly Beach—or at the truly beautiful Beachwalker Park, on Kiawah Island.

But packing a day with too many sights is almost a shame in Charleston. The nicest thing to do there is simply to stroll the old city at leisure, collecting the lovely impressions that will become permanent snapshots in your mind.

Area Code: 843

DRIVING DIRECTIONS   Charleston is located at the intersection of I-26 and US 17. From Atlanta, take I-20 east to Columbia, then I-26 southeast into Charleston, about 286 miles. It is 200 miles from Charlotte, North Carolina, 112 miles from Columbia, South Carolina.

PUBLIC TRANSPORTATION Many airlines serve Charleston; airport shuttles and taxis bring passengers into the city, and those who stay in the town center can easily manage without a car. With a car, avoid parking problems by leaving your car in the visitors center lot, 375 Meeting Street, and using shuttle service into town; shuttles leave every 15 minutes.

ACCOMMODATIONS Lowest rates are in winter. **Historic bed-and-breakfast inns:** *Two Meeting Street,* 2 Meeting Street, 29401, 723-7322, glorious 1890 Victorian facing the water, top choice, E–EE, CP • *John Rutledge House Inn,* 116 Broad Street, 29401, 723-7999 or (800) 476-9741, 1763 historic landmark, spacious and gracious rooms, E–EE, CP • *Maison du Pre,* 317 East Bay Street, 29401, 723-8691 or (800) 662-INNS, a long walk from town but with charm and a lovely courtyard, M–E, CP • *Wentworth Mansion,* 149 Wentworth Street, 29401, 853-1886 or (888) INN-1886, cotton merchant's lavish 1886 mansion, antiques, fireplaces, Jacuzzis, EE, CP • *The Governor's House,* 117 Broad Street, 29401, 720-2070 or (800) 720-9812, 1760 National Historic Landmark, antiques, E–EE, CP • **Less expensive choices:** *Phoebe Pember House,* 25 Society Street, 29401, 722-4186, done in great taste, excellent value, M–E, CP • *Belvedere,* 40 Rutledge Avenue, 29401, 722-0973, fine home, elaborate decor, E, CP • *1837 Bed and Breakfast/Tea Room,* 126 Wentworth Street, 29401, 723-7166, modest but pleasant, M–E, CP • *Cannonboro Inn,* 184 Ashley Avenue, Charleston, 29403, 723-8572, moderately priced but a drive from town, I–E, CP • **Reservation service for private home bed-and-breakfasts:** *Historic Charleston Bed and Breakfast,* 57 Broad Street, 29401, 722-6606 or (800) 743-3583; www.charleston.net/com/ bed&breakfast.

Luxury hotels: *Charleston Place,* 130 Market Street, 29401, 722-4900 or (800) 611-5545, luxury modern hotel with fine service, best location in town, indoor-outdoor rooftop pool, E–EE • *Planters Inn,* 112 N. Market Street, 29401, 722-2345 or (800) 845-7082, historic 62-room inn, elegant Old South ambience with modern conveniences, oversized rooms, fireplaces, whirlpools, member Relais & Chateaux, E–EE • *Mills House Hotel,* 115 Meeting Street, 29401, 577-2400 or (800) 874-9600, refurbished historic hotel, E–EE.

Handsome small hotels with harbor views: *Harbour View Inn,* 2 Vendue Range, 29401, 853-8439, nicely furnished and fairly priced, M–E • *Vendue Inn,* 19 Vendue Range, 29401, 577-7970 or (800) 845-7900, attractively decorated, rooftop terrace, rooms, M–E; suites, EE • *The Anchorage Inn,* 26 Vendue Range, 29401, 723-8300 or (800) 421-2952, M–E, CP.

Convenient small hotels with inn ambience: *Victoria House Inn,*
208 King Street, 29401, 720-2944 or (800) 933-5464, E–EE, CP •
Kings Courtyard Inn, 198 King Street, 29401, 723-7000 or (800) 845-
6119, M–EE, CP • *Fulton Lane Inn,* 202 King Street, 29401, 720-
2600 or (800) 720-2688, E–EE, CP.

DINING   Top picks: *Charleston Grill, Charleston Place Hotel* (see
Accommodations on page 239), fine dining, E–EE • *High Cotton,* 199
East Bay Street, 724-3815, stylish cuisine with Southern roots, E •
Peninsula Grill, Planter's Inn (see Accommodations on page 239) 722-
2345, creative cuisine in handsome surroundings, M–EE • *Louis',* 200
Meeting Street, 853-2550, the town's best-known chef, stylish decor,
and a new take on Southern classics, E • *Magnolias,* 185 East Bay
Street, 577-7771, contemporary Southern, long on everybody's list of
best in town, M–E • **More good choices:** *McCrady's,* 2 Unity Alley,
577-0025, top reviews for the food, served in an atmospheric tavern,
circa 1778, E–EE • *Slightly North of Broad,* 192 East Bay Street, 723-
3434, "Maverick Southern Cooking" is the motto, M–E • *The Library
at Vendue,* Vendue Inn (see Accommodations on page 239), excellent
American fare, M–E • *Anson,* 12 Anson Street, 577-0551, innovative
menu, attractive contemporary setting, M–E • *Carolina's,* 10 Exchange
Street, 724-3800, more modern Carolina cuisine, M–E • *Blossom Café,*
171 East Bay Street, 722-9200, casual choices include homemade pastas, oak-fired pizza, same owners as Magnolia's, M • *The Boathouse
on East Bay,* 549 East Bay Street, 577-7171, seafood in nautical surroundings, M–E • *Pinckney Café & Espresso,* 18 Pinckney Street,
577-0961, informal, funky bistro, good food, I–M • *Hominy Grill,* 207
Rutledge Ave, 937-0930, unpretentious ambience, low country cuisine
at its best, I–M • *Market East Bistro,* 14 North Market Street, 577-
5080, good choice for reasonbly priced bistro fare, I–M • *Papillons,* 32
North Market Street, 723-6510, and *Baker's Café,* 214 King Street,
577-2694, are good choices for lunch, I.

SIGHT-SEEING   *Charleston Museum,* 360 Meeting Street, 722-
2996. Hours: Monday to Saturday 9 A.M. to 5 P.M., Sunday 1 to 5 P.M.
$$$; combination tickets available with the two houses that follow •
Heyward-Washington House, 87 Church Street, 722-0354. Hours:
Monday to Saturday 10 A.M. to 5 P.M., Sunday 1 to 5 P.M. $$$ • *Joseph
Manigault House,* 350 Meeting Street, 723-2926. Hours: Monday to
Saturday 10 A.M. to 5 P.M., Sunday 1 to 5 P.M. $$$ • *Gibbes Museum of
Art,* 135 Meeting Street, 722-2706. Hours: Tuesday to Saturday 10 A.M.
to 5 P.M. $$ • **Historic Charleston Foundation properties:** (combination tickets are available): *Aiken-Rhett House,* 48 Elizabeth Street, 723-
1159. Hours: Monday to Saturday 10 A.M. to 5 P.M., Sunday 2 to 5 P.M.
$$$ • *Nathaniel Russell House,* 51 Meeting Street, 724-8481. Hours:

Monday to Saturday 10 A.M. to 5 P.M., Sunday 2 to 5 P.M. $$$ • *Edmondston-Alston House,* 21 East Battery, 722-7171. Hours: Tuesday to Saturday 10 A.M. to 4:30 P.M., Sunday and Monday 1:30 to 4:40 P.M. $$$$ • *South Carolina Aquarium,* 100 Aquarium Wharf, Calhoun and Concord streets, 720-1990. Hours: July–August, daily 9 A.M. to 7 P.M.; March–June and September–October, 9 A.M. to 5 P.M.; November to February, 10 A.M. to 5 P.M. $$$$$ • *Patriots Point Naval and Maritime Museum,* Charleston Harbor, Mt. Pleasant side of Cooper River Bridge, 884-2727. Hours: Daily 9 A.M. to 5 P.M.; in summer, to 6 P.M. $$$$$.

Boat tours (phone for schedules, rates, reservations): *Fort Sumter Tour Boats and SpiritLine Harbor cruises,* both leave from City Marina or Patriots Point Museum, 722-BOAT • *Charleston Harbor Queen,* Gray Line paddle wheel harbor tours, 722-1112; *Schooner Pride,* 559-9686, sailing tours through Charleston harbor; *Barrier Island Ecotours,* from Isle of Palms Marina, 886-5000; *Outdoor Discovery Tours,* from Patriot's Point, 744-1224.

Walking tours (phone for current schedules, rates, reservations): *Architectural Walking Tours of Charleston,* 893-2327 or (800) 931-7761 • *Charleston Strolls,* 766-2080 • *Anna's House & Garden Tour and Ghost Walk,* 577-5931 • *Charleston by Foot,* 556-0664.

INFORMATION *Charleston Area Convention and Visitors' Bureau,* 81 Mary Street, P.O. Box 975, Charleston, SC 29401, 853-8000 or (800) 868-8118 • *Charleston Visitors' Center,* 375 Meeting Street, no phone listed. Hours: Daily 8:30 A.M. to 5:30 P.M.; www.charlestoncvb.com.

Mardi Gras Mania in Mobile

Alabama's oldest city is a mix of Southern drawl and French accent, a blend best seen in Mobile's lovely neighborhoods, where antebellum columns and fancy iron balconies stand side by side beneath the moss-draped live oak trees.

The lacy wrought iron lends a distinct flavor, but Mobile's favorite French legacy is, without doubt, the nation's first celebration of Mardi Gras, an event repeated each year with merriment and madness for two full weeks, climaxing on the Tuesday before Lent.

Yes, the New Orleans festivities may be bigger and more famous, but they still started later, and partisans will tell you that Mobile's revelry remains number one—more manageable and, therefore, more fun. The city's mystic societies hold costume balls and lavish parades. Spectators jam the streets with hands outstretched to catch the traditional moon pies, beads, doubloons, masks, stuffed animals, artificial roses, and candies tossed by costumed riders on the colorful floats. Many of these riders are Mobile's most elite citizens.

There's another reason Mobile's celebration shouldn't be missed. In this semitropical setting, Mardi Gras usually comes at the beginning of the spring blooming season at Bellingrath Gardens, one of America's great floral showplaces, located about half an hour to the south. The peak varies with the weather, but when the temperature is right, you can wind up a weekend with a dazzle of flowers that will light up the rest of your spring.

Mardi Gras is a sample of the way Mobilians savor and build on their history. By some accounts, this city's first celebration dates back to 1703, just one year after the first French settlers arrived. The parades and masked participants we now associate with the holiday originated in the 1830s and 1840s as celebrations for New Year's Eve.

But it was on Fat Tuesday that festivities were revived, following a suspension during the Civil War. A lover of good times, Joseph Stillwell Cain, determined to raise the spirits of the defeated city in 1866 by holding a one-float parade on a mule-drawn coal wagon. In ensuing years, Cain found plenty of company for his celebration, and eventually a host of new mystic societies were formed, each vying to put on the best show. Cain himself established the Order of Myths, which still parades in Mobile.

Cain rests in an honored place in the historic Church Street Graveyard in downtown Mobile, with an epitaph on his headstone that reads "Here lies old Joe Cain, the heart and soul of Mardi Gras in Mobile." When his body was moved there in 1966 from its original burying place, it wasn't long before a new tradition was born, known as "Raisin' Cain," with speeches and band music around the grave. By 1983 the crowds for this event had grown to 100,000 revelers and become what is sometimes called "the people's Mardi Gras." It is now held downtown on the Sunday preceding Mardi Gras Tuesday. The mock funeral procession includes Joe Cain's "widows," dozens of women dressed and veiled in mourning black.

This parade and two Saturday events, the coronation of King Felix and his queen and the Mystics of Time parade, are highlights of the weekend preceding Mardi Gras, in case you can't be there on Tuesday for the Comic Cowboys and Order of Myths grand parades. For the entire two-week season before Lent, the local newspapers print schedules, routes, and summaries of the float themes for the next day. If you can snag a room at the Admiral Semmes, you'll have a grand vantage point from the balcony, reserved for hotel guests. Veteran viewers say that the intersection of Government and Joachim, in front of WALA-

TV, is a good spot from which to view the festivities because of the lights set up there for television cameras.

The first Mardi Gras monarch, King Felix, the Emperor of Joy, was crowned in 1872, and purple and gold soon became the official colors used for royal robes. The costumes for the king and queen are amazingly ornate affairs. You can see some of the grandest close up when a new Mardi Gras Museum opens in 2002. That will be a big year in the city, for it also marks the reopening of the Museum of Mobile, the place to learn about the city's history, enlarged and ensconced in fine new quarters in the Old City Hall.

And Mobile's history is a rich one indeed. This first permanent white settlement in Alabama was established in 1711 on the west side of the bay, a strategic spot commanding the entrances to major rivers. It became the capital of a French wilderness empire. By the 1850s, Mobile was a prosperous cotton-trading port. Those were the glory years, when brokers and shippers built the town's finest homes. The Battle of Mobile Bay was a major Civil War naval engagement, but the city was occupied only briefly, in 1864.

Recovery came quickly following the war, thanks to railroads and shipbuilding. Mobile was the largest city in the state until Birmingham mushroomed near the turn of the century. The harbor is still a city mainstay. The discovery of natural gas has also brought drilling rigs to the bay.

For a while this was a city whose charms weren't immediately apparent; all you saw was a commercial port and a downtown suffering from defections to the suburbs. An ambitious redevelopment plan is rapidly changing things, starting with a striking new convention center on the waterfront. Dauphin Street, now known as the Arts and Entertainment District, is now chock-a-block with cafés, nightclubs, and a microbrewery, earning it the nickname "The Block That Rocks."

A new family attraction downtown is the Gulf Coast Explorium, a fun-filled, hands-on museum of science that includes an IMAX Theater.

One of the centerpieces for the downtown redevelopment plan is Fort Conde. The administrative and military center of the Louisiana Territory, the fort began in 1711 as a stockade enclosed by 14-inch cedar stakes. From 1724 to 1735, a permanent brick-and-mortar fort went up within the temporary stockade, occupied successively by French, English, Spanish, and American troops.

In 1820, when it was no longer needed for defense, the fortress was blasted with gunpowder and the rubble was used to fill in low-lying riverfront streets. The old fort was carefully reconstructed on the original site in 1976 with the use of drawings from French archives. It now serves as a home for the city welcome center, where you can pick up current information while you learn aboaut the past. Costumed guides lead tours that include cannon and musket demonstrations.

The city's oldest home, the Conde-Charlotte House, dates from 1822 and was used as a jail before it became a residence. It has been restored and furnished in styles from the sixteenth to nineteenth centuries, depicting the periods of Mobile's history under its five flags. An eighteenth-century walled Spanish garden is on the grounds.

From there, you can move on to the neighborhoods that hold many of the city's attractions and charm. You'll see Mobile at its best along its most important and attractive avenue, Government Street, gracefully canopied by century-old live oak trees. Among the notable buildings along the way are the 1857 City Hall, the 1836 Presbyterian Church, the three-story 1860 Ketchum Mansion (which is now the home of Mobile's archbishop), and the 1859 home of Confederate hero Admiral Raphael Semmes, whose statue is also prominently displayed at Government and Royal streets. Semmes commanded the *Alabama,* the most feared ship in the Confederate navy.

Government Street is one part of the Church Street East Historic District, Mobile's second-oldest neighborhood and one of the largest and most varied of the city's many historic districts. Though the earliest homes were destroyed by fires in 1827 and 1839, the remaining buildings are a catalog of American architectural styles.

Each of the historic districts has its own personality. Just north of Government Street is a much-photographed home, the Richards D.A.R. house, famous for its lavish iron lace trim. It was built in 1860 by a wealthy steamboat captain. The house is part of the De Tonti Square District, a nine-block area of flagstone sidewalks, antique gaslights, and fine homes built when Mobile was at its affluent peak.

The Oakleigh Garden District became the city's most fashionable address in the early 1900s and has the finest homes from that period. Oakleigh Mansion dates back to an even earlier time. It is the city's most important antebellum house museum, built by slaves in raised-cottage style in 1833 for a prominent merchant. Elegantly furnished and known for its important early portrait collection, the house was one of Alabama's earliest preservation projects when it was restored in 1955 and is called a Period House Museum. If you can visit only one historic home, make it this one. Next door is the Cox-Deasy House, a raised Creole cottage built around 1850 and a good example of a middle-class home of that time.

The Old Dauphin Way District, adjacent to downtown, is lined with typical Gulf Coast cottages and Victorian middle-class merchants' homes. A prominent resident of this neighborhood is the giant Duffee Oak at 1123 Caroline Avenue, the city's oldest tree, planted before America's independence and having a trunk 25 feet in circumference.

Other historic homes that can be toured include the 1855 Bragg-Mitchell mansion, one of the grandest antebellum homes on the Gulf Coast, boasting 16 graceful fluted columns outside and a sweeping curved staircase and 15-foot ceilings within. The photogenic house is surrounded by a grove of stately live oaks.

The Carlen House Museum, on the grounds of Murphy High School, is an attractive 1842 home in Creole cottage style displaying period fashions in clothing and home furnishings.

The Mobile Museum of Art has a fine collection that spans more than 200 years. Some of the highlights are American and Southern decorative arts, including ceramics, glass, and furniture. The building is in a wooded setting in Langan Park, near a lake.

Mobile's most popular attraction is of much later vintage. The USS. *Alabama* Battleship Park has as its highlight the 680-foot massive floating fortress that earned nine battle stars in the Pacific during World War II. A self-guided tour of the ship takes you along the decks; through the engine room, the crew's sleeping quarters, and the captain's cabin; and into the gun turrets. Berthed next to the giant ship and also open to tours is the submarine USS. *Drum,* veteran of 13 war missions in the Pacific.

March in Mobile means the Azalea Trail and Festival, with parades, house tours, and carefully marked driving tours through the city's flower-filled neighborhoods.

Azaleas usually are at their peak in late March, but you won't have to wait that long to see fantastic floral displays at Bellingrath Gardens. These 65 acres of beauty, patterned after the formal gardens of Europe, are lovely year-round. In late winter and early spring, camellias, the Alabama state flower, are in bloom. You can see hundreds of specimens ranging from delicate shell pink to deep crimson. The early azaleas begin to blossom about the time that an incredible bulb display of some 90,000 daffodils, hyacinths, and tulips bursts into full splendor. Over the long blooming season, the garden shows off 250,000 azaleas representing 200 varieties.

In 1918, Walter Bellingrath, a pioneer in the Coca-Cola bottling industry, bought the property as a fishing camp. It remained a rustic retreat until his wife, Bessie, began transplanting azaleas and camellias from their Mobile garden. Seeing how plants flourished in the acid soil, Walter became interested. The couple traveled abroad to see the great gardens of Europe, and they hired Mobile landscape designer George Royers to create a showplace at home.

Soon there was a gracious brick mansion overlooking the grand lawn, filled with priceless china and porcelain. The former guest house of the estate now is the Delchamps Gallery of Boehm Porcelain, which was begun with the 85-piece private collection of Mobile's Delchamps family and has grown to over 200 pieces, the largest collection in the world of the famous, exquisitely detailed porcelain birds and other figures.

Both home and gallery are part of the Bellingrath Gardens tour, a one-of-a-kind excursion that even Mardi Gras can't beat for color.

<u>Area Code: 334</u>

DRIVING DIRECTIONS Mobile is in southwestern Alabama, reached via I-10 from east or west and I-65 from the north. From Birmingham, follow I-65 south, 241 miles. From Atlanta, take I-85 west, connecting with I-65 at Montgomery, 332 miles.

ACCOMMODATIONS *Adam's Mark Hotel,* 64 Water Street, 36602, 438-4000 or (800) 444-2326, upscale downtowner on the waterfront, attractive rooms, pool and veranda, gym, E • *Radisson Admiral Semmes Hotel,* 251 Government Street, 36602, 432-8000 or (800) 333-3333, elegantly restored landmark, M • *Malaga Inn,* 359 Church Street, 36602, 438-4701, two 1862 town houses turned into a 40-room lodging around a patio, period furnishings, I–M, CP • *Towle House Bed and Breakfast,* 1104 Montauk Avenue, 33604, 432-6440 or (800) 938-6953, old Mobile charm, I–M, CP.

DINING *Justine's Courtyard & Carriageway,* 80 St. Michael Street, 438-4535, Creole and Gulf Coast cuisine in an antebellum setting, Sunday champagne brunch, M–E • *Gus's Azalea Manor Courtyard,* 751 Dauphin Street, 433-4877, Mediterranean cuisine, M–E • *Mayme's,* Malaga Inn (see Accommodations above), excellent seafood in an old carriage house, M • *Riverview Café & Grill,* Adam's Mark Hotel (see Accommodations above), Gulf Coast cuisine, harbor view, M–E • *Roussos,* 166 South Royal Street, next to the welcome center, 433-3322, seafood specialties, I–E • *Ruth's Chris Steak House,* 271 Glenwood Street, 476-0516, best place for steak, M–EE • *Wintzell's Oyster House,* 605 Dauphin Street, 432-4605, old favorite for seafood • *Bella Koozena,* 353 George Street, 438-3400, rustic Italian, M–E, wood-fired-brick-oven pizza, I • *Port City Brewery,* 225 Dauphin Street, 438-2739, build-your-own pizza, pub fare, home brew, I–M • *Pier 4 Restaurant,* Battleship Parkway, 626-6710, seafood on the bay, I–M • *Dreamland Barbecue,* 3314 Old Shell Road, 479-9898, famous for ribs, I • *Brick Pit,* 5456 Old Shell Road, 343-0001, not to be missed for barbecue, I.

SIGHT-SEEING *Bellingrath Gardens,* 12401 Bellingrath Road, off I-10 or US 90, Theodore, 973-2217. Hours: Daily, gardens 8 A.M. to dusk, house 9 A.M. to dusk. Gardens only. $$$; house and gardens. $$$$$ • *USS.* **Alabama** *Battleship Park,* Battleship Parkway exit off I-10, 433-2703. Hours: Daily 8:30 A.M. to dusk. $$$$ • *Gulf Coast Explorium Museum of Science,* Government at Water Street, 208-6873. Hours: Monday to Thursday 9 A.M. to 5 P.M., Friday and Saturday to 9 P.M., Sunday, 10 A.M. to 5 P.M. $$$ • *Fort Conde Mobile Visitor Center,* 150 South Royal Street at Church Street, 434-7304. Hours: Daily 8 A.M. to 5 P.M. Free • *Museum of Mobile and Mardi Gras*

Museum: Both openings expected in 2002. Check with Visitors' Center for current information • *Oakleigh Period House Museum,* 350 Oakleigh Place, 432-1281. Hours: Monday to Saturday 10 A.M. to 4 P.M. $$ • *Richards D.A.R. House,* 256 North Joachim Street, De Tonti Square, 208-7320. Hours: Tuesday to Saturday 10 A.M. to 4 P.M., Sunday 1 to 4 P.M. $$.• *Carlen House Museum,* 54 Carlen Street, 470-7768. Hours: Tuesday to Saturday 10 A.M. to 5 P.M., Sunday 1 to 5 P.M. Free • *Conde-Charlotte Museum House,* 104 Theatre Street, 432-4722. Hours: Tuesday to Saturday 10 A.M. to 4 P.M. $$ • *Bragg-Mitchell Mansion,* 1906 Springhill Avenue, 471-6364. Hours: Tuesday to Friday 10 A.M. to 4 P.M. $$ • *Mobile Museum of Art,* Museum Drive, Langan Park, 471-6364. Hours: Monday to Saturday 10 A.M. to 5 P.M. Sunday 1 to 5 P.M. Free.

INFORMATION *Mobile Convention and Visitors Corporation,* 1 South Royal Street, P.O. Box 204, Mobile, AL 36602, 415-2000 or (800) 5-MOBILE; www.mobile.org.

Making Tracks in High Country

The weather was unseasonal. The calendar said February, but the thermometer read 70 degrees, hardly a promising forecast for skiers in North Carolina's High Country. But up on the mountains they were making tracks down the hills—with jackets off, sunglasses in place. The snowmaking that works overtime to keep the slopes white had provided enough advance cover to survive a temporary blip in the temperature charts.

As long as nights stay cold, skiing is hot in the High Country. When Southern skiing arrived with the advent of mechanical snowmaking, this area quickly emerged as the center. Beech Mountain, opened in 1967, boasts the highest lift-served skiing in the eastern United States, and Sugar Mountain, which began the following year, has the highest elevation.

Near the charming little town of Blowing Rock, the smaller Appalachian Ski Mountain began even earlier, starting with one slope and a rope tow in 1962 and adding the first night skiing in the South in 1965. It is known for its French-Swiss Ski College, using European techniques to teach the sport. They also welcome snowboarders. The amenities include an outdoor skating rink and a restaurant.

Not that running a ski resort in Southern climes is easy. When the nights as well as the days stay warm, business suffers, and all these areas have tottered and actually gone into bankruptcy over the years during economic downturns. But like the skiers, they just keep coming back, and when nature cooperates, they offer a skiing experience to suit every taste and ability. And there's plenty to do and see off the slopes.

Beech Mountain is the closest you'll come to an alpine village this side of the Rockies. Set near the top of a 5,505-foot mountain, the ski slopes rise from a small complex of shops and restaurants, with an outdoor ice-skating rink for a sporting change of pace. Another recently added option is snow tubing. Skiers will find 15 slopes, 10 lifts —and a vertical drop of 830 feet. There are some slopeside condominiums at Beech, but most accommodations are located just down the hill and include lodge-style inns as well as more condos.

When you are at Beech, be sure to stop into Fred's General Mercantile, a modern version of a country store that seems to sell everything from soup to nuts. The soup can be ordered in the very pleasant Backside Deli, in a greenhouse setting. Fred's also includes a ski shop with rentals and a shop for birders, the Wild Bird Company.

There's a bit more challenge for skiers at Sugar Mountain, farther down the hill in Banner Elk. The vertical drop there is 1,200 feet, the elevation is 5,300 feet, and there are 18 slopes. Banner Elk has a couple of motels and inns, but many skiers stay in the host of condominiums surrounding the ski area. It must be said, however, that one of these is a looming high-rise building that seems very out of place in this mountain setting.

Hawksnest, in Seven Devils, has a dozen trails, including Top Gun, a 2,200-foot turn that they bill as "the ski challenge of the South." Snow tubing is available here, as well. A unique feature is night skiing on Friday and Saturday until 2 A.M.

Some of choicest inns in this part of the mountains are seven miles from Banner Elk in Valle Crucis, a village best known as the home of the Mast General Store. This landmark from the past, established in 1883, is still complete with a potbellied stove, a vintage post office, and a variety of wares that keep browsers busy, from rosebud salve to birdhouses.

You can't go wrong with any of the inns in this town. The Mast Farm Inn is a classic farmhouse, with rockers, iron beds, quilts, and rustic accessories. Generous country dinners are served family-style. For soaring vistas, the place is Bluestone Lodge, a contemporary aerie on a mountaintop, with big picture windows and decks to take in the views. Suites here come with fireplaces or woodstoves and whirlpool baths. The columned Baird House is a restored Colonial farmhouse circa 1790, on 16 acres overlooking the Watauga River.

Those who want the gentler slopes and the excellent instruction of Appalachian Ski Mountain will find plenty of tempting choices in Blowing Rock. At the top of the list is the Gideon Ridge Inn, a fieldstone beauty decorated in sophisticated good taste and set on a secluded ridge with spectacular views of the Blackberry and John's River gorges.

Resorts in the Blowing Rock area offer luxury and sports facilities. The Hound Ears Club, set on 700 acres and centered on a velvety golf course, does indeed have the aura of a private club. Accommodations are in lodge rooms or condominiums, and the dining room there is one of the area's best.

Not far away is Yonahlossee Resort and Club, a heavily wooded, 140-acre resort sure to delight tennis players; the racquet club has won awards and offers three indoor tennis courts as well as a 75-foot indoor pool and racquetball courts. Outdoor attractions in season include an equestrian center and a lake for swimming and canoeing.

Chetola Resort is just outside the town of Blowing Rock; though it lacks the acreage of the other resorts, it does offer a recreation center with an indoor pool, racquetball courts, and exercise classes. In summer, there's canoeing, boating, and fishing on Chetola Lake

Perched at an elevation of 4,000 feet just off the Blue Ridge Parkway, the town of Blowing Rock is a strong contender for the title of prettiest town in the mountains. Main Street shops are housed in turn-of-the-century buildings made of local stone, and they offer a range of wares from antiques to crafts to folk art. Those in search of bargains will find over 30 outlet stores at the Shoppes on the Parkway, located on the Highway 321 Bypass.

The Blowing Rock that inspired the town's name is a cliff above the John's River Gorge. The name comes from a believe-it-or-not natural phenomenon. The gorge forms a flume through which the northwest wind sweeps with such force that it will return light objects dropped over the cliff. The entrance to the rock and its observation deck, which has an admission charge, is closed if the weather is not favorable in the winter, but there's no shortage of views if you take a spin along the Blue Ridge Parkway toward Grandfather Mountain. Many people like driving the parkway best of all in winter, when the trees' bare branches reveal distant vistas that are otherwise hidden by leaves.

From mileposts 292 to 295 you'll be in Moses Cone Park, a favorite of photographers, hikers, and horseback riders for its 25 miles of carriage trails. When conditions permit, this is an ideal location for cross-country skiing. In warmer months, this is also headquarters for the Parkway Craft Center, headquarters for the Southern Highland Handicraft Guild.

Flat Rock, at milepost 308.3, is an outcrop with a superb view of Grandfather Mountain and the Linville Valley. A few miles farther on, you'll cross one of the most recently completed parts of the parkway, the Linville Viaduct, with views of the 90-foot Linville Falls roaring through the deepest gorge east of the Grand Canyon. A gentle half-mile trail from the parking area at milepost 316 leads to a magnificent vista of the falls and the beginning of the gorge.

The next stop is Grandfather Mountain in Linville, and a chance to challenge the new mile-high, 228-foot-long Swinging Bridge that gives a lovely, albeit unsteady, view of Linville Peak. The mountainside is a park with 30 miles of nature trails and a recently built nature museum. Six natural habitats for native wildlife, including black bears, cougars, and golden eagles, allow visitors to see and photograph the animals close up.

The mountain was named by pioneers for its profile, resembling a bearded face looking toward the sky. This is the summer site of one of the largest Scottish gatherings in the country, the annual Grandfather Mountain Highland Games, a colorful event well worth a return visit.

You may want to detour into Linville for a stop at the Old Hampton Store, off North Carolina Route 181, another classic general store, circa 1921. The gristmill here turns out delicious cornmeal and grits. This is also the home of Uncle Lee's Barbecue, serving up delicious sandwiches on sourdough buns.

At some point you'll probably want to take a stroll through Boone, a town founded in 1872, whose wood-shingled buildings, sidewalk arcades, and surrounding mountains will likely remind you of a Western town. The town is lively, thanks to the 12,000 students who attend Appalachian State University there. Shoppers will find an outpost of the Mast Store in Boone, and there's a host of local history at the Appalachian Cultural Museum, which displays everything from antique quilts to cars driven by early stock car racers from the area. More local lore can be found in the Appalachian Heritage Museum, between Boone and Blowing Rock.

Just outside of Boone is an excellent lodging, the Lovill House Inn, a beautifully restored 1875 farmhouse bed-and-breakfast on 11 acres, with handsome guest rooms.

North Carolina Route 105, south of Boone toward Foscoe, is the road for those interested in crafts or antiques. There are shopping stops for both, a nice alternative when you've had your fill of the slopes.

Area Code: 828

DRIVING DIRECTIONS Banner Elk and Beech Mountain are on North Carolina Route 184, reached via North Carolina Route 105 or US 221. Major highways into the area are I-77, I-40, I-85, and I-81. From Atlanta to Banner Elk, take I-85 north to US 221 north, merge with North Carolina Route 105 and turn left on North Carolina Route 184, about 255 miles. For Blowing Rock, continue on North Carolina Route 105 through Boone to US 321/221 north, about 275 miles.

PUBLIC TRANSPORTATION The closest airports are Hickory, 45 miles; Tri-Cities, 75 miles; Greensboro, 100 miles; and Charlotte, 110 miles.

ACCOMMODATIONS   Banner Elk: *Beech Alpen Inn and Top of the Beech Lodge,* 700 Beech Mountain Parkway, 28604, 387-2252, adjoining lodges, I–M, CP • *Pinnacle Inn,* 405 Beech Mountain Parkway, P.O. Box 1136, 28604, 387-4276 or (800) 438-2097, condo units, indoor pool, I–E • *Banner Elk Inn Bed and Breakfast,* 407 Main Street, P.O. Box 1953, 28604, 898-6223, M–E, CP • *Archer's Mountain Inn,* 2489 Beech Mountain Parkway, Beech Mountain, 28604, 898-9004, I–E, CP.

Blowing Rock: *Gideon Ridge Inn,* 202 Gideon Ridge Road, P.O. Box 1929, 28605, 295-3644, exceptional, M–E, CP • *Inn at Ragged Gardens,* 203 Sunset Drive, 28605, 295-9703, in-town hideaway in a garden, E–EE, CP • *Rocksberry Inn Bed and Breakfast,* P.O. Box 1417, 28605, 295-3311, M, CP • *Maple Lodge,* Sunset Drive, 28605, 295-3331, in-town inn with warm ambience, M–E, CP • *Meadowbrook Inn,* 711 North Main Street, 28605, 295-4300, in-town lodging, indoor pool, I–M, CP.

Valle Crucis: *Bluestone Lodge Bed and Breakfast,* 850 Bluestone Wild Road, P.O. Box 736, 28691, 963-5177, M–E, CP • *Mast Farm Inn,* 2543 Broadstone Road, P.O. Box 704, 28691, 963-5857 or (888) 963-5857, M–EE, MAP • *Baird House,* 1451 Watauga River Road, 28691, 297-4055 or (800) 297-1342, M–E, CP • *The Inn at the Taylor House,* Highway 194, P.O. Box 713, 38691, 963-5581, attractive choice but closed January to March, E, CP; suites, E–EE.

Boone: *Lovill House Inn,* 404 Old Bristol Road, 28607, 264-4204 or (800) 849-9466, M–E, CP.

Resorts: *Hound Ears Lodge and Club,* P.O. Box 188, Blowing Rock, 28605, 963-4321, luxury resort in mountain setting, ski packages with area slopes, golf packages in summer, M–EE • *Yonahlossee Resort,* 226 Oakley Green, P.O. Box 1397, Boone, 28607, 963-6400 or (800) 692-1986, indoor and outdoor tennis, indoor pool and riding rink, inn lodging, M; cottages, M–E; luxury villas, E–EE • *Chetola Resort,* North Main Street, Blowing Rock, 28605, 295-5500 or (800) 243-8652, indoor pool, racquetball courts, fitness center, lodge rooms, M–E; condominiums, E–EE.

Condominium rentals: *Beech Mountain Slopeside Rentals,* (800) 692-2061 • *Beech Mountain Chalet Rentals,* (800) 368-7404 • *Sugar Mountain Accommodations Center,* (800) 545-9475.

DINING   Blowing Rock: *The Riverwood,* US 321, 295-4162, nouvelle American, highly rated, M–E • *Crippen's Country Inn,* 239 Sunset Drive, fine dining, M–EE • *The Woodlands Barbecue,* 321 Bypass,

295-3651, best barbecue around, I • *Blowing Rock Café,* Sunset Drive, 295-9474, cozy, informal, serves all three meals, mountain trout is the dinner specialty, I–M • *The Best Cellar,* Little Springs Road, 295-3466, rustic log cabin with fireplaces, Continental menu, M–E • *The Manor House,* Chetola Resort, (see Accommodations on page 251), attractive, American menu, M • *The Artists' Palate,* Meadowbrook Inn, (see Accommodations on page 251), well recommended locally, M.

Boone, Beech Mountain, Valle Crucis: *The Bistro,* 115 New Market Center, Boone, 265-0500, upscale, Continental menu, M • *Dan'l Boone Inn,* 130 Hardin Street, Boone, 264-8657, old favorite, country fare, fried chicken, family-style—all you can eat, I • *Makoto's Japanese Steak House,* 815 Blowing Rock Road, Boone, 264-7976, tasty tableside cooking, M • *Casa Rustica,* North Carolina Route 105, Boone, 262-5128, Italian, homemade pasta, I–M • *Pepper's Restaurant,* 240 Shadowline Drive, Boone, 262-1250, longtime local favorite, sandwiches to steaks, I–M • *Peddler Steak House,* 1972 Blowing Rock Road, Boone, 264-4433, steaks and more, salad bar, M • *Mast Farm Inn,* Valle Crucis (see Accommodations on page 251), full dinner, M • *Fred's Backside Deli,* Fred's General Store, Beech Mountain Parkway, Beech Mountain, 387-4838, I.

SIGHT-SEEING *Grandfather Mountain,* US 221, Linville, 733-4337 or (800) 468-7325, nature museum, small outdoor zoo, walking trails, mile-high swinging bridge. Hours: April 1 to October, daily 8 A.M. to 7 P.M.; rest of year, daily to 5 P.M., weather permitting. $$$ • *Appalachian Heritage Museum,* US 321/221, between Boone and Blowing Rock, 264-4726. Hours: October to May, daily 9 A.M. to 5 P.M.; rest of year, to 8 P.M. Donation • *Appalachian Cultural Museum,* University Hall Drive off US 321, Boone, 262-3117. Hours: Tuesday to Saturday 10 A.M. to 5 P.M., Sunday 1 to 5 P.M. $$ • *The Blowing Rock,* off US 321, Blowing Rock, 295-7111. Hours: June to October, daily 9 A.M. to 7 P.M.; rest of year, daily 9 A.M. to 5 P.M., weather permitting, except January, weekends only. $$ • **Ski areas** (www.skinorthcarolina.com) **include:** *Appalachian Ski Mountain,* P.O. Box 106, Blowing Rock, 28605, 295-7828 or (800) 322-2373 • *Beech Mountain Ski Resort,* P.O. Box 1118, Beech Mountain, 28604, 387-2011 or (800) 438-2093 • *Sugar Mountain Ski Resort,* Highway 184, P.O. Box 369, Banner Elk, 28604, 898-4521 or (800) SUGARMT • *Ski Hawksnest,* 1800 Skyland Drive, Seven Devils, 28604, 963-6563 or (800) 429-5763.

INFORMATION *High Country Host,* 1700 Blowing Rock Road, Boone, NC 28607, 264-1299 or (800) 438-7500; www.highcountryhost.com • *Blowing Rock Chamber of Commerce,* Main Street, P.O. Box 406, 295-7851 or (800) 295-7851; www.blowingrock.com.

Watching the Thoroughbreds in Aiken

Champion horses have been the pride of Aiken, South Carolina, for over a century. Many thoroughbreds winter there from October to March at more than 40 local stables, training for national glory later in the year. Aiken's March "Triple Crown," the culmination of the training season, is a preview of future Kentucky Derby, Preakness, and Belmont Stakes winners.

You needn't be a racing fan to enjoy these special events, and the odds are also good that you'll fall in love with the charm of Aiken, a town filled with wide, shady streets and greenery, medians planted with sweet magnolias, and grand homes in the hills around town. Some of the scenic sandy roads are left unpaved to be easy on horses' hooves. There are even equestrian stoplights at some intersections.

Aiken's name honors the first president of the South Carolina Canal and Railroad Company, William Aiken. The town's birth came about with the founding of the company in 1828 to build a railroad from Charleston to the Savannah River. The first train arrived in the newly established town in 1833. The next year, engineers laid out the present wide streets and parkways, and Aiken quickly attracted visitors.

It was the mild winter climate and the sandy soil, perfect for equestrian activities, that began drawing some of America's wealthiest families after the Civil War. They formed an exclusive winter colony, building enormous "cottages" where they could meet and mingle and stables where they trained fleet horses.

The social scene faded after World War II, but the Vanderbilts, Astors, Goodyears, Whitneys, and their set left behind a beautiful legacy of homes—and a tradition of winners that still holds good. Close to 40 champions grace Aiken's Thoroughbred Racing Hall of Fame and Museum, including Kelso, the record breaker named Horse of the Year for five consecutive years in the 1960s, and Swale, who won five consecutive Belmont Stakes from 1982 to 1986.

The newest crop of soon-to-be-winners can be seen on the three successive March weekends known as the Triple Crown. The Aiken Trials show off some of the most promising thoroughbreds in the world having their first go at racing full speed on a quarter-mile track. The Aiken Steeplechase showcases the best of the jumpers going through their paces on a steeplechase course, where elaborate tailgate picnics on the sidelines keep everyone happy between races. The final event is harness racing at McGhees' Mile Track, where the fleetest trotters can be seen.

Even if you miss the big events, you can enjoy watching sleek steeds go through their training paces at local training tracks, or take in a

Sunday polo game or one of the many horse shows where the elite of each class show their breeding. You're liable to encounter a colorful hunt heading into Hitchcock Woods almost any weekend in season, and the Aiken Driving Club takes to the roads of the historic horse districts on the second Saturday of each month, with nattily costumed drivers showing off their shiny horse-drawn carriages and carts.

The first order of business, however, is to see the lovely town and learn more about its history. One way to do this is on the Aiken Tour that leaves every Saturday morning from the Aiken Chamber of Commerce. If you can't make the tour, ask for the walking/driving tour brochure (available at the chamber and in most local inns) and go exploring.

You might start on foot with an easily walkable loop starting from the Willcox Hotel, the *grande dame* on Colleton Avenue. The hotel dates from the early 1900s and was a gathering place for many prominent winter visitors. It is the prime place to stay in town, though there are small bed-and-breakfast inns for those who want a cozier base, and motel accommodations as well.

Walk away from the Willcox down Colleton for three blocks or so, then back again on the other side of the street, to admire the cottages built from 1880 to the early 1900s. The imposing house on the corner across from the hotel was owned by the Astor family of New York.

When you get back to the hotel, turn left on Newberry Street, then take a series of rights on South Boundary Avenue, Laurens Street, Park Avenue, and Chesterfield Street back to Colleton. Near the corner of South Boundary and Laurens is Hitchcock Woods, a lovely 2,000-acre preserve developed at the turn of the century. Currently under the protection of the Hitchcock Foundation, it is a peaceful wooded haven for both walkers and horseback riders, who equally enjoy the winding dirt paths through the tall trees.

On Thanksgiving each year, Hitchcock Woods is the site of the colorful Blessing of the Hounds, performed by a minister on horseback just before the red-jacketed riders take off on a hunt.

On Laurens Street, you'll approach the center of town. Morgan Circle, across from the Municipal Building, was named for Thomas R. Morgan, who was mayor of Aiken in 1899 and 1900. The circle and its cast-iron Victorian fountain were restored in 1963 with funds contributed by residents. Behind the municipal building is the Alley, lined with shops and cafés that are likely spots for lunch.

Then it's time for a drive up Chesterfield Street, zigzagging right on First Avenue, left on Newberry Street, and left again on Easy Street to Whiskey Road, a route that takes in some important sights and some of the grandest remaining residences.

At the corner of Chesterfield and First is Joye Cottage, originally a simple home that was purchased in 1897 by William C. Whitney, a New

York banker, who expanded it into a 50-room showplace. The residence across the street was once the Whitney stables.

At the end of First, turn left onto Newberry and go beyond the serpentine walls to the Aiken County Historical Museum, in the palatial 1850 mansion known as Banksia. The house has 32 rooms, 15 baths, and a full ballroom.

The museum traces Aiken history with exhibits ranging from Indian artifacts to period rooms showing the town's lavish nineteenth-century lifestyle. Also on the grounds are an 1890 one-room schoolhouse and the Ergle log cabin, dating from 1808 and furnished with pieces from the period. One popular exhibit is a 1950s drugstore, moved from nearby Dunbarton, where it was dismantled in 1952 to make way for the Savannah River Plant.

The once-secret government facility where plutonium was produced for nuclear warheads is no longer quite so hush-hush; group tours can be arranged. The plant continues to influence the makeup of Aiken, which boasts more engineers and Ph.D.s than any other town of its size in America.

Behind another serpentine wall, at the corner of Whiskey Road and Dupree Place, is Hopeland, the estate of Hope and Oliver Iselin from the turn of the century until 1970, when it was willed to the city by Mrs. Iselin. Today it is a public park with a 14-acre garden incorporating the lush trees, shrubs, and flowers planted long ago by the Iselins. Two small lakes bordered with weeping willows frame a performing arts stage where summer concerts are held.

The Iselin carriage house was renovated in 1977 by the local Jaycees as the Thoroughbred Racing Hall of Fame, honoring locally bred and trained champions and containing exhibits of racing silks, trophies, and horse-related artwork.

Driving farther through the "horsey" part of town is a delight, a chance to see the dozens of private farms with horses and colts in the fields. Several of the farms offer riding lessons. Write to the chamber of commerce for *The Horseman's Guide to Aiken,* which contains a complete list of the area's horse farms. It will also give you names of more than a dozen equine artists who live in town.

Visitors are welcome to watch the thoroughbreds being trained. October to March is the season, but you'll have to get up early, since that's when most workouts are held. Start with breakfast at the Track Kitchen and you'll be mingling with trainers and owners in their favorite morning gathering place.

The Aiken Training Track is considered one of the best in the world. The timed trials of the Triple Crown event are the first competitive tests under full grandstand conditions for the year's crop of spirited two- and three-year-olds. The bloodlines of the participants are a "Who's Who" of racing.

Standardbred horses, for harness or sulky racing, do their training at McGhees' Mile Track. This is actually one of America's oldest sports, begun when strict codes of behavior did not allow activities so frivolous as racing horses. The horses were kept to a prescribed gait or pace as they pulled two-wheel sulkies. The trotting gait came later and had its greatest popularity in the late 1800s through the early 1900s. Dunbar Bostwick, who established this track in 1936, has been credited to a large degree with reviving interest in harness racing. Owners and drivers participate there to gain experience for their horses and to familiarize spectators with the sport.

The Aiken Steeplechase is the first event of the steeplechasing season. This is a sport in which both horse and rider must have stamina and endurance, combining high speed and split-second timing to clear jumps and gallop long distances. The training of the horses is geared to build up lung power and the muscles of the hindquarters and shoulders. Some of the finest thoroughbreds compete in this event for trophies and prizes of over $80,000.

On any Sunday afternoon from September through November and from March through July, the polo ponies compete at the Whitney Polo Field. In polo, man and horse are truly a team. The idea is to strike the ball from horseback, usually at high speed, either passing it to a teammate or hitting a scoring shot between the goalposts. Eight mounted players create quite a stir galloping up and down the 300 yards of playing area.

Polo has been part of the winter season in Aiken since 1882, just six years after the game was introduced to the United States. At one time, Aiken was the polo center of the South, with 16 fields in use. Bring a blanket or folding chairs and a picnic to get into the spirit of the fun.

If you want different kinds of sporting activity, Aiken has two public golf courses, plus tennis courts and walking trails at the Odell Weeks Recreation Center, off Whiskey Road.

There is a winner's circle of things to see and do in the surrounding area as well. The free Thoroughbred Country Touring Guide folder lists five scenic back-roads tours for bicycle or auto, and more than a dozen historic homes can be seen in North Augusta, 17 miles away on the banks of the Savannah River.

Two nearby state parks offer a choice of moods. Redcliffe State Historic Site includes the 350-acre grounds and 1850s home of Governor James Henry Hammond. Aiken State Park covers 100 acres and features four spring-fed lakes and the meandering South Edisto River, a perfect spot for picnicking, swimming, canoeing, fishing, or walking a nature trail. Canoe rentals are available.

Wine fanciers may want to pay a visit to Montmorenci Vineyards for free tours and tastings.

Whichever way you wander, all roads lead back to Aiken, a champion choice for a weekend.

<u>Area Code: 803</u>

DRIVING DIRECTIONS Aiken is located seven miles south of I-20, via South Carolina Route 19 or US 1. It is 163 miles east of Atlanta and 58 miles west of Columbia.

ACCOMMODATIONS *Willcox Inn,* 100 Colleton Avenue, Aiken, 29801, 649-1377 or (800) 368-1047, M–E. Also many weekend packages • *Sandhurst Estate B & B,* Dupree Place SW, Aiken, 29801, 642-9259, nineteenth-century mansion on five acres, adjoining Hopeland Gardens, M–EE, CP • *White House Inn,* 240 Newberry Street Southwest, Aiken, 29801, 649-2935, Dutch Colonial home in historic area, M–EE, CP • *Carriage House Inn,* 139 Laurens Street NW, Aiken, 29801, 644-5888, 1872 home, I–M, CP • *Town & Country Inn,* 2340 Sizemore Circle, Aiken, 29803, 642-0270, four miles from town, M, CP • *Annie's Inn,* P.O. Box 300, Montmorenci (five miles east of Aiken), 29839, 649-6836, antebellum farmhouse, popovers for breakfast, I, CP • *Crossways Plantation Bed & Breakfast,* 450 East Boundary SE, Aiken, 29801, 644-4746, 1815 antebellum home on landscaped grounds outside town, M–E, CP • *Rosemary & Lookaway Hall,* 804 Carolina Avenue, North Augusta, 29841, 278-6222, pair of elegant turn-of-the-century mansions, high Victorian decor, M–EE, CP • Check with chamber of commerce for motel listings.

DINING *Willcox Inn* (see Accommodations above), M–E • *Riley's Whitby Bull,* 218 York Street, 641-6227, fine dining in an old home, E • *No. 10 Downing Street,* 241 Laurens Street, 642-9062, M • *Up Your Alley,* 222 the Alley, 649-2603, seafood specials, M • *West Side Bowery,* 151 Bee Lane, 648-2900, varied American menu, I–M.

SIGHT-SEEING *Aiken Triple Crown,* three weekends in March featuring steeplechase, thoroughbred, and harness racing. Contact the chamber of commerce (see Information, below) for current dates and information • *Aiken Tours,* 90-minute bus tours from Aiken Chamber of Commerce, 641-1111. Hours: Saturdays at 10 A.M., reservations recommended. $$$ • *Polo Games,* Whitney Field, 643-3611. Hours: September through November and March through July, Sundays at 3 P.M. $ • *Hopeland Gardens,* Dupree Place and Whiskey Road, 642-7630. Hours: Daily 10 A.M. to sunset. Free • *Thoroughbred Racing Hall of Fame and Museum,* Hopeland Gardens, 642-7630. Hours: September to May, Tuesday to Sunday 2 to 5 P.M. Free • *Aiken County Historical Museum,* 433 Newberry Street SW, 642-2015. Hours: Tuesday to Friday 9:30 A.M. to 4:30 P.M.; Saturday and Sunday 2 to 5 P.M. $ • *Montmorenci Vineyards,* US 78, Montmorenci, 649-4870. Hours: Wednesday to Saturday 10 A.M. to 6 P.M. Free • *Aiken State Park,* 1145 State Park Road, Windsor, off US 78, 16 miles from Aiken, 649-2857.

Hours: Daily, daylight hours. Free • *Redcliffe State Historic Site,* 181
Redcliffe Road, off US 278, Beech Island, 827-1473. Hours: Grounds
open Thursday to Monday 9 A.M. to 6 P.M., free; house tours, Thursday
to Monday noon to 4 P.M. $.

INFORMATION *Aiken Chamber of Commerce,* 121 Richland
Avenue East, P.O. Box 892, Aiken, SC 29801, 641-1111 or (800) 542-
4536; www.chamber.aiken.net.

Feeling the Magic in Birmingham

Birmingham may well be the South's best-kept secret. Lots of
people just aren't aware of the new style and spirit today in Alabama's
largest city.

When it is once again open to the public (estimated to be in 2002),
the best overview of what's happening is from atop Red Mountain, gazing down from the observation deck at the base of the statue of Vulcan,
fresh from a major refurbishment. This gigantic figure of the god of
metalworking, forged of locally made cast iron, has presided from his
lofty perch for over 50 years, a visible symbol of the steel industry that
built the city.

People used to come to Birmingham to see the fiery glow of the
open-hearth furnaces. Now they look out on new office towers and the
ever-spreading campus of the University of Alabama at Birmingham.
The big steel mills are in view, but their smokestacks and furnaces are
quiet. Environmental laws rendered them obsolete in the 1970s, and the
last of the original mills that built the city shut down in the 1980s.

That could have been a death knell, but instead Birmingham rein-
vented itself. Now a thriving city of almost a million people, it has
traded hard hats for caps and gowns and scrubs. The university and its
medical center have experienced phenomenal growth, becoming the
city's top employer. Highly educated teachers, medical researchers, and
doctors are attracted from all over the country by the excellence of the
UAB Medical Center and its many specialized hospitals.

The result is a more sophisticated city with emphasis on the arts and
good living, including some very fine dining. Birmingham is now often
included in lists of America's best places to live.

It is an equally good place to visit. The city boasts the largest munic-
ipally owned museum in the South, the biggest zoo in the Southeast,
one of the South's most prestigious library collections, a lovely 67-acre

botanical garden, and moving remembrances of the Civil Rights struggle.

Even some of those old mills have found a new life. The Sloss Furnaces, named a national landmark, have become an industrial museum. One of the sheds serves as an amphitheater, a highly unusual backdrop for concerts and festivals.

Birmingham was never part of the gracious Old South. In fact, it was not founded until 1871, after the Civil War. It was dubbed "the Magic City" for the phenomenal growth that followed when it was discovered that the red rock of the surrounding mountains was actually high-grade iron ore. The steel industry that blossomed produced another nickname: "Pittsburgh of the South."

Then the magic dimmed. During the Civil Rights protests of the 1960s, blue-collar Birmingham became an unhappy symbol of Southern resistance to integration. As a result, the city stagnated. It was only when racial harmony was finally restored that things began to revive.

Ironically, that painful period now accounts for one of Birmingham's attractions, the moving Civil Rights Institute. A walk through the galleries is a pilgrimage through time from the 1920s to the present. There are vivid reminders of the barriers faced by African-Americans in the South, displays of segregated lunch counters and buses, and water fountains labeled "White" and "Colored." Multimedia displays capture the drama and the tumult of Civil Rights protests in the state. A bank of 1960s black-and-white TV sets plays scenes of police clad in riot gear turning fire hoses on unarmed black demonstrators. Among the displays is the actual Birmingham jail cell of the Reverend Dr. Martin Luther King Jr., who led many local marches. The tour ends at a life-size plaster processional depicting blacks and whites together, headed toward windows overlooking Kelly Ingram Park and the Sixteenth Street Baptist Church, across the street.

The park, once the organizing point for downtown marches, was where Public Safety Commissioner "Bull" Conner attacked the marchers with police dogs and hoses, images that remain among our worst memories in the Civil Rights struggle.

The recently restored Sixteenth Street Baptist Church, directly across the street, was headquarters for many protest meetings in the early sixties. It was the only large building where blacks were permitted to assemble. The church was bombed by the Ku Klux Klan in 1963, killing four young black girls preparing for Sunday worship, deaths that horrified the world.

All of these are stops on a self-guided Birmingham Black Heritage Tour. The tour also covers happier memories, such as Tuxedo Junction, a second-floor dance hall that was the social hub for the black community in the 1920s and 1930s. The name, inspired by the streetcar crossing in the Tuxedo Park neighborhood, became famous as the title of a hit song written by Birmingham-born musician Erskine Hawkins.

A recent addition to this area is the Eddie Kendrick Memorial Park honoring the late Birmingham native and lead singer of the Temptations. The park includes a statue of Kendrick, with the other singers in the group sculpted into a granite backdrop.

Athletes of all colors share the spotlight in another favorite downtown attraction, the Alabama Sports Hall of Fame. Ensconced in handsome quarters in the Civic Center, the Hall of Fame celebrates many local heroes who are national legends. Prize exhibits are the trademark checkered hat belonging to the late legendary Alabama coach Paul "Bear" Bryant; the Heisman Trophies won by Auburn's Pat Sullivan and Bo Jackson. Though Birmingham's fans love all their sports teams, college football remains first and foremost. Other displays include golf clubs used by Hubert Green to win the US Open; and memorabilia from such Alabama greats as Joe Louis, Hank Aaron, Joe Namath, Jesse Owens, and Willie Mays, to name just a few.

Golf has many enthusiastic supporters in the city, both spectators and players. The city has hosted PGA Championships, and the Greystone Golf Club hosts the Senior PGA at the Bruno's Memorial Classic. Two Robert Trent Jones–designed Oxmoor golf courses, high atop Little Shades Mountain, are of championship caliber and are open for public use.

The Class-AA Birmingham Barons baseball team draws crowds to the Hoover Metropolitan Stadium, one of the finest fields in the minor leagues, and hockey fans root for the Birmingham Bulls. Birmingham Race Course adds to the sporting agenda with a dog track and simulcast horse racing.

The city also boasts a special attraction for motorcycle enthusiasts. The Barber Vintage Motorsports Museum showcases over 300 cycles from all over the world and from every decade of the twentieth century. Vintage racing cars are on display as well. A new expanded museum due to open in 2001 on the outskirts of the city will include a 2.5-mile racing track as part of the 700-acre complex.

Like many cities, Birmingham is struggling to keep its downtown area competitive with suburban shopping malls. Birmingham Green, a landscaped promenade that prettied up Twentieth Street, the main downtown artery, definitely makes things more attractive, even though some storefronts remain vacant.

The most exciting development downtown is the McWane Center, which occupies the prime corner that was once was the site of the city's leading department store. It is a world-class science museum, with creative interactive exhibits on motion, force, energy, light, and sound. A delightful section for the very young is Just Mice Size, a fantasy environment where everything is ten times bigger than life, as it might look to a tiny mouse. Another notable section is the World of Water, part aquarium, part exhibit area, exploring the importance of water to the planet. The Challenger Learning Center *Alabama* is a technology-packed space mission simulation. An IMAX theater, café, and excellent store aptly named Really Cool Stuff are also part of the multilevel museum.

Birmingham's downtown blocks offer an interesting mix of architecture, from the 1925 art deco Alabama Power Building, topped by a 22-foot golden figure of Electra, to the postmodern AmSouth tower. The restored Alabama Theatre is a 1920s movie queen, with marble columns, gold leaf, and a hall of mirrors. The Tutwiler Hotel, built in 1914 as a luxury apartment complex, has been restored as downtown's most elegant hotel.

The enormous Birmingham-Jefferson Convention Complex is both convention facility and cultural center. Arts venues include a concert hall and a theater that is headquarters for the Birmingham Children's Theatre. The Coliseum arena hosts everything from ice hockey to the circus. The 771-room Sheraton, Alabama's biggest hotel, is connected to the complex by a skywalk.

Not far away is the impressive Birmingham Museum of Art. Among its prides are Renaissance art from the Kress Collection; American art including works by Remington, Sargent, and Mary Cassatt; African masks; Asian art; and the largest collection of Wedgwood porcelain found outside Great Britain.

The main reading room of the nearby Central Library, with its painted ceilings and murals, is one of the city's loveliest interiors. It houses the Tutwiler Collection of Southern History and Literature, a compendium of subjects from Robert E. Lee to Elvis Presley, quilts to early recipes.

Birmingham's one bit of Old South is Arlington, an antebellum mansion that predates the city. Located a mile west of town, the graceful 1840s Greek Revival mansion serves as a museum of Southern decorative arts.

You'll need a car to see Arlington as well as the rest of the sights that are located south of downtown. Drive south on Twentieth Street to visit the sprawling 70-block UAB campus. The UAB Medical Center is recognized nationally for its work in heart surgery, kidney transplants, and many other specialties. It ranks among the nation's top 20 schools in research grants.

Next comes Five Points South, a historic neighborhood focused around a landmark circle at Twentieth Street and Highland Avenue. The city's liveliest bars and best restaurants—and some intriguing shops—can be found there. Cobb Lane, off Twentieth Street just above Five Points, has more shops and a charming café serving lunch.

The intimate Pickwick Hotel, in Five Points, is a convenient place to stay, putting you between downtown and the attractions farther south.

Head up the mountain to Vulcan Park when it reopens to see the largest cast-iron statue ever made, created by Italian-born sculptor Giuseppe Moretti in 1938. An elevator whisks visitors to the observation tower at the foot of the Vulcan statue for a panoramic view of the changing city.

Another wonderful view can be had by driving along the crest of Red Mountain, especially at night, when the city lights twinkle. From Highland Avenue, take Arlington Avenue to Key Circle. At the circle, follow Argyle Road to Stratford Road, overlooking the city, one of the most romantic spots in town.

Continuing beyond Vulcan to the area known as "over the mountain," you'll find the zoo, where some of the rare animals in residence include white rhinoceroses and Siberian tigers. The botanical gardens, nearby, comprise 67 acres, with thousands of different plantings and flowers. Special features include a lovely Japanese garden and a conservatory housing over 5,000 varieties of unusual plants.

Just beyond is the small, charming village of Mountain Brook, a good browsing place for shoppers. It is surrounded by one of the oldest of the city's magnificent hilly, wooded residential areas.

This is the direction in which many of the city's newer neighborhoods are spreading, resulting in blossoming suburban towns such as Hoover. Keep driving south on Highway 31 to see the Riverchase Galleria in Hoover, a posh shopping complex, with 200 stores anchored by the attractive Wynfrey Hotel. Nearby is The Summit, which houses the city's first Saks Fifth Avenue store and many other well-known retailers.

Many first-time visitors are surprised to discover that Birmingham is a city of hills, nestled in the wooded Appalachian foothills. This once-industrial town has always had exceptionally beautiful physical surroundings, but until recently it was a rough-cut gem in a fine setting. Now it is becoming polished, a lively, growing metropolis of nearly a million people with everything to do from football to fine arts.

It's enough to make this native want to go home again.

Area Code: 205

DRIVING DIRECTIONS Birmingham is reached by I-65, US 280, or Highway 31 from north and south, I-20/59 and I-459 from east and west. It is 149 miles from Atlanta, 192 miles from Nashville.

ACCOMMODATIONS *Tutwiler Hotel,* 2021 Park Place North, Birmingham, 35203, 322-2100 or (800) 845-1787, M–E • *Sheraton Birmingham Hotel,* 2101 Civic Center Boulevard, Birmingham, 35203, 324-5000 or (800) 325-3535, M • *Pickwick Hotel,* 1023 20th Street South, Five Points, Birmingham, 35205, 933-9555 or (800) 255-7304, M • *Embassy Suites,* 2300 Woodcrest Place, Birmingham, 35209, 879-7400 or (800) 433-4600, M–E • *Mountain Brook Inn,* 2800 US 280 South, Birmingham, 35223, 870-3100 or (800) 523-7771, M • *Quality Hotel & Suites,* 260 Goodwin Crest Drive, Birmingham,

35209, 290-8000, atop Red Mountain with city views, I–M, CP • *Wynfrey Hotel,* 1000 Riverchase Galleria, Hoover, 35244, 987-1600 or (800) 476-7006, M–E • *Riverchase Inn at the Galleria,* 1800 River Chase Drive, Hoover, 35244, 985-7500, I–M, CP • Contact the Convention and Visitors' Bureau for an extensive list of motels. For accommodations in private homes, phone *Bed and Breakfast Birmingham,* 699-9841.

DINING   Five Points-south area: *Highlands Bar and Grill,* 2011 11th Avenue South, 939-1400, seafood, beef, one of the best in town, M–E • *Bottega,* 2240 Highland Avenue, 939-1000, sophisticated Italian fare, M–E • *Veranda,* 2220 Highland Avenue, 933-1200, contemporary Southern in a restored 1909 home, M–E • *Cobb Lane,* 1 Cobb Lane at Five Points, 933-0462, Southern charm and specialties, lunch, I; dinner, M.

Other recommendations: *Arman's at Park Lane,* 2116 Cahaba Road, 871-5551, contemporary Italian, open kitchen, very popular, M–E • *Bombay Café,* 2839 7th Avenue South, 322-1930, fireplace, art on the walls, varied menu, M–E • *Rossi's,* 2737 US 280, Mountain Brook, 879-2111, American and Italian dishes, I–E • *John's,* 112 North 21st Street, 322-6014, reliable downtown old-timer, I–M • *Winston's,* Wynfrey Hotel (see Accommodations above), fine dining, regional cuisine, pleasant ambience, M–EE • *Magic City Brewery,* 420 21st Street South, 328-BREW, casual food and homemade brew, I–M • *Irondale Café,* 1806 1st Avenue North, 956-5258, the birthplace of fried green tomatoes and inspiration for the movie, best for lunch, I.

Barbecue: Barbecue is big in Birmingham, with lots of choices. Everyone seems to have a favorite; those mentioned most frequently are: *Ollie's,* 1880 Southpark Drive, Hoover, 989-9009 • *Golden Rule,* 1571 Montgomery Highway, 823-7770 or Highway 78, Irondale, 956-2678 • *Jim 'n Nicks* (two locations), 1810 Montgomery Highway, 733-1300, and 744 29th Street, 323-7082 • *Demetri's,* 1901 28th Avenue South, Homewood, 871-1581 • For ribs, the hands-down choice is *Dreamland,* 1400 15th Street South, 933-2133 • All are I.

SIGHT-SEEING   *Alabama Sports Hall of Fame,* 2150 Civic Center Boulevard, 323-6665. Hours: Monday to Saturday 9 A.M. to 5 P.M., Sunday 1 to 5 P.M. $$ • *Arlington,* 331 Cotton Avenue South West, 780-5656. Hours: Tuesday to Saturday 10 A.M. to 4 P.M., Sunday 1 to 4 P.M. $$ • *Birmingham Civil Rights Institute,* 520 16th Street North, 328-9696. Hours: Tuesday to Saturday 10 A.M. to 5 P.M., Sunday 1 to 5 P.M. $$ • *Alabama Jazz Hall of Fame,* Carver Theatre, 1631 4th Avenue North, 254-2731. Hours: Tuesday to Saturday, 10 A.M. to 5 P.M., Sunday 1 to 5 P.M. $ • *Birmingham Botanical Gardens,* 2612 Lane Park Road, 879-1227. Hours: Daily, dawn to dusk. Free • *Birmingham Museum of*

Art, 2000 8th Avenue North, 254-2565. Hours: Tuesday to Saturday 10 A.M. to 5 P.M., Sunday noon to 5 P.M. Free • *Birmingham Zoo,* 2632 Cahaba Road, 879-0408. Hours: Daily 9 A.M. to 5 P.M. $$$$ • *McWane Center,* 200 19th Street North, 714-8300. Hours: Monday to Friday 9 A.M. to 5 P.M., to 6 P.M in summer, Saturday 9 A.M. to 6 P.M., Sunday noon to 6 P.M. $$$ • *Sloss Furnaces National Historic Landmark,* 20 32nd Street North, 324-1911. Hours: Tuesday to Saturday 10 A.M. to 4 P.M., Sunday noon to 4 P.M. Free • *Vulcan Statue,* 20th Street South and Valley Avenue, atop Red Mountain, 328-6198. Check for hours and fees after restoration • *Barber Vintage Motorsports Museum,* check Convention and Visitors' Bureau for information on new location • *Birmingham Race Course,* 1000 John Rogers Drive, 838-7500 or (800) 998-UBET. Phone for currrent racing schedules • *Alabama Ballet, Opera Theater, Children's Theater, Symphony,* for current schedules, contact the Birmingham-Jefferson Convention Complex, 251-4100.

INFORMATION *Greater Birmingham Convention and Visitors' Bureau,* 2200 9th Avenue North, Birmingham, AL 35203, 458-8000 or (800) 458-8085; www.birminghamal.org.

Winning Ways in Augusta

Augusta, the second-oldest city in Georgia, is also the second-largest city in the state, a winning mix of old and new. No city is richer in history, but that's just the first of many reasons to visit.

The attractions in this "second city" include a revitalized waterfront, some prize new museums, a remarkable collection of Southern art, great golf, and the Futurity, where Old South mingles with Old West for the liveliest cowboy event this side of the Rockies.

As if all that weren't enough, less than an hour to the west are smaller towns of picturesque charm, including Washington, another contender for the crown of Georgia's prettiest town.

To get a feel for Augusta, drive past the bland outskirts to discover the landscaped parkways, gracious homes, groves of tall pines, and lively river esplanades in the city's heart. In 1736 this became the second town marked off for settlement by General James E. Oglethorpe, who named it Augusta. An eventful history has left nine distinct historic districts and many monuments.

The 50-foot granite Signer's Monument, at Greene and Gwinnett Streets, commemorates Georgia's signers of the Declaration of Independence. Two of the three, Lyman Hall and George Walton, are buried there. Meadow Garden, Walton's 1791 home, has been restored and is open for tours.

After the Revolutionary War, Augusta served as the state capital from 1785 to 1795. The South's first newspaper, the still-operating *Augusta Chronicle,* began printing in 1785.

The original building of Georgia's first medical academy, completed in 1835, stands at 598 Telfair Street. The school is still in operation, and the city remains a medical center. Among other historic buildings found on Telfair Street is the façade of the restored 1801 Old Government House at number 432 and the Augusta Museum of History, which includes exhibits of local history ranging from the Revolutionary War era to a reconstructed 1930s train station.

The boyhood home of President Woodrow Wilson is located at 419 Seventh Street, on the corner of Telfair, across from the First Presbyterian Church, where his father served as minister. Ware's Folly, at number 540, is a Federal-style structure built in 1818, so named because the construction price of $40,000 seemed so exorbitant at the time. It houses the Gertrude Herbert Memorial Institute of Art, an art school and gallery.

The city's second-oldest structure is the 1798 Ezekiel Harris House, in the Harrisburg Historic District. It has been preserved as an example of a wealthy early merchant's home.

Also in the Harrisburg district is the site of the first Augusta Arsenal, established in 1793 by order of General George Washington. A 176-foot-tall chimney marks the site along the Augusta Canal of the Confederate Powderworks, said to have been the world's largest munitions factory of its time. The castlelike 1881 Sibley Mill, on the same site, resembles the old powderworks.

You can't miss the Confederate Monument in the center of town, on Broad Street between Seventh and Eighth; the marble shaft stands 72 feet high and features life-size figures of Southern heroes, including Robert E. Lee and "Stonewall" Jackson.

Another monument with an interesting tale is the Haunted Pillar at Fifth and Broad. Legend has it that a traveling minister who was not allowed to preach in the Lower Market prophesied that the building would be destroyed. Sure enough, in 1878 a tornado took down everything except this one pillar.

After the Civil War, Augusta became an industrial center for the New South. Before and after the war, it also prospered as the second-largest inland cotton market in the world, right behind Memphis. The elaborate Victorian 1886 Cotton Exchange Building, near the riverfront, has been restored as a cotton museum and the town's visitors' center. A 45-foot blackboard used to post daily market quotes was found intact behind a wall, still chalked with cotton and commodities prices from the early 1900s. It is the hub of the exhibit called "Cotton Pickin' Deals."

Late in the nineteenth century, the city's mild winter climate was discovered by wealthy Northerners. Drive around the Summerville Historic District, on a breezy knoll above town, to see the homes they built in what was known as the "hill section." John D. Rockefeller and Alexander Graham Bell were among the Yankees who rocked on the porch of the Partridge Inn, on Walton Way, and the old Bon Air Hotel, across the street.

Milledge Road is another of Summerville's wealthiest thoroughfares, lined with fine antebellum homes.

Not far away, at 2500 Walton Way, is the campus of Augusta State University. Among the fine old buildings is the 1829 Payne Hall, which served as headquarters for the Augusta Arsenal. This campus is radiant in spring, when its venerable magnolias are in bloom.

Victorian homes can be found in the Old Town neighborhood, closer to downtown. Some of these homes now serve as welcoming inns.

One site that everyone in Augusta points to with pride is the Sacred Heart Cultural Center, an 1898 showplace of Romanesque Revival architecture with imported stained-glass windows and 15 different kinds of brickwork.

One pleasant way to take in the historic side of Augusta is via the historic tour that leaves from the Cotton Exchange each Saturday morning.

The Cotton Exchange borders the pride of modern Augusta, its recently transformed riverfront. The cobbled streets leading to the river, once piled high with cotton bales, are now lined with shops and cafés. Riverwalk, a landscaped park along the water, makes for delightful strolls and includes a 1,500-seat amphitheater that is used for many outdoor entertainments in summer. Augusta's riverfront hosts many special events, including a colorful rowing regatta in late March or early April.

One end of the walk is anchored by a conference center/office complex and an elegant Radisson hotel. On the second floor of one of those office buildings is a not-to-be-missed treasury of Southern art. The Morris Museum of Art is an enlightening view of many facets of Southern life as seen through the artist's eye. Some 2,000 paintings span the years from 1790 to the present, ranging from antebellum portraits to contemporary abstracts. A corridor circling all the galleries is devoted to the Southern landscape in all its beautiful forms.

Attractions on and around the Riverwalk continue to grow. The Augusta Museum of History traces the town's development in exhibits ranging from an American Indian artifacts collection to a vintage steam locomotive, to a space exhibit. There are also displays on the Revolutionary and Civil War periods, and natural history.

An exciting recent addition, the National Science Center's Fort Discovery, has more than 270 interactive exhibits teaching about science and technology, including a high-wire bicycle and a medical helicopter that transmits your vital signs to an aid station. Visitors enter through Science Plaza, with its sensor fountain, power-generating waterwheel, and a liquid Morse code transmitter. Young children have their own Kidscape for activities such as electronic finger-painting on a computer screen.

A new riverwalk hotel is slated to open in 2001, and the Riverfront Convention Center is undergoing expansion that will more than double its meeting space. Anchoring the western end of Riverwalk is the 17-acre Augusta Golf and Gardens, which will be the home of a new Georgia Golf Hall of Fame.

It isn't surprising that the Georgia Golf Hall of Fame will be in Augusta. The city's golf heritage dates back to the post–Civil War era, when the owner of the Bon Air Hotel decided to build a 9-hole golf course. It proved so popular with his wealthy guests that the following year an 18-hole course was built at what is now the Augusta Country Club. In 1933, Bobby Jones founded the Augusta National Golf Club and held the first Masters Tournament, now a world-class event each spring.

Tickets for the Masters are hard to come by, and only members can play the National, but that doesn't mean you can't play golf in Augusta. There are over a dozen public courses, including the Jones Creek Golf Course in nearby Evans, rated among Georgia's top public courses.

Augusta weather is mild most of the year, which means you can often play golf in winter. But regardless of the climate, winter is the season for the city's most unusual event, the Augusta Cutting Horse Futurity, held in late January. Cutting horses are used by cowboys to separate a single cow from the safety of the herd, a maneuver that takes skill and ultimate teamwork between horse and rider. For over a decade the best professional riders have competed for speed, showing off their prowess for a purse of some $500,000 and the title of America's Greatest Cowboy.

The exciting and colorful weeklong event includes a top-notch Western Art Show and a Western Expo with booths selling everything Western, from fringed suede jackets to fancy saddles and Indian jewelry.

If you have time for more sight-seeing, less than an hour to the west is Washington, a beautiful small town dating to 1780 that is now a mellow mix of white antebellum columns and sturdy brick Victorian architecture. The turn-of-the-century town square, dominated by an unusual Flemish-design brick courthouse, is a classic.

Washington's most historic moment came at the end of the Civil War, when Jefferson Davis and the members of his cabinet signed the last official papers dissolving the Confederate government at the Heard House, on the site of the present courthouse. Some still believe that the remainder of the Confederate treasury, estimated at over half a million dollars in gold, was buried somewhere nearby.

A small town with a population of 4,800, Washington can be enjoyed on a brief walking or driving tour, guided with a brochure from the chamber of commerce. Within the city limits are 16 properties on the National Register of Historic Places. Start with a walk around the square, peeking into the old-fashioned gift shops and antiques stores. Look to the left of the courthouse, in the northwest corner, to see the old jail, built in 1891 and recently restored.

Many of the finest older homes are along Robert Toombs Avenue; this includes the Toombs House, a 1794 pillared structure that was the home of the man known as the South's "unreconstructed Rebel." Toombs, a brigadier general and secretary of state of the Confederacy, refused to take the oath of allegiance to the Union after the Civil War, remaining a Rebel to the end of his days. He became a local hero, and his home is now a state historic site.

The Washington Historical Museum, housed in an 1835 structure, contains furnishings from the antebellum era and Civil War memorabilia, including a Confederate gun collection.

Another building worth a visit is the Mary Willis Library, Georgia's first free public library. Founded in 1888, the ornate Victorian building boasts Tiffany stained-glass windows, charming murals of the town, and an impressive collection of rare books.

Callaway Plantation, five miles outside town, portrays a working farm with a columned manor house (circa 1869) and outbuildings. The log kitchen is often used for cooking and other demonstrations.

Several homes in the historic district are now bed-and-breakfast inns. One outstanding choice awaits just outside town. Holly Ridge comprises two homes, a 1780s Colonial and an 1880s Victorian, that were moved to this site, joined, then restored to provide one inn with two distinct characters.

Another top lodging choice is the 1810 West Inn, a short drive away in Thomson. A plantation house built of heart of pine, it has five dependencies, creating a rambling inn of varying moods, tastefully decorated with antiques and offering eight fireplaces.

Thomson, the commercial center of the area, boasts a unique bit of history in the 1785 Rock House, named for its unusual building material. Tours are available; ask at the tourism center in the old railroad depot, where you can also pick up a driving tour through many nearby towns with fine period homes.

Thomson has a strong equestrian bent. The annual Belle Meade Fox Hunts, held from November to March, are renowned; you're likely to spot the red-coated riders on the outskirts of town in the Wrightsborough area.

It's a classic scene, an appropriate image for a region that remains the picture of the classic South.

Area Code: 706

DRIVING DIRECTIONS   Augusta is on the eastern edge of Georgia, off I-20. From Atlanta, follow I-20 east, 145 miles; from Augusta to Washington, follow I-20 west to US 78 north, 45 miles. To reach Washington from Atlanta, take I-20 east to Georgia Route 44 north, 95 miles.

ACCOMMODATIONS   *Radisson Riverfront Hotel Augusta,* 2 10th Street, Augusta, 30901, 722-8900, elegant hotel on the Riverwalk, M • *Partridge Inn,* 2110 Walton Way, Augusta, 30904, 737-8888, restored landmark 1890 hotel, generous buffet breakfast, M–E, CP • *Telfair Inn,* 326 Greene Street, Augusta, 30901, 724-3315, group of Victorian homes, pool, lighted tennis court, M; suites, M–E • *Azalea Inn,* 312-216 Greene Street, Augusta, 30901, 724-3454, elegant Victorian, Jacuzzis, M, CP • *Perrin Guest House Inn,* 208 Lafayette Drive, Augusta, 30901, 731-0920, 1863 home, fireplaces, Jazuzzis, M, CP • *Queen Anne Inn,* 406 Greene Street, Augusta, 30901, 723-0045, in-town Victorian, M, CP • *Maynard's Manor,* 219 East Toombs Avenue, Washington, 30673, 678-4303, nicely restored 1820 home, M, CP • *Holly Ridge Country Inn,* 2221 Sandtown Road, Washington, 30673, 285-2594, I, CP • *Wisteria Hall,* 225 East Robert Toombs Avenue, Washington, 30673, 678-7779 or (770) 993-4633, columned antebellum mansion, M, CP • *1810 West Inn,* 254 North Seymour Drive North West, Thomson, 30824, 595-3156, highly recommended, M–E, CP • *Four Chimneys Bed & Breakfast,* 2316 Wire Road, Thomson, 30824, 597-0220, 1800s country house, I, CP.

DINING   *La Maison on Telfair,* 404 Telfair Street, Augusta, 722-4805, restored 1855 home, Continental, game specialties, M–EE • *Le Café Du Teau,* 1855 Central Avenue, Augusta, 733-3505, quaint café, New Orleans–style menu, live jazz Friday to Sunday, M–E • *Michael's,* 2860 Washington Road, Augusta, 733-2860, contemporary setting, fine dining, M–E • *Calvert's,* 475 Highland Avenue, Augusta, 738-4514, formal dining, a local favorite for special occasions, M–E • *French Market Grille,* 425 Highland Avenue, Augusta, 737-4865, Louisiana cuisine, known for crab cakes and peanut butter pie, M–E • *Partridge Inn,* Augusta (see Accommodations above), fine dining, excellent Sunday brunch, dining room, M–E; bar and grill, M • *T-Bonz Steakhouse* (two Augusta locations), 1654 Gordon Highway, 796-1875, and 1856 Washington Road, 737-8325, casual, friendly, I–M • *T's Restaurant,* 3416 Old Savannah Road, Augusta, 798-4145, catfish and hush puppies, oyster bar, I–M • *King George,* 2 Eighth Street on the Riverwalk, Augusta, 724-4755, pub ambience and menu, I–M • *Sconyers Bar-B-Que,* 2250 Sconyers Way, Augusta, 790-5411, everybody goes there, log cabin decorated with owner's pig collectibles, I • *Another Thyme*

Café, 5 East Public Square, Washington, 678-1672, very informal, I–M • *Plantation Room,* Best Western–White Columns Motel, US 78 at I-10, Thomson, 595-8000 or (800) 528-1234, prime rib, seafood, etc., I–M • *Neal's Bar-B-Que,* US 78/278, Thomson, 595-2594, no atmosphere at all, just good food, I.

SIGHTSEEING Augusta: *Morris Museum of Art,* 1 Tenth Street, Riverfront Center, second floor, 724-7501. Hours: Tuesday to Saturday 10 A.M. to 5:30 P.M., Sunday 12:30 to 5:30 P.M. $$; free on Sunday • *Augusta Museum of History,* 560 Reynolds Street, 722-8454. Hours: Tuesday to Saturday 10 A.M. to 5 P.M., Sunday 1 to 5 P.M. $$ • *Gertrude Herbert Institute of Art,* 506 Telfair Street, 722-5495. Hours: Tuesday to Friday 10 A.M. to 5 P.M.; Saturday 10 A.M. to 2 P.M. Donation • *Sacred Heart Cultural Center,* 1301 Greene Street, 826-4700. Hours: Monday to Friday 9 A.M. to 5 P.M. Free • *Ezekiel Harris Home,* 1822 Broad Street, 724-0436. Hours: Tuesday to Friday 1 to 4 P.M.; Saturday 10 A.M. to 1 P.M. $ • *National Science Center's Fort Discovery,* One Seventh Street on the Riverwalk, 821-0200. Hours: Monday to Saturday 10 A.M. to 6 P.M., Sunday noon to 4 P.M. $$$$ • *Georgia Golf Hall of Fame,* Riverwalk, opening date not determined at press time; check Visitors Bureau for information • *Historic Cotton Exchange Museum and Welcome Center,* 32 Eighth Street, 724-4067. Hours: Monday to Saturday 9 A.M. to 5 P.M., Sunday 1 to 5 P.M. Free • *Historic Guided Tours,* 724-4067. Ninety-minute tours leave Saturday at 10:30 A.M. from Cotton Exchange Welcome Center. Reservations advised. $$$$ • *Augusta Cutting Horse Futurity,* Augusta–Richmond County Civic Center, 823-3417. One week of riding competitions, Western Art Show, and Western Expo, usually late January. Phone Visitors' Bureau for current information • **Washington:** *Washington Historical Museum,* 308 East Robert Toombs Avenue, 678-2105. Hours: Tuesday to Saturday 10 A.M. to 5 P.M., Sunday 2 to 5 P.M. $ • *Robert Toombs House,* 216 East Robert Toombs Avenue, 678-2226. Hours: Tuesday to Saturday 9 A.M. to 5 P.M., Sunday 2 to 5:30 P.M. $ • *Callaway Plantation,* US 78, 678-7060. Hours: Tuesday to Saturday 10 A.M. to 5 P.M., Sunday 2 to 5 P.M. $.

INFORMATION *Augusta Metropolitan Convention and Visitors' Bureau,* 1450 Greene Street, Suite 110, P.O. Box 1331, Augusta, GA 30903, 823-6600 or (800) 726-0243; www.augustaga.org • *Washington-Wilkes Chamber of Commerce,* 104 East Liberty Street, P.O. Box 661, Washington, GA 30673, 678-2013; www.washington ga.org.

Tee Time at Myrtle Beach

Everybody knows about Myrtle Beach, South Carolina, in the summer. Smack in the middle of the 60 miles of sand known as the Grand Strand, this has long been one of the busiest vacation destinations on the Atlantic seaboard. But why in the world are people now heading for the shore in winter? What makes them flock to Myrtle Beach when many people are at home by the fire?

Well, for starters, how about a round of golf? To be more precise, make that 100 rounds of golf. There are 100-plus golf courses in the Myrtle Beach area, enough for a game every day for over three months without repeating the same course twice.

What to do at night in winter? What about a show? Make that a dozen shows. Myrtle Beach is rapidly beginning to rival Nashville and Branson, Missouri, for country music entertainment—plus comedy, ice shows, and dinner theaters.

No wonder the bargain winter rates lure not only a host of all-male golf foursomes but lots of couples and families with nongolfers, who take advantage of a growing list of other diversions while the fanatics are teeing off. Tennis, fishing, indoor pools, shelling, and sight-seeing at one of America's loveliest outdoor sculpture gardens are more off-season activities, all delightfully devoid of crowds.

For the kids, there's a special outing to the Waccatee Zoo to see over 100 animals from llamas to leopards, Ripley's Aquarium, featuring sharks, jellyfish, stingrays, and other exotic creatures of the sea, or a visit to Alligator Adventure, where there are live reptile shows and all kinds of iguanas, lizards, frogs, and turtles—and dozens of alligators in residence, including albino alligators with pink eyes!

The NASCAR SpeedPark, a miniature grand prix entertainment complex, has fans racing against each other on seven tracks, plus displays of racing memorabilia and show vehicles. Families will also find they've come to the world's miniature golf capital, with dozens of lavish layouts that even include towering waterfalls and erupting volcanoes.

Another only-in–Myrtle Beach winter bonus is the chance to see the shaggers in action. The shag is South Carolina's official dance, a Southern cousin of the lindy, replete with show-off dips, glides, and spins. It can be danced to almost any tempo, but best of all is beach music, and the preferred place is North Myrtle Beach. You can see amateurs in action almost any weekend, and many clubs offer lessons if you want to get in on the fun. But if you want to see the best dancers do their thing, you'll find them at the preliminaries for the National Shag Dance Championships in January, with winners going on to the championships in mid-March.

It might be said that Myrtle Beach's phenomenal development in the last few decades is making up for lost time. Separated by water from both the mainland and the Georgetown County plantation country to the south, isolated Horry County was left to the farmers and timbermen, a self-sufficient pocket cut off from development. Until the early 1900s, the beach was accessible only by ferryboat across the Waccamaw River, which is now part of the Intracoastal Waterway.

When a railroad bridge across the river made transportation easier, inland families began building summer cottages along the coast, and in 1901 the first hotel went up. A contest held by the county newspaper produced the name of Myrtle Beach, inspired by the wax myrtles growing wild along the shore.

In 1929 a group of developers built Arcady at the north end of the community, planned as a dream resort for the affluent. It included Pine Lakes, the area's first golf course, and the elegant ten-story Ocean Forest Hotel, which became the center of Myrtle Beach social life for nearly 30 years.

Modern Myrtle Beach was largely the result of Hurricane Hazel, which leveled most of the early beachfront buildings in 1954. New resorts and golf courses sprang up seemingly overnight, this time planned for families with average incomes, and development has never stopped.

The shoreline is now wall-to-wall motels and hotels, the main highway chockablock with restaurants, shopping centers, amusement parks, water slides, and elaborate miniature golf courses that vie for the most waterfalls and other extravaganzas. Property destroyed by Hurricane Hugo in 1989 was rebuilt quickly, and growth continues. It is almost essential to come off-season to see the beauty that attracted development in the first place.

The buildup is slightly less dense at North Myrtle Beach, which also boasts the widest beaches. To the south, the towns of Surfside Beach and Garden City are mostly family cottage colonies. Murrells Inlet, favored by fishermen and seafood lovers, is the dividing line with Georgetown County, and the more secluded beaches of Litchfield and Pawleys Island lie beyond.

Winters are mild, with average temperatures in the fifties and sixties, and spring comes early to the South Carolina shore, so the golfing mania knows no season. Almost every area lodging entices visitors with golf packages galore at phenomenal bargain rates.

If golf is your goal, contact Myrtle Beach Golf Holiday for its free book of golf packages. Over 170 pages thick, it includes color photos of scores of participating properties, from motels to luxury resorts, plus details and pictures of area golf courses.

Ocean Harbour, situated on a peninsula between the Calabash River and the Intracoastal Waterway, is an example of the kind of course that makes this area unique. Nine holes run along marshland and the water.

Golf magazine has ranked it one of the 10 best courses in the world. The six Legends courses—Marsh Harbour, Oyster Bay, Heritage, Moorland, Parkland, and Heathland—are also often ranked among America's top public courses.

More memorable experiences include Waterway Hills, designed by Robert Trent Jones, possibly the only course in the world accessed by a glass-enclosed gondola, and the Witch, with 400 feet of bridges winding through hundreds of acres of wetlands. The Arnold Palmer courses at Myrtle Beach National also feature some legendary water holes, particularly the island greens on the North Course.

Pine Lakes Country Club, the granddaddy of the courses, still shows the Scottish influence of its architect, Robert White. Golfers are greeted by kilted starters, traverse the course in Rolls-Royce golf carts, and are warmed with a mimosa or clam chowder on the course. It was at Pine Lakes that *Sports Illustrated* magazine was conceived in 1954.

Part of the fun of playing in the Myrtle Beach area is the opportunity to try so many courses and pick your own favorites.

If tennis is your game, you'll find that courts are plentiful, 200 at last count. Tennis buffs should consider a stay at the Litchfield Beach and Golf Resort, a 4,500-acre resort in Georgetown County, about 18 miles south of the Myrtle Beach buildup. The Litchfield Racquet Club has the area's largest tennis complex, with 17 outdoor and two indoor courts.

The posh Kingston Plantation features high-rise oceanfront condominium towers, an Embassy Suites hotel and villas, all on 145 oceanfront acres, with tennis, racquetball, and a sport and health club with a pool.

There are more than 60,000 guest rooms in the Myrtle Beach area in every price range, including efficiencies, suites, and cottage rentals. Many are almost interchangeable motel or high-rise accommodations. Those suggested in the listings at the end of this chapter are among the choices that offer both beach access and indoor pools and other facilities for winter visitors. If you want to stay away from it all but within easy reach, also consider the Pawleys Island listings on page 173.

When the sun goes down, Myrtle Beach really lights up these days, with 11 theaters and more on the way. Missouri-born entrepreneur Calvin Gilmore started the trend in 1986 when he opened the Carolina Opry, still going strong after expanding into a lavish theater seating 2,200.

In 1992, part-owner Dolly Parton inaugurated another $7.5 million showplace, the Dixie Stampede, a version of the Dollywood-produced spectacle on horseback that packs in crowds at Pigeon Forge, Tennessee.

The star country music group Alabama, which got its first break in Myrtle Beach, was next to build a supertheater—at the big Barefoot Landing shopping-dining complex, which also includes the House of Blues.

Next came Fantasy Harbour–Waccamaw, an entertainment complex that includes the Crook & Chase Theatre, the Forum Theatre, the Medieval Times Dinner and Tournament (complete with jousting knights on horseback), and the Savoy Theatre featuring ice-skating revues.

The Legends in Entertainment show, located south of Myrtle Beach, quickly found an appreciative audience for its cast, who impersonate show business greats from Elvis to Marilyn Monroe.

Kenny Rogers, Wayne Newton, the Oak Ridge Boys, and top Broadway shows are among the headliners who have played the Palace, the $12 million, 2,700-seat theater that lives up to its name. It is part of a $250 million, see-it-to-believe-it complex called Broadway on the Beach that boasts nearly 100 shops, 20 restaurants, and a lineup of clubs and eating places, including Planet Hollywood, America's first NASCAR cafe and the only Hard Rock Café in the world in the shape of an Egyptian pyramid. In case you get bored, there's an IMAX theater, a 16-movie Cineplex, the NASCAR Speed Park, Ripley's Aquarium, and a carousel park for the kids, and you can take pedal boats out on the man-made lake.

With Broadway at the Beach, Barefoot Landing, and dozens of additional shops along US 17, shoppers will find ample opportunities for their favorite sport. Bargain hunters should make a beeline for US 501 West and Waccamaw Pottery, across the street from the Fantasy Harbour theaters. The original pottery outlet, now selling a huge selection of housewares and home furnishings, is adjacent to an outlet park with more than 100 brand-name factory outlets. Farther west on Route 501 is Myrtle Beach Factory Shoppes, another 125 outlet stores.

No one should miss a visit to Brookgreen Gardens, the main sightseeing attraction in the area, located to the south in Georgetown County. America's first public sculpture garden, it is now the largest outdoor sculpture display in the world, a remarkable blend of nature and art, with over 500 sculptures set on 300 lush, landscaped acres. (Read more about the gardens and all of Georgetown County starting on page 169.)

Across the road, in Huntington Beach State Park, part of the original family land holdings, is Atalaya, the Huntingtons' single-story home, inspired by Moorish watchtowers on the Spanish coast. It is unfurnished but well worth a look.

The park itself includes maritime forests, salt marshes, and sandy beaches. Like much of Myrtle Beach, it is a fine place to be on a mild winter day.

Area Code: 843

DRIVING DIRECTIONS   Myrtle Beach begins at the junction of US 17 north and south with US 501 from the west. From Atlanta and

Columbia, follow I-20 east to Florence, then take US 76 east, which merges into US 501. From I-95, take the Florence exit and follow the directions above. Myrtle Beach is 354 miles from Atlanta, 174 miles from Charlotte, 143 miles from Columbia.

PUBLIC TRANSPORTATION   The Myrtle Beach area has its own airport; easy access and special air and car-rental rates make it easy to visit for a winter weekend. Additional service is from Charleston, 70 miles south.

ACCOMMODATIONS   All have private beach, indoor pool; I rates are usually from November to early March, higher rates in season. *Kingston Plantation,* 9800 Lake Drive, Myrtle Beach, 29572, 449-0006 or (800) 876-0010, towers, *Embassy Suites Hotel,* villas, lighted tennis courts, racquetball, lavish sport and health club, M–EE • *Bluewater Resort,* 2001 South Ocean Boulevard, Myrtle Beach, 29577, 626-8345 or (800) 845-6994, efficiency apartments, racquetball, billiard, and exercise rooms, I–M • *The Breakers Resort Hotel,* 2006 North Ocean Boulevard, Myrtle Beach, 29577, 626-5000 or (800) 845-0688, exercise room, rooms, M; kitchen suites, E–EE • *Captain's Quarters,* 901 South Ocean Boulevard, Myrtle Beach, 29578, 448-1404 or (800) 843-3561, rooms and efficiencies, bowling alley, I–E • *Carolina Winds,* Oceanfront at 76th Avenue North, Myrtle Beach, 29572, 449-2477 or (800) 523-4027, villas with kitchens, spa, exercise and game rooms, I–EE • *Forest Dunes Resort,* 5511 North Ocean Boulevard, Myrtle Beach, 29577, 449-0864 or (800) 845-7787, suites, indoor pool, exercise and game rooms, I–E • *Holiday Inn Resort Hotel,* 1200 North Ocean Boulevard, Myrtle Beach, 29577, 913-5805 or (800) 874-7401, I–E, CP • *Myrtle Beach Martinique Resort Hotel,* 7100 North Ocean Boulevard, Myrtle Beach, 29572, 449-4441 or (800) 542-0048, sauna, exercise and game rooms; hotel rooms and efficiencies, I–E • *Ocean Dunes Resort & Villas,* 201 75th Avenue North, Myrtle Beach, 29578, 449-7441 or (800) 845-0635, indoor fitness center, E; suites, E–EE • *Patricia Grand,* 2710 North Ocean Boulevard, Myrtle Beach, 29577, 448-8453 or (800) 255-4763, game room, sauna, indoor "lazy river," I–M • *Sea Island,* 6000 North Ocean Boulevard, Myrtle Beach, 29577, 449-6406 or (800) 548-0767, I–M • See **Pawleys Island** choices on page 173. Write to chamber of commerce (see Information, below) for full hotel-motel guide or condominium-cottage guide • For a book listing golf packages at all area resorts, contact *Myrtle Beach Golf Holiday,* (800) 506-7511; they can also be accessed on the website www.myrtlebeachlive.com.

DINING   *Sea Captain's House,* Oceanfront at 30th Avenue North, Myrtle Beach, 448-8082, restored beach house, ocean views, area favorite for all three meals, dinners, I–M • *The Crab House,* Broadway at the Beach, US 17 Bypass, Myrtle Beach, 444-2717, informal, blue crabs are the specialty, M • *Collector's Cafe,* 7726 North Kings Highway, Myrtle Beach, 449-9370, art on the walls, Mediterranean menu, M –E • *Latif's Bakery and Cafe,* 503 61st Avenue North, 449-1716, eclectic menu, delicious desserts, M • *The Library,* 1212 Kings Highway North, 448-4527, elegant, M–EE • *Vintage House Cafe,* 1210 North Kings Highway, 626-3918, casual café, interesting menu, M • For **Murrells Inlet** dining, see page 174.

SIGHT-SEEING *Brookgreen Gardens,* US 17, Murrells Inlet, 237-4218. Hours: Daily 9:30 A.M. to 5:30 P.M. $$$$ • *National Shag Dance Championship,* Studebaker's, 2000 North Kings Highway, Myrtle Beach, 448-9747 or 626-3855. Preliminaries usually in late January, championships in March; phone for current dates • *Waccatee Zoo,* 8500 Enterprise Road, Myrtle Beach, 650-8500. Hours: Daily 10 A.M. to 5 P.M. $$ • *Alligator Adventure,* Barefoot Landing, 4604 US 17 South, Myrtle Beach, 361-0789. Hours: Vary with the season; it's best to call. $$$$$ • *Ripley's Aquarium,* 1110 Celebrity Circle, Broadway at the Beach, Myrtle Beach, 916-0888. Hours: Mid-May to Labor Day, daily 9 A.M. to 11 P.M.; phone for hours off-season. $$$$$ • *Waccatee Zoo,* State Route 707 and Enterprise Road, Myrtle Beach, 650-8500. Hours: Daily 10 A.M. to 5 P.M. $$.

ENTERTAINMENT (most shows run year-round, but schedules may be curtailed in late December and January; check all for current show times and rates) *Alabama Theater,* Barefoot Landing, US 17, Myrtle Beach, 272-1111 • *Carolina Opry,* US 17 north, at US 17 Bypass, Myrtle Beach, 238-8888 • *Legends in Concert,* 301 US 17 south, Surfside Beach, 238-7827 • *Dixie Stampede,* junction of US 17 and US 17 Bypass, North Myrtle Beach, 497-9700 • *Fantasy Harbor,* US 501 west, opposite Waccamaw Pottery, Myrtle Beach, includes *The Savoy Theatre ice show,* 236-9700; *Crook & Chase Theatre,* 681-5209; *Medieval Times Dinner and Tournament,* 436-4386; and the *Forum Theatre,* 236-9700 • *Palace Theater,* Broadway at the Beach, US 17 Bypass, Myrtle Beach, 448-0588.

INFORMATION *Myrtle Beach Area Chamber of Commerce,* 1200 North Oak Street, P.O. Box 2115, Myrtle Beach, SC 29578, 626-7444 or (800) 356-3016; www.myrtlebeachlive.com.

The Last Roundup

Southeastern Resorts

Sometimes sight-seeing isn't at all what you have in mind for your weekend. There are times when the most inviting prospect may be a resort where you can stay in one place, relax and refresh, maybe play a little golf or tennis, learn a new sport, take a run around a lake, a walk in the woods, or a hike in the mountains.

Blessed with a mild climate and a spectacular range of scenery, the Southeastern states offer wonderful get-away-from-it-all resorts—by the sea, in the mountains, and in between. They come rustic and fancy, to suit every taste and budget, geared to families as well as to couples. State park resorts in many states are outstanding and are great bargains.

Many top resorts have already been mentioned in previous sections, but some just don't fit neatly into another destination. This final chapter changes the book format, moving state by state to make sure these special places are not overlooked.

Browse through this roundup, then check the index under "Resorts" for a reminder of the other rich choices available when a one-stop getaway is what you have in mind.

ALABAMA

Less than an hour south of Birmingham, in Shelby County, is the kind of hideaway city dwellers often dream about, a rustic resort on 350 wooded acres around a 46-acre private lake. Twin Pines was designed as a conference center, but on weekends the guest rooms in the newly built log houses by the lake are perfect escapes for a minivacation.

Although the setting is definitely country, rooms come with city comforts such as coffeemakers, refrigerators, and cable TV. Suites offer kitchens and fireplaces. Each guest house has a deck with rockers for admiring sunsets over the lake. Country-style meals are served in an airy dining room with a cathedral ceiling, fireplaces, and picture windows.

Besides swimming, canoeing, and fishing, the resort offers a swimming pool and hot tub, tennis, horseshoe-tossing, volleyball, basketball, a white-sand beach lagoon at the lake, a children's playground, jogging, and walking trails. Weekend package rates make this a most affordable getaway.

Even in a state filled with exceptional state resort parks, Lake Guntersville stands out. The majestic wood-and-fieldstone lodge, set atop Little Mountain, provides a superb view of the 66,470-acre Guntersville Reservoir, one of the beautiful Alabama lakes formed by the dam system on the Tennessee River. The lodge rooms have balconies and eye-boggling lake views. Cottages and chalets are also available on the grounds.

Water sports are the big activity here, and the lake is renowned among fishermen, but landlubbers can golf and play tennis on two lighted courts, or enjoy 31 miles of hiking trails along the park's 5,909 acres of ridge tops and in its meadows. Winter eagle-watching weekends led by park naturalists are a special treat.

GEORGIA

It's the ultimate fantasy when worldly worries close in: escape to an island where there are no cars, no commotion, and nothing but serenity. Two Georgia offshore islands can make this fantasy come true.

Little St. Simons is a magical 10,000-acre totally private world of unspoiled marshes, thick maritime forests, moss-draped live oaks, ponds, and seven miles of pristine beaches. It is home to deer, rabbits, 200 species of birds, alligators, and armadillos—and just 30 fortunate guests.

The island was originally purchased in 1908 by Philip Berolzheimer, head of the Eagle Pencil Company, who planned to use the cedar trees as a source of pencil wood. The wood proved unsuitable, but Berolzheimer fell in love with the wild beauty of Little St. Simons and kept it as a personal retreat, building a rustic hunting lodge in 1917. The family still owns Little St. Simons, but they have opened it to visitors as a secluded retreat, where guests stay in five charming modernized cottages dating back to 1917.

Days on the island are spent exploring the tidal marshes and creeks by canoe, beachcombing, or setting out on horseback or on foot to see birds and animals. Resident naturalists lead guided walks, or you can go off on your own. The deserted beach is a shell collector's dream come true. There are also safaris by truck to places like Murtle Pond, a prime spot for seeing alligators. In summer, there are special programs for families to learn together while exploring the island.

At the end of the day, guests gather in the homey, memento-filled main lodge for drinks before dinner and family-style meals. The Lodge on Little St. Simons Island is expensive, but it is a rare experience.

The nature is similar on Cumberland Island, but the ambience is quite different. Located farther south, near the Georgia-Florida border, the island was once a family preserve owned by Thomas Carnegie. The Carnegies lived on a lavish scale, as ruins of the old family mansions reveal.

Greyfield Inn, the only remaining island lodging, was built in 1901 for a daughter, Lucy Carnegie Ferguson, and it was opened as an inn by family descendants in the 1960s. It is still in the Carnegie family. Approached by an oak-lined drive, the 17-room inn retains the ambience of its grander days. High ceilings, paneling, Oriental rugs, and family heirlooms tell you that this was the province of wealth, and the air is still gracious. Dinner, for example, is served by candlelight, and jackets are required for gentlemen, dresses for the ladies. After dinner, everyone usually gathers in the great room for coffee and dessert. A self-service bar is open to guests.

Some 95 percent of Cumberland is now a National Seashore, preserved forever in its unspoiled state. Visitors come over from the mainland by boat to enjoy the beach, to view the birds and the wildlife, and to enjoy the walks and talks offered by national park rangers in season, but the isolation means the island is never crowded. Guests at Greyfield get a jeep tour of the island with a staff naturalist, free use of a bicycle, fishing and beach equipment, and access to a private beach. On nights with a full moon, they often head to the beach to watch for the loggerhead sea turtles, who wait for the light to guide them from the surf to the sand dunes, where they dig their nests.

Two other Georgia resorts are especially convenient to Atlanta weekenders. The Lake Lanier Islands were created when the Buford Dam was built on the Chattahoochee River, forming a 1,200-acre lake with 540 miles of shoreline. The heavily forested hilltops, too high to be submerged, were developed for recreation and are now connected to the mainland by a causeway. These resorts offer just about every facility. Renaissance Pineisle Resort is perhaps a little more posh than the Hilton Lake Lanier Island Resort, but whichever you choose, you'll have your choice of golf, tennis, horseback riding, and boat rentals to enjoy the lake. Kids love the water park, with all manner of rides and slides with names like Triple Threat and Intimidator.

The lavish Chateau Elan in Braselton, Georgia, is unique. It is part winery; part exclusive spa; part golf, tennis, and equestrian resort; part conference center; all done with all the style that money can buy. There are 306 rooms located in the 144-room inn and conference center, in villas near the golf course or in the intimate spa building, where each of the 14 rooms of the deluxe hideaway is done to fanciful themes ranging from high-tech to Oriental, from Greek to Old South. Dining choices are many. In the winery is an informal bistro café and Le Clos, featuring eight-course French meals. In the inn, the Versailles Room offers breakfast and lunch buffets and à la carte dinner service; lighter fare is served in L'Auberge. The Fleur-de-Lis in the spa specializes in healthy cuisine, and the Clubhouse Grille overlooking the eighteenth hole on the golf course serves American fare.

NORTH CAROLINA

Imagine yourself taking a cruise around picturesque Lake Toxaway, surrounded by the dusky Blue Ridge Mountains. When you dock, you need only walk up the stone steps to find your private mansion. That's a typical afternoon scenario at the Greystone Inn. This magnificent 16,000-square-foot "cottage," rambling up six levels to accommodate its rocky terrain, was built by a Savannah heiress, Lucy Moltz, back in 1915 and is now on the National Register of Historic Places. It has become the center of a resort surrounded by 3,000 acres of wilderness, complete with the waterfalls that abound in this enchanted part of the state, about 20 miles north of Highlands.

There are 19 rooms in the main house; they're decorated with antique-style furnishings, canopy and brass beds, and lovely floral fabrics. An oak-paneled library, modeled after the grand library at the Biltmore Estate in Asheville, has been turned into the Presidential Suite, two stories high with huge mullioned windows, wooden beams, and a big fireplace. A newer adjoining lodge makes up for lack of history with fireplaces, Jacuzzis, and private balconies overlooking the lake.

The resort offers a pool, six tennis courts, 18 holes of golf, a velvet-green croquet lawn, and lots of room for hiking. You can take out your own boat or join the afternoon excursions aboard the *Mountain Lily II*. It's a lifestyle designed to make you feel as though you've become an heiress, too.

The mood is just the opposite at Earthshine Mountain Lodge, a rustic retreat also near Lake Toxaway and set on 70 acres across a high mountain meadow. Owners Marion and Kim Boatwright designed and built the one-and-a-half-story cedar log lodge themselves, with only Kim's mother and one employee to help them. Both specialists in outdoor education, the Boatwrights were creating a dream—a place to celebrate the mountains, a center where all ages could come to appreciate and learn more about nature, to fish and hike, ride a horse, and feed the family of farm animals. The hardy can test their mettle on the High Ropes course, a challenging skill akin to rock climbing, or on the 31-foot climbing wall.

The complex keeps growing, but the spirit is unchanged. The owners want guests to take time to enjoy the grandeur of the mountains. The deck is equipped with rockers for contemplating the views, and the long printed list of activities ends with three R's—reading, rocking, and relaxation.

Guest rooms are small and simple, with wooden walls, quilts on the log beds, and nice touches such as tree branches as towel hooks and canning-jar lids as curtain rings. All rooms have a private bath and a loft, making them perfect for families. Some come with decks. The choicest accommodations are the three suites in Sunrise Cottage, with decks, fireplaces, and exceptional views and privacy.

Children are happy here, with activities ranging from special programs such as pond exploration to horse rides in the corral, berry picking, bread baking, learning old-time skills like pressing cider, making candles, spinning wool, and helping with the garden and the animals.

Three miles up a steep winding road, and on a site over 5,000 feet high, Cataloochee Ranch puts you at eye level with the mountains. Just 60 guests share these 1,000 acres above the Maggie Valley, another favorite haven for families. There's good hiking here, as well as tennis and fishing, but most guests go to enjoy the mountains on horseback, letting a trusty steed do the climbing while they enjoy the fabulous scenery.

The ranch was begun by the Alexander family in 1934, and some of the guest families have been coming in successive generations for almost that long. The main ranch house, built of mud-mortared stone, was once the cattle barn, and most of the original walls remain. It is furnished with big, well-worn couches and chairs, lamps made from oxen yokes, and a piano where guests often gather.

Guest rooms are in the main lodge, in seven cabins on the grounds, and in the newer Silverbell Lodge, where suites have fireplaces. Furnishings are rustic, in keeping with the setting. Meals are family-style, followed by entertainment by local musicians, who sing folk songs and teach square dancing and clogging to city folks. In winter Cataloochee offers skiing at the area that was the first for the sport in North Carolina.

Nantahala Outdoor Center doesn't exactly qualify as a resort, but it deserves mention for those who want to get out on the glorious mountain rivers. Sometimes called "the Oxford of whitewater canoe schools," the center has been offering trips through the river's scenic gorge for over 20 years.

This was long before river rafting was "in," and the center has done a great deal to help the sport to grow, while expanding beyond anyone's dreams. Now an employee-owned company with 90 to 100 year-round staff members, it is the prime place in the Southeast for learning rafting. Rock climbing, mountain biking, and backpacking are also offered.

The complex is in two parts. On the river is a reception center, a day-care center, a no-frills motel, a well-stocked outfitters store, and two informal restaurants. Up the hill is Relia's Garden, an attractive cedar chalet-style restaurant overlooking a garden growing vegetables, herbs, and flowers.

Also on the hill are cottages, dorm-style lodgings, and a small modern lodge for students who sign up for courses in canoeing, kayaking, and other sports. Baths are shared, but the accommodations are attractive and comfortable. Participants share meals, which are included in the cost. Discounts are provided if lodging is found elsewhere, and private instruction is also available.

Off North Carolina's Cape Fear coast is Bald Head Island, another very private island, but one that might best be described as a live-in country club at sea. Tranquillity is ensured because no cars are allowed on the island; guests get around by tram, golf cart, bicycle, or on foot.

Visitors are transported to the island by private yacht or by passenger ferry, a 20-minute ride across the Cape Fear River from the landing at Indigo Plantation and Marina in Southport, North Carolina.

Lodgings on the 2,000-acre island are in the 15-room Marsh Harbour Inn or in classy condominiums or vacation homes with every convenience. The comfortable inn has Shaker-style beds, antique wood floors, and modern conveniences such as TV and VCR; many rooms have private decks with water views. Rates include continental breakfast, afternoon hors d'oeuvres, temporary membership in the Bald Head Island Club, and use of an electric golf cart to get around during your stay. There's plenty to do, with miles of beaches plus club facilities that include a pool, marina, and a fine golf course. The club offers many activities such as volleyball games and water aerobics and planned programs for children.

Homes dot much of the area rimming the shore, but there's plenty of untouched beauty in the island's interior and on the 14 miles of unspoiled beach that remain. Bald Head is known for the loggerhead turtles who migrate to the beach each year and share their nesting rituals with turtle-watchers. The Bald Head Island Conservancy conducts walks to see turtles, alligators, and numerous species of birds.

SOUTH CAROLINA

Kiawah Island Resort is living proof that you can have resort facilities without losing the integrity of the environment. Just 21 miles south of Charleston, South Carolina, this is a classic low-country setting with white sand beach, marshes, and wildlife carefully preserved. The Kiawah Island Inn, a low-key, low-rise lodge, and the resort's villas are strategically tucked among the trees so as not to intrude. Views from each villa vary from ocean to forest to dune. Hopefully the luxury oceanfront hotel and spa going up will be done in the same careful manner.

Whitetail deer and some 18 other species of mammals, as well as alligators, sea turtles, and 30 other kinds of reptiles and amphibians share the island with resort guests. Some 140 species of birds have been spotted, including showy varieties such as ospreys, herons, hawks, and egrets. When guests are not using the sports facilities, the beach, or one of four swimming pools, a favorite pastime is "Kiawah Kollege," which includes exploring the island's flora and fauna on marsh biking tours, by canoe, and on walks accompanied by marine biologists and naturalists.

Facilities include five championship golf courses, two tennis clubs, a full-time children's program, and a variety of restaurants and lounges.

TENNESSEE

Fairfield Glade, located in the scenic Cumberland Plateau region, 114 miles east of Nashville, is one of the largest resorts in Tennessee. You will not be bored here. What is there to do? Well, what about one 27-hole and three 18-hole championship golf courses, including Stonehenge, among *Golf Digest*'s top 75 Best Resort Courses in America? You're not a golfer? Try horseback riding, indoor and outdoor tennis courts, indoor and outdoor pools, or a recreation area featuring an 18-hole miniature golf course. Or take your choice of 12 lakes; two marinas offer boat rentals as well as bait and tackle for fishing. Add a putting green and driving range, an exercise room, bicycles, and dancing and entertainment at night—well, you get the idea. Accommodations are hotel-style or in villas.

There's also no shortage of fun at Tennessee's Fall Creek Falls State Resort Park in Pikeville, north of Chattanooga. This is the second-largest in the state park system, and its 160,000 acres offer spectacular scenery—chasms and deep river gorges, virgin forest, and, of course, the dramatic Fall Creek Falls, the highest waterfall east of the Rockies, plunging 256 feet into a shaded pool. And that isn't even all of the show. Smaller falls such as Piney, Cane Creek, and Cane Creek Cascades are almost as impressive.

Take your pick of 144 inn rooms, with balconies overlooking the lake, or cabins. Either way you'll have access to an Olympic-size swimming pool, hiking and biking trails, playgrounds, a game room and fitness room, and an 18-hole golf course that has been listed as one of the top 20 public courses in the country.

Whichever state you choose, the range of wonderful resort facilities for weekenders will likely make you echo the old song "That's What I Like About the South."

RESORT ACCOMMODATIONS *Twin Pines Resort and Conference Center,* 1200 Twin Pines Road, Sterrett, AL 35147, (205) 672-7575, E, MAP • *Lake Guntersville State Resort Lodge,* 1155 Lodge Drive (Alabama Highway 227), Guntersville, AL 35976, (256) 571-5440 or (800) 548-4553, lodge rooms, I; suites, chalets, cottages, M • *The Lodge on Little St. Simons Island,* P.O. Box 1078, St. Simons Island, GA 31522, (912) 638-7472 or (888) 733-5774, EE, AP. Transportation, arranged through the lodge, is by boat from St. Simons, Georgia, or air taxi from the Savannah or Jacksonville airports • *Greyfield Inn,* Cumberland Island, Georgia (mailing address: Drawer B, Fernandina Beach, FL 32034), (904) 261-6408, EE, AP. Transportation is provided from Fernandina Beach, Florida, via the inn's private ferry • *Hilton Lake Lanier Islands Resort,* 7000 Holiday Road, Lake Lanier Islands, GA 30518, (770) 945-8787 or (800) 221-2424, M–E • *Renais-*

sance Pineisle Resort, 9000 Holiday Road, Lake Lanier Islands, GA 30518, (404) 945-8921, M–E • *Chateau Elan,* 7000 Old Winder Highway, Braselton, GA 30517, (770) 932-0900 or (800) 233-WINE, M–EE • *Greystone Inn,* Lake Toxaway, NC 28747, (704) 966-4700 or (800) 824-5766, EE • *Earthshine Mountain Lodge,* Route 1, Box 216-C, Lake Toxaway, NC 28747, (862) 862-4207, EE, AP • *Cataloochee Ranch,* 119 Ranch Drive, Maggie Valley, NC 28751, (828) 926-1401 or (800) 868-1401, E–EE, MAP • *Nantahala Outdoor Center,* 41 Highway 19 west, Bryson City, NC 28713, (828) 488-2175 or (888) 662-1662. Standard courses available for weekends, and three to seven days, EE per person, including instruction, equipment, shared lodging, and all meals. Motel lodgings, I; cabins, E–EE • *Bald Head Island Information Center,* 5079 Southport-Supply Road, Southport, NC 28461, (800) 234-1666, Marsh Harbour Inn rooms, E–EE, CP; condominiums and homes, E–EE. Transportation via ferry from Southport, North Carolina, 30 minutes south of Wilmington • *Kiawah Island Golf and Tennis Resort,* 12 Kiawah Beach Drive, Kiawah Island, SC 29455, (843) 768-2121 or (800) 654-2924, inn, M–E; villas, one to seven bedrooms, E–EE • *Fairfield Glade,* Box 1500, Fairfield Glade, TN 38557, (931) 484-7521, rooms, M; villas, M–E • *Fall Creek Falls State Resort Park,* State Highway 30, Route 3, Pikeville, TN 37369, (423) 881-5241 or (800) 250-8610, inn rooms, I; efficiencies and suites, M–E.

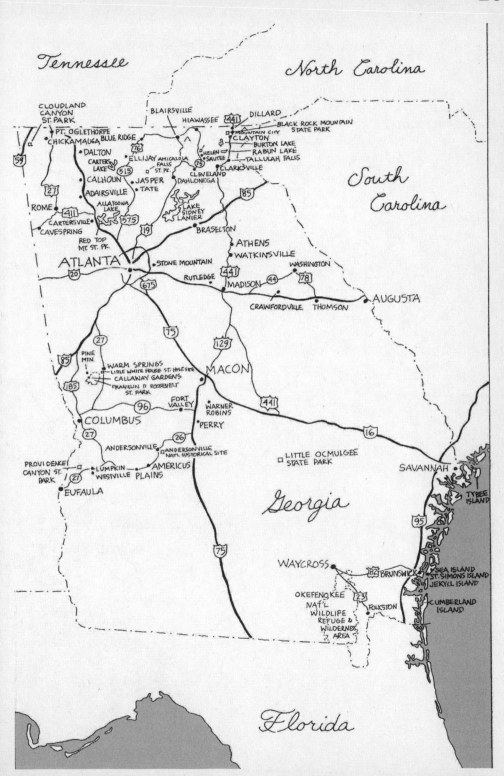

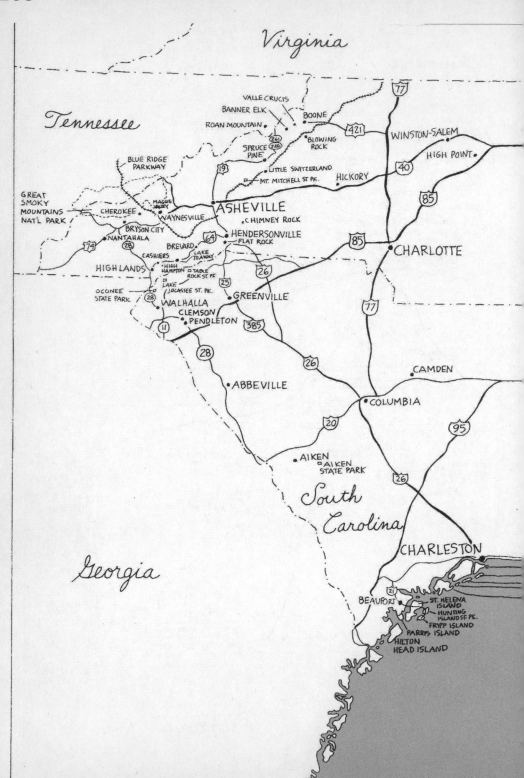

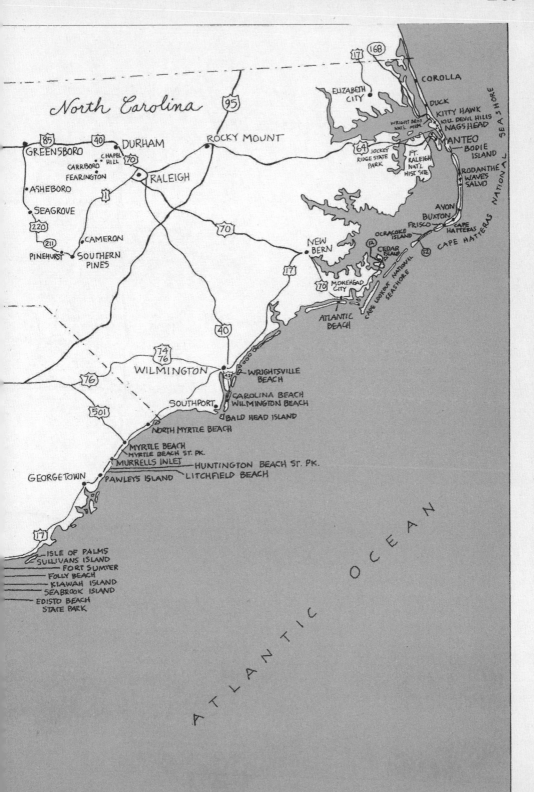

North Carolina

Greensboro
Durham
Chapel Hill
Carrboro
Fearington
Raleigh
Asheboro
Seagrove
Cameron
Pinehurst
Southern Pines
Rocky Mount
New Bern
Morehead City
Atlantic Beach
Wilmington
Wrightsville Beach
Carolina Beach
Wilmington Beach
Southport
Bald Head Island
North Myrtle Beach
Myrtle Beach
Myrtle Beach St. Pk.
Murrells Inlet
Pawleys Island
Georgetown
Huntington Beach St. Pk.
Litchfield Beach

Elizabeth City
Corolla
Duck
Kitty Hawk
Kill Devil Hills
Nags Head
Wright Bros. Nat'l Mem.
Manteo
Bodie Island
Jockey Ridge State Park
Ft. Raleigh Nat'l Hist. Site
Rodanthe
Waves
Salvo
Avon
Buxton
Frisco
Cape Hatteras
Ocracoke Island
Cedar Island
Cape Hatteras National Seashore
Cape Lookout National Seashore

Isle of Palms
Sullivans Island
Fort Sumter
Folly Beach
Kiawah Island
Seabrook Island
Edisto Beach State Park

Atlantic Ocean

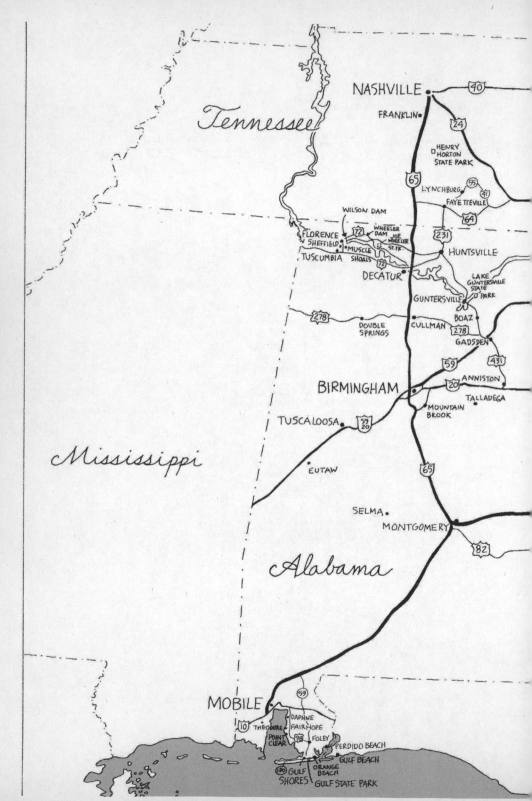

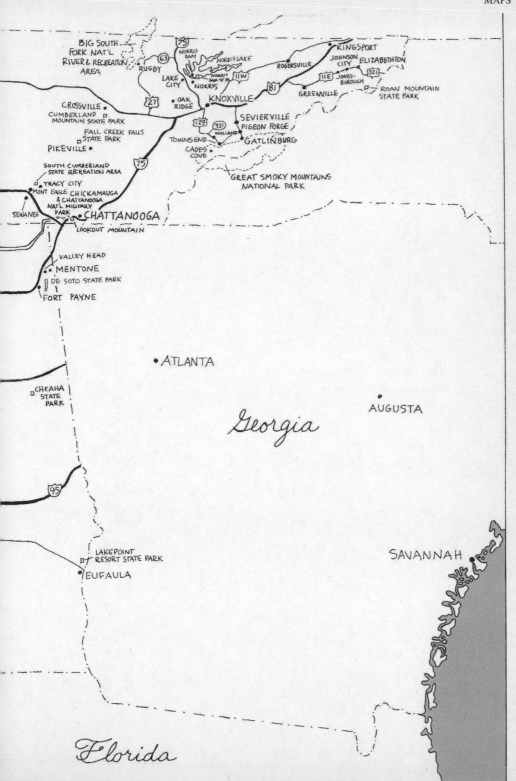

BIG SOUTH
FORK NAT'L
RIVER & RECREATION
AREA

RUGBY

LAKE
CITY

NORRIS
DAM

NORRIS LAKE

NORRIS
DAM ST PK

NORRIS

KINGSPORT

JOHNSON
CITY

ELIZABETHTON

ROGERSVILLE

JONES-
BOROUGH

321

ROAN MOUNTAIN
STATE PARK

CROSSVILLE

CUMBERLAND
MOUNTAIN STATE PARK

FALL CREEK FALLS
STATE PARK

PIKEVILLE

OAK
RIDGE

KNOXVILLE

GREENVILLE

SEVIERVILLE
PIGEON FORGE

TOWNSEND

CADES
COVE

GATLINBURG

WALLAND

SOUTH CUMBERLAND
STATE RECREATION AREA

TRACY CITY

MONT EAGLE

SEWANEE

CHICKAMAUGA
& CHATTANOOGA
NAT'L MILITARY
PARK

CHATTANOOGA

GREAT SMOKY MOUNTAINS
NATIONAL PARK

LOOKOUT MOUNTAIN

VALLEY HEAD

MENTONE

DE SOTO STATE PARK

FORT PAYNE

ATLANTA

CHEAHA
STATE
PARK

Georgia

AUGUSTA

95

SAVANNAH

LAKEPOINT
RESORT STATE PARK

EUFAULA

Florida

INDEX

Eleanor Berman has helped thousands of weekend vacationers successfully navigate their travels with her bestselling *Away for the Weekend* guides. Among them are:

Away for the Weekend: New York
0-609-80596-7. $16.00 paper (Canada: $24.00)

Away for the Weekend: Midwest
0-609-80401-4. $16.00 paper (Canada: $24.00)

Coming in April 2002

Away for the Weekend: Mid-Atlantic
0-609-80905-9. $17.00 paper (Canada: $25.00)

Available from Three Rivers Press wherever books are sold.

THREE RIVERS PRESS • NEW YORK